SOCIAL PSYCHOLOGY OF GENDER

ADVANCES IN GROUP PROCESSES

Series Editors: Edward J. Lawler and Shane R. Thye

Recent Volumes:

Volume 1–17:	Series Editor: Edward J. Lawler
Volume 18:	Series Editors: Edward J. Lawler and Shane R. Thye
Volume 19:	Group Cohesion, Trust and Solidarity – Series Editors: Edward J. Lawler and Shane R. Thye
Volume 20:	Power and Status – Series Editors: Edward J. Lawler and Shane R. Thye
Volume 21:	Theory and Research on Human Emotions – Edited by Jonathan H. Turner
Volume 22:	Social Identification in Groups – Series Editors: Shane R. Thye and Edward J. Lawler
Volume 23:	Social Psychology of the Workplace – Series Editors: Shane R. Thye and Edward J. Lawler

ADVANCES IN GROUP PROCESSES VOLUME 24

SOCIAL PSYCHOLOGY OF GENDER

EDITED BY

SHELLEY J. CORRELL

*Department of Sociology
Cornell University, USA*

Emerald

JAI

United Kingdom – North America – Japan – India – Malaysia – China – Australasia

JAI Press is an imprint of Emerald Group Publishing Limited
Howard House, Wagon Lane, Bingley BD16 1WA, UK

First edition 2007

Copyright © 2008 Emerald Group Publishing Limited

Reprints and permission service
Contact: booksandseries@emeraldinsight.com

No part of this book may be reproduced, stored in a retrieval system, transmitted in any form or by any means electronic, mechanical, photocopying, recording or otherwise without either the prior written permission of the publisher or a licence permitting restricted copying issued in the UK by The Copyright Licensing Agency and in the USA by The Copyright Clearance Center. No responsibility is accepted for the accuracy of information contained in the text, illustrations or advertisements. The opinions expressed in these chapters are not necessarily those of the Editor or the publisher.

British Library Cataloguing in Publication Data
A catalogue record for this book is available from the British Library

ISBN: 978-0-76-231430-0

Awarded in recognition of
Emerald's production
department's adherence to
quality systems and processes
when preparing scholarly
journals for print

INVESTOR IN PEOPLE

CONTENTS

LIST OF CONTRIBUTORS   *ix*

PREFACE   *xiii*

AN INTRODUCTION TO THE SOCIAL PSYCHOLOGY OF GENDER
   Shelley J. Correll, Sarah Thébaud and Stephen Benard   *1*

SEX DIFFERENCES, SEXISM, AND SEX: THE SOCIAL PSYCHOLOGY OF GENDER FROM PAST TO PRESENT
   Laurie A. Rudman and Julie E. Phelan   *19*

GENDER STEREOTYPES IN THE WORKPLACE: OBSTACLES TO WOMEN'S CAREER PROGRESS
   Madeline E. Heilman and Elizabeth J. Parks-Stamm   *47*

THE EFFECTS OF GENDER STEREOTYPES ON JUDGMENTS AND DECISIONS IN ORGANIZATIONS
   Kathleen Fuegen   *79*

COOPERATION ≠ CONSENT: HOW WOMEN REACT TO THEIR PLACE, BASED ON SOCIAL RELATIONS AND AMBIVALENT SEXISM
   Mina Cikara and Susan T. Fiske   *99*

"STREET CRED" AND THE EXECUTIVE
WOMAN: THE EFFECTS OF GENDER
DIFFERENCES IN SOCIAL NETWORKS
ON CAREER ADVANCEMENT
    Susan F. Cabrera and Melissa C. Thomas-Hunt   *123*

FEELING INJUSTICE, EXPRESSING
INJUSTICE: HOW GENDER AND
CONTEXT MATTER
    Cathryn Johnson, Karen A. Hegtvedt,   *149*
    Leslie M. Brody and Krysia Wrobel Waldron

THE DEVIL MADE HER DO IT?
EVALUATING RISK PREFERENCE
AS AN EXPLANATION OF SEX DIFFERENCES
IN RELIGIOUSNESS
    Jeremy Freese and James D. Montgomery   *187*

THE SEXUAL SOCIALIZATION OF YOUNG
CHILDREN: SETTING THE AGENDA FOR
RESEARCH
    Karin A. Martin, Katherine P. Luke and   *231*
    Lynn Verduzco-Baker

STATUS PROCESSES AND GENDER
DIFFERENCES IN SELF-HANDICAPPING
    Jeffrey W. Lucas, Heather Ridolfo,   *261*
    Reef Youngreen, Christabel L. Rogalin,
    Shane D. Soboroff, Layana Navarre-Jackson and
    Michael J. Lovaglia

WOMEN'S PREDOMINANCE IN COLLEGE
ENROLLMENTS: LABOR MARKET AND
GENDER IDENTITY EXPLANATIONS
    Kevin T. Leicht, Douglas Thompkins,   *283*
    Tina Wildhagen, Christabel L. Rogalin,
    Shane D. Soboroff, Christopher P. Kelley,
    Charisse Long and Michael J. Lovaglia

GENDER AS A GROUP PROCESS: IMPLICATIONS
FOR THE PERSISTENCE OF INEQUALITY
    Cecilia L. Ridgeway   *311*

LIST OF CONTRIBUTORS

Stephen Benard	Department of Sociology, Cornell University, Ithaca, NY, USA
Leslie M. Brody	Department of Sociology, Emory University, Atlanta, GA, USA
Susan F. Cabrera	Johnson Graduate School of Management, Cornell University, NJ, USA
Mina Cikara	Department of Psychology, Princeton University, NJ, USA
Shelley J. Correll	Department of Sociology, Cornell University, Ithaca, NY, USA
Susan T. Fiske	Department of Psychology, Princeton University, NJ, USA
Jeremy Freese	Department of Sociology, University of Wisconsin-Madison, Madison, WI, USA
Kathleen Fuegen	Department of Psychology, Northern Kentucky University, KY, USA
Karen A. Hegtvedt	Department of Sociology, Emory University, Atlanta, GA, USA
Madeline E. Heilman	Department of Psychology, New York University, NY, USA
Cathryn Johnson	Department of Sociology, Emory University, Atlanta, GA, USA

LIST OF CONTRIBUTORS

Christopher P. Kelley	Department of Sociology, University of Iowa, IA, USA
Kevin T. Leicht	Department of Sociology, University of Iowa, IA, USA
Charisse Long	Department of Sociology, University of Iowa, IA, USA
Michael J. Lovaglia	Department of Sociology, University of Iowa, IA, USA
Jeffrey W. Lucas	Department of Sociology, University of Maryland, MD, USA
Katherine P. Luke	Department of Sociology, University of Michigan, MI, USA
Karin A. Martin	Department of Sociology, University of Michigan, MI, USA
James D. Montgomery	Department of Sociology, University of Wisconsin-Madison, Madison, WI, USA
Layana Navarre-Jackson	Department of Sociology, University of Iowa, IA, USA
Elizabeth J. Parks-Stamm	Department of Psychology, New York University, NY, USA
Julie E. Phelan	Department of Psychology, Rutgers, the State University of New Jersey, NJ, USA
Cecilia L. Ridgeway	Department of Sociology, Stanford University, CA, USA
Heather Ridolfo	Department of Sociology, University of Maryland, MD, USA
Christabel L. Rogalin	Department of Sociology, University of Iowa, IA, USA

List of Contributors

Laurie A. Rudman	Department of Psychology, Rutgers, the State University of New Jersey, NJ, USA
Shane D. Soboroff	Department of Sociology, University of Iowa, IA, USA
Sarah Thébaud	Department of Sociology, Cornell University, Ithaca, NY, USA
Douglas Thompkins	Department of Sociology, John Jay College – CUNY, NY, USA
Melissa C. Thomas-Hunt	Johnson Graduate School of Management, Cornell University, NJ, USA
Lynn Verduzco-Baker	Department of Sociology, University of Michigan, MI, USA
Krysia Wrobel Waldron	Department of Sociology, Emory University, Atlanta, GA, USA
Tina Wildhagen	Department of Sociology, University of Iowa, IA, USA
Reef Youngreen	Department of Sociology, University of Massachusetts, MA, USA

PREFACE

Advances in Group Processes publishes theoretical analyses, reviews, and theory based empirical chapters on group phenomena. The series adopts a broad conception of "group processes." This includes work on groups ranging from the very small to the very large, and on classic and contemporary topics such as status, power, exchange, justice, influence, decision-making, intergroup relations, and social networks. Previous contributors have included scholars from diverse fields including sociology, psychology, political science, philosophy, mathematics, and organizational behavior.

A number of years ago we began a new trend in the series. Our goal then was to publish a set of interrelated volumes that examine core issues or fundamental themes in the group processes arena. Each volume was to be organized around a particular problem, substantive area, or topic of study, broadly defined to include a range of methodological and theoretical orientations. Previous volumes have included:

- Group Cohesion, Trust, and Solidarity (*v.* 19)
- Power and Status (*v.* 20)
- Human Emotions (*v.* 21)
- Social Identification in Groups (*v.* 22)
- Social Psychology of the Workplace (*v.* 23)

Volume 24, guest edited by Shelley Correll, represents the sixth volume in the series. This volume addresses issues pertinent to the *Social Psychology of Gender*. As described in the introductory chapter, the volume includes papers that reflect a wide range of theoretical approaches to the social psychology of gender, and contributions by major scholars from multiple disciplines who work in this general area.

Shane R. Thye
Edward J. Lawler
Series Co-Editors

AN INTRODUCTION TO THE SOCIAL PSYCHOLOGY OF GENDER

Shelley J. Correll, Sarah Thébaud and Stephen Benard

The social psychology of gender, broadly defined, examines the ways gender shapes and is shaped by social interaction. This includes the cognitive processes through which gender influences the way we perceive, interpret, and respond to our social world; it also includes the mechanisms through which interaction defines and transmits meaning about gender. This definition is congruent with modern theories that increasingly view gender as an institutionalized system of practices for constituting people as two different categories (men and women), and organizing relations of inequality based on this difference (Ferree, Lorber & Hess, 1999; Lorber, 1994; Nakano Glenn, 1999; Ridgeway, 1997; Ridgeway & Correll, 2004; Ridgeway & Smith-Lovin, 1999; Risman, 1998). In other words, gender is not simply (or primarily) a trait of individuals; it is also an organizing principle of all social systems, including families, work, schools, economic and legal systems, and everyday interactions.

Scholarship conceptualizing gender as an institution encompasses three levels of analysis: individual, interactional, and structural (e.g., Risman, 1998). The individual level refers to stable traits of men and women that endure over time, such as differences believed to be rooted in biology or early childhood socialization. The interactional level examines the ways in which social behavior is constrained or facilitated by expectations that people have regarding the traits men and women possess, the ways they should act, and the beliefs they should hold. The structural level addresses how macro level patterns, such as the positions to which people are assigned in society or the rewards attached to those positions, lead to differences in the behavior or experiences of men and women. Current and recent research in the social psychology of gender most often focuses on the interactional level, examining how gendered expectations shape behavior.

The contemporary social psychology of gender, with its focus on interaction, looks considerably different from earlier social psychological approaches to gender. In fact, the current understanding of gender emerged largely out of a critique of the social psychology of gender as it existed in the 1970s and 1980s (for an early critique see Lopata & Thorne, 1978). At that time, individual-level sex role/socialization approaches were predominant within both psychology and sociology. Sex role theories generally argue that gender is a product of socialization: through reinforcement, children learn either the male or female "role," internalize it as an identity, and then enact the behaviors and traits associated with that role as they carry out their adult activities. In this way, gender becomes a mostly stable and durable aspect of who people *are*.

While scholars of gender have been critical of the sex role approach for many reasons described below (see Connell, 1987 or Gerson, 1985 for a review), it is important to understand that sex role theories emerged in response to biological explanations of gender difference. For example, while biological accounts might explain an observed gender difference in a trait such as aggressiveness as resulting from average differences in the level of testosterone between males and females, sex role/socialization accounts might instead locate the source of this observed difference in parenting practices which celebrate aggressive behavior in boys and sanction it in girls. Thus, the movement away from biological theories and towards sex role/ socialization theories introduced more malleability and variability into the process of becoming a gendered individual.

However, as gender scholars routinely note, biological and socialization accounts are not as different as they may at first seem. While socialization or "nurture" theories allow for more malleability than biological or "nature" theories, both ultimately view gender as residing in the individual, whether in her biology or in her psychology. Both sets of theories view gender as a relatively stable and distinguishing aspect of who people are, at least by adulthood. These internalized gender differences are thought to be the source of macro level gender patterns and inequalities, such as the segregation of the labor market by gender, the gender gap in wages, and the gendered division of household labor.

One problem with individual level approaches is that they have historically focused on documenting and then explaining gender differences, while ignoring the similarity between men and women and the vast diversity among men and among women. As Connell (1987) notes, if researchers and readers did not start with the assumption that men and women *are* different, decades worth of "sex differences" research might have been more aptly called "sex similarity" research. Indeed in a recent meta analysis of over 120 studies, psychologist Janet Hyde (2005) provides strong evidence in support of the "gender similarity hypothesis." For 78% of the psychological variables examined in these studies – including measures of preferences for powerful jobs, self-esteem, and mathematics problem solving – the magnitude of the differences between men and women were found to be either small or close to zero. Some gender differences were larger, such as differences in throwing velocity and the frequency of reported masturbation, but interestingly the variables associated with large gender differences are not those that are usually thought to be relevant for explaining gender patterns and inequalities in major life outcomes.

Sex role/socialization theories have also been criticized on a number of other grounds, which we will only briefly note here (for a full review see Connell, 1987). By positing universalistic definitions of the male and female role, these theories fail to appreciate the ways that race and class affect how gender is experienced. More generally, individuals who do not fit within these universalistic definitions can only be understood in terms of failures of socialization or deviants. Defining gender in terms of male and female "roles" creates an imagery of complimentary, separate but equal roles, which prevents an examination of the relations between men and women, which are often unequal. Further, defining gender as a stable part of who someone is obscures an understanding of the situational nature of gender.

Gender theories have, consequently, moved increasingly from understanding gender in terms of sex differences and sex roles to understanding gender as a multilevel structure that includes cultural beliefs and distributions of resources at the macro level, patterns of behavior at the interactional level, as well as roles and identities at the micro level (Ferree & Hess, 1987; Ferree et al., 1999; Ridgeway & Correll, 2004; Risman, 1998). Modern theories emphasize that gender is both a structure and a process. Researchers focusing on gender as a structure have shown that many observed gender differences are actually "deceptive distinctions:" differences that appear because men and women occupy different (and unequal) positions in the social structure (Epstein, 1990; Kanter, 1977). Social psychologists of gender tend to take the complimentary approach of studying gender as a process.

To say that gender is a process is to claim that gender is an on-going interactional accomplishment rather than a given attribute; something one *does* rather than something one *is* (West & Zimmerman, 1987). Rather than being an internalized identity, gender is a set of expectations to which individuals are held accountable while engaging in other seemingly non-gendered activities. Consistent with this idea, research finds that even when men and women are found in similar structural positions, they are often held to different behavioral standards, which can serve to reproduce existing gender inequalities. For example, Rudman (1998) found that, in an interview situation, women interviewees who engaged in self-promoting behavior by describing their past accomplishments were penalized; men who self-promoted incurred no such penalties. Interestingly, self-promotion led to higher competence ratings for both male and female interviewees, but women who self-promoted were judged as less likeable, which decreased the odds that they would be recommended for hire. Thus, what might be considered a "best practice" in interviewing, such as making sure your past accomplishments are known, is less effective for women than men because of the way gender influences the expectations of *others* in interactive settings.

Likewise, in her study of litigators, Pierce (1995) describes a model of litigation that is actively taught to young lawyers and involves the strategic use of displays of anger in dealing with some witnesses and opposing counsel. This model is widely accepted as highly effective; however, it turns out to not be as effective for women litigators because of the way their colleagues, juries, and judges react to women displaying the emotion of anger. Thus, the "best" way of carrying out the role of litigator is blocked from women, who have to adopt a more gender acceptable, but less valued, strategy for carrying out their work.

In sum, while older sex role approaches viewed gendered individuals as existing in gender-neutral social structures and interactions, current understandings of gender as a multilevel system view gendered individuals as occupying gendered positions in society, and their everyday interactions in those positions as being shaped by gender expectations. Gender resides both within and *beyond* individuals.

WHAT CAN SOCIAL PSYCHOLOGY CONTRIBUTE TO OUR UNDERSTANDINGS OF GENDER?

The paradigmatic shift in gender theory, which focuses attention away from the individual and toward structural accounts, has undoubtedly advanced the amount and quality of research on gender as a macro-level phenomenon. However, social psychological accounts of gender have been less frequent among gender scholars in sociology, perhaps due to the perception that studying individuals might reinvigorate sex role and socialization accounts. This concern is especially understandable since sociology as a field has yet to fully incorporate current theories of gender (Stacey & Thorne, 1985; Ferree & Hall, 1996). For example, Ferree and Hall (1996) have shown that many introductory sociology textbooks still present gender as simply the product of socialization, even while examining other bases of inequality, such as race and class, at a structural level. Rather than rehearsing past debates, we argue that social psychological perspectives make a unique contribution to bridging the multiple levels of the gender system, and are especially well suited to helping us understand the ways that gender is achieved through interaction. Understanding gender as an interactive process sheds light on how structural conditions constrain individual choices as well as how structural patterns of gender inequality are generated and recreated. Discovering mechanisms at the micro level, which play an active role in the persistence of inequality, is especially fruitful because they suggest ways by which gender inequality might be lessened.

To illustrate the usefulness of this perspective, we highlight four specific contributions that social psychology can make to our understanding of gender. First, it offers a way to evaluate whether apparently individual gender differences might instead be the product of gendered expectations. Second, it can explain how structural constraints support the emergence of gender inequality through interaction and relegate women to lower status positions. Third, it addresses legitimacy issues that can prevent women in high status positions from benefiting from those positions as much as otherwise equivalent men. Fourth, it can help us understand how gender inequality could emerge in new contexts (such as new organizational forms) that have no history of gender inequality.

As gender theories in sociology and other fields moved towards more macro level theorizing, scholarship within psychological and sociological social psychology also moved away from the static notion of sex roles and towards a more contextual, situational understanding of gender that is inherently interactional (Deaux & Major, 1987). For example, social psychologists have shown that even gender differences in aggression, a trait that has long been associated with definitions of masculinity, are contextually dependent. In one compelling study, Lightdale and Prentice (1994) conducted an experiment where participants played an interactive video game in which they defended their territory and then attacked one another by dropping bombs. In the condition where participants knew that others (the experimenter and other participants) would be aware of their behavior, men dropped significantly more bombs than women, demonstrating the classic gender difference in aggressive behavior. However, in another condition, where participants knew that their behavior would not be monitored, women dropped slightly more bombs than men, although the difference was not significant. In other words, gender differences in aggressive behavior were shown to be the result of accountability to others, rather than internalized differences. Socialization theories within social psychology have similarly become more contextual and have increasingly highlighted the active role of children in the socialization process, thereby focusing more on the process of how individuals acquire gender and allowing more variability in both process and outcomes (Martin, 1998).

An important consequence of this shift in social psychological research toward focusing on the contextual nature of gender in interaction is its ability to explain the emergence of certain types of gender inequality. Integrating social psychological perspectives with macro-level research on structural gender inequality enables scholars to identify how one's position and resources in the context of the broader social structure both shape the type of interactions people encounter, and how those interactions reciprocally shape the social structure itself. For instance, observed patterns of structural inequality, such as occupational sex segregation and the high likelihood of same-sex network ties, indicate that women rarely meet men in status-equal, role-similar interactions (Cabrera & Thomas-Hunt, this volume; Smith-Lovin & McPherson, 1993; Ridgeway & Smith-Lovin, 1999). Instead, they frequently are in interactions where men are in more powerful, agentic roles, and women are in more supportive roles. In this way, the repetition of status unequal interactions between men and women reinforces cultural beliefs about gender differences (Eagly & Steffen, 1984; Ridgeway, 1991). This is particularly problematic because when women do find themselves in interactions where they have a higher status relation to men (e.g., as leaders or managers), they often encounter a series of barriers that can make it more difficult for them to exercise their high status role, as many papers in this volume show.

A third on-going contribution of social psychology toward bridging multiple levels of analysis has been to develop a set of rich, empirically supported accounts of the way gendered beliefs and expectations limit the ability of women to enact high status, or even equal status, roles. Importantly, these accounts outline how individual behavior is constrained, though not fully determined, by macro-level gender beliefs. For example, research in expectation states theory and shifting standards theory has shown that because gender status beliefs include widely shared assumptions that women are generally less competent or status worthy than men, women are frequently judged by a harsher ability standard, both by themselves and others (Biernat & Kobrynowicz, 1997; Fuegen, this volume; Foschi, 1989; Correll, 2004). They likewise face a lack of legitimacy when placed in high status roles (Ridgeway & Berger, 1986).

Research on prescriptive stereotyping has accordingly shown that even when women can overcome doubts about their workplace competence, they are still subjected to discrimination based on beliefs about what roles or behaviors are appropriate for men and women. Heilman (2001) explains that women who violate prescriptive stereotypes by taking on stereotypically masculine roles (such as leadership roles) or behaviors (such as being assertive or self-promoting) face two kinds of reactions. First, they are derogated as interpersonally hostile – cold, deceitful, bitter, selfish, devious, and other negative attributions. Second, they are personally disliked. Even positive stereotypes, such as beliefs that women are warmer or more nurturing, can lead to disadvantages for women in the workplace, such as assigning women more caregiving type roles at work (see Rudman & Phelan, this volume). And, as the Pierce (1995) study cited earlier shows, beliefs about the types of emotional displays that are appropriate for women can also limit women's ability to enact the emotional component of certain high status occupational roles, such as litigator. Taken as a whole, the degree to which individuals are able to negotiate gender expectations in the varied contexts of their interactions largely influences the supply and demand side processes generating macro-structural patterns of gender inequality.

By articulating these interactional processes, social psychology provides a fourth contribution: an explanation for why gender inequality emerges in new settings with no prior history of gender bias, such as new organizational forms. As Ridgeway points out in this volume and elsewhere (Ridgeway & Correll, 2004; Ridgeway & Smith-Lovin, 1999), repeated interactions that are implicitly based on gender status beliefs can reshape the form of gender inequality under new situational conditions and organizational structures. Importantly, social psychology has also suggested ways in which organizations can adjust their policies and practices to avoid perpetuating inequality (for an overview see Valian, 1999). For example, people can avoid unconsciously discriminating against others to the extent that they are motivated to do so (Tetlock, 1983; Kunda & Spencer, 2003; Fein, Hoshino-Brown, Davies, & Spencer, 2003), and able to exert the cognitive effort necessary to monitor their own behavior for the influence of stereotypes

(Devine, 1989; Bodenhausen, 1990; Wilson & Brekke, 1994). To reduce stereotypic gender biases in hiring, organizations can make changes to increase employees' motivation to avoid stereotyping, such as requiring them to account for their hiring decisions to an impartial higher authority (e.g., Foschi, 1996). Organizations can also make changes to ensure that employees have sufficient cognitive resources to self-monitor, for example, by allowing plenty of time for hiring decisions to be made so that decision makers are not forced to make rushed decisions (which may be more likely to be biased) (Valian, 1999).

The ability of social psychology to examine the way gender influences and is influenced by social context is the primary reason why we find this line of work to be especially promising. By specifying the ways in which individuals are held accountable to gender beliefs even while they are enacting seemingly non-gendered roles, social psychology provides insight into the "doing gender" process (West & Zimmerman, 1987). This gives it the potential to shed light on the subtle type of biases that appear to be especially important in limiting women's advancement in today's workplaces (Valian, 1999). However, more research still needs to be done in these areas, such as developing better understandings of how gendered expectations about competence and emotional displays influence men and women's enactment of their occupational roles.

THE USE OF LABORATORY EXPERIMENTS IN STUDYING GENDER

Many of the chapters in this book summarize the results of previous experimental studies, or report the results of new experiments. These chapters reflect the assumption, widespread in social psychology, that the experimental method is a useful tool with which to increase our understanding of the ways in which gender shapes social life. However, many gender scholars have viewed experimental research with reservation or even suspicion (for an excellent review of these concerns see Sprague, 2005). These reservations are understandable in light of the historical context of gender issues in science. Women were long excluded from science as practitioners (Sprague, 2005, pp. 43–44), and were at times used as research subjects in exploitative and unethical ways (Sprague, 2005, pp. 19–20). Furthermore, some scientists explicitly sought to prove that women were inferior to men, and systematically disregarded evidence that contradicted this assumption (Sprague, 2005, pp. 35–36). While sensitive to these concerns, we nonetheless

Introduction

believe that experiments can provide important insights into issues that are of key concern to gender scholars, such as causal evidence for the existence of and mechanisms underlying gender discrimination.

The distinguishing feature of experiments, relative to other quantitative methods, is that the researcher manipulates the independent variable of interest in order to measure its effect on the dependent variable, rather than measuring correlations present in existing data (Aronson, Ellsworth, Carlsmith, & Gonzales, 1990). When manipulation of the independent variable is combined with experimental control of other features of the setting and random assignment of participants into experimental conditions, experiments have the unique ability to establish causality. Importantly for gender scholars, this means experiments can shed empirical light on important processes that tend to be intractable with other methods. Experiments, like all methods, have their limits. But we believe that evidence from experiments can be a valuable part of the knowledge base for scholars working in a given substantive area.

Experiments examining discrimination in labor market settings offer a good example of the unique kind of evidence that experiments can provide. Despite widespread reports of gender inequality, many people remain reluctant to acknowledge that discrimination exists, and some believe that men are systematically disadvantaged relative to women (Rhode, 1997). Establishing that gender discrimination occurs using non-experimental social science data can be difficult. In the case of the gender wage gap, for example, surveys cannot distinguish between discrimination accounts (women are paid less because of bias) and productivity accounts (women are paid less because they are less efficient workers) (see Budig & England, 2001 for an extended discussion of this problem).

However, using an experiment, researchers interested in whether women face gender bias in the hiring process might ask study participants to evaluate a set of job applications, and experimentally vary whether an applicant appears to be a man or a woman, while holding other relevant variables constant (for an overview of the "application files" design, see Foschi, 2006). For example, by asking participants to evaluate identical resumes that vary only on the gender of the applicant, the researcher can rule out the possibility that any systematic differences in the applications (education, experience, etc.) influenced the evaluation of men and women. By ruling out competing explanations, experiments can provide evidence of gender discrimination with a level of certainty unavailable with other methods. The strength of this evidence is apparent in the role experiments have played in the courtroom, as in the historic United States Supreme

Court *Price Waterhouse v. Hopkins* sex discrimination case (see Fiske, Bersoff, Borgida, Deaux, & Heilman, 1991).

Although the experimental method offers several unique advantages to researchers, it has also garnered criticism from some gender scholars. Sprague (2005) reviews two concerns that scholars have raised regarding the experimental method. The first concern is that the abstract nature of an experiment, by removing participants and activities from their normal context, may mask power relations that exist in everyday settings (Sprague 2005, p. 82). The second concern is that, because experiments often use samples composed of undergraduate students, they may disproportionately reflect the experiences of elites (Sprague 2005, p. 89). We now turn to addressing both of these concerns.

We acknowledge that, when conducting an experiment, one runs the risk of overlooking the importance of power relations in a particular setting. However, it is important to note that this is a potential shortcoming of any given research design, rather than a flaw inherent in the experimental method. In fact, we believe that a well-designed experiment can be ideally suited to addressing issues of power relations in interactional contexts. The exercise of power in interpersonal relations is often difficult to observe in natural settings, as it is covariant with other factors. By methodically varying elements of the situation, experiments can expose the existence of power and the mechanisms behind aspects of it that would otherwise be difficult to detect. For example, experimental research has shown that men's sexual harassment of women varies with contextual factors such as threats to masculine identity and the apparent legitimacy of male privilege (Maass, Cadinu, Guarnieri, & Grasselli, 2003).

The second concern is one of external validity (Sprague 2005, p. 89). Most experiments are conducted on college and university campuses, and as a result, study participants tend to be drawn from students at those institutions. Using college students as research participants may limit the conclusions one can draw from this research; in particular, the results of such research may disproportionately represent the experiences of elites.

It is true that college students do not represent a random sample from the population. The behavior of college students thus may not generalize to other populations, but the extent to which this is true depends on the particular research question being asked. For example, the application file experiments mentioned above seek to predict the decisions managers will make when faced with hiring decisions. Research comparing the behavior of college students to actual managers in this setting suggests that they tend to offer very similar appraisals of applicants (Cleveland & Berman, 1987). In a meta-analysis, Olian and Schwab (1988) found no significant difference between managers and student evaluators in the effect size of applicant gender on applicant ratings and hiring decisions. Correll, Benard, and Paik (2007) examined discrimination against mothers using both a laboratory resumé evaluation study and an audit study in which the researchers sent resumés to actual firms and measured the rate at which prospective employers contacted the applicants. They found the same pattern of means and similar effect sizes across both studies, which suggests that, at least for some research questions, college student samples can approximate real-world samples quite well. In general, the question of how well the characteristics of a college student sample approximate those of another population of interest is an important one, and the answer varies depending on the specific research question.

The broader response to concerns about external validity is that experiments are designed to test causal arguments, not to generalize to broader populations (Zelditch, 1969). Thus, to criticize experiments for a lack of external validity is equivalent to criticizing survey research for failing to prove causality or ethnographic research for failing to generalize beyond the specific place and time in which it was conducted. While these criticisms may be technically valid, they overlook the goals and unique contributions of each method.

Importantly, the strengths and weaknesses of these and other methods tend to be complimentary – each can answer questions that the others cannot. For example, experimental resumé evaluation studies, survey data on work experiences and earnings, and ethnographic fieldwork within organizations intersect to provide much richer information regarding the role of gender in structuring the labor market experiences of men and women than any of these methods alone.

OVERVIEW OF THE VOLUME

This volume contains contributions from scholars in sociology, psychology, and organizational behavior. While scholars working in the group processes tradition and those working in the area of sociology of gender share many insights about what gender is and how it functions, the literatures from these two fields are all too rarely in conversation with each other. Both tend to see gender as a property of structure rather than a trait of individuals learned in childhood. Both view gender as contextual and variable, rather than fixed and durable. One of the goals of this volume then is to help bridge this divide.

The first paper, Laurie A. Rudman and Julie E. Phelan's "Sex Differences, Sexism, and Sex: The Social Psychology of Gender from Past to Present," reviews the history of gender research in psychology, and in particular provides excellent accounts of research on "benevolent sexism" and "backlash effects." Benevolent sexism is the tendency to attribute qualities to women that are positively valued, but which also undermine their status in the workplace; backlash effects most commonly occur when agentic women are punished for violating normative assumptions about how women should behave. Both concepts play a role in explaining why women continue to experience disadvantages in the labor market, despite changing attitudes about women's overall competence. This paper will be especially valuable to researchers interested in inequality or work and occupations.

The next chapter, Madeline E. Heilman and Elizabeth J. Parks-Stamm's, "Gender Stereotypes in the Workplace: Obstacles to Women's Career Progress," is an outstanding overview of work by the authors and others on gender stereotyping. The authors' theoretical framework includes both descriptive stereotypes (beliefs about how men and women are), and prescriptive stereotypes (beliefs about how men and women should be) and their effects on the career outcomes of women and men. They describe a wealth of studies documenting the conditions under which descriptive stereotypes bias evaluations of women's performance, and prescriptive stereotypes lead evaluators to view women negatively even when their performance decisively refutes descriptive stereotypes. The authors also discuss ways in which organizations might structure their evaluation processes to avoid bias. This paper makes a significant contribution by providing thorough and engaging accounts of two forms of bias that affect women's careers.

Kathleen Fuegen's chapter, "The Effects of Gender Stereotypes on Judgments and Decisions in Organizations," discusses recent research on how gendered expectations change the standards that evaluators use in making hiring and firing decisions. The key findings from this research are that women tend to be held to lower minimum standards but higher confirmatory standards in assessments of competence, and higher minimum standards but lower confirmatory standards in assessments of *in*competence. However, these findings are contingent on the gender of the evaluator. Fuegen closes by identifying a number of open research questions in the field. This chapter should be an important resource for anyone interested in developing a more nuanced and sophisticated understanding of how gender affects organizational decision-making.

The following chapter by Mina Cikara and Susan T. Fiske builds on earlier chapters by bringing together the abundant literatures supporting status characteristics theory, the stereotype content model, and ambivalent sexism theory (which addresses hostile and benevolent sexism). In doing so, they highlight how women's choices often reflect a pragmatic approach to their alternatives, rather than explicit consent to hierarchical gender relations. The authors outline how a variety of processes, such as stereotyping that generates paternalistic pity and envious prejudice, nonverbal behavior eliciting dominance and submissiveness, and the interdependent quality of heterosexual relations, often leave women in a double bind that provides few options for attaining "soft" power through interaction, which is dependent upon being both liked and respected. This review will be fruitful for researchers interested in the especially subtle qualities of interactional processes that reproduce unequal relationships between men and women across a wide variety of settings.

Next, a chapter by Susan F. Cabrera and Melissa C. Thomas-Hunt, "'Street Cred' and the Executive Woman: The Effects of Gender Differences in Social Networks on Career Advancement," provides an exceptional example of the value of examining the interaction between structural and social psychological factors. Their paper proposes a model predicting executive hiring patterns, and reviews network research relevant to establishing credibility, one key facet of the model. An important theme of their paper is that homophily – the psychological principle stating that people tend to seek interactions with similar others – can be differentially effective for men and women, as men tend to occupy more high status positions within organizations. Their work is broadly relevant for scholars interested in gender, inequality, organizations, and networks.

The next chapter by Cathryn Johnson and colleagues begins with an engaging review of the theoretical and empirical literature on gender and emotions that should be useful to social psychologists and others who are new to this important area of gender scholarship. The authors then present results from an experimental vignette study that examines how gender and contextual factors affect participants' emotional responses to a situation where they have experienced injustice by not being chosen for a position even though they are well qualified. Interestingly, and consistent with research in other areas of social psychology, they find that contextual factors matter more than an individual's gender. In particular, they find that the gender of the decision maker has a stronger effect on participants' emotional responses than does their own gender.

The subsequent chapter by Jeremy Freese and James D. Montgomery empirically and formally evaluates the hypothesis that women are more religious than men because they are more risk-averse and therefore are more motivated by the threat of punishment in the afterlife. As the authors note, women have been shown to be more religious than men in the U.S. and elsewhere. Using a cross-national sample they find that, contrary to the predictions of risk-preference theory, gender differences in religiosity are no smaller for those individuals who do not believe in hell compared with those who do. What might explain this consistent gender difference if not differences in risk-aversion? As the authors note, this question raises the more general issue of whether observed differences in men and women's behavior are the results of men and women facing different "choice problems" with similar psychology versus facing similar choice problems with different psychology (regardless of the origins of those psychological differences). This question is important as it pushes us to consider foundational questions about what the social psychology of gender is and how in a given decision-making context, it might produce gender differences in observed behavior.

Karin A. Martin and colleagues similarly speak to foundational questions by invigorating a new perspective on the process of childhood socialization, during which children alter, resist, and manage conflicting discourses, interactions, and social structures. Using this framework, they make a strong case for the need for more research on the sexual socialization of young children, that is, how children come to understand sexuality and the structures that support it, given their exposure to partial and potentially conflicting sources of meaning. The authors discuss research agendas that could speak to a broad array of issues, such as childhood sexual abuse, the strategies and behaviors of adolescent sexuality, how sexuality comes to be socially constructed as it intersects with other forms of identity, and how children play an active role in this process. In doing so, they provide a good starting point for anyone interested in the links between gender and sexuality, or the mechanisms reinforcing the hegemony of heterosexuality.

The following chapter by Jeffrey W. Lucas and colleagues presents results from two experiments that examine the effect of gender and status processes on self-handicapping (selecting actions that can impair future performances). The widespread finding that men tend to self-handicap more than women has been surmised to play a role in women's relative academic success. However, the results of this study suggest that men's higher likelihood of self-handicapping is related to concerns about protecting their status or self image: Both experiments find that men, but not women, are more likely to self-handicap when they are in a high status position. These findings are noteworthy in that they demonstrate how gender processes may inform one's strategies for preserving their status position in a given situation.

The next paper by Kevin T. Leicht and colleagues proposes a novel social psychological explanation for the predominance of women on college campuses, a recent trend that has puzzled scholars and the public alike. After presenting evidence that labor market factors cannot account for the increasing proportion of women college students, the authors develop a social identity explanation, suggesting that men may avoid college because cultural understandings of the student role, while congruent with feminine identities, are in conflict with masculine identities. In other words, students respond to gendered cultural expectations about the student role in developing educational aspirations and orientations. Results from a survey of students on five college campuses provide tentative support for the social identity explanation. The authors then develop a new experimental paradigm that promises to provide rich data that will allow us to better understand how gender identities shape educational performance and outcomes.

The volume concludes with Cecilia L. Ridgeway's chapter, "Gender as a Group Process: Implications for the Persistence of Inequality," which tackles the important question of why gender inequality persists in the face of economic and institutional changes that increasingly de-emphasize difference based on gender. She argues that viewing gender as a group process, rather than an individual phenomenon, is crucial in this regard. Gender is a broadly encompassing cultural tool for coordinating behavior at the interpersonal level, such that gender has become, at some level, a part of every sphere of social life. Additionally, cultural beliefs about difference and status based on gender greatly impact behavior and bias judgments. Due to confirmation bias and the institutionalization of shared gender stereotypes through the media, laws and social policies, and the organization of public places, there is a lag between changes in men and women's material experience and changes in gender stereotypes. It is precisely during this window of opportunity that people fall back on old stereotypes to help them make sense of new structural conditions. Despite these hurdles, the author argues that the erosion of such stereotypes can occur with enough repetition of the material changes that continue to shape men and women's lives.

REFERENCES

Aronson, E., Ellsworth, P. C., Carlsmith, J. M., & Gonzales, M. H. (1990). *Methods of research in social psychology.* New York, NY: McGraw-Hill.

Biernat, M., & Kobrynowicz, D. (1997). Gender- and race-based standards of competence: Lower minimum standards but higher ability standards for devalued groups. *Journal of Personality and Social Psychology, 66,* 5–20.

Bodenhausen, G. V. (1990). Stereotypes as judgmental heuristics: Evidence of circadian variations in discrimination. *Psychological Science, 1,* 319–322.

Budig, M., & England, P. (2001). The wage penalty for motherhood. *American Sociological Review, 66,* 204–225.

Cleveland, J. N., & Berman, A. H. (1987). Age perceptions of jobs: Agreement between samples of students and managers. *Psychological Reports, 61,* 565–566.

Connell, R. W. (1987). *Gender & power.* Stanford, CA: Stanford University Press.

Correll, S. J. (2004). Constraints into preferences: Gender, status, and emerging career aspirations. *American Sociological Review, 69,* 93–113.

Correll, S. J., Benard, S., & Paik, I. (2007). Getting a job: Is there a motherhood penalty? *American Journal of Sociology,* 1297–1338.

Deaux, K., & Major, B. (1987). Putting gender into context: An integrative model of gender-related behavior. *Psychological Review, 94,* 369–389.

Devine, P. G. (1989). Stereotypes and prejudice: Their automatic and controlled components. *Journal of Personality and Social Psychology, 56,* 5–18.

Eagly, A. H., & Steffen, V. J. (1984). Gender stereotypes stem from the distribution of men and women into social roles. *Journal of Personality and Social Psychology, 46,* 735–754.

Epstein, C. F. (1990). *Deceptive distinctions: Sex, gender and the social order.* New Haven, CT: Yale University Press.

Fein, S., Hoshino-Brown, E., Davies, P. G., & Spencer, S. J. (2003). Self-image maintenance goals and sociocultural norms in motivated social perception. In: S. J. Spencer, S. Fein, M. P. Zanna & J. M. Olson (Eds), *Motivated social perception: The Ontario symposium* (pp. 21–44). Mahwah, NJ: Erlbaum.

Ferree, M. M., & Hall, E. J. (1996). Rethinking stratification from a feminist perspective: Gender, race and class in mainstream textbooks. *American Sociological Review, 61,* 1–22.

Ferree, M. M., & Hess, B. B. (1987). Introduction. In: M. M. Ferree & B. B. Hess (Eds), *Analyzing gender: A handbook of social science research* (pp. 9–30). Thousand Oaks, CA: Sage Publications.

Ferree, M. M., Lorber, J., & Hess, B. B. (1999). Introduction. In: M. M. Ferree, J. Lorber & B. B. Hess (Eds), *Revisioning gender* (pp. xv–xxxvi). Thousand Oaks, CA: Sage Publications.

Fiske, S. T., Bersoff, D. N., Borgida, E., Deaux, K., & Heilman, M. E. (1991). Social science research on trial: Use of sex stereotyping research in *Price Waterhouse v. Hopkins. American Psychologist, 46,* 1049–1060.

Foschi, M. (1989). Status characteristics, standards, and attributions. In: J. Berger, M. Zelditch, Jr. & B. Anderson (Eds), *Sociological theories in progress: New formulations* (pp. 58–72). Newbury Park, CA: Sage Publications.

Foschi, M. (1996). Double standards in the evaluation of men and women. *Social Psychology Quarterly, 59,* 237–254.

Foschi, M. (2006). On the application-files design for the study of competence and double standards. *Sociological Focus, 39,* 115–132.

Gerson, K. (1985). *Hard choices: How women decide about work, career and motherhood.* Berkeley, CA: The University of California Press.

Heilman, M. E. (2001). Description and prescription: How gender stereotypes prevent women's ascent up the organizational ladder. *Journal of Social Issues, 57,* 657–674.

Hyde, J. S. (2005). The gender similarities hypothesis. *American Psychologist, 60,* 581–592.

Kanter, R. M. (1977). *Men and women of the corporation.* New York, NY: Basic Books.

Kunda, Z., & Spencer, S. J. (2003). When do stereotypes come to mind and when do they color judgment? A goal-based theoretical framework for stereotype activation and application. *Journal of Personality and Social Psychology, 129,* 522–544.

Lightdale, J. R., & Prentice, D. A. (1994). Rethinking sex differences in aggression: Aggressive behavior in the absence of social roles. *Personality and Social Psychology Bulletin, 20,* 34–44.

Lopata, H. Z., & Thorne, B. (1978). On the term sex roles. *Signs, 3,* 718–721.

Lorber, J. (1994). *Paradoxes of gender.* New Haven, CT: Yale University Press.

Maass, A., Cadinu, M., Guarnieri, G., & Grasselli, A. (2003). Sexual harassment under social identity threat: The computer harassment paradigm. *Journal of Personality and Social Psychology, 85,* 853–870.

Martin, K. A. (1998). Becoming a gendered body: Practices of preschools. *American Sociological Review, 63,* 494–511.

Nakano Glenn, E. (1999). The social construction and institutionalization of gender and race: An integrative framework. In: M. M. Ferree, J. Lorber & B. B. Hess (Eds), *Revisioning gender* (pp. 3–43). Thousand Oaks, CA: Sage Publications.

Olian, J. D., & Schwab, D. P. (1988). The impact of applicant gender compared to qualifications on hiring recommendations: A meta-analysis of experimental studies. *Organizational Behavior and Human Decision Processes, 41,* 180–195.

Pierce, J. (1995). *Gender trials: Emotional lives in contemporary law firms.* Berkeley, CA: University of California Press.

Rhode, D. L. (1997). *Speaking of sex: The denial of gender inequality.* London: Cambridge University Press.

Ridgeway, C. L. (1991). The social construction of status value: Gender and other nominal characteristics. *Social Forces, 70,* 367–386.

Ridgeway, C. L. (1997). Interaction and the conservation of gender inequality: Considering employment. *American Sociological Review, 62,* 218–235.

Ridgeway, C. L., & Berger, J. (1986). Expectations, legitimation, and dominance behavior in task groups. *American Sociological Review, 51,* 603–671.

Ridgeway, C. L., & Correll, S. J. (2004). Unpacking the gender system: A theoretical perspective on gender beliefs and social relations. *Gender & Society, 18,* 510–531.

Ridgeway, C. L., & Smith-Lovin, L. (1999). The gender system and interaction. *Annual Review of Sociology, 25,* 191–216.

Risman, B. J. (1998). *Gender vertigo: American families in transition.* New Haven, CT: Yale University Press.

Rudman, L. A. (1998). Self-promotion as a risk factor for women: The costs and benefits of counter-stereotypical impression management. *Journal of Personality and Social Psychology, 74,* 629–645.

Smith-Lovin, L., & McPherson, M. (1993). You are who you know: A network perspective on gender. In: P. England (Ed.), *Theory on gender/feminism on theory* (pp. 223–251). New York, NY: Aldine.

Sprague, J. (2005). *Feminist methodologies for critical researchers: Bridging differences.* Walnut Creek, CA: Altamira Press.

Stacey, J., & Thorne, B. (1985). The missing feminist revolution in sociology. *Social Problems, 32*, 301–316.
Tetlock, P. E. (1983). Accountability and complexity of thought. *Journal of Personality and Social Psychology, 45*, 74–83.
Valian, V. (1999). *Why so slow? The advancement of women.* Cambridge, MA: The MIT Press.
West, C., & Zimmerman, D. (1987). Doing gender. *Gender & Society, 1*, 125–151.
Wilson, T. D., & Brekke, N. (1994). Mental contamination and mental correction: Unwanted influences on judgments and evaluations. *Psychological Bulletin, 116*, 117–142.
Zelditch, M. (1969). Can you really study an army in the laboratory? In: A. Etzoni (Ed.), *A sociological reader on complex organizations* (pp. 528–539). New York, NY: Holt, Rinehart & Winston.

SEX DIFFERENCES, SEXISM, AND SEX: THE SOCIAL PSYCHOLOGY OF GENDER FROM PAST TO PRESENT

Laurie A. Rudman and Julie E. Phelan

ABSTRACT

Early research on sexism presumed the traditional model of prejudice as an antipathy. This research focused on negative stereotypes of women as less competent than men and hostility toward gender equality. More recently, sexism has been revealed to have a "benevolent" component; although it reflects positive beliefs about women, it also supports gender inequality by implying that women are weaker than men. In addition, although disconfirming stereotypes should provide women with a means of thwarting sex discrimination, recent research shows that even ambitious and successful women are punished for violating prescriptive stereotypes that assign them to subordinate roles.

THE SOCIAL PSYCHOLOGY OF GENDER FROM PAST TO PRESENT

Whether it be the controversy sparked by the president of Harvard over putative sex differences in science aptitude, a film exploring the hostile work environment of female miners, the continued debate over the struggle to balance careers and families for working mothers, or the steady stream of newly-published relationship guidebooks, it is clear that gender issues consistently occupy the media and the public mind. Popular interest in sex differences, sexism, and sex has both inspired and been informed by scientific research. Ranging from investigations of male dominance in leadership roles (e.g., Eagly & Karau, 2002), to the causes and consequences of sexual harassment and gender discrimination (e.g., Burgess & Borgida, 1999; Fiske, Bersoff, Borgida, Deaux, & Heilman, 1991), to studies examining how sexuality and romance inform sexism (e.g., Rudman & Heppen, 2003; Sanchez, Crocker, & Boike, 2005), social psychological gender research has important implications for the boardroom, the courtroom, and the bedroom.

In this chapter, we begin with a brief overview of the history of gender research, examining how gender issues were first explored by social psychologists and how this knowledge has evolved and shaped subsequent areas of inquiry. The remainder of the chapter focuses on two current avenues of research, which, in concert, help to explain why women's advancement since the advent of the feminist movement has been surprisingly slow (Valian, 1999). Specifically, we consider: (a) how seemingly positive female stereotypes and attitudes pose a unique threat to gender equity; and (b) how negative reactions toward ambitious and capable women present a difficult barrier for women in performance settings. Thus, the goal of the present chapter is to tie social psychological theorizing about gender to its specific applications in the workplace, with particular attention to obstacles that impact women's career mobility and earnings.

THE BIRTH OF GENDER RESEARCH IN SOCIAL PSYCHOLOGY

Beginning in the 1930s, stereotyping and prejudice captured social psychologists' attention, but their focus was on biases based on ethnicity, religion, and occupation (e.g., Allport, 1935, 1954/1979; Katz & Braly, 1933). Remarkably, gender was ignored, perhaps because sex discrimination was so normative that even women were largely complacent with the status quo (i.e., historically and cross-culturally, men have been the dominant sex). With the advent of the Women's Movement in the 1970s, gender issues began to receive empirical attention. In the beginning, gender researchers largely focused on two broad themes, described below. The first of these themes concerns sexist attitudes, defined as antipathy toward women's rights and the endorsement of beliefs of male superiority. The second (and related) theme concerns gender stereotypes, defined as beliefs about sex differences.

Sexist Attitudes

Guided by Allport's (1935) definition of prejudice as antipathy, early gender researchers set out to assess hostility toward women's increasing demands for equal rights and status in society. This led to the first individual difference measure of sexism, the Attitudes Toward Women Scale (ATWS; Spence & Helmreich, 1972a), which assessed beliefs about women's rights (e.g., "A woman should not expect to go to exactly the same places or to have quite the same freedom of action as a man") and roles (e.g., "On average, women should be regarded as less capable of contributing to economic production than are men"). In support of the measure's validity, high scores on the ATWS predicted negative reactions to competent women (Spence & Helmreich, 1972b), greater male aggression toward women (Scott & Tetreault, 1987), and more favorable perceptions of men who harm women (e.g., domestic abusers and rapists; Hillier & Foddy, 1993; Weidner & Griffitt, 1983). These findings are consistent with the argument that the ATWS measures antipathy toward women. However, the measure is limited in the scope of its predictive utility (see Spence, 1999, for a review). For example, it does not predict gender identity, women's career choices, or gender stereotypes, perhaps because it measures attitudes toward women's *rights*, not attitudes toward women themselves.

As with all direct measures of prejudice, a further limitation is the scale's susceptibility to social desirability bias (i.e., the tendency to provide "politically correct" responses). As egalitarian norms increased, ATWS scores decreased correspondingly – to the point where the measure is no longer useful for college student samples (Spence, 1999). To counter this limitation, researchers have developed more subtle instruments, including the Modern Sexism Scale (Swim, Aiken, Hall, & Hunter, 1995) and the Neo-Sexism Scale (Tougas, Brown, Beaton, & Joly, 1995), which assess opposition to women's progress and the policies that support it (e.g., affirmative action). Nonetheless, like the ATWS, these scales assess attitudes toward gender equality, not attitudes toward women as a group.

Gender Stereotypes

In contrast to the early gender attitude research, initial gender stereotype research directly targeted beliefs about women as a group. Beginning with

Rosencrantz, Vogel, Bee, Broverman, and Broverman (1968), much of this research has asked respondents to indicate whether traits are more typical of the average adult female or the average adult male. People consistently reported perceived sex differences in achievement-oriented and people-oriented traits (see Basow, 1986; Williams & Best, 1990, for reviews). In particular, men were often characterized as competent, independent, ambitious, and decisive (i.e., *agentic*), whereas women were viewed as kind, helpful, and concerned about others (i.e., *communal*; Bakan, 1966). Further, women were seen as lacking agentic qualities and men as lacking communal qualities, underscoring the common expression, "the opposite sex."

The perceived discrepancy between male and female attributes largely aligns with traditional expectations for gender roles, with men serving as breadwinners and women as homemakers (Eagly, 1987). However, as women began to enter the workforce in numbers commensurate with men (i.e., 46% of today's workers are female; U.S. Bureau of Labor Statistics, 2006), researchers turned their attention to the ways in which persisting sex stereotypes might impact women's work roles. Gutek and Morasch (1982) argued that gender-based expectancies "spill over" into professional environments; for example, female supervisors are expected to be more nurturing than male counterparts, which may undermine their authority (see also Gutek, 1985). Moreover, characteristics expected of managers and leaders (e.g., competitiveness and self-reliance) align more closely with male agency than with female communality (Schein, 1973). As a result, Heilman (1983) argued that even when women and men were identically qualified, women were often viewed as unsuitable managers because they were presumed to lack the masculine qualities necessary for the job (the "lack of fit" hypothesis). Moreover, even when women are undeniably successful, evaluators may make faulty attributions for their success, such that female accomplishments are attributed to luck or effort, whereas male accomplishments are seen as a result of natural talent or skill (Swim & Sanna, 1996). Recent research suggests that denying credit to women is particularly likely when women work in male-female teams, a frequent occurrence in the workplace (Heilman & Haynes, 2005).

Although women now make up 36% of managers in the U.S. workplace (U.S. Bureau of Labor Statistics, 2006), the perceived incongruity between women and leaders still hinders women's ability to ascend to the upper echelon of power. In lower and mid-level management positions, communal skills such as fostering cooperation and motivating subordinates are deemed important, in addition to competence. However, in top executive positions (Martell, Parker, Emrich, & Crawford, 1998), and high-powered arenas such as politics (Huddy & Terkildsen, 1993) and the military (Boyce & Herd, 2003), the emphasis is solely on agentic qualities, such as ruthlessness, competitiveness, and decisiveness. Thus, women's disadvantage may increase as positions increase in power. For example, within Fortune 500 companies, only 15.7% of all corporate officers and 1.4% of all CEOs are women (Catalyst, 2002). Within politics, women make up only 15% of congressional representatives, 14% of senators, and 16% of state governors (White House Project, 2006).

In sum, although women's career opportunities have greatly improved since the first studies of sexism were conducted, women still show enormous deficits when it comes to obtaining prestigious leadership positions. Although early research on sexist attitudes and stereotypes was fruitful, it cannot fully account for the durability of sex discrimination given women's dramatic influx into the workplace and the contemporary acceptance of career women. Consequently, gender researchers have sought new explanations for the continuing shortage of women in positions of power that extend beyond traditional notions of sexism. Instead of antipathy toward women's rights, more subtle, yet potentially more insidious forms of bias can operate to prevent women from fully achieving gender equity. Below, we describe research on benevolent sexism and backlash effects to illustrate these barriers.

BENEVOLENT SEXISM

The limitations of the original conceptualization of sexism (as antipathy) became evident as research showing strongly positive attitudes toward women accumulated (Eagly & Mladinic, 1989; Eagly, Mladinic, & Otto, 1994; Glick & Fiske, 1996, 2001). The "women are wonderful" effect first described by Eagly and Mladinic (1989) was driven by the favorable attitudes both women and men hold toward key aspects of the communal stereotype (e.g., to be warm and supportive of others). Because women are viewed as more communal than men, this resulted in greater reported liking for women (as compared to men). Similarly, Glick and Fiske (1996) found that women were viewed as more moral, pure, and worthy of protection as compared with men. These findings were initially very surprising, as they seemed to suggest the existence of "reverse sexism." At the very least, it became clear that women's lower status could not be fully explained by antipathy and intergroup hostility.

However, ostensibly favorable attitudes toward women were found to be derived from the stereotype of women as wonderful but *weak* (e.g., incapable and child-like), and therefore in need of protection (Glick & Fiske, 1996, 2001). Thus, although women's communality may lead to pro-female attitudes, it can also lead to discrimination, in the form of benevolent sexism. Benevolent sexism refers to putatively positive beliefs and behaviors toward women that serve to undermine their status. For example, the belief that women are more nurturing than men assigns them to low-status caregiver roles both at home and in the workplace. Further, the belief that women are in need of protection can lead to seemingly pro-social behaviors (e.g., overhelping, taking over, or limiting responsibilities) that reinforce assumptions of women's incompetence and help to maintain their lower status.

Benevolent sexism may also manifest in the form of patronizing praise, whereby female subordinates receive more praise, but less valued resources (e.g., promotions) than male subordinates (Vescio, Gervais, Snyder, & Hoover, 2005). Further, although women who perform well in masculine domains may receive high competence ratings (Deaux & Taylor, 1973; Rudman, 1998), this may reflect lowered initial expectations and shifting standards for excellence (i.e., "She's excellent ... for a woman"), and therefore not translate into tangible rewards (Biernat & Fuegen, 2001).

Prescriptive versus Descriptive Stereotypes

As described above, benevolent sexism has been linked to gender stereotypes, and gender stereotypes to traditional sex roles. With contemporary women occupying more leadership and authority roles, one might expect gender stereotypes to reflect this change. However, in addition to a descriptive component reflecting how men and women typically are perceived, gender stereotypes also contain a strong prescriptive component which reflects how men and women "should be" and importantly, how they "should not be" (Burgess & Borgida, 1999; Eagly & Karau, 2002; Fiske & Stevens, 1993; Rudman & Glick, 1999, 2001). As Eagly (1987) noted, "[gender] beliefs are more than beliefs about the attributes of women and men: Many of these expectations are normative in the sense that they describe qualities or behavioral tendencies believed to be desirable for each sex" (p. 13). Indeed, prescriptive and descriptive stereotypes tend to overlap, with the communal qualities viewed as typical of women seen as ideal for women (but proscribed for men) and the agentic qualities viewed as typical of men seen as ideal for men (but proscribed for women).

Recent research has examined the effect of women's occupying more agentic roles on gender stereotypes. The evidence suggests that while descriptive beliefs may be changing to reflect the more agentic roles women now possess, prescriptive beliefs remain static (Diekman & Eagly, 2000; Prentice & Carranza, 2002; Spence & Buckner, 2000). For example, when developing the Bem Sex Role Inventory (BSRI), Bem (1974) assessed the 20 traits deemed most desirable for women and men, thus providing a measure of the content of prescriptive gender stereotypes. Although constructed over three decades ago, recent investigations of the BSRI have shown that the same traits deemed most desirable for women in the 1970s continue to be viewed as most desirable for women today (Auster & Ohm, 2000; Harris, 1994; Holt & Ellis, 1998). Prentice and Carranza (2002) provide further evidence for the persistence of traditional gender prescriptions, despite changes in descriptive gender stereotype content. They asked participants to rate a series of attributes on whether they were more typical for one gender or the other and whether they were more desirable for one gender or the other. Although traits pertaining to competence (e.g., intelligent, rational, and worldly) were rated as equally typical for men and women (descriptive stereotype), they were rated as less desirable for women than men (prescriptive stereotype). That is, even though women have successfully changed descriptive stereotype content, traditional gender prescriptions remain intact. Further, Gill (2004) asked evaluators to choose between a male and female candidate for a managerial role in a business consulting firm. Because candidates were described as equally suitable, this information should successfully undercut gender bias due to descriptive stereotyping, and it did. However, evaluators who possessed strong gender stereotype prescriptions were still likely to show bias against the female applicant even though descriptive stereotypes had successfully been thwarted. Thus, despite dramatic changes in women's career opportunities and work roles, perceptions that women *should* differ from men in ways that negatively reflect on their ability to perform high-powered jobs persist as a barrier to gender equity.

Heterosexuality and Benevolent Sexism

In contrast to other groups, men and women are uniquely intimate and interdependent, which can influence the persistence of prescriptive gender stereotypes (Fiske & Stevens, 1993). In particular, the strength of the female communality stereotype may be bolstered by men's dependence on women (e.g., for sexual intimacy, reproduction, and child care; Glick & Fiske, 1996, 2001). According to benevolent sexism theory, men tend to positively reinforce women's communal qualities to ensure that women remain compliant with these roles. As Jackman (1994) argues, oppression in the guise of kindness (the velvet glove) is more effective than coercion (the iron fist) because subordinates are less likely to resist "soft" prejudice (i.e., paternalism). Moreover, women may embrace the paternalistic attitudes and prescriptive stereotypes that deem them worthy of male protection. For example, they may enact prescriptions for niceness in order to favorably distinguish themselves from men (Brewer, 1991), or as a means of receiving positive male regard (Kilianski & Rudman, 1998). In essence, positive reinforcement for fulfilling feminine ideals may co-opt women into accepting the status quo, and cause them to be (unwitting) conspirators in gender hegemony (Jackman, 1994).

Paternalistic prejudice may also be tied to the fact that men and women are uniquely intimate and interdependent in romantic relationships and domestic life (Glick & Fiske, 1996, 2001). Traditionally, romance has idealized femininity, placing women "on a pedestal." However, it may also teach women (e.g., through romantic fairytales) to depend on men for economic and social rewards. In particular, the romantic idealization of men as chivalric rescuers (e.g., Prince Charming) might encourage women to seek their fortune indirectly, through men. If so, romantic fantasies might be negatively linked to women's interest in personal power. Rudman and Heppen (2003) tested this hypothesis using the Implicit Association Test (IAT; Greenwald et al., 2002) because it measures beliefs and attitudes that people may not be aware they possess in a manner that cannot be easily controlled. Not surprisingly, as inheritors of the Women's Movement, women were reluctant to report associating male romantic partners with chivalry (e.g., Prince Charming, White Knight, protector, hero); nonetheless, they demonstrated this association on the IAT. Furthermore, women who possessed implicit romantic beliefs also showed less interest in personal power across multiple measures. For example, they expected to make less income in their careers, and had lower educational goals. They also showed less interest in prestigious occupations (e.g., CEOs, corporate lawyers, and politicians) and were less willing to volunteer for a leadership role in an upcoming experiment. Taken together, the results provide tentative support for a possible "glass-slipper" effect, such that women who implicitly idealize men may be more interested in pursuing power indirectly, through their romantic relationships, than by seeking their own fortunes. Because romantic ideologies are subjectively pro-female, they represent an important example of how women can be co-opted by benevolent sexism in ways that can be harmful for gender equity (Rudman, 2005).

Because benevolent sexism reflects less hostility than traditional conceptions of sexism, it may appear to be relatively benign. However, this also makes it particularly problematic because it may be difficult for both recipients and perpetrators to recognize it as a form of discrimination (Barreto & Ellemers, 2005; Jackman, 1994). In order to confront prejudice, prejudice must first be perceived. Unfortunately, it is easy to see how people can dismiss the soft bigotry of paternalism. Indeed, women themselves show support for paternalistic men (Kilianski & Rudman, 1998), and they routinely score higher on measures of benevolent sexism, as opposed to hostile sexism (i.e., beliefs that feminists seek to gain power over men; Glick & Fiske, 1996). Further, at least some women may happily receive patronizing help and attention from men, either because they fail to realize how this reinforces their lower status, or because they believe that it is better to be patronized than to face overt hostility. In fact, women's enthusiasm for paternalism can sometimes exceed men's, but this pattern coincides with norms for hostile sexism. In a cross-cultural examination of 26 nations, women scored higher than men on benevolent sexism in the five nations in which men most strongly endorsed hostile sexism (Glick et al., 2000, 2004).

In sum, despite being subjectively positive, paternalistic prejudice may be a particularly difficult barrier to gender equity. Benevolence toward women who fulfill the communal stereotype maintains the status quo by rewarding women for eschewing agency and enacting subordinate roles. Interestingly, research reveals that benevolent sexism positively correlates with hostile sexism around the world (Glick et al., 2000). That is, people who have hostile attitudes toward women also view women benevolently. There is evidence that these contradictory attitudes can be linked to female subtypes. Specifically, paternalistic benevolence is reserved for women in low-status feminine roles, whereas women who strive to achieve success in nontraditional roles (i.e., feminists and career women) are subject to more hostile sexism (Glick, Diebold, Bailey-Werner, & Zhu, 1997). In essence, women are rewarded for conforming to the communal stereotype and punished when they refuse. The next section reviews research examining negative reactions to women who contradict the traditional female stereotype.

BACKLASH EFFECTS FOR DISCONFIRMING GENDER STEREOTYPES

As reviewed above, the female communality stereotype can result in gender bias in myriad ways, including devaluing women's competence and denying them credit for their success (e.g., Heilman & Haynes, 2005; Swim & Sanna, 1996), as well as putatively benevolent behaviors that reinforce the status quo (e.g., praise without a raise; Vescio et al., 2005). These forms of sexism stem from perceptions that women are less agentic than men, and therefore not suited for prestigious, male-dominated occupations (Cejka & Eagly, 1999; Eagly, 1987; Glick, Wilk, & Perreault, 1995; Heilman, 1983). The observation of a perceived "lack of fit" between femininity and leadership led researchers to hypothesize that in order for women to break the glass ceiling, they would have to actively disconfirm the female gender stereotype by acting "more like men" (Wiley & Eskilson, 1985). Research confirmed this, showing that only when women were described as *successful* managers were they viewed as equally competent as identically described men (Heilman, Block, & Martell, 1995; see also Dodge, Gilroy, & Fenzel, 1995). Indeed, unless she provides irrefutable counterstereotypical information, a female candidate for a masculine-type occupation is likely to be judged as less suitable than a man (Glick, Zion, & Nelson, 1988).

These findings are consistent with impression formation models, which emphasize the need for clear, unambiguous information about a person's counterstereotypical attributes in order to undermine stereotypes (e.g., Brewer, 1988; Fiske & Neuberg, 1990). From this perspective, to impede the influence of gender stereotypes in the workplace, women need only to present themselves as competent, independent, and assertive (i.e., as possessing the requisite agentic qualities necessary for leadership). Although research supports the notion that clear evidence of a woman's agency counteracts gender-stereotypical inferences regarding her competence (Dodge et al., 1995; Glick et al., 1988; Heilman et al., 1995), unintended negative consequences of stereotype disconfirmation have subsequently been revealed.

In fact, evidence now abounds that female agency can result in *backlash effects*, defined as social and economic repercussions for disconfirming prescriptive stereotypes (Rudman, 1998; Rudman & Glick, 1999, 2001). Although women must present themselves as self-confident, assertive, and competitive to be viewed as qualified for leadership roles, when they do so, they violate prescriptive female communality prescriptions and therefore, risk social and economic reprisals. Specifically, although agentic women are rated as highly competent and capable of leadership, they are also viewed as socially deficient and unlikable by both male and female perceivers (Rudman, 1998; Rudman & Glick, 1999, 2001). This type of bias is evident in the epithets often applied to powerful women, such as "dragon lady" and "battleaxe" (Tannen, 1994). As Fiske and Stevens (1993) elucidate:

> Women are [in] a double bind. Do they behave in a way that meets the sex stereotypic prescriptive demands to be feminine? Or, do they act competently and aggressively in order to fill job-specific demands? If they work to fill the job-specific demands they run the risk of being evaluated negatively for displaying behavior antithetical to the stereotypic expectation for women. On the other hand, if they fill the gender-prescriptive demands they run the risk of being viewed as incapable of having a successful career. Interestingly, both of these scenarios could result in sexual discrimination. In one case, discrimination would result from not behaving like a woman should, and, in the other case, from behaving too much like a woman. (p. 181)

In other words, ambitious women may have to choose between being liked but not respected (by displaying communal qualities) or being respected but not liked (by displaying agentic qualities), a dilemma not faced by men. As reviewed below, evidence of backlash effects exists at every stage of employment, from hiring and salary negotiations to promotion and leadership evaluations.

Backlash Effects on Hiring

To obtain a leadership position, applicants need to project a confident image to would-be employers by engaging in self-promotion (e.g., highlighting past accomplishments and emphasizing one's skills). Self-promotion during job interviews is important for both genders, but it matters especially for women, who face a double standard (Rudman, 1998). In order to counteract stereotypical expectations of female subordination and incompetence, women must present themselves as confident and capable. However, in a series of experiments, Rudman (1998) showed that while self-promotion is necessary for high competence ratings, it decreases women's likeability ratings and consequently, their likelihood of being hired (see also Rudman & Glick 1999, 2001). By contrast, self-promoting men were viewed as highly competent, likable, and hirable, suggesting that only women face normative pressures to be modest (Daubman, Heatherington, & Ahn, 1992; Gould & Slone, 1982; Heatherington et al., 1993). It is noteworthy that results were similar whether self-promoting men and women used the same or different scripts, and whether live or videotaped applicants were presented (Rudman, 1998). Similarly, Buttner and McEnally (1996) found that women who used a direct and assertive strategy when applying for a job were less likely to be recommended for it than men who used the same strategy. Thus, agentic women (but not men) may pay a price for behaviors that are necessary to embark on a successful career.

In the recent past, corporations have begun to recognize the value of an inclusive, participatory approach to leadership (Offermann & Gowing, 1990; Peters, 1988; Rosener, 1990). The trend toward "feminization" of management, with corporations increasingly valuing interpersonal skills, would seem to be a positive development for women. By softening the traits required of managerial positions, the discrepancy between female stereotypes and requisite job characteristics should be somewhat ameliorated. However, when communal qualities are required for the job, hiring discrimination may especially be likely against agentic women (Rudman & Glick, 1999; 2001). Essentially, agentic women (but not men) are viewed as insufficiently feminine for the position. Although agentic men are not seen as particularly nice (Eagly & Mladinic, 1989), they are judged less harshly on interpersonal skills than the agentic women (Eagly, Makhijani, & Klonsky, 1992; Rudman & Glick, 1999, 2001). Because agentic men do not violate prescriptions for communality, they are viewed as more likable, and thus, are more likely to be hired for a management position, even when it is feminized, than identically described women (Rudman & Glick, 1999, 2001). In support of this interpretation, negative evaluations of agentic women were predicted by evaluators' implicit gender stereotype beliefs, such that people who more strongly associated female gender with communality and male gender with agency also rated an agentic female applicant as socially unattractive (Rudman & Glick, 2001).

Backlash Effects on Salary Negotiations

Even when women are hired, the risk of sanctions for agentic behavior can put women at a serious financial disadvantage. Although assertiveness is necessary for success in the business world, in women it is viewed negatively (Costrich, Feinstein, Kidder, Maracek, & Pascale, 1975; Crawford, 1988; Powers & Zuroff, 1988), even when involved in self-defense (Branscombe, Crosby, & Weir, 1993). This constraint on women's behavior can have serious economic effects during salary negotiations (Janoff-Bulman & Wade, 1996). For example, even when controlling for other factors that may influence salary negotiations, female MBAs routinely accept lower salary offers than male MBAs (Bowles, Babcock, & McGinn, 2005; Gerhart & Rynes, 1991; Stevens, Bavetta, & Gist, 1993), especially when the appropriate salary range is unclear (Bowles et al., 2005b). In a study of professional school graduates, only 7% of female graduates attempted to negotiate their initial salary offers (as compared to 57% of male graduates; Babcock & Laschever, 2003).

Women's unwillingness to negotiate for more compensation is likely explained in part by differential treatment of male and female negotiators. Bowles, Babcock and Lai (2005) found that male evaluators were more inclined to work with "nice" women who accepted their compensation offers, compared with women who attempted to negotiate for more money; by contrast, negotiating for a higher salary had no effect on men's willingness to work with male candidates. These findings suggest that women "do not ask" (e.g., for higher pay, more responsibility, or greater recognition; Babcock & Laschever, 2003) because they (correctly) fear negative reactions from others.

Backlash Effects on Promotion and Evaluations

Once a woman navigates the double standard for agency to obtain a high-powered job, she may continue to pay a price for stereotype disconfirmation, even though it may be required for career success (Eagly et al., 1992; McIlwee & Robinson, 1992). The classic example is Ann Hopkins, a successful accountant who was denied promotion to partnership in her firm for being too masculine. Her evaluators suggested she needed "a course in charm school," where she might learn to speak and dress more femininely, even though stereotypically masculine qualities were necessary for her job (Fiske et al., 1991). In other words, violating feminine niceness prescriptions can result in poor performance evaluations and adversely affect promotion considerations (Heilman, 2001; Lyness & Judiesch, 1999). In one series of experiments, agentic women who had demonstrated their clear professional competence were viewed as interpersonally hostile (e.g., abrasive, pushy, and manipulative); as a result, they were not recommended for higher paying, prestigious positions (Heilman, Wallen, Fuchs, & Tamkins, 2004).

Research investigating leadership style provides further evidence of sanctions for female agency. Women are expected to be nice, and when their leadership behavior deviates from this expectation, their evaluations suffer. For example, business students evaluated female managers who led in a stereotypically feminine style positively, but those who led in a stereotypically masculine style were rated more negatively than men (Bartol & Butterfield, 1976). In a meta-analysis, Eagly et al. (1992) found a small overall tendency for male leaders to receive more positive evaluations than female leaders;

however, when women led in a stereotypically masculine style, this gender difference was exacerbated. Further, they found that only women were penalized for leading in a stereotype inconsistent fashion (i.e., men who led in a stereotypically feminine style did not receive correspondingly low evaluations). An additional meta-analysis showed that stereotype inconsistency influenced effectiveness; the more female supervisors strayed from stereotypically feminine leadership styles (e.g., by leading autocratically), the less effective they were as leaders (Eagly, Karau, & Makhijani, 1995).

Women leaders are also evaluated more negatively than male leaders when they use intimidation strategies as a method of accomplishing goals (Bolino & Turnley, 2003), or when they deliver discipline (Atwater, Carey, & Waldman, 2001; Brett, Atwater, & Waldman, 2005). Finally, Sinclair and Kunda (2000) found that after receiving negative feedback from a female instructor, participants viewed her as less competent than when she administered praise, whereas male instructors were free to criticize without penalty. These findings are consistent with considerable research demonstrating that women have less latitude in their communication style, compared with men (Carli, 1990, 2001; Carli, LaFleur, & Loeber, 1995). As Tannen (1990) notes: "Women in authority find themselves in a double bind. If they speak in ways expected of women, they are seen as inadequate leaders. If they speak in ways expected of leaders, they are seen as inadequate women. The road to authority is tough for women, and once they get there it's a bed of thorns" (p. 244).

Emotional and Implicit Reactions to Agentic Women

Research has also demonstrated negative responses to agentic women using less controlled indicators, including emotional responses (Carranza, 2004; Butler & Geis, 1990; Koch, 2005) and implicit attitudes (e.g., Rudman & Kilianski, 2000). For example, using facial EMG, Carranza (2004) found that women were likely to frown in response to self-promoting women, whereas men were likely to smile at them derisively. Being laughed at or frowned upon reflects severe social punishment, and is likely to curb women's ability to speak in a confident, assertive manner. Butler and Geis (1990) and Koch (2005) examined nonverbal reactions toward female leaders, including facial display and body language. In both the initial study (Butler & Geis, 1990) and replications in the lab and field (Koch, 2005), results indicated that negative affect was displayed more frequently to female leaders than to male leaders.

In addition to negative emotional reactions, female leaders may elicit more negative implicit attitudes (Carpenter & Banaji, 1998; Richeson & Ambady, 2001; Rudman & Kilianski, 2000). For example, Richeson and Ambady (2001) found that men showed negative implicit attitudes toward women when they anticipated working with a female superior. By contrast, men showed positive implicit attitudes toward women when they anticipated a superior role, or an equal status interaction. In addition, Rudman and Kilianski (2000) found more negative implicit attitudes toward female than male authority figures (e.g., doctors and professors), particularly on the part of respondents who automatically associated male gender with high status roles (e.g., leader, boss) and female gender with low status roles (e.g., subordinate, helper). These results suggest that deeply ingrained beliefs about gendered status hierarchies can contribute to spontaneously negative reactions to female leaders.

Consequences of Backlash for Gender Parity

Thus far, we have shown how violating prescriptive stereotypes can negatively impact women's financial health and professional status by influencing their ability to obtain employment, fair compensation, career promotions, and positive performance evaluations. Because backlash effects are common, it is not surprising that women are aware of the interpersonal penalties for stepping outside prescribed gender bounds (Rudman & Fairchild, 2004). As a result, women are less willing and able to both ask for and receive promotions (Wade, 2001). Although women are encouraged to advocate on behalf of others, they are socialized to believe that self-advocacy is not appropriately feminine (Bowles et al., 2005a). The threat of backlash effects may help to explain why women wait longer than men for managerial promotions (Maume, 1999), and why gender wage gaps widen over career spans (Olson & Frieze, 1987). According to the U.S. Census Bureau (2002), women earn 73 cents for every dollar earned by men. Further, in a study tracking the advancement of over 30,000 managers, Lyness and Judiesch (1999) found that this disadvantage increases in higher-level positions, with women in upper levels of management receiving fewer promotions and salary increases than comparable men. In addition, while the ratio of men to women in positions with salaries in the $25,000–$35,000 range is roughly equal, the ratio at the highest salary bracket ($1 million or more) is around 13 men to every 1 woman (Sailer, Yao, & Rehula, 2002). Despite a dramatic increase of women in the workforce, there is little evidence that this gender gap in earnings is narrowing (Lips, 2003). The U.S. General Accounting Office (2001) found that in 7 of the 10 industries under investigation, the earnings gap between men and women widened between 1995 and 2000.

As reviewed above, backlash likely promotes gender inequity by reducing hiring and promotion opportunities for ambitious women, and curbing women's ability to negotiate equitable salaries and other benefits. Thus, it likely hinders women from realizing their full financial and professional potential. Although backlash effects research has focused primarily on reactions to women who enact agency, recent work suggests that women who do not enact communality also suffer reprisals. For example, Moss-Racusin and Heilman (2006) found that women who failed at a female sex-typed job were disliked and viewed as more interpersonally hostile than women who failed at a male sex-typed job. Since women are expected to possess the communal characteristics required for success at female-typed jobs, when they fail they are seen as insufficiently feminine and therefore risk backlash in the form of interpersonal sanctions. Similarly, Heilman and Chen (2005) showed that (non-required) helping on the job was evaluated differently for men and women. Being helpful is central to the communal female stereotype. Therefore, when women do not engage in helping behaviors, they are viewed less favorably than identically behaving men. Furthermore, when they do behave altruistically, it is less noted and applauded than when men behave altruistically. Taken together, these findings indicate that helping behavior is less "optional" for women, with women benefiting less from helping and being penalized more for not helping than men. The likely result is that women will be expected to engage in more service-oriented activities, which are undervalued (socially and economically), leaving them less time to pursue financially rewarding activities.

Backlash Effects for Men

Because of its consequences for gender parity, we have focused on negative reactions to agentic women. However, counterstereotypical men also risk backlash effects. For example, compared with agentic counterparts, communal male applicants are rated as less competent and hireable for managerial roles (Rudman, 1998; Rudman & Glick, 1999, 2001). Men who simply show proficiency in feminine domains may be sabotaged by their peers, and thereby prevented from earning financial rewards (Rudman & Fairchild, 2004). These findings are consistent with earlier research showing that men who violate gender stereotypes are likely to experience backlash (Cherry & Deax, 1978; Costrich et al., 1975; Derlega & Chaiken, 1976). For example, a man described as being at the top of his nursing class was perceived to be at risk for future victimization (Cherry & Deax, 1978). Further, when a man was described as having disclosed an emotional problem to a stranger, he was rated as more psychologically disturbed than a self-disclosing woman (Derlega & Chaiken, 1976).

Turning to the developmental literature, cross-sexed behavior in boys is judged more negatively than is cross-sexed behavior in girls (Cahill & Adams, 1997; Martin, 1990; Sandnabba & Ahlberg, 1999), with the result that more boys than girls are diagnosed with gender identity disorders (Zucker, Bradley, & Sanikhani, 1997). Thus, backlash can be more severe for boys than for girls, possibly because parents and teachers fear that cross-sexed behavior signals latent homosexuality (Kite & Deaux, 1987). This fear may pertain more to boys, given that girls can be "tomboys" without raising doubts about their sexuality. By contrast, the social psychological literature has primarily focused on backlash for agentic behavior in women because of its implications for the glass ceiling.

Consequences of Backlash for Stereotype Maintenance

In addition to contributing to gender inequities, backlash also plays a role in maintaining cultural stereotypes (Rudman & Fairchild, 2004). When atypical job applicants are devalued and discriminated against (e.g., for leadership roles and promotions), it curbs their ability to stand out as stereotype disconfirming role models – an important mechanism by which stereotypes are thwarted (e.g., Fiske & Neuberg, 1990). By thwarting the ambitions of agentic women and communal men, evaluators contribute to preserving stereotypes in the culture-at-large.

Moreover, to the extent that people fear backlash for counterstereotypical behaviors, they are likely to closet their actions, which prevents them from becoming stereotype-disconfirming exemplars. Recent research suggests how this process occurs (Rudman & Fairchild, 2004). Men and women were assigned to receive false positive feedback on gender knowledge tests. Participants were randomly assigned to believe they had scored high in their own gender test (normatives) or the opposite gender test (deviants). They were then afforded the opportunity to publicize their success in various ways (e.g., on a Website advertising the project). They were also given the chance to win a lottery prize by depositing a ticket in a box clearly marked "feminine" or "masculine" knowledge test winners. Compared with normatives, deviants were more likely to hide their success by refusing publicity, deceiving the experimenter (by claiming success in the wrong test), and depositing their ticket in the wrong box. Moreover, deviants reported greater interest in gender stereotypical occupations and activities, suggesting a need to increase their efforts to conform to gender norms. However, these effects were moderated by fear of backlash. That is, successful gender deviants engaged in these strategies (hiding, deception, and norm conformity) in response to the threat of being socially rejected. As Rudman and Fairchild (2004) note, "To the extent that people hide their counterstereotypical behavior, feign normative achievement, or redouble their efforts to conform to gender norms, gendered beliefs are allowed to persist unchallenged" (p. 169).

In sum, backlash effects help to preserve gender stereotypes by keeping atypical men and women out of the spotlight (when evaluators sanction them), or dampening atypical actors' enthusiasm for publicizing their success (when they fear sanctions). As a result, stereotypes are allowed to thrive in the culture-at-large. Because cultural expectancies are the reason why atypical individuals are perceived as deviants, the result is a vicious cycle; until there is more latitude for stereotype-disconfirming behaviors, gender stereotypes and backlash effects are likely to remain strong.

Potential Moderators of Backlash

While research evidence clearly points to negative consequences for female agency, studies have also suggested ways for agentic women to overcome backlash. Women who temper their agentic qualities with a display of communal warmth can convey their competence and be influential with a much lower risk of backlash, as compared with women who solely display agentic traits (e.g., Carli, 2001; Carli et al., 1995; Rudman & Glick, 2001). Heilman and Okimoto (in press) found that when successful women managers were also described as communal they were rated as far more likeable than successful women managers for whom no communal information was provided. This is also consistent with the finding that female leaders who lead in an interpersonally oriented democratic style were less likely to receive negative evaluations than females who led in a task-oriented or autocratic style (Eagly et al., 1992). Further it seems that women are aware of this, and tend to lead in more androgynous styles (Eagly, Johannesen-Schmidt, & van Engen, 2003). Although displaying communal qualities in addition to displaying competence may be an effective method of alleviating backlash, it is not an ideal solution as it presents an additional burden for female leaders. Men do not suffer repercussions for assertive behavior; therefore they have more freedom to lead without the risk of sanctions.

Are there gender differences in backlash effects? For most of the part, research shows that men and women equally sanction counterstereotypical targets, but there are a few exceptions. Communications studies find that, compared with women, men are more likely to judge assertive speech harshly in women (Carli, 1990, 2001; Carli et al., 1995). In addition, Carranza (2004) found that women reacted more positively toward feminine men on measures of facial feedback, compared with men. In one study, men selected evenly between an agentic woman and an agentic man as a partner for a competitive task when they believed their own success was dependent on their partners' competence; by contrast, women uniformly chose the agentic man (Rudman, 1998). Nonetheless, the routine absence of gender differences is consistent with the fact that (a) implicit gender stereotypes predict backlash (Rudman & Glick, 2001), and (b) sex differences are rarely found on these measures (Greenwald et al., 2002).

CONCLUSION

The social psychology of gender has made tremendous advancements since the advent of the Women's Movement and the first individual difference measure of sexism (Spence & Helmreich, 1972a). Early researchers fruitfully established the importance of attitudes toward women's rights, as well as gender stereotypes, when predicting reactions to ambitious women. Although the initial belief that people feel antipathy toward women was subsequently discharged by the "women are wonderful" effect (Eagly & Mladinic, 1989), the results of benevolent sexism and backlash effect research suggest we ought to label this phenomenon the "women are wonderful *when*" effect – when they are communal, and when they are not in charge (Eagly & Karau, 2002).

This development is clearly a theoretical advance over the simple definition of prejudice as group-based antipathy (Allport, 1954), which is currently being refined by intergroup relations researchers (Dovidio, Glick, & Rudman, 2005). Benevolent sexism has also played a significant role in this advance, as subjectively favorable attitudes toward women are revealed to negatively reflect on their competence, thereby maintaining gender hegemony. Because paternalism is "soft" bigotry (relative to overt hostility), women themselves may be co-opted into maintaining the status quo (Jackman, 1994). In this chapter, we attempted to show the many ways that benevolent sexism hinders gender parity and how it operates at home, in the workplace, and within women's minds (e.g., as romantic fantasies that curb interest in personal power).

Finally, backlash effects are a particularly pernicious barrier to gender equity because they prevent the very women who might be best suited for leadership roles from achieving their ambitions, as well as from serving as role models. Moreover, backlash stems from traditional stereotype prescriptions that seem particularly resistant to change. Research on backlash effects has theoretically advanced impression formation models, which have assumed that counterstereotypical actors reap positive outcomes when they thwart gender stereotypes (because they avoid category-based judgments; Brewer, 1988; Fiske & Neuberg, 1990). On the contrary, violating prescriptive stereotypes tends to boomerang so that actors suffer negative consequences for stereotype disconfirmation. Furthermore, recognizing the multifarious ways that backlash operates to preserve cultural stereotypes, from the standpoint of perceivers and actors alike, is an important conceptual advance (Rudman & Fairchild, 2004).

In sum, contemporary gender researchers are beginning to understand the complex barriers that women face as they strive to gain equal status with men. The research agenda is already filled with numerous challenges and multiple directions to pursue; we are confident that this situation will only multiply in the future. Uncovering the diverse ways in which gender bias manifests itself expands our understanding of prejudice and allows us to create more efficient means of combating it. For example, benevolent sexism research has shown the deleterious effects of subjectively positive sentiments on women's ability to achieve gender equity. Although convincing laypeople that benevolence can be a form of discrimination may prove a daunting task, the accumulating research evidence makes a persuasive case. Similarly, backlash research expands our understanding of the way gender stereotypes operate in the workplace, allowing for intervention strategies to be developed that not only help to ameliorate bias due to descriptive stereotypes, but also take into account gender stereotype prescriptions. Future research in these domains will continue to revise and expand theoretical frameworks, which can only further the ultimate aim of achieving gender equity.

ACKNOWLEDGMENTS

Preparation of this chapter was partially supported by Grant BCS-0417335 from National Science Foundation. We thank Peter Glick and Corrine Moss-Racusin for their helpful comments. Correspondence concerning this article may be addressed to Laurie A. Rudman, Department of Psychology, Tillett Hall, Rutgers University, 53 Avenue E, Piscataway, NJ, 08854-8040. Electronic mail may be addressed to rudman@rci.rutgers.edu

REFERENCES

Allport, G. W. (1935). *A handbook of social psychology.* Worcester, MA: Clark University Press.
Allport, G. W. (1954/1979). *The nature of prejudice.* Cambridge, MA: Perseus Books.
Atwater, L. E., Carey, J. A., & Waldman, D. A. (2001). Gender and discipline in the workplace: Wait until your father gets home. *Journal of Management, 27,* 537–561.
Auster, C. J., & Ohm, S. C. (2000). Masculinity and femininity in contemporary American society: A reevaluation using the Bem Sex-Role Inventory. *Sex Roles, 43,* 499–528.
Babcock, L., & Laschever, S. (2003). *Women don't ask: Negotiation and the gender divide.* Princeton, NJ: Princeton University Press.
Bakan, D. (1966). *The duality of existence.* Chicago, IL: Rand McNally.
Barreto, M., & Ellemers, N. (2005). The burden of benevolent sexism: How it contributes to the maintenance of gender inequalities. *European Journal of Social Psychology, 35,* 633–642.
Bartol, K. M., & Butterfield, D. A. (1976). Sex effects in evaluating leaders. *Journal of Applied Psychology, 61,* 446–454.
Basow, S. A. (1986). *Gender stereotypes: Traditions and alternatives* (2nd ed.). Monterey, CA: Brooks/Cole.
Bem, S. L. (1974). The measurement of psychological androgyny. *Journal of Clinical and Consulting Psychology, 42,* 155–162.
Biernat, M., & Fuegen, K. (2001). Shifting standards and the evaluation of competence: Complexity in gender-based judgment and decision making. *Journal of Social Issues, 57,* 707–724.
Bolino, M. C., & Turnley, W. H. (2003). Counternormative impression management, likeability, and performance ratings: The use of intimidation in an organization setting. *Journal of Organizational Behavior, 23,* 237–250.
Bowles, H. R., Babcock, L., & Lai, L. (2005a). *It depends who is asking and who you ask: Social incentives for sex differences in the propensity to initiate negotiation.* KSG Working Paper No. RWP05-045.
Bowles, H. R., Babcock, L., & McGinn, K. L. (2005b). Constraints and triggers: Situational mechanics of gender in negotiation. *Journal of Personality and Social Psychology, 89,* 951–965.
Boyce, L. A., & Herd, A. M. (2003). The relationship between gender role stereotypes and requisite military leadership characteristics. *Sex Roles, 49,* 365–378.
Branscombe, N. R., Crosby, P., & Weir, J. A. (1993). Social inferences concerning male and female homeowners who use a gun to shoot an intruder. *Aggressive Behavior, 19,* 113–124.
Brett, J. F., Atwater, L. E., & Waldman, D. A. (2005). Effective delivery of workplace discipline: Do women have to be more participatory than men? *Group and Organization Management, 30,* 487–513.
Brewer, M. B. (1988). A dual process model of impression formation. In: T. K. Skrull & R. S. Wyer, Jr. (Eds), *Advances in social cognition* (Vol. 1, pp. 1–36). Hillsdale, NJ: Erlbaum.
Brewer, M. B. (1991). The social self: On being the same and different at the same time. *Personality and Social Psychology Bulletin, 17,* 475–482.
Burgess, D., & Borgida, E. (1999). Who women are, who women should be: Descriptive and prescriptive gender stereotyping in sex discrimination. *Psychology, Public Policy, and Law, 5,* 665–692.

Butler, D., & Geis, F. L. (1990). Nonverbal affect responses to male and female leaders. Implications for leadership evaluations. *Journal of Personality and Social Psychology, 58,* 48–59.

Buttner, E. H., & McEnally, M. (1996). The interactive effect of applicant gender, influence tactics, and type of job on hiring recommendations. *Sex Roles, 34,* 581–592.

Cahill, B., & Adams, E. (1997). An exploratory study of early childhood teachers' attitudes toward gender roles. *Sex Roles, 36,* 517–529.

Carli, L. L. (1990). Gender, language, and influence. *Journal of Personality and Social Psychology, 59,* 941–951.

Carli, L. L. (2001). Gender and social influence. *Journal of Social Issues, 57,* 725–741.

Carli, L. L., LaFleur, S. J., & Loeber, C. C. (1995). Nonverbal behavior, gender, and influence. *Journal of Personality and Social Psychology, 68,* 1030–1041.

Carpenter, S., & Banaji, M. R. (1998, April). Implicit attitudes and behavior toward female leaders. Paper presented at the annual meeting of the Midwestern Psychological Association, Chicago, IL.

Carranza, E. (2004). *Is what's good for the goose derogated in the gander? Reactions to masculine women and feminine men.* Unpublished doctoral dissertation. Princeton University, Princeton, NJ.

Catalyst. (2002). *2002 Catalyst census of women corporate officers and top earners in the Fortune 500.* Retrieved May 04, 2006, from http://www.catalyst.org/files/fact/COTE%20Factsheet%202002updated.pdf

Cejka, M. A., & Eagly, A. H. (1999). Gender-stereotypic images of occupations correspond to the sex segregation of employment. *Personality and Social Psychology Bulletin, 25,* 413–423.

Cherry, F., & Deax, K. (1978). Fear of success versus fear of gender-inappropriate behavior. *Sex Roles, 4,* 97–101.

Costrich, N., Feinstein, L., Kidder, L., Maracek, J., & Pascale, L. (1975). When stereotypes hurt: Three studies of penalties for sex-role reversals. *Journal of Experimental Social Psychology, 11,* 520–530.

Crawford, M. (1988). Gender, age, and the social evaluation of assertion. *Behavior Modification, 12,* 549–564.

Daubman, K. A., Heatherington, L., & Ahn, A. (1992). Gender and the self-presentation of academic achievement. *Sex Roles, 27,* 187–204.

Deaux, K., & Taylor, J. (1973). Evaluation of male and female ability: Bias works two ways. *Psychological Reports, 32,* 261–262.

Derlega, V. J., & Chaiken, A. L. (1976). Norms affecting self-disclosure in men and women. *Journal of Consulting and Clinical Psychology, 44,* 376–380.

Diekman, A. B., & Eagly, A. H. (2000). Stereotypes as dynamic constructs: Women and men of the past, present, and future. *Personality and Social Psychology Bulletin, 26,* 1171–1188.

Dodge, K. A., Gilroy, F. D., & Fenzel, L. M. (1995). Requisite management characteristics revisited: Two decades later. *Journal of Social Behavior and Personality, 10,* 253–264.

Dovidio, J. F., Glick, P., & Rudman, L. A. (2005). *On the nature of prejudice: Fifty years after Allport.* Malden, MA: Blackwell Publishing.

Eagly, A. H. (1987). *Sex differences in social behavior: A social-role interpretation.* Hillsdale, NJ: Erlbaum.

Eagly, A. H., Johannesen-Schmidt, M. C., & van Engen, M. L. (2003). Transformational, transactional, and laissez-faire leadership styles: A meta-analysis comparing women and men. *Psychological Bulletin, 129,* 569–591.

Eagly, A. H., & Karau, S. J. (2002). Role congruity theory of prejudice toward female leaders. *Psychological Review, 109*, 573–598.
Eagly, A. H., Karau, S. J., & Makhijani, M. G. (1995). Gender and the effectiveness of leaders: A meta-analysis. *Psychological Bulletin, 111*, 3–22.
Eagly, A. H., Makhijani, M. G., & Klonsky, B. G. (1992). Gender and the evaluation of leaders: A meta-analysis. *Psychological Bulletin, 111*, 3–22.
Eagly, A. H., & Mladinic, A. (1989). Gender stereotypes and attitudes toward women and men. *Personality and Social Psychology Bulletin, 15*, 543–558.
Eagly, A. H., Mladinic, A., & Otto, S. (1994). Cognitive and affective bases of attitudes toward social groups and social policies. *Journal of Experimental Social Psychology, 30*, 113–137.
Fiske, S. T., Bersoff, D. N., Borgida, E., Deaux, K., & Heilman, M. E. (1991). Social science research on trial: Use of sex stereotyping research in Price Waterhouse v. Hopkins. *American Psychology, 46*, 1049–1060.
Fiske, S. T., & Neuberg, S. L. (1990). A continuum of impression formation, from category-based to individuating processes: Influence of information and motivation on attention and interpretation. In: M. Zanna (Ed.), *Advances in experimental social psychology* (Vol. 23, pp. 1–74). New York: Academic Press.
Fiske, S. T., & Stevens, L. E. (1993). What's so special about sex? Gender stereotyping and discrimination. In: S. Oskamp & M. Costanzo (Eds), *Gender issues in contemporary society* (pp. 173–196). Thousand Oaks, CA: Sage Publications, Inc.
Gerhart, B., & Rynes, S. (1991). Determinants and consequences of salary negotiations by male and female MBA graduates. *Journal of Applied Psychology, 76*, 256–262.
Gill, M. J. (2004). When information does not deter stereotyping: Prescriptive stereotyping can foster bias under conditions that deter descriptive stereotyping. *Journal of Experimental Social Psychology, 40*, 619–632.
Glick, P., Diebold, J., Bailey-Werner, B., & Zhu, L. (1997). The two faces of Adam: Ambivalent sexism and polarized attitudes toward women. *Personality and Social Psychology Bulletin, 23*, 1323–1334.
Glick, P., & Fiske, S. T. (1996). The ambivalent sexism inventory: Differentiating hostile and benevolent sexism. *Journal of Personality and Social Psychology, 70*, 491–512.
Glick, P., & Fiske, S. T. (2001). Ambivalent sexism. In: M. P. Zanna (Ed.), *Advances in experimental social psychology* (Vol. 33, pp. 115–188). Thousand Oaks, CA: Academic Press.
Glick, P., Fiske, S. T., Mladinic, A., Saiz, J. L., Abrams, D., Masser, B., et al. (2000). Beyond prejudice as simple antipathy: Hostile and benevolent sexism across cultures. *Journal of Personality and Social Psychology, 79*, 763–775.
Glick, P., Lameiras, M., Fiske, S. T., Eckes, T., Masser, B., Volpato, C., et al. (2004). Bad but bold: Ambivalent attitudes toward men predict gender inequality in 16 nations. *Journal of Personality and Social Psychology, 86*, 713–728.
Glick, P., Wilk, K., & Perreault, M. (1995). Images of occupations: Components of gender and status in occupational stereotypes. *Sex Roles, 32*, 564–582.
Glick, P., Zion, C., & Nelson, C. (1988). What mediates sex discrimination in hiring decisions? *Journal of Personality and Social Psychology, 55*, 178–186.
Gould, R. J., & Slone, C. G. (1982). The "feminine modesty" effect: A self-presentational interpretation of sex differences in causal attribution. *Personality and Social Psychology Bulletin, 8*, 477–485.

Greenwald, A. G., Banaji, M. R., Rudman, L. A., Farnham, S. D., Nosek, B. A., & Mellott, D. S. (2002). A unified theory of implicit attitudes, stereotypes, self-esteem, and self-concept. *Psychological Review, 109,* 3–25.

Gutek, B. A. (1985). *Sex and the workplace.* San Francisco, CA: Jossey Bass.

Gutek, B. A., & Morasch, B. (1982). Sex-ratios, sex-role spillover, and sexual harassment of women at work. *Journal of Social Issues, 38,* 55–74.

Harris, A. C. (1994). Ethnicity as a determinant of sex role identity: A replication study of item selection for the Bem Sex Role Inventory. *Sex Roles, 31,* 241–273.

Heatherington, L., Daubman, K. A., Bates, C., Ahn, A., Brown, H., & Preston, C. (1993). Two investigations of "female modesty" in achievement situations. *Sex Roles, 29,* 739–754.

Heilman, M. E. (1983). Sex bias in work settings: The lack of fit model. *Research in Organizational Behavior, 5,* 269–298.

Heilman, M. E. (2001). Description and prescription: How gender stereotypes prevent women's ascent up the organizational ladder. *Journal of Social Issues, 57,* 657–674.

Heilman, M. E., Block, C. J., & Martell, R. F. (1995). Sex stereotypes: Do they influence perceptions of managers? *Journal of Social Behavior and Personality, 10,* 237–252.

Heilman, M. E., & Chen, J. J. (2005). Same behavior, different consequences: Reactions to men's and women's altruistic citizenship behavior. *Journal of Applied Psychology, 90,* 431–441.

Heilman, M. E., & Haynes, M. C. (2005). No credit where credit is due: Attributional rationalization of women's success in male-female teams. *Journal of Applied Psychology, 90,* 905–916.

Heilman, M. E., & Okimoto, T. G. (in press). Averting penalties for women's success: Rectifying the perceived communality deficiency. *Journal of Applied Psychology.*

Heilman, M. E., Wallen, A. S., Fuchs, D., & Tamkins, M. M. (2004). Penalties for success: Reactions to women who succeed at male gender-typed tasks. *Journal of Applied Psychology, 89,* 416–427.

Hillier, L., & Foddy, M. (1993). The role of observer attitudes in judgments of blame in cases of wife assault. *Sex Roles, 29,* 629–644.

Holt, C. L., & Ellis, J. B. (1998). Assessing the current validity of the Bem Sex-Role Inventory. *Sex Roles, 39,* 929–941.

Huddy, L., & Terkildsen, N. (1993). The consequences of gender stereotypes for women candidates at different levels and types of office. *Political Research Quarterly, 46,* 503–525.

Jackman, M. R. (1994). *The velvet glove: Paternalism and conflict in gender, class, and race relations.* Berkeley, CA: University of California Press.

Janoff-Bulman, R., & Wade, M. B. (1996). The dilemma of self-advocacy for women: Another case of blaming the victim? *Journal of Social and Clinical Psychology, 15,* 445–446.

Katz, D., & Braly, K. (1933). Racial stereotypes of one hundred college students. *Journal of Abnormal and Social Psychology, 28,* 280–290.

Kilianski, S. E., & Rudman, L. A. (1998). Wanting it both ways: Do women approve of benevolent sexism? *Sex Roles, 39,* 333–352.

Kite, M. E., & Deaux, K. (1987). Gender belief systems: Homosexuality and the implicit inversion theory. *Psychology of Women Quarterly, 11,* 83–96.

Koch, S. C. (2005). Evaluative affect display toward male and female leaders of task-oriented groups. *Small Group Research, 36,* 678–703.

Lips, H. M. (2003). The gender pay gap: Concrete indicator of women's progress toward equality. *Analyses of Social Issues and Public Policy, 3,* 87–109.

Lyness, K. S., & Judiesch, M. K. (1999). Are women more likely to be hired or promoted into management positions? *Journal of Vocational Behavior, 54*, 158-173.

Martell, R. F., Parker, C., Emrich, C. G., & Crawford, M. S. (1998). Sex stereotyping in the executive suite: "Much ado about something". *Journal of Social Behavior and Personality, 13*, 127-138.

Martin, C. L. (1990). Attitudes and expectations about children with nontraditional and traditional gender roles. *Sex Roles, 22*, 151-165.

Maume, D. J. (1999). Glass ceilings and glass escalators: Occupational segregation and race and sex differences in managerial promotions. *Work and Occupations, 26*, 483-509.

McIlwee, J. S., & Robinson, J. G. (1992). *Women in engineering: Gender, power, and workplace culture.* Albany, NY: State University of New York Press.

Moss-Racusin, C., & Heilman, M. (2006). Failure to be feminine: Interpersonal penalties for failure behavior on sex-consistent domains. Paper presented at the 7th Annual Meeting of the Society for Personality and Social Psychology, Palm Springs, CA, January 27.

Offermann, L. R., & Gowing, M. K. (1990). Organizations of the future: Changes and challenges. *American Psychologist, 45*, 95-108.

Olson, J. E., & Frieze, I. H. (1987). Income determinants for women in businesss. In: A. H. Stromberg, L. Larwood & B. A. Gutek (Eds), *Women and work: An annual review* (Vol. 2, pp. 173-206). Thousand Oaks, CA: Sage Publications, Inc.

Peters, T. (1988). Restoring American competitiveness: Looking for new models of organizations. *Academy of Management Executive, 2*, 103-109.

Powers, T. A., & Zuroff, D. C. (1988). Interpersonal consequences of overt self-criticism: A comparison with neutral and self-enhancing presentations of self. *Journal of Personality and Social Psychology, 54*, 1054-1062.

Prentice, D. A., & Carranza, E. (2002). What women and men should be, shouldn't be, are allowed to be, and don't have to be: The contents of prescriptive gender stereotypes. *Psychology of Women Quarterly, 26*, 269-281.

Richeson, J. A., & Ambady, N. (2001). Who's in charge? Effects of situational roles on automatic gender bias. *Sex Roles, 44*, 493-512.

Rosencrantz, P., Vogel, S., Bee, H., Broverman, I., & Broverman, D. (1968). Sex-role stereotypes and self-concepts in college students. *Journal of Consulting and Clinical Psychology, 32*, 287-295.

Rosener, J. B. (1990). Ways women lead. *Harvard Business Review, 68*, 119-125.

Rudman, L. A. (1998). Self-promotion as a risk factor for women: The costs and benefits of counterstereotypical impression management. *Journal of Personality and Social Psychology, 74*, 629-645.

Rudman, L. A. (2005). Rejection of women? Beyond prejudice as antipathy. In: J. F. Dovidio, P. Glick & L. A. Rudman (Eds), *On the nature of prejudice: Fifty years after Allport* (pp. 106-120). Malden, MA: Blackwell.

Rudman, L. A., & Fairchild, K. (2004). Reactions to counterstereotypic behavior: The role of backlash in cultural stereotype maintenance. *Journal of Personality and Social Psychology, 87*, 157-176.

Rudman, L. A., & Glick, P. (1999). Feminized management and backlash toward agentic women: The hidden costs to women of a kinder, gentler image of middle managers. *Journal of Personality and Social Psychology, 77*, 1004-1010.

Rudman, L. A., & Glick, P. (2001). Prescriptive gender stereotypes and backlash toward agentic women. *Journal of Social Issues, 57*, 732-762.

Rudman, L. A., & Heppen, J. B. (2003). Implicit romantic fantasies and women's interest in personal power: A glass slipper effect? *Personality and Social Psychology Bulletin, 29,* 1357–1370.

Rudman, L. A., & Kilianski, S. E. (2000). Implicit and explicit attitudes toward female authority. *Personality and Social Psychology Bulletin, 25,* 1315–1328.

Sailer, P., Yao, E., & Rehula, V. (2002). Income by gender and age from information returns. *Statistics of Income Bulletin, 21,* 83–102.

Sanchez, D. T., Crocker, J., & Boike, K. R. (2005). Doing gender in the bedroom: Investing in gender norms and the sexual experience. *Personality and Social Psychology Bulletin, 31,* 1445–1455.

Sandnabba, N. K., & Ahlberg, C. (1999). Parents' attitudes and expectations about children's cross-gender behavior. *Sex Roles, 40,* 249–263.

Schein, V. E. (1973). The relationship between sex role stereotypes and requisite management characteristics. *Journal of Applied Psychology, 57,* 95–100.

Scott, R. L., & Tetreault, L. A. (1987). Attitudes of rapists and other violent offenders toward women. *Journal of Social Psychology, 127,* 375–380.

Sinclair, L., & Kunda, Z. (2000). Motivated stereotyping of women: She's fine if she praised me but incompetent if she criticized me. *Personality and Social Psychology Bulletin, 26,* 1329–1342.

Spence, J. T. (1999). Thirty years of gender research: A personal chronicle. In: W. B. Swann, J. H. Langlois & L. A. Gilbert (Eds), *Sexism and stereotypes in modern society: The gender science of Janet Taylor Spence* (pp. 255–289). Washington, DC: American Psychological Association.

Spence, J. T., & Buckner, C. E. (2000). Instrumental and expressive traits, trait stereotypes, and sexist attitudes. *Psychology of Women Quarterly, 24,* 44–62.

Spence, J. T., & Helmreich, R. (1972a). The Attitudes Toward Women Scale: An objective instrument to measure attitudes toward the rights and roles of women in contemporary society. *JSAS Catalog of Selected Documents in Psychology, 2,* 66–67 (Ms. 153).

Spence, J. T., & Helmreich, R. (1972b). Who likes competent women? Competence, sex role congruence of interests, and subjects' attitudes towards women as determinants of interpersonal attraction. *Journal of Applied Social Psychology, 2,* 197–213.

Stevens, C. K., Bavetta, A. G., & Gist, M. E. (1993). Gender differences in the acquisition of salary negotiation skills: The role of goals, self-efficacy, and perceived control. *Journal of Applied Psychology, 78,* 723–735.

Swim, J. K., Aiken, K. J., Hall, W. S., & Hunter, B. A. (1995). Sexism and racism: Old-fashioned and modern prejudices. *Journal of Personality and Social Psychology, 68,* 199–214.

Swim, J. K., & Sanna, L. J. (1996). He's skilled, she's lucky: A meta-analysis of observers' attributions for women's and men's successes and failures. *Personality and Social Psychology Bulletin, 22,* 507–519.

Tannen, D. (1990). *You just don't understand: Women and men in conversation.* New York, NY: Morrow.

Tannen, D. (1994). *Talking from 9 to 5: Women and men in the workplace: Language, sex, and power.* New York, NY: Morrow.

Tougas, F., Brown, R., Beaton, A. M., & Joly, S. (1995). Neosexism: Plus ça change, plus c'est pareil. *Personality and Social Psychology, 21,* 842–849.

U.S. Bureau of Labor Statistics. (2006). *Household data: Monthly household data* (Table A-19: Employed persons by occupation, sex, and age). Retrieved May 04, 2006 from ftp://ftp.bls.gov/pub/suppl/empsit.cpseea19.txt

U.S. Census Bureau. (2002). *Historical income tables* - People. (Table P-38: Full-time, year-round workers [all races] by median earning and sex: 1960 to 2000). Retrieved May 04, 2006 from http://www.census.gov/hhes/income/histinc/p38.html

U.S. General Accounting Office. (2001, October). *Women in management: Analysis of selected data from the current population survey* (GAO-02-156). Retrieved May 04, 2006 from http://www.equality2020.org/women.pdf

Valian, V. (1999). *Why so slow? The advancement of women.* Cambridge, MA: The MIT Press.

Vescio, T. K., Gervais, S. J., Snyder, M., & Hoover, A. (2005). Power and the creation of patronizing environments: The stereotype-based behaviors of the powerful and their effects on female performance in masculine domains. *Journal of Personality and Social Psychology, 88,* 658–672.

Wade, M. E. (2001). Women and salary negotiation: The costs of self-advocacy. *Psychology of Women Quarterly, 25,* 65–76.

Weidner, G., & Griffitt, W. (1983). Rape: A sexual stigma? *Journal of Personality, 51,* 152–166.

White House Project. (2006). *Snapshots of current political leadership.* Retrieved May 04, 2006 from http://www.thewhitehouseproject.org/v2/researchandreports/snapshots.html

Wiley, M. G., & Eskilson, A. (1985). Speech style, gender stereotypes, and corporate success: What if women talk more like men? *Sex Roles, 12,* 993–1007.

Williams, J. E., & Best, D. L. (1990). *Measuring sex stereotypes: A multination study.* Newbury Park, CA: Sage.

Zucker, K. J., Bradley, S. J., & Sanikhani, M. (1997). Sex differences in referral rates of children with gender identity disorder. *Journal of Abnormal Child Psychology, 25,* 217–227.

GENDER STEREOTYPES IN THE WORKPLACE: OBSTACLES TO WOMEN'S CAREER PROGRESS

Madeline E. Heilman and Elizabeth J. Parks-Stamm

ABSTRACT

This chapter focuses on the implications of both the descriptive and prescriptive aspects of gender stereotypes for women in the workplace. Using the Lack of Fit model, we review how performance expectations deriving from descriptive gender stereotypes (i.e., what women are like) can impede women's career progress. We then identify organizational conditions that may weaken the influence of these expectations. In addition, we discuss how prescriptive gender stereotypes (i.e., what women should be like) promote sex bias by creating norms that, when not followed, induce disapproval and social penalties for women. We then review recent research exploring the conditions under which women experience penalties for direct, or inferred, prescriptive norm violations.

Gender stereotypes have both descriptive and prescriptive properties. Each of these aspects of gender stereotypes give rise to biased perceptions that can affect both how women are evaluated and the career-related decisions that are made about them. In this chapter we will discuss our ideas about how and why gender stereotypes lead to negative consequences for women in work settings. We also will discuss research based on these ideas that seeks to identify the conditions most likely to bring about sex bias in evaluative judgments and organizational decision-making.

Descriptive gender stereotypes designate what women and men are like. Prescriptive gender stereotypes indicate what women and men should be like. We propose that both descriptive and prescriptive gender stereotypes can compromise women's ability to gain acceptance and achieve upper-level positions in the workplace. First we will consider how performance expectations about women deriving from descriptive gender stereotypes can adversely affect the perceived suitability of women for organizational advancement. Using the Lack of Fit model (Heilman, 1983), we will describe how a perceived mismatch between the characteristics women possess and the characteristics needed for success in male-typed jobs can create expectations of failure for women – expectations that can have a powerful effect on judgments and decisions.

Second, we will explore the more subtle but no less pernicious effects of prescriptive gender stereotypes for women in the workplace. We will review research demonstrating the penalties that successful women face for directly or indirectly violating gender norms. Together, we argue, descriptive and prescriptive gender stereotypes put working women in a very difficult position, forcing them to prove either their competence or their femininity.

DESCRIPTIVE STEREOTYPES ABOUT WOMEN

Beliefs about how men and women differ (i.e., how men and women each typically are) are known as descriptive stereotypes. Agency is often cited as the defining characteristic of the male stereotype, and communality as the defining characteristic of the female stereotype (Bakan, 1966; Broverman, Vogel, Broverman, Clarkson, & Rosenkrantz, 1972; Deaux & Lewis, 1984; Eagly, 2000; Heilman, 2001). Whereas men are thought to be more agentic (i.e., independent, assertive, decisive), women are thought to be more communal (i.e., unselfish, friendly, concerned with others). These agentic versus communal characteristics are sometimes simplified into two pervasive dimensions: competent and nice (Fiske, 1998); women are believed to be less competent but nice, and men are believed to be competent but less nice. Although conceptions of men and women differ, each description is positive in its own way. So, although women are not thought to be independent or decisive, they are believed to be warmer, kinder, and less selfish than men (Diekman & Eagly, 2000).

The characterizations of men and women deriving from descriptive gender stereotypes are surprisingly consistent across cultures and time. Williams and Best (1990) examined gender stereotypes in 25 countries by asking participants to rate if each adjective in a list was more frequently associated with men, women, or neither group. They found a good deal of consistency in gender stereotypes across cultures. Adjectives related to agency (e.g., dominance, autonomy, and achievement) were more likely to be applied to men, whereas adjectives related to communality (e.g., deference, nurturance, and affiliation) were more likely to be applied to women. Even with changes in sex roles and attitudes over time, descriptive gender stereotypes remain remarkably stable (Lueptow, Garovich, & Lueptow, 1995). Moreover, there is evidence that descriptive stereotypes influence how women and men are characterized in employment settings as well as in social and domestic settings (Dodge, Gilroy, & Fenzel, 1995; Heilman, Block & Martell, 1995; Heilman, Block, Martell, & Simon, 1989; Schein, 2001). Evidently, the increase in the numbers of working women, as well as their presence in positions of power and authority, has not eliminated gender-stereotypic assumptions about what women are like.

These widely shared beliefs about men and women can have broad effects. Descriptive stereotypes serve as heuristics or shortcuts for forming impressions about individuals. Research has shown stereotypes serve as energy-saving devices, allowing perceivers to form impressions quickly so that they may more easily respond to and make more predictable an "incomprehensibly complex social world" (Macrae, Milne, & Bodenhausen, 1994, p. 37). Moreover, research has shown that stereotypes can exert influence without the perceiver's awareness. There is evidence that stereotypes are often activated automatically upon contact with a member of a stereotyped group, although not necessarily acted upon (Dovidio, Evans, & Tyler, 1986; Devine, 1989), and also that people often are unaware of the impact of gender stereotypes on their views of a given category member and the effect of these views on their judgments, such as on the interpretation of ambiguous behaviors (Banaji, Hardin, & Rothman, 1993). Because stereotypes are widely held, automatically activated, and highly influential, descriptive gender stereotypes have a remarkable ability to dominate in impression formation.

One's first reaction might be to expect that the effects of descriptive gender stereotypes would always be detrimental for women. However, it should be noted that the characterizations deriving from these stereotypes do not always produce negative consequences. In fact, there is evidence that women and the attributes believed to characterize them are generally favorably regarded and highly valued (Eagly & Mladinic, 1989; Eagly, Mladinic, & Otto, 1991). Rather, stereotypical conceptions of what women are like are detrimental in their career-relevant consequences only when they negatively affect expectations about how successful women will be when working at a particular job. These performance expectations are determined not only by characterizations of a woman's attributes but also by how well they "fit" with the attributes thought to be required to perform the job well (Heilman, 1983, 2001; see also Eagly & Karau, 2002).

Lack of Fit and the Formation of Performance Expectations

Descriptive stereotypes about women can create problems in the workplace because there is a perceived "lack of fit" between women's assumed capabilities and the presumed requirements of a position (Heilman, 1983). This should cause particular problems for women attempting to gain access to high-level jobs, as the qualities believed to be necessary for jobs that are highest in authority and prestige are typically ones that are considered to be male in gender-type (Lyness, 2002). The requirements believed necessary for success in these positions are attributes such as decisiveness, toughness, and leadership skill – attributes that are consistent with stereotypes of men, but not with stereotypes of women. Consequently, women are often thought to be deficient in the qualities required for success at upper-level positions (Heilman et al., 1989; Schein, 2001). This perceived lack of fit between female stereotypic attributes and male gender-typed job requirements leads to the conclusion that women are not equipped to handle these jobs, and the expectation that they are not likely to succeed in positions that are traditionally considered male. This is the essence of the Lack of Fit model (Heilman, 1983, 1995), which proposes that these expectations of failure will proceed to bias employment decisions regarding women.

There is much evidence that there is a perceived lack of fit between the occupational demands of high-level jobs and how women typically are characterized. Schein asked male managers (Schein, 1973) and female managers (Schein, 1975) to identify the attributes of successful managers as well as the attributes of men in general and women in general. She found that the described profile of a successful manager was closer to the described profiles of typical men than of typical women. Heilman et al. (1989) replicated Schein's findings, demonstrating 15 years later that the perceived attributes of a successful manager were much more similar to those of men in general than of women in general. Because of concerns that depictions of "women in general" may not capture conceptions of working women, Heilman et al. (1989) also asked the managers who were participating in their study for descriptions of typical male and female *managers*. Although when specified as managers women were characterized as more similar to successful managers than women in general, female managers were still described as more different from successful managers than were male managers. Subsequent research has verified that a good manager is described in masculine terms (Powell, Butterfield, & Parent, 2002; Willemsen, 2002; Dennis & Kunkel, 2004), and that the attributes believed to be necessary to succeed as an executive are stereotypically male (Martell, Parker, Emrich, & Crawford, 1998).

Performance Expectations and Information Processing

Because descriptive stereotypes about women create expectations that they are unlikely to successfully perform male gender-typed jobs, these performance expectations can influence the way information about a target individual is processed. Expectations have a self-fulfilling quality; they tend to bias information processing in the service of maintaining themselves. Performance expectations therefore affect what information about an individual is attended to, how it is interpreted, and which information is recalled about an individual when evaluations and decisions are made in the workplace.

Attention
One may think that the first step of processing information about a person – observing behaviors – is relatively straightforward. However, expectations can influence what information is focused upon and attended to. Social psychology research has demonstrated that expectations act as a perceptual filter, directing attention toward consistent information and away from inconsistent information (Johnson & Judd, 1983). Thus, information that is inconsistent with expectations often is ignored even in this initial observation. Alternatively, such behaviors may be observed, but not included in one's overall impression. Expectation-inconsistent information may be considered irrelevant and attributed to temporary situational components or external factors, making it uninformative for judgments or evaluations of the individual (Swim & Sanna, 1996). By either ignoring expectation-inconsistent information, or treating it as indicative of the situation rather than the individual (Crocker, Hannah, & Weber, 1983; Hastie, 1984; Kulik, 1983), prior expectations persist unchallenged. It is not surprising, then, that

raters have been found to spend less time attending to work behaviors of individuals about whom there are stereotype-based expectations, such as women, than those about whom no such expectations exist (Favero & Ilgen, 1989).

Interpretation
Even when expectation-inconsistent information is attended to, stereotype-based expectations tend to be perpetuated through the interpretation of the information in a way that remains consistent with the expectation. When a behavior is performed by individuals about whom there exist different expectations, its meaning may be interpreted very differently (Kunda, Sinclair, & Griffin, 1997). So, the same change of course of action may be seen as "flexible" when performed by a man, but as "flighty" or "indecisive" when performed by a woman; the same work demeanor may be seen as "laid-back" when exhibited by a man, but as "passive" or "timid" when exhibited by a woman. Thus, treatment of even behavioral information may be quite malleable, with its meaning varying depending upon what is expected.

Recall
Expectations can also bias memory in the direction of these expectations (Cantor & Mischel, 1979; O'Sullivan & Durso, 1984). People have been shown to greatly manipulate events in their memory, recalling more expectation-consistent than inconsistent behaviors, even falsely recalling expectation-consistent behaviors that did not occur (Fiske & Neuberg, 1990; Higgins & Bargh, 1987). Indeed, expectations have been shown to be more powerful than actual memories of observed events in making behavioral ratings (Baltes & Parker, 2000; Cooper, 1981; DeNisi, Cafferty, & Meglino, 1984; Feldman & Lynch, 1988; Martell, Guzzo, & Willis, 1995). This research suggests that a woman's behavior that validates negative performance expectations held about her may be readily recalled whereas her behavior that contradicts these negative performance expectations is more likely to be forgotten by an evaluator.

Moreover, in order to save cognitive resources, individuals typically engage in only a limited memory search to recall relevant information for an evaluation. Therefore, the most accessible information – that which is most readily remembered – is most likely to provide the basis for evaluations. This is apt to occur even if more diagnostic (but less accessible) information actually is stored in memory (Feldman & Lynch, 1988). Because expectation-consistent information is typically the most accessible information, this is the information likely to be recalled and used in evaluative judgments.

Career-related Consequences of Stereotype-based Performance Expectations

Because performance expectations originating from gender stereotypes are so tenacious, and their effects on information processing so potentially powerful, these expectations can have important and wide-ranging consequences for how women are treated in the workplace (Heilman, 1995, 2001). Expectations can create sex bias in evaluative judgments both at the time of organizational entry and in subsequent career relevant employment decisions. By promoting the view that she is unequipped for a job and unlikely to succeed at it, stereotype-based performance expectations are likely to directly affect the chances a woman will be selected for traditionally male positions or that she will be placed into them if she is hired. Additionally, because of the selective attention, interpretation, and recall of behaviors these expectations produce, they can taint assessments of a woman's on-the-job competence and her attainment of organizational advancement and rewards.

Moreover, the more negative these performance expectations, the more we might expect biased career-related outcomes. According to the Lack of Fit model, the greater the apparent discrepancy between the characteristics of the individual and the requirements of the job, the more negative the resulting performance expectations and the evaluative outcomes they produce. Support for this idea has been provided by investigations in which there are variations in the degree of lack of fit.

One factor the Lack of Fit model would predict should amplify the lack of fit effect for women is the extent to which the job is considered male in gender-type. Lack of fit should only create negative performance expectations, and therefore negative career consequences, for women when the job is deemed to be "male." This occurs when the nature of the work responsibilities are those typically associated with men or when the percentage of individuals working at that job are overwhelmingly male. Indeed, negative evaluations in selection processes have been found to occur particularly for male gender-typed jobs (Davison & Burke, 2000). There are similar findings in investigations concerning competence assessments and performance evaluations. Results of a study of performance evaluations in a large multinational financial services company indicated that women were rated less favorably than men in line jobs (which tend to be highly male gender-typed), but not in staff jobs (Lyness & Heilman, 2006). Also, a large scale field study of over 3,000 senior officers in the Israeli Defense Forces conducted by Pazy and Oron (2001) indicated that women's competence and performance was rated significantly lower than men's in organizational units in which women were underrepresented but not in those in which they were not.

The Lack of Fit model would also predict that the extent of negative performance expectations (and their resulting negative career consequences) for women should depend on the other aspect of the fit formulation, the perceived femininity of the woman. Accordingly, it has been shown that women with personal attributes that increase the saliency of their gender, such as physical attractiveness (Heilman & Stopeck, 1985a, 1985b) or motherhood status (Fuegen, Biernat, Haines, & Deaux, 2004; Heilman & Okimoto, 2007b), elicit more negative performance expectations and evaluations, and therefore less favorable employment decisions, than women without these personal attributes. Moreover, organizational factors that highlight a woman's gender, such as token or minority status (Heilman & Blader, 2001; Sackett, DuBois, & Noe, 1991) or association with affirmative action or diversity initiatives (Heilman, Block, & Stathatos, 1997; Heilman & Welle, 2006), have been shown to result in more negative performance expectations and evaluations for women when the job is male gender-typed. The increased distinctiveness of women's gender, which accentuates their femininity and exacerbates perceptions of lack of fit with a male gender-typed job, can therefore increase the negative performance expectations for women, and the negative career consequences that they produce.

Thus, descriptive gender stereotypes and the negative performance expectations that they give rise to can lead to greater sex bias and discrimination in traditionally male work settings, with the potential seriousness of these outcomes dependent on how negative the performance expectations are. But it is not only the degree of lack of fit that determines whether negative performance expectations about women have detrimental effects; the extent to which there is ambiguity inherent in the decision process also is important. This is because ambiguity facilitates the influence of expectations when decisions are made.

The Effect of Ambiguity

The more ambiguity there is, the more inference is required for evaluation, and the less guidance there is about the "correct" outcome of an evaluation. Thus, ambiguity creates a vacuum in which expectations can forcefully exert their influence, fueling subjectivity in evaluative decision-making, and therefore providing a facilitative context for sex bias (Nieva & Gutek, 1980; Heilman & Haynes, in press). In work settings, ambiguity is high when the information available is impoverished or not job-relevant, when the criteria for the decision or the structure for evaluation is poorly defined, and when there is confusion about the source of performance outcomes.

Ambiguity in the Amount and Type of Information Available
Research has consistently demonstrated that ambiguity in the information available to an evaluator is related to bias in evaluative judgments (Davison & Burke, 2000; Heilman, Wallen, Fuchs, & Tamkins, 2004; Tosi & Einbender, 1985), with information that is more sparse facilitating the use of stereotype-based expectations. Thus, in their meta-analysis of "Joan versus John" studies (i.e., in which participants evaluated the work of a fictitious individual whose sex is manipulated), Swim, Borgida, Maruyama, and Myers (1989) found that women are rated less favorably than men particularly when less information is provided about the target.

But information quality is also critical. Unless highly job-relevant and diagnostic of performance success, information has been found to do little to limit the effect of expectations in evaluation (Heilman, 1984). In fact, there is evidence that irrelevant information results in no less bias in evaluations than the absence of information (Heilman, 1984; Rasinski, Crocker, & Hastie, 1985). And, even if the information is relevant, there is indication that it must be very specific and virtually impossible to distort if it is to preclude the impact of negative stereotype-based expectations in evaluative judgments (Heilman, Martell, & Simon, 1988). For example, it was found that even when targets were said to have performed in the highest performance category on a rating sheet, it was only if the category was labeled as "the top 2% of employees" that women in male gender-typed jobs were rated as favorably as men; if the top category was labeled "the top 25% of employees," women were rated significantly less competent than men (Heilman et al., 1997; Heilman & Haynes, 2005).

Ambiguity in Evaluative Criteria
Research in social psychology has generally indicated that the more vague and poorly defined the judgment criteria, the more easily information can be distorted to fit an expected outcome (Fiske & Taylor, 1991). When evaluative decisions about women are being made, the evaluative criteria can be vague in multiple ways. One issue is the nature of the performance outcome itself. It is more difficult to distort test scores or dollars earned, for example, than to distort work output that is abstract or lacking a prescribed reference point for comparison. A related issue is the evaluative focus. Distortion is less likely to enter into assessments of actual work behaviors

than of assessments of inferred characteristics, such as whether an individual is "resilient," "charismatic," or "a team player." There is evidence, for example, that supervisors rate performance of communication competence and interpersonal competence less reliably than they rate productivity or work quality (Viswesvaran, Ones, & Schmidt, 1996).

Ambiguity in the Evaluative Structure
Lack of clear specification about how various evaluative criteria are to be weighted and combined also invites expectation-based distortion (Baltes & Parker, 2000; Bauer & Baltes, 2002). If raters are left to devise their own systems for integrating information into an evaluative judgment, then they are not constrained to consider multiple sources of information in the same way, or to conform to a predetermined set of criteria. A structured evaluation process, in contrast, ensures that particular features of performance are assessed for everyone, and that these features are given equal weight in the evaluation process no matter who the particular target is. Thus, ambiguous evaluative structure can encourage non-uniform evaluative standards, a situation that is highly susceptible to the influence of expectations. It is a particular problem given the general move toward more flexible definitions of work roles and the view of jobs as dynamic (Arvey & Murphy, 1998), suggesting that gender-based expectations can influence which standards are operative at any given time.

Ambiguity about the Source of Performance
The source of responsibility for joint performance outcomes can also create ambiguity. When there is this kind of "source ambiguity," stereotype-based expectations are likely to influence inferences about who actually is deserving of credit. Research has indicated, for example, that when a woman works together with a man on a joint task, she is given less credit for a successful joint outcome, is viewed as having made a more trivial contribution to it, and is viewed as less competent than her male teammate (Heilman & Haynes, 2005). This effect was found to occur unless the task was structured so that individual contribution was made evident or the woman's competence was explicitly reported. Source ambiguity is not limited to situations in which women are working in structured dyads with men on a single project. In today's work world, work is rarely accomplished in solo fashion and, in addition, there often are institutionalized mentoring and coaching programs that make it impossible to squarely place responsibility for work outcomes on one person rather than another. Source ambiguity, whatever its form, is likely to give power to expectations as the basis of inference in evaluative

judgments. Consequently, even when work is done well, expectations can preclude women from getting credit for their successful performance when the source of their success is ambiguous.

Motivation as a Deterrent

Performance expectations of course do not always determine the outcome of evaluative judgments. Even when expectations are strongly negative and ambiguity is high, evaluators will rely less on them when there is strong motivation to make accurate judgments. According to the Heuristic-Systematic Model (HSM; Chaiken, 1980), people's default processing strategy is to rely on schemas, stereotypes, and expectancies. People generally operate on a least-effort principle, where they expend as little cognitive resources as possible to perform a task, whether it be forming an impression or making a decision. It is only when individuals are motivated to be accurate that they will expend more energy and systematically process information.

Accuracy is likely to be a motivator when the evaluator is in an interdependent relationship with the target of evaluation so that his or her outcomes are directly tied to the evaluated person's performance (Fiske, 2000). Because in these cases the evaluators benefit from being keenly aware of the target's strengths and weaknesses, this is a situation that encourages the careful consideration of individuating information rather than the more cognitively lazy reliance on expectations. Another situation in which evaluators are motivated to be accurate is when evaluators are held accountable for the judgments they make (Tetlock, 1983a, 1983b; Simonson & Nye, 1992). Accountability, if it motivates people to appear competent by being accurate, can curb the use of expectations by encouraging more effort in information search and less superficial processing of information. Accountability can also prompt a different type of motivation for evaluators – the motivation to present oneself in a favorable light. In this case also, the effects of expectations are likely to be weakened, trumped by the tendency to make judgments that are consistent with the views of, and likely to curry favor with, the audience evaluators are striving to impress (Klimoski & Inks, 1990; Tetlock, 1985; Tetlock, Skitka, & Boettger, 1989).

Thus, in situations in which evaluators are motivated to be accurate and therefore willing to expend more cognitive resources, or are motivated by approval and therefore simply say what they think others want to hear, the influence of expectations on evaluative decision-making is apt to be curtailed. This would be likely despite the level of ambiguity in the decision process or the degree to which there are negative expectations produced by perceptions of lack of fit. When, however, the evaluator has a smaller stake in the outcome of his or her decision, there is little reason not to rely on expectations in making judgments. Indeed, it is more efficient to do so, especially when there are limited cognitive resources available, such as when the evaluator is doing several things simultaneously (Gilbert & Hixon, 1991) or the evaluator is highly pressed for time (Pratto & Bargh, 1991), conditions very common to today's work settings.

So, it is clear that descriptive gender stereotypes can be the precipitant for negative competence judgments and evaluative decisions for women in work settings. But what happens when the ill-effects of descriptive gender stereotypes and the negative performance expectations they produce are overcome and women are acknowledged to be successful despite the male gender-typed nature of the job? Are women then free of the biasing effects of gender stereotypes? We would argue no. In fact, we believe that it is precisely at this point that processes arising from the prescriptive aspect of gender stereotypes are set in motion, with a different set of negative consequences for working women. We now turn to consider this other aspect of gender stereotypes and the way in which it, also, can obstruct women's career progress.

PRESCRIPTIVE GENDER STEREOTYPES

Gender stereotypes not only are descriptive, they also are prescriptive. That is, they not only provide information about how women and men *are* but also provide information about how they *should* be. Prescriptive stereotypes are what Cialdini and Trost (1998) labeled "injunctive norms;" they dictate what attributes and behaviors are appropriate for individuals from particular groups. Thus, gender stereotype-based prescriptions provide guidance about what behaviors are suitable for men and women to engage in (Burgess & Borgida, 1999; Eagly & Karau, 2002; Heilman, 2001; Rudman & Glick, 2001).

There is a good deal of overlap between the content of the prescriptive and descriptive elements of gender stereotypes, with the attributes and behaviors prescribed for each sex being the ones that are positively valued. Thus, the attributes for which women are so positively valued (Eagly et al., 1991; Eagly & Mladinic, 1989) are central to their "shoulds." Prescriptive stereotypes about women specify that women should behave communally, demonstrating socially sensitive and nurturing attributes that reflect their concern for the welfare of others, such as being kind, understanding, and sympathetic. In addition to "shoulds," prescriptive gender stereotypes denote "should nots" (Heilman, 2001; Heilman et al., 2004; Heilman & Okimoto, 2007a). For women, these include behaviors that are associated with men that are thought to be incompatible with the behaviors prescribed for women. Thus, agentic behavior – behavior that demonstrates the self-assertion, dominance, and achievement orientation that is so highly valued for men – is typically prohibited for women.

Violating Prescriptive Stereotypes

Gender-stereotypic prescriptions can affect reactions to women. They function as norms to be fulfilled, and their perceived violation is likely to produce disapproval and promote negativity, as normative violations generally do (Cialdini & Trost, 1998). Social sanctions, or penalties, for the violator are the likely result.

Violating gender prescriptions to act femininely can have generally negative effects on women. For example, women who do not exhibit "womanly" attributes have been shown to be judged as less psychologically healthy and are evaluated less favorably than more feminine women (Costrich, Feinstein, Kidder, Marecek, & Pascale, 1975). Moreover, nontraditional women are evaluated less favorably than women categorized in a more traditional way, with "housewives" preferred to "feminists" (Haddock & Zanna, 1994). Thus, women who violate prescriptive norms about femininity in the broadest sense face social penalties that are likely to carry over to the workplace.

Engaging in "Should Nots" in the Workplace

What happens when a woman aggressively competes for a management position in her organization? By acting independently and competitively, she violates prescriptive gender stereotypes for women. She then is likely to experience disapproval and subsequent social sanctions for this norm-violating behavior, reactions that potentially can affect her career progress. Thus, even when a woman is able to beat the odds and individuate herself from expectations derived from descriptive gender stereotypes, she may be subjected to negative consequences – but this time for acting in a norm-violating way.

Research has demonstrated the dangers for women who contradict prescriptive gender stereotypes in work settings. Negative consequences have been documented for several specific stereotype-inconsistent work behaviors. Women who exhibit norm-deviant behavior in terms of leadership style, communication, and self-promotional behavior have been found to incur penalties for violating prescriptive gender norms.

The penalties imposed for deviating from prescribed norms have included reductions in liking, social acceptance, and influence.

Leadership Style
One aspect of a manager's leadership style is the degree of participation he or she encourages. Women who lead with a dominant, autocratic style deviate from prescriptive norms for women to be communal and non-aggressive. Eagly, Makhijani, and Klonsky's (1992) meta-analysis found that women were evaluated more negatively than men when they were assertive and direct (i.e., an autocratic leadership style reserved for men), but women were not evaluated more negatively than their male counterparts when they used a more democratic style (more consistent with prescribed behavior for women). Another aspect of leadership style is the manner in which discipline is administered. Consistent with our ideas, Brett, Atwater, and Waldman (2005) found female leaders are most effective when they discipline their subordinates in private and with a two-way interaction (a leadership style they call "considerate"). Both of these findings demonstrate that women are punished for engaging in leadership behaviors that are rewarded in men. Thus, prescriptions about how women should be in turn affect perceptions about the best way for women to lead, with violations resulting in negative reactions.

Communication Style
Communication is essential to being effective in organizational settings; it typically is the vehicle for having impact on others. Carli (2001) found that women who spoke in a direct and competent manner were less able to influence male listeners than those with a tentative, mitigating style. It appears that women's violation of stereotypic prescriptions through competent and confident behavior results in reductions in their influence. These results are consistent with other research in which men were found to be less influenced by a competent woman than either a competent man or an incompetent woman (Carli, LaFleur, & Loeber, 1995). Thus, the very behaviors that increase men's influence decrease women's influence. This can make it very difficult for women to learn how to be influential from

models and mentors, as the behaviors they observe to be beneficial for men are actually detrimental for women.

Self-Promotion
Rudman (1998) investigated self-promotion as a work-relevant behavior that is positively related to hiring and promotion, but contrary to prescriptive gender stereotypes for women to be submissive and uncompetitive. Self-promotion involves explicitly expressing one's accomplishments, strengths, and talents. This creates a difficult situation for women who both need to engage in self-promotion (e.g., to compete with male candidates for a position in a job interview), but risk violating prescriptive gender norms by doing so. In this and other studies (e.g., Rudman & Glick, 1999, 2001; Rudman & Fairchild, 2004) Rudman found that women who act in a norm-violating way experience a "backlash effect," suffering economic or social sanctions for their behavior. Men, on the other hand, were not disliked for self-promoting. Like women who speak with a confident, direct style, these women are disliked for the very behaviors that are valued and rewarded in men.

It thus is clear that women who violate prescriptive stereotypes by behaving in a manner deemed inappropriate for them experience disapproval. Expectations about the way women should be are powerful, and women who violate these prescriptive norms by acting in ways that would be beneficial for male colleagues are socially sanctioned for their behavior. Women who intend to succeed in a male gender-typed work environment are therefore limited in their professional repertoire: behaviors that are consistent with the female descriptive stereotype reaffirm the perceived lack of fit between women's attributes and the male position, but behaviors that demonstrate a good fit with the job are considered "out of bounds" for women according to prescriptive stereotypes. Women engaging in these male gender-typed work behaviors experience negative reactions for their prescriptive stereotype violations. And these negative reactions can have serious organizational consequences.

Failing to Engage in "Shoulds" in the Workplace

Up until now we have discussed only reactions to women who violate normative prescriptions by engaging in behaviors that are typically prescribed for men and prohibited for women. But there also can be penalties for failing to engage in the behaviors prescribed for women. That is, prescription violation can take the form of doing what one should not do or, alternatively, failing to do what one should. An example of the latter is the failure to be helpful when called upon for assistance.

Altruistic Citizenship Behavior

A central part of the female normative prescription is that women "be kind and caring" and provide help to others when they are in need. It therefore is believed that women should engage in altruistic behavior when given the opportunity. This has relevance for the work environment because altruism has been identified as one of several dimensions of organizational citizenship behavior (Organ, 1988), behavior that is considered to be voluntarily performed for the benefit of the organization and, as such, can affect performance evaluations and organizational rewards (Allen & Rush, 1998; Podsakoff, MacKenzie, Paine, & Bachrach, 2000; Werner, 1994).

If indeed altruism is a prescribed behavior for women, then their altruistic deeds are likely to be seen as constrained by this prescription (Ames, Flynn, & Weber, 2004), and therefore considered inconsequential; however, their failure to be altruistic is likely to induce disapproval in ways that do not occur for men. Research by Heilman and Chen (2005) supports this idea. They found that whereas men were benefited by their willingness to provide work-related help to a colleague, women were not. Moreover, when they chose not to help a colleague, women suffered in their evaluations but men did not. Thus, the prescriptive injunction requiring women to be helpful nullified a positive effect on evaluations when help was given, and induced a negative effect when help was not given. These findings demonstrate that women are penalized for failing to do what they are supposed to do (help) as well as for engaging in behaviors that are prohibited for them (i.e., being autocratic, communicating forcefully, promoting oneself).

Success: A Violation of Prescriptive Gender Stereotypes for Women

Interestingly, it is not necessary that women explicitly contradict prescriptive stereotypes through engaging in norm-violating behavior to experience penalties in work settings. In fact, research has demonstrated that the mere fact of being successful in a male domain is regarded as a violation of prescriptive gender stereotypes. Women, simply put, are not supposed to excel at jobs and tasks that are designated as male in our culture. And although they may have irrefutably debunked the negative performance expectations that are induced by descriptive gender stereotypes and have come to be viewed as competent and successful, successful women then face another obstacle – the disapproval and negativity that derives from the violation of prescriptive norms. This means that despite their success they may be disadvantaged relative to men at their organizational level when career decisions are made. These ideas are consistent with data provided by Lyness and Judiesch (1999) that tracked the advancement of 30,000 managers and showed that as women moved up the organizational hierarchy, their likelihood of being promoted was less than that of similarly positioned men. Thus, although they may be allowed to move ahead up to a point, competent women are in jeopardy of ultimately being hindered by their own success.

Penalties for Implied Deficits
Several studies have found that when given the information that a woman has been highly successful as a manager in an organization, research participants make strong inferences about what she is like. They infer not only that this successful female manager possesses the agentic qualities necessary for such success, but also that she lacks the communal qualities prescribed for women. Indeed, they characterize her in interpersonally hostile terms antithetical to the prescribed female stereotype: e.g., selfish, deceitful, cold, and manipulative (Heilman et al., 1995; 2004). She also is consistently judged to be unlikable. Men, on the other hand, do not elicit interpersonal rejection when they are depicted as highly successful. Success for men does not imply that they are interpersonally hostile or unlikable. Evidently, when women are clearly competent at handling male positions, the traditionally favorable interpersonal image of them no longer holds. In fact, the inferences drawn are notably unflattering. Success is taken to imply not just that they are low in communality; rather, the inference is that they are overtly counter-communal. That is, they are viewed not just as not warm or sweet; they are seen as cold and bitter. And they are viewed not just as not selfless or kind; they are seen as selfish and deceitful. It is no wonder that they are disliked!

There is evidence that lends credence to the idea that negative reactions to successful women managers stem from the perception that they have violated prescriptive stereotypes. Heilman et al. (2004) demonstrated that although there was interpersonal derogation and reported dislike of women who were successful managers when they held a male gender-typed position (i.e., manager of a unit providing financial and investment advice), these reactions did not occur when they held a managerial job that was female in gender-type (i.e., manager of a unit providing assistance with personal and family problems). Thus, the antipathy toward women managers was limited to situations in which their success was a violation of stereotype prescribed behavior; success in and of itself did not invite interpersonal derogation and dislike.

Career-related Consequences for Women's Success

The cost of not being liked can be serious. Affect has been shown to bias performance ratings (Dipboye. 1985; Ilgen & Feldman, 1983), and liking has been found to interfere with performance rating accuracy in a way that favors the liked ratee (Cardy & Dobbins, 1986). But the effects of not being liked not only impact performance ratings. Research has indicated that people need to be likable in order to have influence in the workplace (Carli, 2001). Moreover, being judged "unlikable" has been shown to have a cost in terms of gaining access to social networks (Casciaro & Lobo, 2005) and special career opportunities and salary recommendations (Heilman et al., 2004). Likability is also important because it can serve as a buffer for work-based norm violations. Bown and Abrams (2003) found that the negative effect of workplace norm deviance (e.g., by showing low commitment to the company's policies) on personality-related evaluations was mitigated by being likable. Thus, it is clear that being deemed unlikable can be costly for individuals in the workplace.

There also are costs for the inferred negative interpersonal attributes that ensue when women are successful. These perceptions can pave the way for not uncommon characterizations of powerful and successful women, such as "bitch," "dragon-lady," "battle-axe," and "ice queen" – all of which can serve as an excuse for not advancing women in their careers. A clear example of the organizational consequences of such characterizations was brought to light in a Supreme Court case involving a highly successful female in a male gender-typed occupation (Fiske, Bersoff, Borgida, Deaux, & Heilman, 1991). Ann Hopkins had more billable hours than any other person proposed for partner, and brought in business worth $25 million at Price Waterhouse. When she claimed she had not been made partner because of her gender, citing sexual discrimination, the decision makers insisted it was because as a "lady partner candidate" she was too "macho," "overcompensated for being a woman," and needed a "course at charm school" (Fiske et al., 1991, p. 1050). The career penalties she incurred were not a result of perceived deficiencies in competence or skill (i.e., not from the influence of descriptive stereotypes on the evaluation of her performance), but from the way she was perceived personally as a successful woman in a traditionally male job.

The Impetus for Success-Based Penalties

What, precisely, is responsible for social penalties resulting from information about a woman's success? Heilman and Okimoto (2007a) explored whether these penalties occur because their success implies women are acting in a way that only men are supposed to act (i.e., in an agentic manner), or because their success implies that they are not acting as women should (i.e., in a communal manner). They found that when information implying communality accompanied information about her success (e.g., information that the manager created a supportive work environment or encouraged cooperation among subordinates), the negativity produced by a woman's success in a male gender-typed job was averted. Interestingly, the evidence for a successful woman's communality did not need to be behavioral or explicit; it could also be conveyed through a role inferred to require communal traits, such as motherhood (Heilman & Okimoto, 2007a, Study 3). Because the negative reactions to successful women are alleviated with evidence of communality, this research suggests that it is the perceived violation of feminine "shoulds," not the enactment of masculine "should nots," that is responsible for the penalties successful women incur for their success. Research demonstrating that feminizing information can reduce penalties for gender norm violations provides additional support for this idea (e.g., Matschiner & Murnen, 1999; Carli, 2001).

Thus, to summarize, the mere knowledge that a woman is successful at a traditionally male job implies prescriptive norm violations. Furthermore, it is the inferred violation of the feminine injunction to be communal that appears to drive the negative response to successful women and the judgments that they are interpersonally hostile and unlikable. In fact, counteracting this inference by providing information about femininity can reduce the penalties experienced by successful women.

Further support for the idea that it is the violation of the communality prescription that provides the impetus for the penalization of counter-normative women can be found in research investigating what happens when women fail to be successful in feminine work roles. Such women also have violated stereotype-based norms about how women should behave, but in this case the implied lack of feminine attributes is more direct than when women are successful at male gender-typed jobs. Moss-Racusin and

Heilman (2006) explored the perceptions of women who fail in traditionally feminine endeavors. They found that women experience the same interpersonal penalties (in terms of liking and interpersonal derogation) by failing when they are supposed to succeed (in female gender-typed jobs) as by succeeding when they are supposed to fail (in male gender-typed jobs). Importantly, no perceived increase in agenticism accompanied this perceived decrease in communal qualities associated with the failure. These findings thus strongly imply that it is the violation of prescriptions to be communal that are at the heart of women's vulnerability to social penalties.

Deterrents against the Use of Prescriptive Gender Stereotypes

In contrast to the bias that arises from the descriptive aspect of gender stereotypes, the bias that arises from the prescriptive aspect is value-based and a consequence of beliefs about how things should be. This means that prescription-based bias is less responsive to contextual variation or efforts by the organization aimed at precluding its effects (Gill, 2004). Even motivational elements of the organizational context that energize people to act in their own best interests are not likely to constrain these tendencies. The effects of prescriptive stereotypes on evaluations create a difficult problem for organizational leadership striving to minimize bias in the workplace. What is required to overcome these effects is not merely the imposition of conditions that bring about more meticulous and thoughtful information processing in the evaluator as is necessary to overcome the effect of descriptive stereotypes; rather, it requires each evaluator to disengage from deeply-held beliefs.

This is not to imply that there are no moderators of the occurrence of penalties for women's perceived stereotype violation. Situational factors that affect the perceived level of incompatibility between the gender prescription and a woman's behavior can no doubt mitigate the perceived degree of violation, and therefore the likelihood and gravity of penalties. The masculine ethos of certain work domains (e.g., law enforcement) or positions (e.g., investment banker) increases the extent to which the job is seen as requiring agentic attributes for success and therefore is likely to increase the perceived violation of female gender role prescriptions when a woman succeeds. What is known about a woman also is likely to have an effect; information that depicts or contains clues about a woman's communal tendencies (e.g., volunteering with children) is likely to protect her against being seen as a norm breaker, softening the negativity associated with violation of prescriptive stereotypes. But the gender-typing of jobs and work domains is culturally determined and often intransigent, and the availability of information about a particular female employee typically rests with her rather than the organization where she works. Thus, the problem of negative reactions to a woman's success, and to women's violation of stereotypic prescriptions more generally, appears to be difficult to combat and not particularly responsive to organizational intervention.

Implications for Men

An interesting question that arises from these findings is: do gender stereotypes negatively affect men as well as women? In particular, if the ideas we have presented are correct, then men should also experience penalties for stereotype-based norm violation. Certainly there are prescriptive stereotypes for men, expected norms for the way that men should act. Additionally, there are jobs that are traditionally feminine in nature. Just as success in traditionally-male positions implies a lack of femininity for women, success in traditionally-female positions may imply a lack of masculinity for men. But what would the penalties men experience look like? Penalties for women are in the communality domain, including interpersonal traits and likability, which is central to the female stereotype. It would be expected, therefore, that penalties for men would be in the agency domain, which is central to the male stereotype.

Heilman and Wallen (2006) examined the evaluation of men who succeed in traditionally feminine workplace positions. Their findings supported these hypotheses. Whereas women who were reported to be clearly successful at a position typically held by men were seen as interpersonally hostile and were not liked, men who were reported to be clearly successful at a position typically held by women were seen as wimpy and passive, and were not respected. These results indicate that there is indeed a symmetrical process in penalties for stereotype violation for men as well as women, and therefore lends additional support to the theoretical ideas underlying our claims about the effects of prescriptive gender stereotypes.

The consequences of stereotype violation for men who perform female jobs is, however, less clear. There is evidence that men tend to ride the "glass escalator" in female occupations, receiving greater organizational rewards relative to similarly qualified women (Williams, 1992). But there also is evidence that men's comparative advantage over women in both pay and promotions in female-dominated jobs is actually smaller than in male or gender-mixed jobs (Budig, 2002). Thus, how the violation of prescriptive gender stereotypes ultimately affects the career progress of men as opposed to women, and, specifically, whether men continue to benefit from being men even when the work domain is female in sex-type, is yet to be determined.

SOME OTHER ISSUES CONCERNING GENDER STEREOTYPES

The Effects of Gender Stereotypes on the Behavior of Women

Effects of Descriptive Stereotypes

If stereotypes about men and women are widespread and culturally shared, then women are likely to apply them to themselves. In fact, research on women has produced findings that indicate that they subscribe to descriptive gender stereotypes, accepting the general societal view of themselves as being high on communal and low on agentic attributes. Consequently, many women still approach male gender-typed roles and tasks with less confidence in their performance capability than equivalently qualified men (Heilman, Lucas, & Kaplow, 1990).

There are a host of consequences that derive from women's negative performance expectations for themselves. One is the failure to take responsibility for their successes. Recent research has demonstrated that women, when working in teams paired with men, are unwilling to take equal credit for successful outcomes and are likely to see themselves as less competent than their male partners (Haynes, 2006). Another potential consequence is that women may directly engage in self-limiting behavior because of fears of not being up to the task – minimizing risks, choosing to not be "visible," and not putting oneself forward for opportunities and experiences that are conduits to advancement.

Effects of Prescriptive Stereotypes

Women also are likely to internalize prescriptive gender stereotypes, holding them as standards for themselves. In fact, prescriptive stereotypes have been found to be evident in the ought and ideal selves of both men and women (Wood, Christensen, Hebl, & Rothgerber, 1997). Together with the awareness of societal expectations about what behavior is appropriate for them, this can have serious consequences for women's career progress. Their concerns about being "ladylike" and not presenting themselves too forcefully may inhibit the behaviors that are critical to making inroads in work settings (Battle & Heilman, 2006). Thus, women may engage in self-censorship either in advancing their interests (e.g., failing to ask for benefits or demand for better work conditions), or in being assertive (e.g., failing to stand up for what they believe, resist bullying, or energetically compete for resources). Whether because of concerns about how others will react to them, or because of their own prescription-based standards for their behavior, in each of these instances the reluctance to violate gender stereotypic injunctions about how women "should" behave can hinder their career progress.

Potential Differences between Female and Male Perceivers

In the vast majority of studies conducted on gender stereotypes, no differences have been found in the reactions of male and female respondents. While this makes sense in a general way – stereotypes are widely shared in our culture – it is perplexing in others. One would expect that women would empathize with other women, be sensitive to the bias that thwarts them, and therefore process individuating information about them more carefully, resulting in less negative evaluative judgments. One would also expect that women would be sensitive to the burden of normative strictures that constrain other women, and therefore somewhat ease these standards in responding to them. Moreover, one would think that men have more of a vested interest than women in maintaining gender stereotypes. Burgess and Borgida (1999) proposed that prescriptive stereotypes serve to maintain gender status norms in the workplace, and according to this hypothesis, men, more than women, should be motivated to enforce prescriptive gender norms. A similar case can be made for descriptive gender stereotypes. Why, then, do studies consistently show that female and male perceivers do not differ?

It is conceivable that although there is no difference in the way men and women respond to women in the workplace, there is a difference in why they respond the way they do. Recent research lends some support to this idea. Results from a set of studies suggests that female perceivers penalize successful women because they are threatened by them, and that characterizing a successful woman as unlikable and interpersonally hostile allows female judges to exclude her as a personal standard of comparison, releasing them from a harmful upward comparison (Parks-Stamm, Heilman, & Hearns, 2007). Thus, female participants were shown to feel more competent after penalizing a successful female manager than when they were precluded from doing so (because of additional communal information), and to not penalize a successful female manager when they had first been made to feel highly competent about their own managerial potential. These findings suggest that although female and male perceivers similarly penalize women who violate prescriptive norms, they may do so for different reasons. There are analogues with descriptive gender stereotypes. For example, the "queen bee syndrome" (Staines, Tavris, & Jayaratne, 1974) suggests that women's motives for their negative evaluative judgments and employment decisions about other women may decidedly differ from those of their male colleagues. Additional research is needed to better understand this issue and its implications for career-aspiring women.

SUMMARY AND CONCLUSIONS

In this chapter we have considered how gender stereotypes, both descriptive and prescriptive, can contribute to sex bias in work settings and the impeding of women's career progress. We have discussed how descriptive gender stereotypes promote sex bias because of the negative performance expectations that result from the perception that the attributes of women do not "fit" with the attributes deemed necessary for success at male gender-typed jobs. Accordingly, we identified organizational conditions that – either because they promote ambiguity, or because they create self-interested motivation – encourage or discourage the expectation-confirming information processing that fuels sex-biased evaluations. We also have discussed how prescriptive gender stereotypes promote sex bias by creating normative standards about how women should behave that, when not met, induce disapproval and social penalties. We have explored how women's direct violation of stereotype-based prescriptions, as well as the inferred violations that arise when they are successful, can negatively affect their career prospects, and the limited actions organizations can take to counteract these effects.

Throughout this chapter we claim that gender stereotypes are the basis of sex bias in evaluative judgments and discriminatory treatment of women in work settings. We have tried to elucidate the psychological processes that are instigated by gender stereotypes and to identify conditions that regulate their detrimental effects. Nonetheless, the message provided here is not a happy one. It appears that career-oriented women are not yet free of the consequences of gender stereotypes. When the position to which women aspire is male gender-typed, they are prone to being viewed as ill-equipped to handle it. When they step out of the constricted band of often ineffectual behaviors acceptable for females, they tend to pay a steep price. And, most disconcerting of all, when their success is obvious and irrefutable, they are disliked and interpersonally derogated. It appears that despite the tremendous gains of recent years, the effects of gender stereotypes are still very much with us.

REFERENCES

Allen, T. D., & Rush, M. C. (1998). The effects of organizational citizenship behavior on performance judgments: A field study and a laboratory experiment. *Journal of Applied Psychology, 83,* 247–260.

Ames, D. R., Flynn, F. J., & Weber, E. U. (2004). It's the thought that counts: On perceiving how helpers decide to lend a hand. *Personality and Social Psychology Bulletin, 30,* 461–474.

Arvey, R. D., & Murphy, K. R. (1998). Performance evaluation in work settings. *Annual Review of Psychology, 49,* 141–168.

Bakan, D. (1966). *The duality of human existence: An essay on psychology and religion.* Chicago, IL: Rand McNally.

Baltes, B. B., & Parker, C. P. (2000). Reducing the effects of performance expectations on behavioral ratings. *Organizational Behavior and Human Decision Processes, 82*(2), 237–267.

Banaji, M. R., Hardin, C., & Rothman, A. J. (1993). Implicit stereotyping in person judgment. *Journal of Personality and Social Psychology, 65*(2), 272–281.

Battle W. S., & Heilman M. E. (2006). *Women's reluctance to self-advocate: A result of internal or social factors?* Manuscript in preparation.

Bauer, C. C., & Baltes, B. B. (2002). Reducing the effects of gender stereotypes on performance evaluations. *Sex Roles, 47*(9–10), 465–476.

Bown, N. J., & Abrams, D. (2003). Despicability in the workplace: Effects of behavioral deviance and unlikability on the evaluation of in-group and out-group members. *Journal of Applied Social Psychology, 33,* 2413–2426.

Brett, J. F., Atwater, L. L., & Waldman, D. A. (2005). Effective delivery of workplace discipline: Do women have to be more participatory than men? *Group and Organization Management, 30,* 487–513.

Broverman, I. K., Vogel, S. R., Broverman, D. M., Clarkson, F. E., & Rosenkrantz, P. S. (1972). Sex-role stereotypes: A current appraisal. *Journal of Social Issues, 28,* 59–78.

Budig, M. J. (2002). Male advantage and the gender composition of jobs: Who rides the glass escalator? *Social Problems, 49,* 258–277.

Burgess, D., & Borgida, E. (1999). Who women are, who women should be: Descriptive and prescriptive gender stereotyping in sex discrimination. *Psychology, Public Policy, and Law, 5*(3), 665–692.

Cantor, N., & Mischel, W. (1979). Prototypicality and personality: Effects on free recall and personality impressions. *Journal of Research in Personality, 13*(2), 187–205.

Cardy, R. L., & Dobbins, G. H. (1986). Affect and appraisal accuracy: Liking as an integral dimension in evaluating performance. *Journal of Applied Psychology, 71,* 672–678.

Carli, L. L. (2001). Gender and social influence. *Journal of Social Issues, 57,* 725–741.

Carli, L. L., LaFleur, S. J., & Loeber, C. C. (1995). Nonverbal behavior, gender, and influence. *Journal of Personality and Social Psychology, 68,* 1030–1041.

Casciaro, T. & Lobo, M. S. (2005). Competent jerks, lovable fools, and the formation of social networks. *Harvard Business Review, 83*, 92–99.

Chaiken, S. (1980). Heuristic versus systematic information processing and the use of source versus message cues in persuasion. *Journal of Personality and Social Psychology, 39*, 752–766.

Cialdini, R. B., & Trost, M. R. (1998). Social influence: Social norms, conformity, and compliance. In: D. T. Gilbert, S. T. Fiske & L. Gardner (Eds), *The handbook of social psychology* (Vol. 2, pp. 151–192). New York, NY: McGraw-Hill.

Cooper, W. H. (1981). Conceptual similarity as a source of illusory halo in job performance ratings. *Journal of Applied Psychology, 66*(3), 302–307.

Costrich, N., Feinstein, J., Kidder, L., Marecek, J., & Pascale, L. (1975). When stereotypes hurt: Three studies of penalties for sex-role reversals. *Journal of Experimental Social Psychology, 11*, 520–530.

Crocker, J., Hannah, D. B., & Weber, R. (1983). Person memory and causal attributions. *Journal of Personality and Social Psychology, 44*(1), 55–66.

Davison, H. K., & Burke, M. J. (2000). Sex discrimination in simulated employment contexts: A meta-analytic investigation. *Journal of Vocational Behavior, 56*, 225–248.

Deaux, K., & Lewis, L. L. (1984). Structure of gender stereotypes: Interrelationships among components and gender label. *Journal of Personality and Social Psychology, 46*(5), 991–1004.

Dennis, M. R., & Kunkel, A. D. (2004). Perceptions of men, women, and CEOs: The effects of gender identity. *Social Behavior and Personality, 32*(2), 155–172.

DeNisi, A. S., Cafferty, T. P., & Meglino, B. M. (1984). A cognitive view of the performance appraisal process: A model and research propositions. *Organizational Behavior and Human Performance, 33*(3), 360–396.

Devine, P. G. (1989). Stereotypes and prejudice: Their automatic and controlled components. *Journal of Personality and Social Psychology, 56*, 5–18.

Diekman, A. B., & Eagly, A. H. (2000). Stereotypes as dynamic constructs: Women and men of the past, present, and future. *Personality and Social Psychology Bulletin, 26*, 1171–1188.

Dipboye, R. L. (1985). Some neglected variables in research on discrimination in appraisals. *Academy of Management Review, 10*(1), 116–127.

Dodge, K. A., Gilroy, F. D., & Fenzel, M. L. (1995). Requisite management characteristics revisited: Two decades later. *Journal of Social Behavior and Personality, 10*(6), 253–264 Special Issue: Gender in the workplace.

Dovidio, J. F., Evans, N., & Tyler, R. B. (1986). Racial stereotypes: The contents of their cognitive representations. *Journal of Experimental Social Psychology, 22*, 22–37.

Eagly, A. H. (2000). Gender roles. In: A. E. Kazdin (Ed.), *Encyclopedia of psychology* (Vol. 3, pp. 448–453). New York, NY: Oxford University Press.

Eagly, A. H., & Karau, S. J. (2002). Role congruity theory of prejudice toward female leaders. *Psychological Review, 109*(3), 573–598.

Eagly, A. H., Makhijani, M. G., & Klonsky, B. G. (1992). Gender and the evaluation of leaders: A meta-analysis. *Psychological Bulletin, 111*, 3–22.

Eagly, A. H., & Mladinic, A. (1989). Gender stereotypes and attitudes toward women and men. *Personality and Social Psychology Bulletin, 15*(4), 538–543.

Eagly, A. H., Mladinic, A., & Otto, S. (1991). Are women evaluated more favorably than men? An analysis of attitudes, beliefs, and emotions. *Psychology of Women Quarterly, 15*, 203–216.

Favero, J. L., & Ilgen, D. R. (1989). The effects of ratee prototypicality on rater observation and accuracy. *Journal of Applied Social Psychology, 19*(11), 932–946.

Feldman, J. M., & Lynch, J. G. (1988). Self-generated validity and other effects of measurement on belief, attitude, intention, and behavior. *Journal of Applied Psychology, 73*(3), 421–435.

Fiske, S. T. (1998). Stereotyping, prejudice, & discrimination. In: D. T. Gilbert, S. T. Fiske & G. Lindzey (Eds), *The handbook of social psychology* (Vol. 2, pp. 357–414). New York, NY: McGraw Hill.

Fiske, S. T. (2000). Interdependence and the reduction of prejudice. In: S. Oskamp (Ed.), *Reducing prejudice and discrimination: "The Claremont Symposium on Applied Social Psychology"* (pp. 115–135). Mahwah, NJ: Larry Erlbaum Associates, Publishers.

Fiske, S. T., Bersoff, D. N., Borgida, E., Deaux, K., & Heilman, M. E. (1991). Social science research on trial: Use of sex stereotyping research in *Price Waterhouse v. Hopkins*. *American Psychologist, 46*, 1049–1060.

Fiske, S. T., & Neuberg, S. L. (1990). A continuum of impression formation, from category-based to individuating processes: Influences of information and motivation on attention and interpretation. In: M. P. Zanna (Ed.), *Advances in experimental social psychology* (Vol. 23, pp. 1–74). San Diego, CA: Academic Press.

Fiske, S. T., & Taylor, S. E. (1991). *Social cognition* (2nd ed.). New York, NY: McGraw Hill Book Company.

Fuegen, K., Biernat, M., Haines, E., & Deaux, K. (2004). Mothers and fathers in the workplace: How gender and parental status influence judgments of job-related competence. *Journal of Social Issues, 60*(4), 737–754.

Gilbert, D. T., & Hixon, J. G. (1991). The trouble of thinking: Activation and application of stereotypic beliefs. *Journal of Personality and Social Psychology, 60*(4), 509–517.

Gill, M. J. (2004). When information does not deter stereotyping: Prescriptive stereotyping can foster bias under conditions that deter descriptive stereotyping. *Journal of Experimental Social Psychology, 40*, 619–632.

Haddock, G., & Zanna, M. P. (1994). Preferring "housewives" to "feminists": Categorization and the favorability of attitudes toward women. *Psychology of Women Quarterly, 18*, 25–52.

Hastie, R. (1984). Causes and effects of causal attribution. *Journal of Personality and Social Psychology, 46*(1), 44–56.

Haynes, M. C. (2006). *Did I do that? Women's attributional rationalization of their contribution to successful work outcomes.* Manuscript in preparation.

Heilman, M. E. (1983). Sex bias in work settings: The lack of fit model. In: B. Staw & L. Cummings (Eds), *Research in organizational behavior* (Vol. 5, pp. 269–298). Greenwich, CT: JAI.

Heilman, M. E. (1984). Information as a deterrent against sex discrimination: The effects of applicant sex and information type on preliminary employment decisions. *Organizational Behavior and Human Performance, 33*, 174–186.

Heilman, M. E. (1995). Sex stereotypes and their effects in the workplace: What we know and what we don't know. *Journal of Social Behavior and Personality, 10*(6), 3–26.

Heilman, M. E. (2001). Description and prescription: How gender stereotypes prevent women's ascent up the organizational ladder. *Journal of Social Issues, 57*(4), 657–674.

Heilman, M. E., & Blader, S. L. (2001). Assuming preferential selection when the admissions policy is unknown: The effects of gender rarity. *Journal of Applied Psychology, 86*(2), 188–193.

Heilman, M. E., Block, C. J., & Martell, R. F. (1995). Sex stereotypes: Do they influence perceptions of managers? *Journal of Social Behavior and Personality, 10,* 237–252.

Heilman, M. E., Block, C. J., Martell, R. F., & Simon, M. C. (1989). Has anything changed? Current characterizations of men, women, and managers. *Journal of Applied Psychology, 74*(6), 935–942.

Heilman, M. E., Block, C. J., & Stathatos, P. (1997). The affirmative action stigma of incompetence: Effects of performance information ambiguity. *Academy of Management Journal, 40*(3), 603–625.

Heilman, M. E., & Chen, J. J. (2005). Same behavior, different consequences: Reactions to men's and women's altruistic citizenship behavior. *Journal of Applied Psychology, 90,* 431–441.

Heilman, M. E., & Haynes, M. C. (2005). No credit where credit is due: Attributional rationalization of women's success in male–female teams. *Journal of Applied Psychology, 90,* 905–916.

Heilman, M. E., & Haynes, M. C. (in press). Subjectivity in the appraisal process: A facilitator of gender bias in work settings. In: E. Borgida & S. T. Fiske (Eds), *Psychological science in court: Beyond common knowledge.* Mahwah, NJ: Larry Erlbaum Associates, Publishers.

Heilman, M. E., Lucas, J. A., & Kaplow, S. R. (1990). Self-derogating consequences of sex-based preferential selection: The moderating role of initial self-confidence. *Organizational Behavior and Human Decision Processes, 46*(2), 202–216.

Heilman, M. E., Martell, R. F., & Simon, M. C. (1988). The vagaries of sex bias: Conditions regulating the undervaluation, equivaluation, and overvaluation of female job applicants. *Organizational Behavior and Human Decision Processes, 41*(1), 98–110.

Heilman, M. E., & Okimoto, T. G. (2007a). Why are women penalized for success at male tasks?: The implied communality deficit. *Journal of Applied Psychology, 92,* 81–92.

Heilman, M. E., & Okimoto, T. G. (2007b). *Parenthood: Hindrance to women's (but not men's) career advancement.* Manuscript submitted for publication.

Heilman, M. E., & Stopeck, M. H. (1985). Attractiveness and corporate success: Different causal attributions for males and females. *Journal of Applied Psychology, 70*(2), 379–388.

Heilman, M. E., & Stopeck, M. H. (1985). Being attractive – advantage or disadvantage? Performance-based evaluations and recommended personnel actions as a function of appearance, sex, and job type. *Organizational Behavior and Human Decision Processes, 35*(2), 202–215.

Heilman, M. E., & Wallen, A. S. (2006). *Men as wimpy and women as bitchy: Perceptions of managers who violate gender stereotype prescriptions.* Manuscript in preparation.

Heilman, M. E., Wallen, A. S., Fuchs, D., & Tamkins, M. M. (2004). Penalties for success: Reactions to women who succeed at male gender-typed tasks. *Journal of Applied Psychology, 89,* 416–427.

Heilman, M. E., & Welle, B. (2006). Disadvantaged by diversity? The effects of diversity goals on competence perceptions. *Journal of Applied Social Psychology, 206,* 1291–1319.

Higgins, E. T., & Bargh, J. A. (1987). Social cognition and social perception. *Annual Review of Psychology, 38,* 369–425.

Ilgen, D. R., & Feldman, J. M. (1983). Performance appraisal: A process focus. *Research in Organizational Behavior, 5,* 141–197.

Johnson, J. T., & Judd, C. M. (1983). Overlooking the incongruent: Categorization biases in the identification of political statements. *Journal of Personality and Social Psychology, 45*(5), 978–996.

Klimoski, R., & Inks, L. (1990). Accountability forces in performance appraisal. *Organizational Behavior and Human Decision Processes, 45*(2), 194–208.
Kulik, J. A. (1983). Confirmatory attribution and the perpetuation of social beliefs. *Journal of Personality and Social Psychology, 44*(6), 1171–1181.
Kunda, Z., Sinclair, L., & Griffin, D. (1997). Equal ratings but separate meanings: Stereotypes and the construal of traits. *Journal of Personality and Social Psychology, 72*(4), 720–734.
Lueptow, L. B., Garovich, L., & Lueptow, M. B. (1995). The persistence of gender stereotypes in the face of changing sex roles: Evidence contrary to the sociocultural model. *Ethology and Sociobiology, 16*, 509–530.
Lyness, K. S. (2002). Finding the key to the executive suite: Challenges for women and people of color. In: R. Silzer (Ed.), *The 21st century executive: Innovative practices for building leadership at the top* (pp. 229–273). San Francisco, CA: Jossey-Boss.
Lyness, K. S., & Heilman, M. E. (2006). When fit is fundamental: Performance evaluation and promotions of upper-level female and male managers. *Journal of Applied Psychology, 91*, 777–785.
Lyness, K. S., & Judiesch, M. K. (1999). Are women more likely to be hired or promoted into management positions? *Journal of Vocational Behavior, 54*(1), 158–173.
Macrae, C. N., Milne, A. B., & Bodenhausen, G. V. (1994). Stereotypes as energy-saving devices: A peek inside the cognitive toolbox. *Journal of Personality and Social Psychology, 66*, 37–47.
Martell, R. F., Guzzo, R. A., & Willis, C. E. (1995). A methodological and substantive note on the performance-cue effect in ratings of work-group behavior. *Journal of Applied Psychology, 80*(1), 191–195.
Martell, R. F., Parker, C., Emrich, C. G., & Crawford, M. S. (1998). Sex stereotyping in the executive suite: "Much ado about something". *Journal of Social Behavior and Personality, 13*, 127–138.
Matschiner, M., & Murnen, S. K. (1999). Hyperfemininity and influence. *Psychology of Women Quarterly, 23*, 631–642.
Moss-Racusin, C., & Heilman, M. E. (2006, January). *Failure to be feminine: Interpersonal penalties for failure behavior on sex-consistent domains.* Poster session presented at the 7th Annual Meeting of the Society for Personality and Social Psychology, Palm Springs, CA
Nieva, V. G., & Gutek, B. A. (1980). Sex effects on evaluation. *Academy of Management Review, 5*, 267–276.
Organ, D. W. (1988). *Organizational citizenship behavior: The good soldier syndrome.* Lexington, MA: Lexington Books.
O'Sullivan, C. S., & Durso, F. T. (1984). Effect of schema-incongruent information on memory for stereotypical attributes. *Journal of Personality and Social Psychology, 47*(1), 55–70.
Parks-Stamm, E. J., Heilman, M. E., & Hearns, K. A. (2007). *Motivated penalization: Why women derogate successful women?* Manuscript submitted for publication.
Pazy, A., & Oron, I. (2001). Sex proportion and performance evaluation among high-ranking military officers. *Journal of Organizational Behavior, 22*(6), 689–702.
Podsakoff, P. M., MacKenzie, S. B., Paine, J. B., & Bachrach, D. G. (2000). Organizational citizenship behaviors: A critical review of the theoretical and empirical literature and suggestions for future research. *Journal of Management, 26*(3), 513–563.
Powell, G. N., Butterfield, D. A., & Parent, J. D. (2002). Gender and managerial stereotypes: Have the times changed? *Journal of Management, 28*(2), 177–193.

Pratto, F., & Bargh, J. A. (1991). Stereotyping based on apparently individuating information: Trait and global components of sex stereotypes under attention overload. *Journal of Experimental Social Psychology, 27*(1), 26–47.

Rasinski, K. A., Crocker, J., & Hastie, R. (1985). Another look at sex stereotypes and social judgments: An analysis of the social perceiver's use of subjective probabilities. *Journal of Personality and Social Psychology, 49*(2), 317–326.

Rudman, L. A. (1998). Self-promotion as a risk factor for women: The costs and benefits of counterstereotypical impression management. *Journal of Personality and Social Psychology, 74*, 629–645.

Rudman, L. A., & Fairchild, K. (2004). Reactions to counterstereotypic behavior: The role of backlash in cultural stereotype maintenance. *Journal of Personality and Social Psychology, 87*, 157–176.

Rudman, L. A., & Glick, P. (1999). Feminized management and backlash towards agentic women: The hidden costs to women of a kinder, gentler image of middle managers. *Journal of Personality and Social Psychology, 77*, 1004–1010.

Rudman, L. A., & Glick, P. (2001). Prescriptive gender stereotypes and backlash toward agentic women. *Journal of Social Issues, 57*, 743–762.

Sackett, P. R., DuBois, C. L., & Noe, A. W. (1991). Tokenism in performance evaluation: The effects of work group representation on male-female and White-Black differences in performance ratings. *Journal of Applied Psychology, 76*(2), 263–267.

Schein, V. E. (1973). The relationship between sex role stereotypes and requisite management characteristics. *Journal of Applied Psychology, 57*, 95–100.

Schein, V. E. (1975). Relationships between sex role stereotypes and requisite management characteristics among female managers. *Journal of Applied Psychology, 60*, 340–344.

Schein, V. E. (2001). A global look at psychological barriers to women's progress in management. *Journal of Social Issues, 57*, 675–688.

Simonson, I., & Nye, P. (1992). The effect of accountability on susceptibility to decision errors. *Organizational Behavior and Human Decision Processes, 51*(3), 416–446.

Staines, G., Tavris, C., & Jayaratne, T. E. (1974). The queen bee syndrome. *Psychology Today, 7*, 55–60.

Swim, J., Borgida, E., Maruyama, G., & Myers, D. G. (1989). Joan McKay versus John McKay: Do gender stereotypes bias evaluations?. *Psychological Bulletin, 105*(3), 409–429.

Swim, J. K., & Sanna, L. J. (1996). He's skilled, she's lucky: A meta-analysis of observers' attributions for women's and men's successes and failures. *Personality and Social Psychology Bulletin, 22*(5), 507–519.

Tetlock, P. E. (1983). Accountability and complexity of thought. *Journal of Personality and Social Psychology, 45*(1), 74–83.

Tetlock, P. E. (1983). Accountability and the perseverance of first impressions. *Social Psychology Quarterly, 46*(4), 285–292.

Tetlock, P. E. (1985). Accountability: The neglected social context of judgment and choice. *Research in Organizational Behavior, 7*, 297–332.

Tetlock, P. E., Skitka, L., & Boettger, R. (1989). Social and cognitive strategies for coping with accountability: Conformity, complexity, and bolstering. *Journal of Personality and Social Psychology, 57*(4), 632–640.

Tosi, H. L., & Einbender, S. W. (1985). The effects of the type and amount of information in sex discrimination research: A meta-analysis. *Academy of Management Journal, 28*(3), 712–723.

Viswesvaran, C., Ones, D. S., & Schmidt, F. L. (1996). Comparative analysis of the reliability of job performance ratings. *Journal of Applied Psychology, 81*(5), 557–574.

Werner, J. M. (1994). Dimensions that make a difference: Examining the impact of in-role and extra-role behaviors on supervisory ratings. *Journal of Applied Psychology, 79*(1), 98–107.

Willemsen, T. M. (2002). Gender typing of the successful manager: A stereotype reconsidered. *Sex Roles, 46*, 385–391.

Williams, C. L. (1992). The glass escalator: Hidden advantages for men in the "female" professions. *Social Problems, 39*, 253–266.

Williams, J. E., & Best, D. L. (1990). *Measuring sex stereotypes: A multinational study* (revised edition). Beverly Hills, CA: Sage Publications.

Wood, W., Christensen, P. N., Hebl, M. R., & Rothgerber, H. (1997). Conformity to sex-typed norms, affect, and the self-concept. *Journal of Personality and Social Psychology, 73*, 523–535.

THE EFFECTS OF GENDER STEREOTYPES ON JUDGMENTS AND DECISIONS IN ORGANIZATIONS

Kathleen Fuegen

ABSTRACT

I describe the shifting standards model of stereotyping and explain the implications of this model for organizational decisions. I present research showing that the standards one sets for inferring competence and incompetence affect important organizational decisions, including short listing, hiring, probation, and firing decisions. I also present research documenting that gender stereotypes interact with parental status to affect standards set for hiring a mother and father. I conclude by offering recommendations for future research that delineates the subtle ways stereotypes affect judgments of work-related competence.

That gender stereotypes affect many work-related judgments and decisions is a well-established fact. Research in social and organizational psychology shows that gender stereotypes affect perceptions of job suitability (Biernat & Fuegen, 2001; Davison & Burke, 2000; Heilman, 1983, 1995; Operario & Fiske, 2001; Schein, 1973, 2001), leadership ability (Biernat, Crandall,

Young, Kobrynowicz, & Halpin, 1998; Boldry, Wood, & Kashy, 2001; Eagly, 2005; Eagly & Karau, 2002; Eagly, Makhijani, & Klonsky, 1992), and the likelihood of obtaining promotions (Fiske, Bersoff, Borgida, Deaux, & Heilman, 1991; Lyness & Judiesch, 1999; Lyness & Heilman, 2006; Tomkiewicz, Brenner, & Adeyemi-Bello, 1998). Women who attempt to gain entry into male-dominated occupations, such as the military, or women who attempt to secure coveted positions, such as partner in a law firm, are often targets of negative stereotypes. In many cases, the amount of evidence of good performance needed to infer that an individual has ability is significantly greater for women than for men.

Because stereotypes affect what we notice, attend to, and remember about others (for a review, see Fiske, 1998), reliance on stereotypes affects a variety of decisions. When a supervisor notices and remembers an employee's successful project, it is likely the employee will be offered new task assignments, training opportunities, a raise, and/or a promotion (Cleveland, Murphy, & Williams, 1989). Conversely, when an employee's mistakes are noticed and remembered, he or she may be assigned to less desirable tasks, transferred, demoted, and/or terminated (Struthers, Weiner, & Allred, 1998). To the extent that negative stereotypes exist regarding women's competence in traditionally masculine domains, evaluators are likely to notice and attend to stereotype-consistent behavior and interpret such behavior as diagnostic of ability. Poor performance by women is more likely to be attributed to internal factors (e.g., lack of ability) than poor performance by men (Deaux, 1984; Greenhaus & Parasuraman, 1993; Jackson, Sullivan, & Hodge, 1993; Swim & Sanna, 1996). Favorable performance by women is more likely to be attributed to external factors (e.g., luck) than similar performance by men.

Among the factors thought to augment the influence of stereotypes in the workplace are ambiguous qualifications (Dovidio & Gaertner, 2000), performance measures that are not easily quantified or subjective in nature (Heilman, 1995), and vague evaluative criteria (Gupta, Jenkins, & Beehr, 1983; Nieva & Gutek, 1980; Sessa, 2001). For example, an experiment investigating the effects of race stereotypes on employment decisions showed that well-qualified and poorly qualified black job applicants were as likely to be hired as similarly qualified white applicants. However, a black applicant whose credentials were only moderately good was less likely to be hired than a comparable white applicant (Gaertner & Dovidio, 2000). In the realm of performance appraisal, judgments based on vague evaluative criteria (e.g., is the applicant "executive material?") are often based on similarities between the evaluator and the person being evaluated. Thus, a male evaluator is more likely to bestow coveted promotions upon a male than a female subordinate (Gupta et al., 1983).

While the form of bias directed toward women may be blatant (e.g., as in the expectation that a candidate for promotion dress more femininely; see Fiske et al., 1991), stereotypes are frequently subtle in their influence. The form of bias directed toward women may be manifested as a backlash against women who are too agentic or too successful as managers (Heilman, Wallen, Fuchs, & Tamkins, 2004; Rudman & Glick, 1999), who criticize subordinates (Sinclair & Kunda, 2000), or who adopt an autocratic leadership style (Eagly et al., 1992). Another subtle manifestation of gender stereotypes is the practice of holding women to higher performance standards than men.

SHIFTING STANDARDS

The shifting standards model of stereotyping is based on the premise that stereotypes activate standards according to which individual members of stereotyped groups are judged (Biernat, 2003). These standards reflect our expectations regarding the characteristics of a group of people. For example, if one holds the stereotype that men are better leaders than women, that individual applies different standards when judging the leadership competence of a particular woman and the leadership competence of a particular man. A woman is judged relative to lower standards for women in general, and a man is judged relative to higher standards for men in general. Thus, the same behavior (e.g., coordinating a political campaign) may be judged as indicative of high leadership ability in a woman ("for a woman, she's really good") but only moderate leadership ability in a man. The implication is that subjective judgments (i.e., trait ratings) of men and women are not directly comparable. The label "good leader" does not mean the same thing when applied to a woman as it does when applied to a man.

The shifting standards model of stereotyping predicts that stereotyping effects will be masked or even reversed when subjective scales (e.g., Likert-type trait ratings, semantic differentials) are used in judgments of individual members of stereotyped groups. The use of objective scales (e.g., rankings, standardized test scores) is more likely to reveal the influence of stereotypes, because these scales force an individual to array *all* targets on a given dimension. Instead of making within-group comparisons, one is forced to make between-groups comparisons. Research shows that persons shift standards when rating women and men on verbal ability, writing competence, aggression, parenting involvement, leadership, and job-related competence

(Biernat, Manis, & Nelson, 1991; Biernat et al., 1998; Biernat & Kobrynowicz, 1997; Biernat & Manis, 1994; Kobrynowicz & Biernat, 1997). That is, while a woman may be judged to have high leadership ability on a subjective scale (where she is compared with other women), she may nevertheless be ranked a less able leader than a man on an objective scale, consistent with gender stereotypes (see also Roth, Bobko, & Huffcuff, 2003, for evidence of shifting standards in the evaluation of Black and White employees).

MINIMUM AND CONFIRMATORY STANDARDS

While this research documents that the pattern of stereotyping depends on the *form* of judgment (i.e., scale type), patterns of stereotyping also depend on the *type* of standard being assessed. When judging the degree to which an individual possesses a certain attribute, persons apply both minimum and confirmatory standards. A minimum standard reflects one's expectations for what members of a particular group are like and thus reflects the stereotype. A confirmatory standard is the threshold that reflects *certainty* that an individual has an attribute. Confirmatory standards require more evidence of the attribute in question than do minimum standards. For example, when the attribute is leadership ability, persons holding gender-based stereotypes about leadership have lower expectations for women than men. Because a woman is held to a lower minimum standard, she may not need to work as hard as a man to surpass low expectations. Nevertheless, precisely because of these lower expectations, the amount of evidence needed to *certify* that she has leadership ability will be greater.

The setting of higher confirmatory standards for women than men is consistent with research on double standards for competence derived from expectation states theory (Foddy & Smithson, 1989; Foschi, 1989, 2000; Foschi & Foddy, 1988). According to this theory, standards reflect broad-based inferences about an attribute. As such, more evidence of the attribute is needed from members of low-status groups (e.g., women) than members of high-status groups (e.g., men) to confirm its presence, particularly when the task is associated with attributes of the high-status group. The setting of higher confirmatory standards for women is also consistent with recent research by Lyness and Heilman (2006). Using archival organizational data, these researchers showed that women in upper-level management who were promoted received more favorable performance evaluations than men who were promoted. To be promoted, women needed to demonstrate higher levels of key attributes than men.

The prediction that members of negatively stereotyped groups will be held to lower minimum but higher confirmatory standards for inferring ability was first tested in an experiment using undergraduate participants (Biernat & Kobrynowicz, 1997). Participants reviewed the résumé of a female or male job applicant and indicated the level of competence they would require in order to hire the applicant. Half the participants indicated the number of job-relevant skills they would require of the applicant before feeling that he or she "meets the minimum standard" to be successful in the position. The other half indicated the number of job-relevant skills they would require to decide that the applicant "has the ability" to perform the job. As expected, participants required fewer skills of a female applicant than a male applicant to meet the minimum standard. In other words, they conveyed their low expectations of women's task competence by setting a lower hurdle for inferring some minimal level of competence. However, despite this lower minimum standard, participants set stricter confirmatory standards for a female than male applicant. That is, they required more evidence of skill from a woman to confirm that she had the ability to perform a job.

In subsequent research, we extended this work on gender-based minimum and confirmatory standards by mapping these standards onto important organizational decisions. We were interested not only in how minimum and confirmatory standards apply to decisions related to inferring competence (as in judgments of whether to hire someone for a job), but also how these standards apply to decisions related to inferring incompetence (as in judgments of whether to fire someone based on poor performance). I first describe research applying minimum and confirmatory standards to steps in the hiring process followed by research applying these standards to steps in the firing process. I then describe research focusing just on confirmatory standards (i.e., hiring). This latter research addresses how gender stereotypes regarding job-relevant competence interact with the parenting role to affect perceptions of mothers' and fathers' job suitability.

STANDARDS AND ORGANIZATIONAL DECISIONS

Short-Listing and Hiring Studies

Biernat and Fuegen (2001) examined how minimum and confirmatory standards relate to important steps in the hiring process. We hypothesized that minimum standards may correspond to that point in the decision-making process where one determines which candidates are still in the running for a position, as in the creation of a short list. Confirmatory standards may correspond to the decision of which person from the short list to hire. Our prediction was that women would be more likely to make the short list, though men would be more likely to be hired. That is, lower minimum standards for women should make it easier to pass an initial screening process, but higher confirmatory standards should make it more difficult for women to pass the scrutiny required to be hired.

We asked 175 undergraduate participants to roleplay the position of a manager in charge of evaluating applicants for a job. Each was given a folder containing instructions on short listing and hiring, a job description, a résumé, and an evaluation form. The job description was the same for all participants, that of an assistant to a senior executive. In half the cases, this description was labeled "executive secretary," and in half it was labeled "executive chief of staff." Though the position labeled "executive chief of staff" was judged to be of higher status and deserving of a higher salary than the "executive secretary" position, this manipulation did not affect the setting of standards or short listing and hiring decisions. The résumé was identical for all participants, except that half received a résumé with a female name and half received a résumé with a male name. Participants were randomly assigned to set standards either for placing the applicant on the short list or for hiring the applicant.

To assess short listing and hiring standards, we asked participants "what level of performance would indicate that this applicant should be placed on the short list?" (*or* "should be hired?"). Participants judged the level of performance on standardized ability tests, letters of recommendation, and several specific ability tests. These judgments were made using percentile rankings, i.e., "this applicant would need to be ranked in the X percentile relative to all other applicants." Because percentile rankings force an individual to judge an applicant relative to *all* others, they represent an objective scale. As such, these judgments should reveal the effects of stereotypes. After setting standards, *all* participants indicated whether they would short list or hire the applicant.

Consistent with hypothesis, we found that lower standards were set for placing a female than a male on the short list, though higher standards were set for hiring a female. However, this pattern was evident only among female participants. (Male participants set higher standards for hiring than short listing, and this did not differ by applicant gender.) Interestingly, the only time standards were lower for hiring than short listing was when female participants set standards for hiring a male. Regarding short listing and hiring decisions, we found that a female applicant was more likely to make the short list than a male applicant but was less likely to be hired (though these effects were evident only among participants exposed to a female experimenter). This finding of greater short listing but lesser hiring of a female applicant was replicated in a second experiment in which participants viewed a pool of applicants, instead of just one applicant. Participants selected 3 applicants from a pool of 14 to short list and, from the short-listed applicants, selected 1 to hire. Among the female participants, a female applicant was significantly less likely to be hired than placed on the short list. Among the male participants, a female applicant was over-hired relative to the representation of females on the short list. Across all participants, the rate at which a female was hired decreased when participants were made to feel accountable for their decisions.

Taken together, the results of these studies suggest that women are not immune to bias against other women. While we have no definitive explanation for women's harshness toward other women, it may reflect a disdain for self-promoting women (Rudman, 1998), a tendency to view other women as competitors in what is considered a zero-sum game (Staines, Travis, & Jayaratne, 1974), or an expectation that their own credibility will be questioned if they do not judge other women according to strict standards (Broder, 1993).

Probation and Firing Study

While the short listing and hiring studies showed that more evidence of competence was needed to hire a woman than a man, it is also worthwhile to examine how minimum and confirmatory standards affect decisions relevant to diagnosing incompetence. In the short listing and hiring studies, we asked participants how much evidence of competence was needed to confirm that women have ability. We may also ask the obverse: how much evidence of *in*competence is needed to confirm that women *lack* ability? For example, when an individual is employed and that individual's work performance begins to suffer, what kind of evidence is needed before a termination decision is made?

Our prediction here is the mirror opposite of our prediction regarding inferring competence: persons will set *higher minimum* but *lower confirmatory* standards for judging lack of task competence in women relative to men. Poor performance may not be surprising if one expects it. Thus, it may take more evidence of poor performance by a woman than a man to set off alarms or arouse concern. Nevertheless, the amount of evidence needed to *certify* that a woman lacks the ability to perform a job will be less. The prediction of lower confirmatory standards for women than men resonates with theorizing on double standards (Foddy & Smithson, 1989; Foschi, 2000). When low-status individuals (i.e., women in traditionally masculine domains) fail, they are not given the benefit of the doubt awarded to their high-status counterparts. Indeed, the higher the status, the more convincing the demonstration of incompetence will have to be before inferring inability.

Applying minimum and confirmatory standards to organizational decisions, we hypothesized that minimum standards may correspond to that point when one initially becomes alarmed about performance. Confirmatory standards may correspond to the decision to terminate a poorly performing employee. We predicted that higher minimum standards would make it more difficult for a woman than a man to be placed on probation, though lower confirmatory standards would make it easier for a woman to be fired.

Method
One hundred thirty-seven undergraduate participants were asked to roleplay the position of a manager in charge of evaluating employees (Fuegen & Biernat, 2006a). Similar to the short listing and hiring studies, participants were given a folder containing instructions, a job description, a résumé, and an evaluation form. They also received a summary of the employee's (predominantly negative) job performance during the past year. The job was labeled either "executive secretary" or "executive chief of staff," though again, this manipulation of sex-typing did not affect the results. The résumé was identical for all participants, except that half received a résumé with a female name and half received a résumé with a male name. Participants were randomly assigned to set standards for either placing the employee on probation or firing the employee. Probation was described as a "warning signal" to the employee that he or she "must improve to keep the job." After the probationary period had ended, the employee would be re-evaluated, and his or her future with the company would then be determined. Being fired was described as a sign that "the employee is not meeting the expectations of others, and the employee is not qualified for the job."

To assess probation and firing standards, we asked participants "what level of performance would indicate that this employee should be placed on probation?" (*or* "fired?"). Participants indicated a percentile ranking score on standardized ability tests, written evaluations from supervisors, and several specific ability tests. They also indicated the number of missed deadlines and missed days of work they would allow before deciding to place the employee on probation or fire the employee. Regardless of whether they were assigned to set standards for probation or firing, all participants were asked to indicate whether they would place the employee on probation *and* whether they would fire the employee.

Results

Standards. We analyzed the standards participants set for placing the employee on probation and firing the employee using a Participant Gender × Employee Gender × Instructional Standard (probation vs. fire) MANOVA. This analysis revealed no significant effects. Thus, there was no evidence that participants set higher standards for placing a female employee on probation but lower standards for firing her, relative to a male employee.

Decisions. We conducted a Decision (probation vs. fire) × Participant Gender × Employee Gender × Instructional Standard ANOVA on the proportions of probation and firing decisions. There was a main effect of Decision, $F(1, 88) = 194.49$, $p < .001$, such that employees were placed on probation 82% of the time and fired only 6% of the time. Of key interest was the significant Decision × Participant Gender × Employee Gender × Instructional Standard interaction, $F(1, 88) = 7.47$, $p < .01$ (see Table 1). We conducted separate Decision × Employee Gender × Instructional Standard ANOVAs for female and male participants. The interaction was not significant for females, though it was significant for males, $F(1, 88) = 16.69$, $p < .01$.

As shown in the top panel of Table 1, male participants who had been oriented toward setting standards for probation were equally likely to place a female and male employee on probation (64% and 70%, respectively). The employee was never fired. A different pattern emerged among male participants oriented toward setting standards for firing. Here, males placed the male employee on probation 100% of the time, though they never fired him. By contrast, they placed the female employee on probation only 50% of the time and fired her 40% of the time.

Why was the expected pattern of lesser probation but greater firing of a female employee evident only among male participants who set standards for firing? It seems plausible that the standard toward which participants had been oriented primed decisions. When male participants set standards for probation, they recommended probation (or no action) in all cases. Perhaps under a probation mind set, firing was perceived

Table 1. Percentage of Participants Choosing to Place Employee on Probation or Fire Employee, by Participant Gender, Instructional Standard, and Employee Gender.

Employee	Probation (%)	Fire (%)
Male participants		
Probation instructional standard		
Female	64	0
Male	70	0
Firing instructional standard		
Female	50	40
Male	100	0
Female participants		
Probation instructional standard		
Female	100	0
Male	100	0
Firing instructional standard		
Female	93	0
Male	73	13

as especially punitive. When male participants set standards for firing, gender stereotypes were revealed. Because the possibility of firing had already been made salient, participants may have felt "freed" to exercise this option when it arose.

Summary

The previous studies show that stereotypes can affect important organizational decisions in complex ways. A woman whose qualifications were identical to those of a man was less likely to be hired (among females and accountable participants) but more likely to be fired (among male participants). A couple of questions remain unanswered. First, while women were held to lower minimum but higher confirmatory standards in the short listing and hiring studies, there was no evidence that women were held to higher minimum but lower confirmatory standards in the probation and firing study. One reason for this difference may be that while it is relatively easy to imagine the sorts of hurdles one would need to jump before securing a job offer, it is more difficult to imagine how many mistakes one would be allowed before being terminated. The inclusion of different types of dependent measures (e.g., behavioral measures) may help in setting standards for inferring lack of competence.

A second question in need of answering is why the judgments of male participants conformed to hypothesis in the probation and firing study but the judgments of female participants conformed to hypothesis in the short listing and hiring studies. While more research is needed before definitive conclusions may be drawn, one possibility is that gender stereotypes are differentially salient for women and men in different employment contexts. Among female participants, the difficulty in securing a coveted position may be more salient than the fear of losing one's job once one is employed. Indeed, the scientific literature and popular media are replete with examples of the challenges women face as they attempt to break into male-dominated fields (e.g., comments by former Harvard president Lawrence Summers that women's under-representation in math and science reflects biological gender differences). Though women may not endorse gender stereotypes, culturally shared stereotypes regarding women's lesser task competence than men can still affect judgments of individual women pursuing non-traditional careers. Among male participants, concerns about appearing fair or non-sexist may have prompted a high rate of hiring women. Such fairness concerns may not be salient once women have secured positions. Given that men hold less positive attitudes toward affirmative action programs than women (Harrison, Kravitz, Mayer, Leslie, & Lev-Arey, 2006), they may be quicker than women to construe a woman's poor performance as indicative of inability if they believe the woman benefited from preferential treatment. Future research examining how motivations to be fair and attitudes about affirmative action affect standards and decisions is needed to test these assumptions (see Fuegen & Biernat, 2006b, for a related discussion relevant to race stereotyping).

PARENTS IN THE WORKPLACE

Though gender stereotypes are often subtle in their influence (as in the setting of stricter standards for women), they may also be blatant, as in the evaluation of mothers' and fathers' parenting skills and work-related competence (Bridges & Etaugh, 1995; Correll, Benard, & Paik, 2007; Cuddy, Fiske, & Glick, 2004; Etaugh & Folger, 1998). Research in the shifting standards tradition documents that subjective descriptions of parenting behavior mean different things when applied to women and men.

Kobrynowicz and Biernat (1997) asked participants to decode subjective descriptions of parenting effectiveness (e.g., being a "very good" or "all right" parent) into objective judgments (i.e., how many parenting behaviors does this individual perform?). Though mothers and fathers were judged equally effective at parenting, mothers were judged to perform *more* parenting behaviors than fathers. That is, to be labeled a "good" parent, a mother needed to perform more childcare behaviors than a father. Similarly, Bridges, Etaugh, and Barnes-Farrell (2002) asked participants to estimate the frequency with which stay-at-home and employed mothers and fathers performed various childcare behaviors and to judge their effectiveness as parents. Whereas an employed mother was judged to provide more physical care than an employed father, an employed father was regarded as a *better* parent than an employed mother. Furthermore, though a stay-at-home mother and a stay-at-home father were regarded as equally effective parents, a stay-at-home mother was judged to perform *more* physical and emotional care-giving than a stay-at-home father. Together, these studies show that gender stereotypes serve as standards for decoding subjective descriptions of parenting effectiveness. Stereotypes about women's greater involvement in parental care (i.e., their greater nurturing ability) led observers to evaluate male and female parents relative to different standards.

In the following study, we focused on how the setting of confirmatory standards (in this case, hiring) is affected by the knowledge that the job applicant is also a parent. To the extent that motherhood exaggerates stereotypes of women (i.e., that women are nurturing and kind), a job applicant who is a mother may be judged according to a stricter standard than a job applicant who is a father. This prediction is consistent with status characteristics theory which suggests that, to the extent that motherhood is salient at work, it should exaggerate gender stereotypes and negatively affect judgments of women's workplace competence (Correll et al., 2007; Ridgeway & Correll, 2004).

Fuegen, Biernat, Haines, and Deaux (2004) examined how gender and parental status interact to affect perceptions of job-related competence. One hundred ninety-six undergraduate participants role-played the position of a manager in charge of evaluating applicants for a job. Each of them was provided with a job description for the position of an immigration law attorney and an applicant's résumé. The applicant was either male or female and was depicted as either single without children or married with two young children. Participants set standards for what level of performance they would require of the applicant in order to hire him or her for the position. The performance standards measures were the same as those used in the short listing and hiring studies (i.e., participants judged what scores on ability tests and recommendation letters they would require of the applicant to hire him or her). In addition to performance standards, we also assessed time commitment standards. Participants indicated the number of hours per week the applicant would need to be available to work, as well as the maximum number of days per month the applicant would be allowed to call in sick and arrive late or leave early in order to be hired. Lastly, participants indicated whether they would hire the applicant and whether he or she would make a good candidate for promotion.

Consistent with the hypothesis, we found that performance and time commitment standards were higher for a mother than for a father. That is, an applicant who was a mother needed to be available more often and achieve a higher performance score than an applicant who was a father in order to be hired. In addition, a male applicant was held to lower performance and time commitment standards when he was a parent than when he was not a parent. Though not anticipated, a female applicant without children was *not* held to stricter standards than a male applicant without children. In terms of decisions, parenthood lessened a female applicant's chances of being hired and promoted, though it had no impact on a male applicant's chances.

These data suggest that parental status has a polarizing effect on judgments of individual men and women. While being a parent prompted the setting of relatively harsh standards for a woman, it prompted the setting of relatively *lenient* standards for a man. While being a good father may be construed as providing financially for one's family, being a good mother is still thought to involve extensive care-giving. Thus, the lenient pre-employment standards set for the father may reflect the belief that the father as provider "needs the job more" than a mother. The strict pre-employment standards set for the mother are consistent with research showing that the traits deemed necessary to be successful in the workplace are inconsistent with those deemed necessary to be a good mother (Halpert, Wilson, & Hickman, 1993).

IMPLICATIONS AND EXTENSIONS

The research described here documents how gender stereotypes activate judgment standards and how these standards affect important organizational decisions. Studies that map standards onto other organizational decisions and that utilize different types of dependent measures and samples would increase the generalizability of these findings. For example, the standards one needs to meet to be promoted or tenured are higher than the standards one needs to meet to be hired. Would there be stricter (confirmatory) standards for promoting women relative to men (Lyness & Heilman, 2006)? Research in this vein would further our understanding of the mechanisms that limit women's advancement in organizations. Second, while the research described here uses percentile ranking scores as a measure of standards, one could also use behavioral dependent measures. Behavioral evidence could take the form of number of projects completed, years of experience, or questions adequately answered in an interview. Third, more archival research and experiments with older, employed participants are needed to increase the external validity of these findings. Additional research that would advance our understanding of the subtle ways stereotypes are applied in the workforce is described below.

Implications of Subjective Evaluation Criteria for Advancement in Organizations

Considerable evidence exists that as one advances in an organization, the criteria used to evaluate one's suitability for promotion become increasingly subjective in nature (Agars, 2004; Gupta et al., 1983; Heilman, 2001; Stumpf & London, 1981). In addition to objective measures of performance (e.g., dollars earned, number of projects completed), subjective judgments play a major role in promotion decisions (e.g., is the individual a "good team player," does he or she "fit" in the organization). Though no one can exactly define what constitutes "fit" in an organization, executives "know it when they see it" (Sessa, 2001, p. 96). Because subjective judgments reflect a shifting standard based on the individual performing the behavior (and are therefore inherently "slippery" in their meaning; Biernat et al., 1991), it seems likely that subjective judgments are relatively easy to distort, depending on the target's social category membership. Because objective performance evaluations give specific, verifiable information, they mean the same thing regardless of the person performing the action. Hence, objective performance evaluations should be impervious to distortion. To the extent that subjective performance evaluations are open to interpretation, they may reveal the bias of the evaluator.

A hypothesis worthy of testing is whether subjective performance feedback is easier to distort than objective performance feedback, and whether persons distort subjective feedback to make it stereotype consistent. That is, would being "a team player" be construed as a sign of strength in a man but weakness in a woman? If so, what are the implications for reward distribution and organizational advancement?

Overlooking "Known Quantities"

Barnes-Farrell (2001) observed that performance appraisal frequently requires a manager to observe multiple employees. Because a manager cannot devote full attention to any one employee, he or she may choose to focus on those employees who either appear to be especially talented. The challenge for appraisers is to go beyond collecting "just enough" information to draw inferences about employees' abilities.

An important question worth addressing is whether managers overlook important information or fail to monitor the performance of particular employees they consider to be "known quantities." Stereotypes are likely to guide judgments of which employees are "known quantities" and which employees deserve further attention. "Known quantities" may be those individuals who work in occupations where their gender predominates (e.g., women in clerical jobs) and whose performance is moderately good (i.e., not stellar or poor). To the extent such individuals tend to be overlooked, signs of trouble may not be noticed until it is too late. At the other end of the spectrum, the successful completion of several challenging tasks may be necessary before talent is noticed and suitably rewarded.

Solo Status

One key factor in research addressing how stereotypes affect judgments of competence is whether the person being evaluated is numerically rare. Pazy and Oron (2001) found that women's performance ratings varied as a function of the gender composition of their work unit: Women who comprised less than 10% of a work group received the lowest performance ratings. Women's performance ratings increased as their representation in the work group increased (see also Sackett, DuBois, & Wiggens Noe, 1991). Persons whose social category membership is salient in a workgroup attract increased attention that often leads to stereotypical judgments of their ability (Fuegen & Biernat, 2002; Heilman, 1995; Kanter, 1977; Pettigrew & Martin, 1987; Taylor, Fiske, Etcoff, & Ruderman, 1978). Because women are still a distinct minority in the upper echelons of large companies (Lyness, 2002), it is likely that many women are solos in their workgroups.

A question worthy of future research is whether evaluators are more likely to apply different standards to applicants (or employees) when one is solo in the applicant pool (or workgroup). If stricter standards are applied to solos, to what degree does this reflect a fear that mistakes committed by persons who are highly visible reflect poorly upon supervisors and mentors (Fitt & Newton, 1981)? Alternatively, would stricter standards be applied because solos are assumed to have benefited from affirmative action programs and are regarded as less competent than others (Heilman & Blader, 2001; Heilman, Block, & Stathatos, 1997)? Research that investigates the effects of solo status on standards and the allocation of desired rewards such as bonuses and promotions would be valuable.

Answers to these questions would further our understanding of the subtle ways in which gender stereotypes affect work-related judgments and decisions. Additional research that explores the conditions under which stereotypes are *least* likely to affect organizational judgments and decisions would be of tremendous benefit.

ACKNOWLEDGMENTS

Correspondence should be directed to Kathleen Fuegen, Department of Psychology, 347 Business-Education-Psychology Center, Northern Kentucky University, Highland Heights, KY 41099. Electronic mail may be sent to fuegenk1@nku.edu. I thank Monica Biernat for her insightful comments on an earlier draft.

REFERENCES

Agars, M. D. (2004). Reconsidering the impact of gender stereotypes on the advancement of women in organizations. *Psychology of Women Quarterly, 28*, 103–111.
Barnes-Farrell, J. L. (2001). Performance appraisal: Person perception processes and challenges. In: M. London (Ed.), *How people evaluate others in organizations* (pp. 135–153). Mahwah, NJ: Lawrence Erlbaum.
Biernat, M. (2003). Toward a broader view of social stereotyping. *American Psychologist, 58*, 1019–1027.
Biernat, M., Crandall, C. S., Young, L. V., Kobrynowicz, D., & Halpin, S. M. (1998). All that you can be: Stereotyping of self and others in a military context. *Journal of Personality and Social Psychology, 75*, 301–317.
Biernat, M., & Fuegen, K. (2001). Shifting standards and the evaluation of competence: Complexity in gender-based judgment and decision making. *Journal of Social Issues, 57*, 707–724.

Biernat, M., & Kobrynowicz, D. (1997). Gender- and race-based standards of competence: Lower minimum standards but higher ability standards for devalued groups. *Journal of Personality and Social Psychology, 72*, 544–557.

Biernat, M., & Manis, M. (1994). Shifting standards and stereotype-based judgment. *Journal of Personality and Social Psychology, 66*, 5–20.

Biernat, M., Manis, M., & Nelson, T. E. (1991). Stereotypes and standards of judgment. *Journal of Personality and Social Psychology, 60*, 485–499.

Boldry, J., Wood, W., & Kashy, D. A. (2001). Gender stereotypes and the evaluation of men and women in military training. *Journal of Social Issues, 57*, 689–705.

Bridges, J. S., & Etaugh, C. (1995). College students' perceptions of mothers: Effects of maternal employment-childrearing pattern and motive for employment. *Sex Roles, 32*, 735–751.

Bridges, J. S., Etaugh, C., & Barnes-Farrell, J. (2002). Trait judgments of stay-at-home and employed parents: A function of social role and or shifting standards? *Psychology of Women Quarterly, 26*, 140–150.

Broder, I. E. (1993). Review of NSF economic proposals: Gender and institutional patterns. *American Economic Review, 83*, 964–970.

Cleveland, J. N., Murphy, K. R., & Williams, R. E. (1989). Multiple uses of performance appraisal: Prevalence and correlates. *Journal of Applied Psychology, 74*, 130–135.

Correll, S. J., Benard, S. B., & Paik, I. P. (2007). Getting a job?: Is there a motherhood penalty? *American Journal of Sociology, 112*, 1297–1338.

Cuddy, A. J. C., Fiske, S. T., & Glick, P. (2004). When professionals become mothers, warmth doesn't cut the ice. *Journal of Social Issues, 60*, 701–718.

Davison, H. K., & Burke, M. J. (2000). Sex discrimination in simulated employment contexts: A meta-analytic investigation. *Journal of Vocational Behavior, 56*, 225–248.

Deaux, K. (1984). From individual differences to social categories: Analysis of a decade's research on gender. *American Psychologist, 39*, 105–116.

Dovidio, J. F., & Gaertner, S. L. (2000). Aversive racism and selection decisions: 1989 and 1999. *Psychological Science, 11*, 315–319.

Eagly, A. H. (2005). Achieving relational authenticity in leadership: Does gender matter? *Leadership Quarterly, 16*, 459–474.

Eagly, A. H., & Karau, S. J. (2002). Role congruity theory and prejudice toward female leaders. *Psychological Review, 109*, 573–598.

Eagly, A. H., Makhijani, M. G., & Klonsky, B. G. (1992). Gender and the evaluation of leaders: A meta-analysis. *Psychological Bulletin, 111*, 3–22.

Etaugh, C., & Folger, D. (1998). Perceptions of parents whose work and parenting behaviors deviate from role expectations. *Sex Roles, 39*, 215–223.

Fiske, S. T. (1998). Stereotyping, prejudice, and discrimination. In: D. T. Gilbert, S. T. Fiske & G. Lindzey (Eds), *The handbook of social psychology* (pp. 357–411). New York, NY: McGraw-Hill.

Fiske, S. T., Bersoff, D. N., Borgida, E., Deaux, K., & Heilman, M. E. (1991). Social science research on trial: Use of sex stereotyping research in *Price Waterhouse v. Hopkins. American Psychologist, 46*, 1049–1060.

Fitt, L. W., & Newton, D. A. (1981). When the mentor is a man and the protégé a woman. *Harvard Business Review, 59*, 56–60.

Foddy, M., & Smithson, M. (1989). Fuzzy sets and double standards: Modeling the process of ability inference. In: J. Berger, M. Zelditch, Jr. & B. Anderson (Eds), *Sociological theories in progress: New formulations* (pp. 73–99). Newbury Park, CA: Sage.

Foschi, M. (1989). Status characteristics, standards, and attributions. In: J. Berger, M. Zelditch, Jr. & B. Anderson (Eds), *Sociological theories in progress: New formulations* (pp. 58–72). Newbury Park, CA: Sage.
Foschi, M. (2000). Double standards for competence: Theory and research. *Annual Review of Sociology, 26*, 21–42.
Foschi, M., & Foddy, M. (1988). Standards, performance, and the formation of self-other expectations. In: M. Webster, Jr. & M. Foschi (Eds), *Status generalization: New theory and research* (pp. 248–260). Stanford, CA: Stanford University Press.
Fuegen, K., & Biernat, M. (2002). Reexamining the effects of solo status for women and men. *Personality and Social Psychology Bulletin, 28*, 913–925.
Fuegen, K., & Biernat, M. (2006a). [*Gender-based standards of incompetence*]. Unpublished raw data.
Fuegen, K., & Biernat, M. (2006b). *Inferring incompetence: How stereotypes affect judgments of inability*. Manuscript submitted for publication.
Fuegen, K., Biernat, M., Haines, E., & Deaux, K. (2004). Mothers and fathers in the workplace. How gender and parental status influence judgments of job-related competence. *Journal of Social Issues, 60*, 737–754.
Greenhaus, J. H., & Parasuraman, S. (1993). Job performance attributions and career advancement prospects: An examination of gender and race effects. *Organizational Behavior and Human Decision Processes, 55*, 273–297.
Gupta, N., Jenkins, G. D., & Beehr, T. A. (1983). Employee gender, gender similarity, and supervisor-subordinate cross-evaluations. *Psychology of Women Quarterly, 8*, 174–184.
Halpert, J. A., Wilson, M. L., & Hickman, J. L. (1993). Pregnancy as a source of bias in performance appraisals. *Journal of Organizational Behavior, 14*, 649–663.
Harrison, D. A., Kravitz, D. A., Mayer, D. M., Leslie, L. M., & Lev-Arey, D. (2006). Understanding attitudes toward affirmative action in employment: Summary and meta-analysis of 35 years of research. *Journal of Applied Social Psychology, 91*, 1013–1036.
Heilman, M. E. (1983). Sex bias in work settings: The lack of fit model. In: B. Staw & L. Cummings (Eds), *Research in organizational behavior* (Vol. 5, pp. 269–298). Greenwich, CT: JAI.
Heilman, M. E. (1995). Sex stereotypes and their effects in the workplace: What we know and what we don't know. *Journal of Social Behavior and Personality, 10*, 3–26.
Heilman, M. E. (2001). Description and prescription: How gender stereotypes prevent women's ascent up the organizational ladder. *Journal of Social Issues, 57*, 657–674.
Heilman, M. E., & Blader, S. L. (2001). Assuming preferential selection when the admissions policy is unknown: The effects of gender rarity. *Journal of Applied Psychology, 86*, 188–193.
Heilman, M. E., Block, C. J., & Stathatos, P. (1997). The affirmative action stigma of incompetence: Effects of performance information ambiguity. *Academy of Management Journal, 40*, 603–625.
Heilman, M. E., Wallen, A. S., Fuchs, D., & Tamkins, M. M. (2004). Penalties for success: Reactions to women who succeed at male gender-typed tasks. *Journal of Applied Psychology, 89*, 416–427.
Jackson, L. A., Sullivan, L. A., & Hodge, C. N. (1993). Stereotype effects on attributions, predictions, and evaluations: No two social judgments are quite alike. *Journal of Personality and Social Psychology, 65*, 69–84.

Kanter, R. M. (1977). *Men and women of the corporation*. New York, NY: Basic Books.
Kobrynowicz, D., & Biernat, M. (1997). Decoding subjective evaluations: How stereotypes provide shifting standards. *Journal of Experimental Social Psychology, 33*, 579–601.
Lyness, K. S. (2002). Finding the key to the executive suite: Challenges for women and people of color. In: R. Silzer (Ed.), *The 21st century executive: Innovative practices for building leadership at the top* (pp. 229–273). San Francisco, CA: Jossey-Bass.
Lyness, K. S., & Heilman, M. E. (2006). When fit is fundamental: Performance evaluations and promotions of upper-level female and male managers. *Journal of Applied Psychology, 91*, 777–785.
Lyness, K. S., & Judiesch, M. K. (1999). Are women more likely to be hired or promoted into management positions? *Journal of Vocational Behavior, 54*, 158–173.
Nieva, V. F., & Gutek, B. A. (1980). Sex effects on evaluation. *Academy of Management Review, 5*, 267–276.
Operario, D., & Fiske, S. T. (2001). Causes and consequences of stereotypes in organizations. In: M. London (Ed.), *How people evaluate others in organizations* (pp. 45–62). Mahwah, NJ: Lawrence Erlbaum.
Pazy, A., & Oron, I. (2001). Sex proportion and performance evaluation among high-ranking military officers. *Journal of Organizational Behavior, 22*, 689–702.
Pettigrew, T. F., & Martin, J. (1987). Shaping the organizational context for Black American inclusion. *Journal of Social Issues, 43*, 41–78.
Ridgeway, C. L., & Correll, S. J. (2004). Motherhood as a status characteristic. *Journal of Social Issues, 60*, 683–700.
Roth, P. L., Bobko, P., & Huffcutt, A. I. (2003). Ethnic group differences in measures of job performance: A new meta-analysis. *Journal of Applied Psychology, 88*, 694–706.
Rudman, L. A. (1998). Self-promotion as a risk factor for women: The costs and benefits of counter-stereotypical impression management. *Journal of Personality and Social Psychology, 74*, 629–645.
Rudman, L. A., & Glick, P. (1999). Feminized management and backlash toward agentic women: The hidden costs to women of a kinder, gentler image of middle managers. *Journal of Personality and Social Psychology, 77*, 1004–1010.
Sackett, P. R., DuBois, C. L. Z., & Wiggens Noe, A. (1991). Tokenism in performance evaluation: The effects of work group representation on male-female and White-Black differences in performance ratings. *Journal of Applied Psychology, 76*, 263–267.
Schein, V. (1973). The relationship between sex role stereotypes and requisite management characteristics. *Journal of Applied Psychology, 57*, 95–100.
Schein, V. (2001). A global look at psychological barriers to women's progress in management. *Journal of Social Issues, 57*, 675–688.
Sessa, V. I. (2001). Executive promotion and selection. In: M. London (Ed.), *How people evaluate others in organizations* (pp. 91–110). Mahwah, NJ: Lawrence Erlbaum.
Sinclair, L., & Kunda, Z. (2000). Motivated stereotyping of women: She's fine if she praised me but incompetent if she criticized me. *Personality and Social Psychology Bulletin, 26*, 1329–1342.
Staines, G., Travis, C., & Jayaratne, T. (1974). The Queen Bee syndrome. *Psychology Today, 9*, 55–60.
Struthers, C. W., Weiner, B., & Allred, K. (1998). Effects of causal attributions on personnel decisions: A social motivation perspective. *Basic and Applied Social Psychology, 20*, 155–166.

Stumpf, S. A., & London, M. (1981). Management promotions: Individual and organizational factors influencing the decision process. *Academy of Management Review, 6*, 539–549.

Swim, J. K., & Sanna, L. J. (1996). He's skilled, she's lucky: A meta-analysis of observers' attributions for women's and men's successes and failures. *Personality and Social Psychology Bulletin, 22*, 507–519.

Taylor, S. E., Fiske, S. T., Etcoff, N. L., & Ruderman, A. J. (1978). Categorical and contextual bases of person memory and stereotyping. *Journal of Personality and Social Psychology, 36*, 778–793.

Tomkiewicz, J., Brenner, O. C., & Adeyemi-Bello, T. (1998). The impact of perceptions and stereotypes on the managerial mobility of African Americans. *Journal of Social Psychology, 138*, 88–92.

COOPERATION ≠ CONSENT: HOW WOMEN REACT TO THEIR PLACE, BASED ON SOCIAL RELATIONS AND AMBIVALENT SEXISM

Mina Cikara and Susan T. Fiske

ABSTRACT

This chapter examines the tension between interdependence and dominance. First, we briefly review prominent social psychological theories regarding the development and maintenance of status systems. Next we briefly describe how these structures help distribute social power in modern society. We then examine how prejudice, stereotyping, and discrimination stem from status systems and interdependence, using the Stereotype Content Model (Fiske, Xu, Cuddy & Glick, 1999; Fiske, Cuddy, Glick, & Xu, 2002). Next, we consider the unique circumstances of gender relations and how they give way to complementary justifications of gender inequality, using Ambivalent Sexism Theory (Glick & Fiske, 1996, 1999, 2001a, 2001b). Last, we review evidence to support our argument that women do not necessarily acquiesce joyfully to the present hierarchical arrangement, but rather guide their choices by their pragmatic alternatives, as dictated by benevolent and hostile ideologies.

THE GAME OF LIFE

To play a game, one must be familiar with the rules. If not familiar, one quickly learns the rules as one goes along or else risks being ejected from the game. In the game of life, status systems comprise a major part of the social structure that shapes our perceptions, thoughts, and behaviors as we move through our daily lives. In any game, the patterns of cooperation and competition matter as well, and players have to know whose side they share. That is, they need to know the interdependence structures as well as the status system, to stay in the game.

The Rules: Status Systems

Status refers to one's position in a social hierarchy. By some definitions, status is a reward that people *earn* by being exemplary group members. People are seen as good group members if they conform to group norms, facilitate achievement of the group's goals, and put the group's interests before their own (Cohen & Zhou, 1991). This would be one form of achieved status. Accomplishments earn another form of achieved status. Lay people often view status as earned, assuming that people get what they deserve, as demonstrated by Just World Theory (Lerner, 1980), and world-wide correlations between perceived status and perceived competence (Cuddy et al., in press; Oldmeadow & Fiske, in press).

Rather than always being earned, however, status is also *ascribed* to certain individuals or groups, based on innate characteristics such as gender, race, age, attractiveness, etc. (Ridgeway, 1991). Expectation States Theory (Berger, Fisek, Norman, & Zelditch, 1977; Webster & Foschi, 1988) suggests that social groups are inextricably linked to social hierarchies because stereotypes encompass explicit ideas regarding different groups' status (or contribution to the group), in addition to traits and roles (Ridgeway, 2001). Status beliefs consistently associate higher status groups with greater competence and valued skills (Webster & Foschi, 1988).

Status beliefs could be particularly potent if both dominant and subordinate groups endorse them, as a result of individuals' need to justify their social systems (Jost & Banaji, 1994). The dominant group maintains social power and wider access to material resources because the shared expectation is that they are more competent, and thus better qualified to perform in instrumental capacities (self–other performance expectations; Ridgeway, 2001). Greater skills and the resulting legitimacy, afforded by the dominant group, lead to more power (Carli, 1991). It is thus easy to imagine how the dominant group might subscribe to the status quo.

Furthermore, shared status beliefs are most likely to develop among groups who *must* cooperate with one another to get what they want and need (Glick & Fiske, 1999). This poses the more problematic case: Although women need men as much as vice versa, their lower-status position would hardly seem something to celebrate and cherish. And yet women cooperate, for the most part, in the existing status relation. System Justification Theory (Jost & Banaji, 1994) argues that subordinate groups endorse status hierarchies because system stability affords security. We will argue that when women are aware of the rules of the game, they may feel compelled to go along, even if they do not necessarily endorse the status beliefs.

The Prize: Social Power

As with all games, the game of life has a prize for which players compete: Power. Whether conscious or unconscious, the choice to compete for power comes with the game; status systems automatically make one a competitor.

Power may be defined as "relative control over another's valued outcomes" (Fiske, 1993; see also Fiske & Berdahl, in press; Keltner, et al., 2003). This definition casts power in terms of its structural properties in social relations. In lay terms, one might consider power to mean brute force, which ignores the target's volition (Raven, 1993, 2001). However, brute force is not useful in the context of gender relations because at a group level, most men do not often express this kind of power over women (although, arguably, the mere threat of such brute force can effectively deter rebellion).

Instead we will focus on the distinction between soft and harsh power, as conceptualized in the Interpersonal Power Inventory (IPI; Raven, Schwarzwald, & Koslowsky, 1998). Soft power uses social outcomes (liking and respect), whereas harsh power uses physical and economic outcomes (necessities for health and material well-being, respectively). The use of power is easier to recognize as outcomes become more objective and tangible (e.g., control over food or employee promotions); power use is more difficult to recognize as outcomes become more subjective and intangible (e.g., liking and respect). The latter, more subtle type of power better characterizes gender relations than does brute force. Note that soft power specifies a range of valued outcomes that men and women might seek from each other, as the rest of this chapter emphasizes.

Despite what the labels might seem to imply, harsh power is no more effective than soft power is; the strength of power is determined by the value of the controlled outcome, which depends on the situation. Men have systemic power because women depend on them for economic support more than vice versa. Women have close-relationship power because men depend on them for offspring and emotional support; here women's level of power equals or surpasses men's power.

The power dynamic between men and women is less about one group's conscious need to influence and dominate a subordinate group and more about power as a derivative of the hierarchical gender system that is in place, combined with intimate interdependence. Whether or not the dominant group wishes to influence the subordinate group, and whether or not the subordinate group wants to acquiesce, the mere fact of one group's relatively greater control over valued outcomes yields power differentials (Fiske, 1993). As just noted, the pervasive nature of status beliefs about men and women legitimizes a system in which men have relatively more control than women in public domains (e.g., professional settings), whereas women are thought to have relatively more control than men in private domains (e.g., the home). These widely held beliefs about control and the legitimacy of how control is distributed among men and women serve to justify and maintain the current system.

Note that status is not tantamount to power. Status refers to one's position in a hierarchy, whereas power concerns outcome control. While the two are deeply intertwined, status and power are distinct constructs in that one can have high status and low outcome control (e.g., debutante, lame-duck politician), as well as low status and high outcome control (e.g., garbage collector, corrupt DMV worker). Power and status can also shift depending on the context and the groups in question. Nevertheless, status and group interdependence play an enormous role in the content of the beliefs groups maintain about each other, the emotions they feel toward one another, and the behavior they enact if and when they engage one another.

WHOSE SIDE ARE YOU ON?

In any game people are quick to identify allies as well as foes. It is important for people to know which players they should help and rely on for help, as well as which players they should watch carefully. As we will see, this information guides interaction not only between women and men, but also among all groups.

People like to have a distinctive and positive group membership, according to Social Identity Theory (Tajfel & Turner, 1986). Group identity and its boundaries engender ingroup favoritism, which in turn reinforces social categories (Hewstone, Rubin, & Willis, 2002). Favoritism involves resources, such that groups reserve resources for those they favor and withhold resources from those they derogate. Though evidence for ingroup favoritism outweighs outgroup derogation, ingroup favoritism hurts the outgroup by exclusion. However, as we know from the power literature, resources can be widely construed, and power derives from the *value* of the resource in a given context. One possible resource is the reputation of a group or of an individual as a member of that group. As discussed earlier, soft power, or control over social resources (e.g., liking, respect), is no less effective than harsh power in maintaining the status quo. Groups in power may control the distribution of intergroup images, or at least the images they hold carry more impact because they also control other resources such as money and access (e.g., white directors' depictions of minorities as villains in films). The stereotypes people hold about various cultural groups thus manifest soft power. Consider the generally positive evaluations (liking and respect) of culturally dominant groups (e.g., Whites, Christians), and the overtly negative evaluations (disliking and disrespect) of less culturally valued groups (e.g., drug addicts, welfare recipients).

The prejudice, or antipathy (as it is defined in Allport, 1954) reflected in negative outgroup stereotypes also stems from the perceived incompatibility of the ingroup's and outgroup's goals (Fiske & Ruscher, 1993) ("if you're not with me, you're against me"). In other words, competition should breed antipathy, but recent research demonstrates that the situation is more complicated than that. Given the stereotype-setting role of the dominant group, what happens when the dominant group needs the outgroup? What attitudes are reserved for outgroups on which the ingroup relies? What about groups that pose no threat to their status? How are boundaries and hierarchy between dominant and subordinate groups maintained, if not by antipathy?

The Teams: The Importance of Warmth and Competence

Gender represents one category boundary along which team lines can be drawn. Men and women differ in their stereotypic specialties, which help explain how they resolve the tension between intimacy and disparity. The Stereotype Content Model (SCM; Cuddy, Fiske, & Glick, in press; Fiske, Xu, Cuddy, & Glick, 1999; Fiske, Cuddy, Glick, & Xu, 2002) organizes beliefs about cultural groups (including gender groups) along two dimensions: competence and warmth. The SCM posits that the content of a stereotype and type of prejudice reserved for a social group follows from their perceived cooperation and status in society. In other words, the way an ingroup feels about an outgroup will depend on the perceived *intent* and *capability* of the outgroup to harm the ingroup. Whether an outgroup is cooperative or competitive will determine if they have intent to harm the ingroup, which will guide perceptions of the outgroup's warmth. Likewise, whether an outgroup does or does not have high status will determine if they have capability to harm the ingroup, which will guide perceptions of the outgroup's competence. This 2 (intent: low/high warmth) × 2 (capability: low/high competence) mapping of intergroup space yields four classes of stereotypes. Groups high on both warmth and competence are the ingroup and its allies; groups low on both are the worst off (homeless, addicted, or poor people). Groups high on one dimension but low on the other are most relevant to gender relations: Paternalistic pity targets allegedly warm but incompetent groups such as older or disabled people and (in some samples) housewives. Envious prejudice targets allegedly competent but cold groups, such as rich, Jewish, or Asian people in American samples.

According to the SCM, structural relations between groups cause specific stereotypes, which in turn maintain the status quo and defend the position of societal reference groups. As mentioned, favorable stereotypes are reserved for the ingroup, its allies, and cultural default groups. These groups are perceived as both warm and competent as a function of ingroup favoritism. They have no reason, nor intent, to compete with themselves and are therefore liked and respected. Liking and respect, in turn, legitimize the social power of the ingroup. Cultural prototypes (middle-class, heterosexual, Christian) exemplify this quadrant.

Conversely, derogatory stereotypes describe outgroups that are seen as competitive and having low status (e.g., homeless people). Because these groups are thought to usurp economic and political capital that would otherwise go to higher status groups in society, they are seen as competing in a zero-sum distribution of resources. These groups are seen as having low warmth and low competence, and are disliked and disrespected as a result. Disliking and disrespect undermine the social power of these groups.

In addition to uniform favoritism and derogation, the SCM allows for mixed content stereotypes in which groups can be seen as having high warmth and low competence, or as having low warmth and high competence. Paternalistic stereotypes depict groups that are neither inclined nor capable of competing with the ingroup, meaning they have low status and are not seen as competitive (e.g., elderly people, and in some samples, homemakers; e.g., Eckes, 2002). These groups do not threaten the ingroup and are therefore seen as incompetent but warm. This stereotype encourages paternalistic prejudice, which disrespects competence and rewards socially desirable, but deferent qualities (Glick & Fiske, 2001a, 2001b; Ridgeway, 2001). Paternalistic prejudice promotes compliance from subordinates with minimal conflict, allowing dominant groups to feel that their higher status is justified or earned (Jackman, 1994). The White Man's Burden (colonists allegedly civilizing purported savages) provides one example, as does the stereotypic chivalrous man saving the damsel in distress.

In contrast, envious stereotypes are reserved for groups that have attained high status and are therefore seen as competitive (e.g., Asians, career women). Envious prejudice guides the ingroup to elevate its ratings of the outgroup's competence due to the outgroup's apparent power or success, but to lower its ratings of warmth to justify the ingroup's negative reactions toward the outgroup.

In short, the origin of each of these four classes of stereotypes may vary, but their function is the same in each case: They legitimize the current social structure and as long as they persist, continue to reinforce it.

Blocking or rejecting the power of disliked and/or disrespected groups maintains existing power hierarchies. As individuals' power increases, their evaluations of others become increasingly negative, and their evaluations of self become increasingly positive (Georgesen & Harris, 1998, 2000), potentially leading powerholders to believe that they know what is best for everyone. Even disadvantaged groups may identify with certain aspects of the culturally dominant group and endorse its viewpoint. Not only do low-status groups explicitly (Haines & Host, 2000) and implicitly (Jost, Pelham, Brett, & Carvallo, 2002) favor high-status groups, but the more disadvantaged a group is, the more likely that group is to defend the status quo (Jost, Pelham, Sheldon, & Sullivan, 2003).

Note that a great deal of prejudice is enacted by ingroups withholding resources and positive attributes from outgroups (Dovidio, Kawakami, & Gaertner, 2000; Mummendey, 1995). When the ingroup is men and the context is a professional setting (i.e., a setting where men are the culturally dominant group), different kinds of resources, when withheld, can undermine the social power of women (the outgroup, in this case). The SCM tells us that liking and respect are two of the most important social resources in determining how much power a group has relative to other groups in society. Cooperation is associated with warmth, which earns liking, but not respect. Competition is associated with status, which wins respect, but not liking.

Thus women, depending on how competent and warm they appear to be, may be denied liking and/or respect. We will return to this idea later.

Subtypes of Women

In the case of gender, paternalistic prejudice rewards women who relegate themselves to traditional roles by attributing to them more socially desirable traits (e.g., patience, warmth). In essence, warmth is a consolation prize for forgoing competition with men for social power. When women transgress gender norms of femininity by taking on a nontraditional role, one way to penalize their increase in status or their competition is to cast their behavior in a negative light, though this is not always done consciously. As predicted by envious prejudice and explained by the SCM, the negative reactions that arise as a result of competition posed by nontraditional women justify the dominant group's resentment of them, penalizing women's traditional advantage on the perceived warmth dimension. Note that most of the time professional women are perceived to be neither as warm nor as competent as men, but occasionally people confront women whom they cannot help but see as qualified due to their glaring successes (e.g., eBay CEO, Meg Whitman).

Contemporary subtypes of women exemplify groups that would fall in the mixed (i.e., paternalistic or envious) stereotype categories. On average, women are thought to have less status than men, but status can vary depending on the role of the woman in question. Once her status is assessed, the resulting nature of her relationship with men (i.e., cooperative or competitive) follows, ultimately determining whether she elicits paternalistic or envious prejudice. For example, a female homemaker is seen as cooperative because she has taken on a traditionally female role, but is also seen as low-status because she is presumed to have little to no income and relatively less education than a typical man; she is perceived as warm, but not competent. A female professional, on the other hand, contradicts stereotypes regarding women's normal status, and, given the associations between status and power, can be seen as a formidable competitor. She is seen as having high status because she is presumed to have acquired a certain level of education and a considerable income, and is seen as competitive because she has managed to take on a traditionally male role. Thus, she is admittedly competent, but not warm.

Where a woman falls in the SCM depends on what "kind" of woman she is. Rather, evaluations of a woman will depend on the context or role in which she is being evaluated. Different subtypes of women include, but are not limited to: respected but disliked women (e.g., business women, feminists) and disrespected but liked women (e.g., housewife, secretary) (Deaux, Winton, Crowley, & Lewis, 1985; Eckes, 1994, 2002; Noseworthy & Lott, 1984; Six & Eckes, 1991).

The SCM says that content of stereotypes and emotions elicited by different social groups can be predicted by how competitive or cooperative groups are (perceived warmth), in addition to how able they are to make good on any threat to the ingroup (perceived competence). While the relative status and nature of groups' interdependence are clear factors in determining the social structures that shape male–female relations, several factors unique to gender further complicate the multiple forms of prejudice put forth by the SCM. In the specific case of men and women, Ambivalent Sexism Theory (AST) digs deeper to explicate the institutions and mechanisms by which gender inequality persists.

KNOWING THE PLAYERS: UNIQUE NATURE OF GENDER RELATIONS

Ambivalent Sexism Theory: Benevolent and Hostile Sexism

When the players of the game are men and women, slightly different rules apply. As we will review, three factors, unique to gender relations, complicate the manner in which the game is played and determine how much players ultimately win from playing.

The extremity with which people generate and rate different subtypes of women provides some insight into the complexity of attitudes people have about them. Like the SCM, AST (Glick & Fiske, 1996, 1999, 2001a, 2001b) contends that prejudice against women is not rooted in absolute antipathy. Rather, sexism combines complimentary gender ideologies (respectively, positive and negative in flavor), held by men and women worldwide (Glick et al., 2000). These ideologies promote the persistence of gender inequality. Benevolent sexism is a paternalistic ideology that views women as subordinate, best suited for traditional, low-status roles; women need to be protected, cherished, and revered for their virtue. Hostile sexism, a closer relative of mere antipathy, is a combative ideology maintaining that women seek to control men and use sexuality or feminist ideology as a means to achieving status.

Hostile Sexism and Benevolent Sexism follow predictably from the power differences and interdependence between men and women in all domains of everyday life. Specifically, patriarchy, gender differentiation, and heterosexual relations constitute the structural foundations of Ambivalent Sexism. To some extent, these foundations mirror SCM's structural concepts of "status" and "interdependence." Patriarchy or male societal power mirrors the SCM status concept. The SCM interdependence concept appears in the simultaneous deeply cooperative but potentially contentious nature of heterosexuality and the cooperative nature of women and men's traditional role differentiation but the competitive nature of nontraditional role enactments. Hence, patriarchy, gender differentiation, and heterosexual relations specifically are unique to gender relations, and give rise to a specific set of behavioral outcomes for men and women in both the private and public domains. As AST describes, each of these institutions has a benevolent and a hostile component, giving way to complementary justifications for gender inequality.

The institution of patriarchy (male hegemony) yields paternalism, the ideological justification of male dominance. The hostile elements of patriarchy are based in dominative paternalism, the prescription that men ought to have more power than women and the contention that women might usurp men's power. As a complement, the benevolent elements of patriarchy are based in protective paternalism, the belief that men need to protect and provide for the women because they are weak.

Gender differentiation refers to the social distinctions all cultures make between men and women, and the importance of gender identity in social hierarchy (Harris, 1991). Competitive gender differentiation, rooted in antipathy theories of prejudice, accounts for the idea that, because of women's lower status, stereotypes associated with women inherently comprise inferiority and incompetence. On the other hand, complementary gender differentiation stresses the functionality of women in gender-conventional roles and accounts for the view that women are "wonderful" because they are nurturing and supportive (Eagly & Mladinic, 1993) or possess a moral purity.[1]

Finally, the necessary condition of heterosexual relations and sexual reproduction highlight the interpersonal interdependence of men and women. The hostile interpretation of this interdependence is that women are purportedly able to use sex to control men, whereas the benevolent interpretation asserts that women are a valuable resource (e.g., essential for men's true happiness), even if they are inferior.

Both men and women report subscribing to these ideologies, albeit to varying degrees (Glick & Fiske, 1996; Killianski & Rudman, 1998), and these ideologies suggest how gender inequality persists. Men are socially dominant by many accounts (e.g., higher-status roles, greater income) (United Nations Development Programme, 2005), so several mechanisms follow for their role as the higher-status group. As noted, System Justification Theory argues that people are motivated to create beliefs that reinforce the status quo so that they can see the social system in which they live as fair and legitimate (Jost & Banaji, 1994); Social Dominance Theory also posits that people create ideologies ("legitimating myths") to support the hierarchy (Sidanius & Pratto, 1999). Therefore gender stereotypes emerge that reflect the current system. The dominant group also has incentive to reward subordinates, on whom they rely, for warmth and cooperation. Additionally, being hostile alone would never work to keep the subordinates in check (Glick & Fiske, 1999). According to the Metamorphic Theory of power (Kipnis, 1976, 1984), overt control leads powerholders and targets to attribute targets' behavior to force, which leads the powerholder to perceive the target as weak, and the target to resent the powerholder. As soon as the powerholder is no longer present, the target will cease to enact the desired behavior. On the other hand, relational tactics lead both parties to perceive choice in the target's behavior, which allows the target to maintain self-respect and encourages self-sustaining behavior. Relational tactics suggest one way that women maintain the system, by some degree of perceived choice. This is essential, for the hierarchical gender system would never sustain itself for this long if it were maintained only by brute force.

Instead, dominant groups endorse paternalistic ideologies that offer help and protection to subordinates in order to justify the hierarchy (Jackman, 1994). The system is arranged so that dominants confer benefits upon the subordinates to keep them complacent. Subordinates, ever sensitive to their position and the cultural view, are influenced by status beliefs in their own behavior, and cooperate to maintain amicable conditions (Seachrist & Stangor, 2001). In part, Benevolent Sexism stems from the perceived willing cooperation of the subordinates. Additionally, seemingly "protective" gestures allow dominants to see subordinates as less competent while turning a blind eye to discriminatory acts (Glick & Fiske, 1996, 2001a, 2001b). In other words, dominants can deny subordinates education, organizational power, and economic participation under the guise of protection (Glick et al., 2000). If the subordinates go along with the arrangement, dominants are free to assume subordinates' consent. If subordinates reject the "benefits," thereby refusing to cooperate, the dominants will react with hostility toward the subordinates, because they believe it is their right to maintain the system.

AST builds on the existing theories of gender inequality by demonstrating why it is that both hostile and benevolent ideologies contribute to persistent prejudice and discrimination against women. First, although Benevolent Sexism is seemingly innocuous, and in certain situations perceived as beneficial, it is problematic because it is yoked to hostile sexism; Benevolent Sexism does not exist without Hostile Sexism and the resulting prejudice and discrimination. Data from more than 15,000 participants in 19 countries illustrate that Benevolent and Hostile Sexism are highly correlated with one another, and negatively correlated with other indicators of gender equality in economic and political life (Glick et al., 2000). Second, Benevolent Sexism is selectively favorable only toward women who occupy traditional female roles. Ambivalent sexists reconcile their presumably conflicting ideologies about women by reserving benevolent beliefs for traditional women and hostile beliefs for nontraditional women (Glick, Diebold, Bailey Werner, & Zhu, 1997). Third, Benevolent Sexism reduces women's resistance to prejudice and discrimination, because benevolence is often used to justify hostile acts. For example, women with higher Benevolent Sexism scores rated both interpersonal discrimination (e.g., husband forbids wife from going out at night) and professional discrimination (e.g., boss promotes male employee instead of female employee, even though she is more qualified) as less serious when the perpetrator cited benevolent justifications (e.g., for their protection). Furthermore, higher Benevolent Sexism scores predicted women's greater tolerance for husbands' overtly hostile discrimination, though this last finding only held for women without paid employment (Moya, Exposito, & Casado, 1999). Lastly, Benevolent Sexism is dangerous because it highlights stereotypic differences between men and women contributing to the belief in innate gender differences.

Recent work reveals that Benevolent and Hostile Sexism are related to several practices, individual differences, and behaviors that predict prejudice and discrimination against women. The likelihood of individuals passing on female- and male-disparaging jokes, as well as how funny men think they are is predicted by Hostile Sexism, and the relationship between Hostile Sexism and likelihood to pass on disparaging jokes is mediated by perceived funniness (Thomas & Esses, 2004). Education is negatively related to Benevolent and Hostile Sexism, and Catholicism predicts more Benevolent, but not Hostile Sexism (Glick, Lameiras, & Castro, 2002). In Turkey and Brazil, Hostile Sexism predicts men and women's justification of violence against wives. Furthermore, the alleged protection promoted by Benevolent Sexism is contingent on wives occupying traditional roles and remaining subordinate to husbands' authority (Glick, Sakali-Urgulu, Ferreira, & Aguiar de Souza, 2002).

So do women go along to avoid brutality? Or do they really endorse the system, because they want it both ways (protection *and* equal rights)? Only one study that we are aware of addresses this question directly. Women rated profiles of benevolent sexists and hostile sexists as mildly favorable and highly unfavorable, respectively, and 44% of them simultaneously approved of the benevolent sexist and disapproved of the hostile sexist (Killianski & Rudman, 1998). Nevertheless, on average participants thought it was unlikely that the two profiles described the same person indicating that they underestimate ambivalent prejudice.

Implications of Status Beliefs and Roles for Women

As discussed, Expectation States Theory (Berger et al., 1977; Webster & Foschi, 1988) tells us that gender is inextricably linked to social hierarchy because gender stereotypes explicitly describe men's and women's status in addition to traits and roles (Ridgeway, 2001). Furthermore, men and women have to work together in order to get what they need and want. Two significant trends emerge as a result of this cooperative interdependence: (1) the status differentiating qualities of both groups are more likely to be highlighted than are other qualities, and (2) the dominant group, when unchallenged, is likely to interpret cooperation of the subordinate group as consent. So, on the surface, men and women contentedly continue the present arrangement, and both groups do the necessary cognitive gymnastics to make sense of the way things are (Jost & Banaji, 1994).

Another possible interpretation is that it's not just system justification in the sense of sacrificing the self for the sake of the system. It may be that women are just choosing the lesser of two evils. Gender is one, if not the most, salient social category (Fiske, 1998; Stroessner, 1996) and gender stereotyping is often automatic or unconscious (Dunning & Sherman, 1997). In other words, the mere sight of a woman can immediately elicit a specific set of traits and attributions, depending on context (category-based perception; Fiske & Neuberg, 1990). Social-role theory (Eagly, 1987) suggests that gendered division of labor is the source of the stereotypes we hold about women and men to this day. Women are associated with domestic roles (e.g., mother), which require communal qualities (e.g., warmth, patience), whereas men are associated with high-status roles (e.g., professional), which require agentic traits (e.g., competence, independence). Thus, the "work" roles associated with each gender have shaped the content of the stereotypes people hold about men and women. While the content of stereotypes for women may seem subjectively positive, public domains make it clear that these "favorable" attitudes are predicated on women occupying low-status roles.

People have learned to think about women in a certain way, and women can go along with it or not go along with it. Given the features of gender relations – the clearly defined and deeply embedded hierarchy, the automatically accessed roles, and the pervasive benevolent and hostile ideologies that dictate social rewards and punishments – women in the public domain face a Catch-22 every day. They have to make a choice: Will they cooperate or compete? What risk do they run if they compete, choosing to challenge the status quo?

PAY TO PLAY?

In many domains, men continue to surpass women in power and status (Pratto & Walker, 2001). Even when their objective behavior is equivalent, men and women are perceived as displaying divergent behaviors and possessing attributes indicative of differences in power, status, and dominance (Heilman, 2001). Moreover, particularly in masculine domains, women's relative power and status may be misperceived as being much lower than objectively indicated. Women have to work harder than men do in order to be perceived as equally competent (Foschi, 2000).

As explained, some dominant group members endorse negative stereotypes that legitimize their privilege and withhold social power from subordinate groups. AST makes specific predictions about possible negative outcomes for women who operate in the public domain while having to navigate the fall-out from benevolent and hostile ideologies. Some negative outcomes include patronizing discrimination, backlash, and sexual harassment, to which we now turn.

Playing by the Rules

In this case, playing by the rules means adopting traditional gender roles and operating within the status system that is already in place. However, as we will see, even when women try to play by the rules, they do not necessarily benefit.

Women are allegedly communal, and men are allegedly agentic (Eagly, 1987), but employees in professional settings who are seen as warm and incompetent elicit patronizing discrimination (Glick & Fiske, in press). Patronizing behaviors have serious consequences for women in professional settings. Because stereotypes about gender comprise status beliefs (i.e., women have less status than men), less agentic traits, and more communal traits, superiors will tend to hold women to lower stereotyped-based standards in performance settings (Biernat, Manis, & Nelson, 1991; Biernat & Kobrynowicz, 1997; Biernat & Manis, 1994; Biernat, Vescio, & Manis, 1998). In masculine domains, this activation of low or patronizing standards for women can lead evaluators to be more impressed with female candidates than male candidates because the female candidate readily surpasses minimum standards for a woman (a "wow effect"), whereas the male candidate is held to higher, male stereotype-based standards and therefore seems comparatively less impressive (Biernat & Kobrynowicz, 1997). Still, this "advantage" does not translate into getting the job because of an enormous behavioral gap between praising an applicant's qualities and actually putting applicants on the payroll (Biernat & Fuegen, 2001). These decisions distinguish between zero-sum and non-zero-sum behaviors (Biernat et al., 1998), such that zero-sum choices allocate limited but valuable resources (e.g., money, promotions), and non-zero-sum choices dole out unlimited but less-valued resources (e.g., verbal praise, positive nonverbal cues). Non-zero-sum behaviors contrast to stereotypes, as a consequence of shifting standards (e.g., "She did a really great job giving that presentation, for a woman. We should definitely consider her for the job."). However, the really valuable, limited zero-sum choices assimilate to stereotypes (e.g., men are more competent than women, so hire the man) (Biernat & Fuegen, 2000; Biernat & Vescio, 2002). Thus, while minimum competence standards are often lower for women, ability standards are actually higher (Foschi, 2000). In other words, while female applicants are likely to appear on the short list, they still lag in hiring, raises, and promotions.

Other more overt manifestations of patronizing discrimination include: handicapping via over-helping (e.g., "there's no reason why you should have to learn this program, I'll do it for you"), taking over (e.g., "let me do this project, you seem in over your head"), and limiting the responsibilities of targets (e.g., "you have enough to do as it is; I'll give this project to him") (Rudman, Glick, & Phelan, in press). Subordinates (either male or female) respond with anger to patronizing behaviors of powerholders, but men subsequently perform better, whereas women perform worse (Vescio, Gervais, Snyder, & Hoover, 2005).

Patronizing discrimination is embedded in benevolent sexism and serves to maintain the dominant group's higher status. The double-edged nature of patronizing discrimination is precisely what makes benevolent sexism so insidious. It is not overtly hostile and in many cases is seemingly beneficial to the recipient. Furthermore, perpetrators may think they are helping recipients. Women who accept paternalistic gestures do so either because they are not aware that they are reinforcing their own low-status role, or because they understand that they have to cooperate, and accepting benevolent gestures is a better alternative to enduring overt hostility.

Not Playing by the Rules

As noted, women do not necessarily benefit by enacting traditional gender roles; so what happens when they do try to compete? Given existing pervasive gender–status associations, women have to weigh the alternatives of cooperation versus perceived competition. Everyday, women face a paradox in performance settings: They have to provide strong counter-stereotypic information (e.g., that they are agentic and competent) in order to demonstrate that they are qualified for high-status professional roles (Glick, Zion, & Nelson, 1988), but this deviation from prescribed and proscribed gender norms can elicit a *backlash effect* (Rudman, 1998).

Consider the consequences of refusing benevolent gestures or violating feminine norms. If a woman elects to reject patronizing assistance, she is seen uncooperative. As a result, the benefits of paternalism reserved for women who stick to traditional gendered behavior are revoked and backlash rooted in hostile sexism can take its place. Manifestations of backlash include hiring discrimination (Heilman, Wallen, Fuchs, & Tamkins, 2004), being judged more harshly (Eagly, Makhijani, & Klonsky, 1992), being sabotaged (Rudman & Fairchild, 2004), social exclusion (Jackman, 1994), and being sexually harassed (Fiske & Stevens, 1993). Indeed, research demonstrates that high Hostile Sexism scores, but not Benevolent Sexism scores, are related to more negative evaluations and fewer management recommendations for female candidates, but more management recommendations for male candidates (Masser & Abrams, 2004). Moreover, women are bound by workplace culture norms; research indicates that the social costs of making attributions to discrimination prevent stigmatized individuals from dealing with the discrimination (Kaiser & Miller, 2001).

Hostile ideologies elicited by competitive or counter-normative behaviors promote ideas that can be used to justify resentment. A hostile interpretation of heterosexual intimacy can motivate individuals to infer that female coworkers acquired their positions illegitimately (e.g., by sleeping with a superior), because sexuality is supposedly the domain in which women have the perceived ability to control men. It is hardly a coincidence that men who are most concerned with protecting their status are also the most likely to harass (Maass, Cadinu, Guarnieri, & Grasselli, 2003), and that individuals (male or female), who threaten men's status are most likely to become the targets of harassment (Berdahl, 2004; Dall'Ara & Maass, 2000; Maass et al., 2003). Furthermore, being perceived as "sexy" can elicit hostile reactions, from both men and women, and lead people to perceive sexual harassment as justified (Muehlenhard & MacNaughton, 1988). Thus, when women compete and threaten to destabilize the current status system, sexual harassment may be one way others attempt to reinforce their place in the hierarchy.

To make matters more complicated, the nonverbal behavioral research suggests that women are facing an uphill battle to preserve their legitimacy once they are in positions of authority. Dominant nonverbal behavior is a major cue to power, as well as a subtle but crucial midpoint along the continuum between covert and overt displays of control (Carli, LaFleur, & Loeber, 1995; Henley, 1995; LaFrance, Hecht, & Paluck, 2003). Henley (1977, 1995) has proposed that many of the nonverbal behaviors that we have learned to attribute to gender differences (e.g., men take up more space, women smile more) can be better explained by dominance and submissiveness (e.g., dominant people maintain a steady gaze, submissive people look away/down more). This proposal does not eliminate gender as a factor as it is true that men tend to display more dominance behaviors while women tend to display more submissive behaviors (Hall, 1984). The trouble lies in the many nonverbal behaviors that function both as dominance cues and cues of intimacy, depending on who is expressing them, when, and where. For example, individuals who touch are seen as more dominant than the target they are touching (Major, 1981), but physical touch between two people is also a clear signal of intimacy and closeness. Given that dominant nonverbal behavior is a central avenue for control that also serves the dual function of communicating intimacy, women who enact these behaviors in an effort to communicate their authority run the risk of being misinterpreted. Indeed, research shows exactly this pattern: not only are dominant behaviors seen as less dominant when displayed by women, they are also seen as more sexual in both dyadic interactions (Henley & Harmon, 1985) and when they are presented alone (Cikara & Morrow, 2004).

When women enact dominant nonverbal behaviors, simultaneously deviating from gender norms and not playing by the rules, they run the risk of being seen as overtly sexual. The misperception of women's dominance behaviors as sexual may be particularly pernicious and may disserve women in at least two ways. First, behavioral confirmation may work in concert with attributions, to restrict women's ability to influence situations and other people. Perhaps rightly, women do not believe that they can be seen simultaneously as competent and sexual (Gutek, 1989). Second, being seen as sexual rather than powerful, women are objectified and diminished, thus making them more likely targets for harassment and unwanted sexual advances. As one might expect, flirtatiousness and harassment have negative consequences for women's self-confidence (Satterfield & Muehlenhard, 1997).

While women tolerate harassment less than men do, Ambivalent Sexism and hostility toward women predicts tolerance of harassment regardless of gender (Russell & Trigg, 2004). And enacting submissiveness is not a solution. Not only does it undermine people's perception of social power, being seen as submissive can also lead to exploitation (Richardson, Rollerson, & Phillips, 1970). Our take home message is this: Attributing women's professional success to sexuality, aggression, or coldness strips competence of its relation to legitimate forms of social power and the likelihood of making these attributions can be predicted by the extent to which individuals ascribe to benevolent and hostile ideologies.

SUMMARY

This chapter examines the tension between interdependence and dominance in gender relations. We reviewed how status systems affect the distribution of social power in modern society as well as how prejudice, stereotyping, and discrimination stem from said status systems and intergroup processes. Using AST, we discussed the way male hegemony, gender differentiation, and heterosexual intimacy yield complementary justifications of gender inequality and find that women in the public domain face a difficult choice: cooperate or compete. We reviewed evidence to support our argument that women do not necessarily acquiesce joyfully to the present hierarchical arrangement, but rather guide their decisions by weighing the outcomes of going along to get along against challenging the status quo. Finally, we examine some of the negative consequences women face when they cooperate and when they compete. All this evidence suggests that when women do cooperate in their subordinate status, they do not necessarily accept it.

NOTE

1. Note that the SCM warmth dimension links both friendly intent and trustworthiness, so it combines these ideas.

REFERENCES

Allport, G. W. (1954). *The nature of prejudice.* Reading, MA: Addison-Wesley.
Berdahl, J. L. (2004). *The sexual harassment of "masculine" women.* Unpublished manuscript, University of Toronto, Toronto, Canada.
Berger, J., Fisek, M. H., Norman, R. Z., & Zelditch, M., Jr. (1977). *Status characteristics and social interaction: An expectation states approach.* New York: Elsevier.
Biernat, M., & Fuegen, K. (2001). Shifting standards and the evaluation of competence: Complexity in gender-based judgments and decision making. *Journal of Social Issues, 57,* 707–724.
Biernat, M., & Kobrynowicz, D. (1997). Gender- and race-based standards of competence: Lower minimum standards but higher ability standards for devalued groups. *Journal of Personality and Social Psychology, 72,* 544–557.
Biernat, M., & Manis, M. (1994). Shifting standards and stereotype-based judgments. *Journal of Personality and Social Psychology, 66,* 5–20.
Biernat, M., Manis, M., & Nelson, T. F. (1991). Comparison and expectancy processes in human judgment. *Journal of Personality and Social Psychology, 61,* 203–211.
Biernat, M., & Vescio, T. K. (2002). She swings, she hits, she's great, she's benched: Shifting judgment standards and behaviors. *Personality and Social Psychology Bulletin, 28,* 66–76.
Biernat, M., Vescio, T. K., & Manis, M. (1998). Judging and behaving toward members of stereotyped groups: A shifting standards perspective. In: C. Sedikides, J. Schopler & C. A. Insko (Eds), *Intergroup cognition and intergroup behavior* (pp. 151–175). Mahwah, NJ: LEA.
Carli, L. L. (1991). Gender, status, and influence. In: E. J. Lawler, B. Markovsky, C. L. Ridgeway & H. Walker (Eds), *Advances in group processes* (Vol. 8, pp. 89–113). Greenwich, CT: JAI.
Carli, L. L., LaFleur, S. J., & Loeber, C. C. (1995). Nonverbal behavior, gender, and influence. *Journal of Personality and Social Psychology, 68,* 1030–1041.
Cikara, M, & Morrow, J. (May, 2004). Effects of gender and dominance on perceptions of overt sexuality, sexual attractiveness, warmth, and competence. Presented at the American Psychological Society Meeting, Chicago, IL.
Cohen, B. P., & Zhou, X. (1991). Status processes in enduring work groups. *American Sociological Review, 56,* 179–188.
Cuddy, A. J. C., Fiske, S. T., & Glick, P. (in press). Competence and warmth as universal trait dimensions of interpersonal and intergroup perception: The Stereotype Content Model and the BIAS Map. In: M. P. Zanna (Ed.), *Advances in experimental social psychology.* New York: Academic Press.
Cuddy, A. J. C., Fiske, S. T., Kwan, V. S. Y., Glick, P., Demoulin, S., Leyens, J-Ph., et al. (in press). Is the stereotype content model culture-bound? A cross-cultural comparison reveals systematic similarities and differences. *British Journal of Social Psychology.*
Dall'Ara, E., & Maass, A. (2000). Studying sexual harassment in the laboratory: Are egalitarian women at higher risk? *Sex Roles, 41,* 681–704.
Deaux, K., Winton, W., Crowley, M., & Lewis, L. (1985). Level of categorization and content of gender stereotypes. *Social Cognition, 3,* 145–167.
Dovidio, J. F., Kawakami, K., & Gaertner, S. L. (2000). Reducing contemporary prejudice: Combating explicit and implicit bias at the individual and intergroup level. In: S. Oskamp (Ed.), *Reducing prejudice and discrimination* (pp. 137–163). Mahwah, NJ: Lawrence Erlbaum Associates Publishers.

Dunning, D., & Sherman, D. A. (1997). Stereotypes and tacit inference. *Journal of Personality and Social Psychology, 73,* 459–471.

Eagly, A. H. (1987). *Sex differences in social behavior: A social-role interpretation.* Hillsdale, NJ: Erlbaum.

Eagly, A. H., Makhijani, M. G., & Klonsky, B. G. (1992). Gender and the evaluation of leaders: A meta-analysis. *Psychological Bulletin, 111,* 3–22.

Eagly, A. H., & Mladinic, A. (1993). Are people prejudiced against women? Some answers from research on attitudes, gender stereotypes and judgments of competence. In: W. Strobe & M. Hewstone (Eds), *European review of social psychology* (Vol. 5, pp. 1–35). New York: Wiley.

Eckes, T. (1994). Features of men, features of women: Assessing stereotypic beliefs about gender subtypes. *British Journal of Social Psychology, 33,* 107–123.

Eckes, T. (2002). Paternalistic and envious gender stereotypes: Testing predictions from the Stereotype Content Model. *Sex Roles, 47,* 99–114.

Fiske, S. T. (1993). Controlling other people: The impact of power on stereotyping. *American Psychologist, 48,* 621–628.

Fiske, S. T. (1998). Prejudice, stereotyping, and discrimination. (In: D. T. Gilbert, S. T. Fiske & G. Lindzey (Eds), *The handbook of social psychology* (4th ed., pp. 357–411). New York: McGraw-Hill.

Fiske, S. T., & Berdahl, J. (in press). Social power. In: A. Kruglanski & E. T. Higgins (Eds), *Social psychology: A handbook of basic principles* (2nd ed.). New York: Guilford.

Fiske, S. T., Cuddy, A. J. C., Glick, P., & Xu, J. (2002). A model of (often mixed) stereotype content: Competence and warmth respectively follow from perceived status and competition. *Journal of Personality and Social Psychology, 82,* 878–902.

Fiske, S. T., & Neuberg, S. L. (1990). A continuum of impression formation, from category-based to individuating processes: Influences of information and motivation on attention and interpretation. In: M. Zanna (Ed.), *Advances in experimental social psychology* (Vol. 23, pp. 1–74). New York: Academic Press.

Fiske, S. T., & Ruscher, J. B. (1993). Negative interdependence and prejudice: Whence the affect? In: D. M. Mackie & D. L. Hamilton (Eds), *Affect, cognition, and stereotyping: Interactive processes and group perception* (pp. 239–268). San Diego, CA: Academic Press.

Fiske, S. T., & Stevens, L. E. (1993). What so special about sex? Gender stereotyping and discrimination. In: S. Okamp & M. Costanzo (Eds), *Gender issues in contemporary society* (pp. 173–196). Thousand Oaks, CA: Sage Publications, Inc.

Fiske, S. T., Xu, J., Cuddy, A. C., & Glick, P. (1999). (Dis)respecting versus (dis)liking: Status and interdependence predict ambivalent stereotypes of competence and warmth. *Journal of Social Issues, 55,* 473–489.

Foschi, M. (2000). Double standards for competence: Theory and research. *Annual Review of Sociology, 26,* 21–42.

Georgesen, J. C., & Harris, M. J. (1998). Why's my boss always holding me down? A meta-analysis of power effects on performance evaluations. *Personality and Social Psychology Review, 2,* 184–195.

Georgesen, J. C., & Harris, M. J. (2000). The balance of power: Interpersonal consequences of differential power and expectation. *Personality and Social Psychology Bulletin, 26,* 1239–1257.

Glick, P., Diebold, J., Bailey Werner, B., & Zhu, L. (1997). The two faces of Adam: Ambivalent sexism and polarized attitudes toward women. *Personality and Social Psychology Bulletin, 23,* 1323–1334.

Glick, P., & Fiske, S. T. (1996). The Ambivalent Sexism Inventory: Differentiating hostile and benevolent sexism. *Journal of Personality and Social Psychology, 70,* 491–512.
Glick, P., & Fiske, S. T. (1999). Sexism and other "isms": Interdependence, status, and the ambivalent content of stereotypes. In: W. B. Swan, J. H. Langlois & L. A. Gilbert (Eds), *Sexism and stereotypes in modern society* (pp. 193–221). Washington, DC: American Psychological Association.
Glick, P., & Fiske, S. T. (2001a). An ambivalent alliance: Hostile and benevolent sexism as complementary justifications for gender inequality. *American Psychologist, 56,* 109–118.
Glick, P., & Fiske, S. T. (2001b). Ambivalent sexism. In: M. P. Zanna (Ed.), *Advances in experimental social psychology* (Vol. 33, pp. 115–188). Thousand Oaks, CA: Academic Press.
Glick, P., & Fiske, S. T. (in press). Sex discrimination: The psychological approach. In: F. J. Crosby, M. S. Stockdale & S. A. Ropp (Eds), *Sex discrimination in the workplace.* Malden, MA: Blackwell.
Glick, P., Fiske, S. T., Mladinic, A., Saiz, J., Abrams, D., Masser, B., Adetoun, B., Osagie, J., Akande, A., Alao, A., Brunner, A., Willemsen, T. M., Chipeta, K., Dardenne, B., Dijksterhuis, A., Wigboldus, D., Eckes, T., Six-Materna, I., Exposito, F., Moya, M., Foddy, M., Kim, H.-J., Lameiras, M., Sotelo, M. J., Mucchi-Faina, A., Romani, M., Sakalli, N., Udegbe, B., Yamamoto, M., Ui, M., Ferreira, M. C., & Lopez, W. L. (2000). Beyond prejudice as simple antipathy: Hostile and benevolent sexism across cultures. *Journal of Personality and Social Psychology, 79,* 763–775.
Glick, P., Lameiras, M., & Castro, Y. R. (2002). Education and catholic religiosity as predictors of hostile and benevolent sexism toward women and men. *Sex Roles, 47,* 433–441.
Glick, P., Sakali-Urgulu, N., Ferreira, M. C., & deSouza, M. A. (2002). Ambivalent sexism and attitudes toward wife abuse in Turkey and Brazil. *Psychology of Women Quarterly, 26,* 292–297.
Glick, P., Zion, C., & Nelson, C. (1988). What mediates sex discrimination in hiring decisions? *Journal of Personality and Social Psychology, 55,* 178–186.
Gutek, B. A. (1989). Sexuality in the workplace: Key issues in social research and organizational practice. In: J. Hearn, D. L. Sheppard, P. Tancred-Sheriff & G. Burell (Eds), *The sexuality of organization* (pp. 56–70). London: Sage Publications.
Haines, E. L., & Host, J. T. (2000). Placating the powerless: Effects of legitimate and illegitimate explanation on effect, memory, and stereotyping. *Social Justice Research, 13,* 219–236.
Hall, J. A. (1984). *Nonverbal sex differences: Communication accuracy and expressive style.* Baltimore: Johns Hopkins University Press.
Harris, M. (1991). *Cultural anthropology* (3rd ed.). New York: Harper Collins.
Heilman, M. E. (2001). Description and prescription: How gender stereotypes prevent women's ascent up the organizational ladder. *Journal of Social Issues, 57,* 657–674.
Heilman, M. E., Wallen, A. S., Fuchs, D., & Tamkins, M. M. (2004). Penalties for success: Reactions to women who succeed at male gender-typed tasks. *Journal of Applied Psychology, 89,* 416–427.
Henley, N. M. (1977). *Body politics: Power, sex, and nonverbal communication.* Englewood Cliffs, NJ: Prentice-Hall.
Henley, N. M. (1995). Body politics revisited: What do we know today? In: P. J. Kalbfleisch & M. J. Cody (Eds), *Gender, power, and communications in human relationships* (pp. 27–61). Hillsdale, NJ: LEA.

Henley, N. M., & Harmon, S. (1985). The nonverbal semantics of power and gender: A perceptual study. In: S. L. Ellyson & J. F. Dovidio (Eds), *Power, dominance, and nonverbal behavior* (pp. 151–164). New York: Springer-Verlag.

Hewstone, M., Rubin, M., & Willis, H. (2002). Intergroup bias. In: S. T. Fiske, D. L. Schacter & C. Zahn-Waxler (Eds), *Annual review of psychology* (Vol. 53, pp. 575–604). Palo Alto, CA: Annual Reviews.

Jackman, M. R. (1994). *The velvet glove: Paternalism and conflict in gender, class and race relations*. Berkeley, CA: University of California Press.

Jost, J. T., & Banaji, M. R. (1994). The role of stereotyping in system-justification and the production of false consciousness. *British Journal of Social Psychology, 33*, 1–27.

Jost, J. T., Pelham, B. W., Brett, W., & Carvallo, M. R. (2002). Non-conscious forms of system justification: Implicit and behavioral preferences for higher status groups. *Journal of Experimental Social Psychology, 38*, 586–602.

Jost, J. T., Pelham, B. W., Sheldon, O., & Sullivan, B. N. (2003). Social inequality and the reduction of ideological dissonance on behalf of the system: Evidence of enhanced system justification among the disadvantaged. *European Journal of Social Psychology, 33*, 13–36.

Kaiser, C. R., & Miller, C. T. (2001). Stop complaining! The social costs of making attributions to discrimination. *Personality and Social Psychology Bulletin, 27*, 254–263.

Keltner, D., Gruenfeld, D. H., & Anderson, C. (2003). Power, approach, and inhibition. *Psychological Review, 110*, 265–284.

Killianski, S., & Rudman, L. A. (1998). Wanting it both ways: Do women approve of benevolent sexism? *Sex Roles, 39*, 333–352.

Kipnis, D. (1976). *The powerholders*. Chicago, IL: University of Chicago Press.

Kipnis, D. (1984). The use of power in organization and in interpersonal settings. *Applied Social Psychology Annual, 5*, 179–210.

LaFrance, M., Hecht, M. A., & Paluck, E. L. (2003). The contingent smile: A meta-analysis of sex differences in smiling. *Psychological Bulletin, 129*, 305–334.

Lerner, M. J. (1980). *The belief in a just world: A fundamental delusion*. New York: Plenum.

Maass, A., Cadinu, M., Guarnieri, G., & Grasselli, A. (2003). Sexual harassment under social identity threat: The computer harassment paradigm. *Journal of Personality and Social Psychology, 85*, 853–870.

Major, B. (1981). Gender patterns in touching behavior. In: C. Mayo & N. M. Henley (Eds), *Gender and nonverbal behavior* (pp. 15–37). New York: Springer-Verlag.

Masser, B. M., & Abrams, D. (2004). Reinforcing the glass ceiling: The consequences of hostile sexism for female managerial candidates. *Sex Roles, 51*, 609–615.

Moya, M., Exposito, F., & Casado, P. (1999). *Women's reactions to hostile and benevolent sexist situations*. Oxford, UK: European Association of Experimental Social Psychology.

Muehlenhard, C. L., & MacNaughton, J. S. (1988). Women's beliefs about women who "lead men on". *Journal of Clinical Psychology, 7*, 65–79.

Mummendey, A. (1995). Positive distinctiveness and social discrimination: An old couple living in divorce. *European Journal of Social Psychology, 25*, 657–670.

Noseworthy, C. M., & Lott, A. J. (1984). The cognitive organization of gender-stereotypic categories. *Personality and Social Psychology Bulletin, 10*, 474–481.

Oldmeadow, J., & Fiske, S. T. (in press). Ideology moderates status = competence stereotypes: Roles for belief in a just world and social dominance orientation. *European Journal of Experimental Social Psychology*.

Pratto, F., & Walker, A. (2001). Dominance in disguise: Power, beneficence, and exploitation in personal relationships. In: A. Lee-Chai & J. A. Bargh (Eds), *The use and abuse of power* (pp. 93–114). Philadelphia, PA: Taylor and Francis.

Raven, B. H. (1993). The bases of power: Origins and recent developments. *Journal of Social Issues, 49,* 227–251.

Raven, B. H. (2001). Power interaction and interpersonal influence. In: A. Lee-Chai & J. A. Bargh (Eds), *The use and abuse of power* (pp. 217–240). Philadelphia, PA: Taylor and Francis.

Raven, B. H., Schwarzwald, J., & Koslowsky, M. (1998). Conceptualizing and measuring a power/interaction model of interpersonal influence. *Journal of Applied Social Psychology, 28,* 307–332.

Richardson, L., Rollerson, B., & Phillips, J. (1970). Perceptions of submissiveness: Implications for victimization. *The Journal of Psychology, 4,* 407–411.

Ridgeway, C. (1991). The social construction of status value: Gender and other nominal characteristics. *Social Forces, 70,* 367–386.

Ridgeway, C. (2001). Gender, status, and leadership. *Journal of Social Issues, 57,* 637–655.

Rudman, L. A. (1998). Self-promotion as a risk factor for women: The costs and benefits of counter-stereotypical impression management. *Journal of Personality and Social Psychology, 74,* 629–645.

Rudman, L. A., & Fairchild, K. (2004). Reactions to counterstereotypical behavior: The role of backlash in cultural stereotype maintenance. *Journal of Personality and Social Psychology, 87,* 157–176.

Rudman, L. A., Glick, P., & Phelan, J. E. (in press). From the laboratory to the bench: Gender stereotyping research in the courtroom. In: E. Borgida & S. T. Fiske (Eds), *Beyond common sense: Psychological science in the courtroom.* Malden, MA: Blackwell.

Russell, B. L., & Trigg, K. Y. (2004). Tolerance of sexual harassment: An examination of gender differences, ambivalent sexism, social dominance, and gender roles. *Sex Roles, 50,* 565–573.

Satterfield, A. T., & Muehlenhard, C. L. (1997). Shaken confidence: The effects of an authority figure's flirtatiousness on women's and men's self-rated creativity. *Psychology of Women Quarterly, 21,* 395–416.

Seachrist, G. B., & Stangor, C. (2001). Perceived consensus influences intergroup behavior and stereotype accessibility. *Journal of Personality and Social Psychology, 80,* 645–654.

Sidanius, J., & Pratto, F. (1999). *Social dominance: An intergroup theory of social hierarchy and oppression.* New York, NY: Cambridge University Press.

Six, B., & Eckes, T. (1991). A closer look at the complex structure of gender stereotypes. *Sex Roles, 24,* 57–71.

Stroessner, S. J. (1996). Social categorization by race or sex: Effects of perceived non-normalcy on response times. *Social Cognition, 14,* 247–276.

Tajfel, H., & Turner, J. C. (1986). The social identity theory of intergroup behavior. In: J. Worchel & W. G. Austin (Eds), *Psychology of intergroup relations* (pp. 7–24). Chicago, IL: Nelson.

Thomas, C. A., & Esses, V. M. (2004). Individual differences in reaction to sexist humor. *Group Processes and Intergroup Relations, 7,* 89–100.

United Nations Development Programme (2005). *Human development report 2005.* HDR Statistics [On-line]. Available: http://hdr.undp.org/statistics/data/indicators.cfm

Vescio, T. K., Gervais, S. J., Snyder, M., & Hoover, A. (2005). Power and the creation of patronizing environments: The stereotype-based behaviors of the powerful and their effects on female performance in masculine domains. *Journal of Personality and Social Psychology, 88*, 658–672.

Webster, M., & Foschi, M. (1988). *Status generalization: New theory and research.* Stanford, CA: Stanford University Press.

"STREET CRED" AND THE EXECUTIVE WOMAN: THE EFFECTS OF GENDER DIFFERENCES IN SOCIAL NETWORKS ON CAREER ADVANCEMENT

Susan F. Cabrera and Melissa C. Thomas-Hunt

ABSTRACT

Drawing upon Cabrera and Thomas-Hunt's (2006) theoretical framework for the advancement of executive women, we identify gender differences in social networks as an important determinant of the relative perceived credibility of men and women and the opportunities for hire and promotion available to them. A review of the existing research literature on gender and social networks is presented and several potentially fruitful avenues for future research in this area are discussed.

On the face of it, 2006 was a spectacular year for women executives. In just one year, the number of women CEOs in Fortune 100 companies increased by 100% and the number in Fortune 500 companies increased by 22%.

Underlying these startling increases were just two factors – well, to be precise ... just two women: Patricia Woertz of Archer Midland Daniels and Indra Nooyi of PepsiCo. With the appointment of just these two women as CEO in 2006, the representation of women at the top of the U.S. business world increased dramatically – from zero to two (0–2%) among Fortune 100 companies and from 9 to 11 (1.8% to 2.2%) among Fortune 500 companies (Fortune, 2006). These discouraging statistics improve moderately when women's representation across non-CEO senior corporate positions is considered. A recent report by Catalyst (2006) indicated that in Fortune 500 companies in 2005, women held only 16.4% of corporate officer positions, 9.4% of the most powerful "clout" positions, and even worse, made up only 6.4% of the aggregate of the five highest paid individuals within each of these companies. Further, the average growth in the percentage of women holding corporate officer positions fell to its lowest level in 10 years (Catalyst, 2006). While perhaps more extreme within the business world than in other arenas, this pattern of significant under-representation of women in positions of power is repeated across American society. In 2006, women made up only 15.1% of Congress (14% of the Senate), 16% of state governors, were mayors of 12 of the top 100 U.S. cities (Rutgers University, 2006), were 21.1% of university presidents (in 2001, the latest date where data is available) (Corrigan, 2002), and just one of the nine members of the U.S. Supreme Court was a woman, despite the fact that women make up 50.7% of the U.S. population (U.S. Census Bureau, 2006).

Recently, we proposed a model to help explain this dearth of women in senior leadership positions (Cabrera & Thomas-Hunt, 2006). Central to this model are the risk assessments made by employers during the hiring process. However, as illustrated in Fig. 1, before individuals are subject to these hiring risk assessments, they first must be included on the roster of candidates being considered for the position. Logically, for any given job, most individuals are not considered because, either they are not, in reality, qualified for the position, they are not perceived to be qualified, they do not know about the position or the employer does not know about them, or perhaps they do not seem to fit the usual prototype for the position. We have argued that the determination of whether individuals "make the list" is driven by their *opportunity structure,* defined as the universe of possible positions which they actually have and are perceived to be qualified for, which they know about, and to which they thus have access. This opportunity structure, in turn, is determined by factors such as individuals' previous positions, their education, their socioeconomic status, where they grew up, the information regarding employment that they have access to, as well as many others.

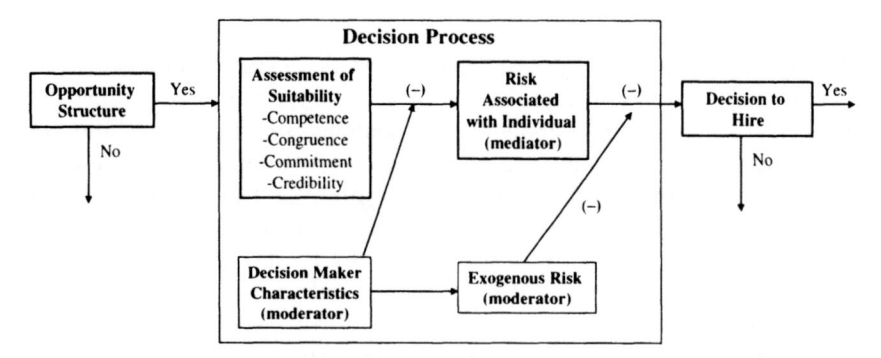

Fig. 1. An Illustration of the Risk Model of Executive Advancement. *Source:* Cabrera and Thomas-Hunt (2006).

According to our model, once individuals have "made the list" and are considered for promotion or hire, employers engage in an assessment of both the individual *candidate* risk and the *exogenous* risk associated with the hiring decision (Cabrera & Thomas-Hunt, 2006). In their assessments of candidate risk, employers evaluate the suitability of individuals on four dimensions – competence, commitment, congruence, and credibility. As candidates are evaluated as more suitable on each of these dimensions, the individual risk associated with hiring them (i.e. their candidate risk) decreases; conversely, as candidates are assessed as less suitable, their candidate risk increases. Candidate risk, in turn, mediates the decision to hire any particular individual such that the riskier the individual is perceived to be, the less likely he or she is to be hired.

In our model, we explicitly define exogenous risk as "risk in the hiring decision that is external to the particular candidate being evaluated" and suggest that it reflects the degree of exposure associated with a particular hiring decision. In assessing exogenous risk, decision makers consider factors such as the type of position and its importance to the organization, as well as the potential implications of the hiring decision for the prospects of the company. Assessments of exogenous risk act as a moderator on the relationship between the level of candidate risk and the decision to hire; for individuals with a given level of assessed candidate risk, if the exogenous risk is higher, they are less likely to be hired and vice versa. Put another way, if a position is critical to an organization, then to be successful in the hiring process, a candidate must be highly suitable for the job and thus, considered "low risk." Finally, our model includes one other important element: the characteristics of the decision maker. Specifically, we have argued that the characteristics of individual decision makers, including their status, demographic attributes, gender beliefs, previous experiences, appetite for taking risk as well as other factors, will to some degree determine their particular perspective of individual candidates and situations, and thus influence their assessments of both candidate risk and exogenous risk.

Drawing on this model, we argued that with respect to each dimension of the individual risk assessment, as well as the evaluation of exogenous risk, women will tend to be at least subtly disadvantaged, relative to men (Cabrera & Thomas-Hunt, 2006). Further, while each of these differences may be subtle and therefore, not individually concerning, it is the accumulation of small differences over the span of a career that results in dramatically fewer women in leadership positions across society. In contemplating ways in which to ameliorate the disadvantage that women face, we also suggested that female job candidates' credibility may be a key lever which can offset the lower assessments of competence, congruence, and commitment that women receive throughout the hiring process. Consequently, in this chapter we have chosen to examine the factors that enhance and thwart females' development of credibility. In particular, we focus on the impact of social networks, which may work to either support or undermine any individual's credibility. We begin by considering the different opportunity structures to which men and women have access and specifically examine how the social structural aspects of job opportunity impact the credibility which any individual job candidate brings to the hiring and promotion process.

OPPORTUNITY STRUCTURE

The accumulation of "small differences," referred to above, affects the opportunity structure within which an individual is situated. At the beginning of any individual's career, a certain set of job opportunities is available, based on the abilities and cumulative history of that person's experiences to date. As individuals progress in their careers, their opportunity structure keeps changing constantly, influenced by all prior hiring and promotion decisions and the implications of those decisions on outcomes such as the human capital the individuals develops, the relationships and networks they build, and even their attitude and feelings about work and career. As these decision processes are repeated throughout a career, individuals are funneled either toward or away from the executive suite. One particularly important determinant of any individual's opportunity structure is the social network of relationships within which he or she is embedded. Substantial research has shown that social networks determine access to a variety of important resources and are influential in both identification of jobs and hiring and promotion decisions (Brass, 1985; Burt, 1992, 1998; Campbell, Marsden, & Hurlbert, 1986; Granovetter, 1974). Social networks may also provide access to high-status sponsors that can dramatically change the opportunity structure within which an individual is positioned, by providing informal information about job openings and lending legitimacy to any application for promotion or hire. As we discuss below in more detail, there are important differences in men's and women's social networks which, in turn, drive differences in the opportunity structures available to them. In order to understand how the varying opportunity structures of men and women contribute to the dearth of women at the top, and in particular, the way in which they impact the credibility of job candidates, we first explore the nature of credibility and then the convergence and divergence of men's and women's social networks and the consequences of these differences for candidate credibility and advancement.

CREDIBILITY

Numerous researchers have suggested that credibility is crucial to the advancement of women; unfortunately, they have also demonstrated that, frequently, women are not perceived as credible as their male counterparts (Burt, 1998; Carli, 2001; Hollander, 1992; Ridgeway, 2001; Valian, 1998; Yoder, 2001; Yoder, Schleicher, & McDonald, 1998). Consistent with these findings, in our model we highlighted credibility as a particularly important determinant of women's career outcomes (Cabrera & Thomas-Hunt, 2006). Defining credibility as "the believability and legitimacy of an individual's credentials and future potential," we suggested that it is "both a function of perceptions of the individual's competence, congruence and commitment, and a contributing factor to those perceptions" (Cabrera & Thomas-Hunt, 2006). Given this influence of perceived credibility on each key dimension considered in individual risk assessments, and the fact that greater perceived credibility should also reduce the level of exogenous risk assigned to a candidate, we argued that closing the "credibility gap" between men and women is one of the most promising avenues for leveling the hiring and promotion process. We further pointed to two mechanisms which drive positive credibility assessments for women. First, existing research has shown that women can be legitimated in the hiring and promotion process through indisputable displays of competence and ability (Pugh & Wahrman,

1983); for example, by demonstrating clear success in a position similar to the one for which the candidate is being considered (Steinpreis, Anders, & Ritzke, 1999). In other words, for women to be successful in moving up the executive ladder, they have to be *perceived* as successful, which, given the biases against women often implicit in performance evaluations, often requires that women must actually be *more* successful than their male counterparts. A potentially more useful mechanism is suggested by a second body of research; specifically, that women may be perceived as more credible when they are "sponsored" by a high-status third party (Burt, 1998; DeMatteo, Dobbins, Myers, & Facteau, 1996; Hogue, Yoder, & Ludwig, 2002; Ibarra, 1997; Yoder, 2001; Yoder et al., 1998). This finding logically suggests further questions such as: Where do women find these sponsors? Do they have the same access to important high-status relationships as men? And, what are the implications of the answers to these questions on women's career outcomes? We believe that some of these questions can be answered by understanding similarities and differences in the social networks of men and women, as well as identifying the causes and outcomes of these differences. Given the important influence of social networks on the relative opportunity structures and credibility of men and women professionals, it is to this topic that we turn our attention.

THE IMPORTANCE OF SOCIAL NETWORKS

Implicit in the well-known quip "It's not what you know, but who you know" is the commonly held understanding that social networks *matter*. In the half-century since this term was coined by Barnes (1954), the study of social networks has exploded. Across a large and growing body of research, it has been shown that social networks have important and wide-ranging effects on many aspects of social life, including access to information, support, advice, influence, and power (Burt, 1992, 1998; Campbell et al., 1986). The nature of these social networks helps to determine outcomes as varied as the ease with which one can find a job (Granovetter, 1974) and the status of that job (Lin, Ensel, & Vaughn, 1981), whether one attains promotions or greater influence in an organization (Brass, 1985; Burt, 1992), achieves higher income or greater mobility in the workplace (Carroll & Teo, 1996; Podolny & Baron, 1997), and even whether one is healthy or lives long (House, Landis, & Umberson, 1988; Moen, Dempster-McClain, & Williams, 1989).

It has also long been known that women do not have equal access to many of the social networks most important for attaining information, power, influence, and support within and across organizations, thus limiting women's access to the many benefits provided by them (Bartol, 1978; Kanter, 1977; Lincoln & Miller, 1979; Miller, 1986; Miller, Labovitz, & Fry, 1975). Despite this recognition, it is only during the last two decades that research in the area of social networks has been systematically applied to the issues of gender differentiation and inequality in our society. Traditionally, most social theories and disciplines have explained differences in the behavior, status, and social position of men and women as resulting from differences in individual-level attributes; attributes such as tastes and preferences (economists), genetics (sociobiologists), or socialization (social psychologists) (Smith-Lovin & McPherson, 1992). Importantly, each of these interpretations suggests that men and women differ in fundamental and largely unchanging ways. In contrast, network theory provides an alternative and structural perspective in which "social processes and individual outcomes are determined by patterns of relationships among actors" (Smith-Lovin & McPherson, 1992, p. 223). Because men and women are embedded in different networks of relationships, they have different access to information, resources, and opportunities, in particular hiring and promotion opportunities.

While considerable progress has been made in advancing a social network perspective of gender (Brass, 1985; Burt, 1998; Ibarra, 1992, 1997; Lincoln & Miller, 1979; McPherson & Smith-Lovin, 1987; McPherson, Smith-Lovin, & Cook, 2001; Mehra, Kilduff, & Brass, 1998; Miller, Lincoln, & Olson, 1981; Moore, 1990; Smith-Lovin & McPherson, 1992; van Emmerik, 2006), clearly additional work is needed. In 1993, Herminia Ibarra, one of the leading researchers in the field, proposed a conceptual framework for furthering study in this area. Focusing on personal or "ego-centric" informal interaction networks, the framework suggests a new perspective that "views network differences as reflections of purposeful strategic action within a context characterized by structural constraint" (Ibarra, 1993, p. 57). Specifically, attributes of the organizational context such as the overall gender composition of the organization, the hierarchical distribution by gender, and turnover and mobility rates by gender both produce and interact with organizational dynamics such as the degree of gender stereotyping and the quality of gender relations to produce important differences in the networks of men and women (Ibarra, 1993). Examples of some of the mechanisms underlying this process include: lower availability of high-status, same-sex ties for women in organizations dominated by men;

less perceived desirability of ties to women in organizations that rely on stereotypes of women as less competent than men; and less instrumental value of weak ties for women in organizations where women are viewed as illegitimate players.

In addition to directly affecting the personal networks of individuals, organizational factors also indirectly affect these networks by shaping the strategies available to individuals as well as the relative costs of these strategies. Importantly, Ibarra (1993) notes that although they are subject to organizational constraints, individuals are not simply passive tabula rasa upon which structure is enacted. Instead, "individuals play an active role in structuring their social networks to achieve their goals and maximize the benefits they seek" (Ibarra, 1993, p. 74); however, the strategies that individuals use are prescribed and shaped by the social context in which they are embedded. For example, in forming network ties, individuals typically demonstrate a preference for both homophily (the tendency for individuals to interact with those who have similar attributes such as race, gender, religion, or values) (McPherson et al., 2001) and for high-status network partners. In an unconstrained environment, presumably both men and women would pursue a strategy of creating homophilous and high-status networks. However, in many organizational contexts in which there are few high-status women professionals, this strategy is not available to women; in this way, the "purposeful strategic actions" of individuals are constrained by the structure of the organization (Ibarra, 1993). In other words, women, despite seeking to further their career progression by associating with high-status individuals, are constrained in their ability to connect with those best positioned to enhance their credibility.

Ibarra (1993) argued for a multi-prong approach to future research on gender differences in personal networks, in which she first called upon researchers to move beyond simple identification of women's exclusion from informal interaction networks and toward a more specific understanding of the practical and theoretical ways in which men's and women's networks differ. Second, she argued that we must identify what causes network differences, focusing specifically on organizational constraints and differences in the strategies used by men and women to develop networks. Third, researchers must investigate the relationship between differences in social networks and real-world outcomes; in other words, what are the consequences of these differences? Finally, Ibarra noted the importance of conducting this type of analysis over time. While most existing research tends to be discrete in nature, taking snapshots of various networks at a given point in time, this approach is seriously limited. Duncan Watts expounded on the powerful and dynamic nature of networks in his book "*Six Degrees: The Science of a Connected Age*":

> "Networks are dynamic objects not just because things happen in networked systems, but because the systems themselves are evolving and changing in time, driven by the activities or decisions of those very components. In the connected age, therefore, *what happens and how it happens depend on the network*. And the network in turn depends on what has happened previously. It is this view of a network – as an integral part of a continuously evolving and self-constituting system – that is truly new about the science of networks." (Watts, 2003, pp. 28–29)

Thus, in order to truly understand the causes, realities, and implications of gender differences in social networks, we must study them *dynamically* and *longitudinally*. While we fully endorse Ibarra's approach, we argue that given the broader context of our model (Cabrera & Thomas-Hunt, 2006) – that is, the cross-organizational, career-spanning process through which individuals progress toward the executive suite – her approach should be extended even further to include an investigation of how the evolution of individuals' social networks are affected by societal forces such as our system of gender beliefs. Specifically, we believe that such an approach will more effectively elucidate the structural constraints which limit women's opportunities to establish credibility and their potential for attaining senior executive positions.

As will be discussed in the literature review below, substantial empirical work has been done to address the first research question posed in Ibarra's framework (i.e. identifying actual gender differences in social networks). Across a variety of contexts and using numerous different measurements, researchers have identified many of the key differences in the social networks of men and women (Brass, 1985; Burt, 1998; Ibarra, 1992, 1997; Lincoln & Miller, 1979; McPherson & Smith-Lovin, 1987; McPherson et al., 2001; Mehra et al., 1998; Miller et al., 1981; Moore, 1990; Smith-Lovin & McPherson, 1992; van Emmerik, 2006). Further, some of this work has explored outcomes resulting from these differences, including impacts on influence, rate of promotion, and status in organizations (Brass, 1985; Burt, 1998; Ibarra, 1992, 1997; Lincoln & Miller, 1979; Miller et al., 1981). To date, however, very little work has been done to systematically identify the societal and organizational factors which result in gender differences in social networks (for exceptions, see McPherson & Smith-Lovin, 1987; South, Bonjean, Markham, & Corder, 1982) or the different strategies used by men and women to develop these networks (for an exception, see Ibarra, 1992). Further, virtually no research has explored how men's and women's social networks change over time.

EXISTING RESEARCH ON SOCIAL NETWORKS AND GENDER

Over the last two decades, we have seen the development of a substantial body of research which has advanced our understanding of how the social networks of men and women differ across a number of contexts and using a variety of measurement methods. Not surprisingly, these streams of research are often overlapping and occasionally contradictory. However, in an effort to identify and describe some of the key findings, we will proceed with a discussion of the literature delineated on the basis of the specific characteristic of social networks that is being measured. This will include some of the key studies and findings around differences in network composition, as measured by homophily (Brass, 1985; Ibarra, 1992, 1997; McPherson & Smith-Lovin, 1987; McPherson et al., 2001; Mehra et al., 1998; South et al., 1982), and range (Ibarra, 1997; Moore, 1990), and differences in relationship characteristics, as measured by tie strength (Ibarra, 1997), multiplexity (Ibarra, 1992), network centrality (Brass, 1985; Ibarra, 1992; Lincoln & Miller, 1979; Mehra et al., 1998; Miller et al., 1981), and network constraint (Burt, 1998). In addition, throughout the discussion we will touch on what existing literature can tell us about differences in the way in which men and women translate social networks into tangible benefits (Burt, 1998; Ibarra, 1992, 1997; Lincoln & Miller, 1979; van Emmerik, 2006) and we will identify instances where existing research investigates or informs either the societal or organizational factors influencing gender differences in social networks or the outcomes resulting from these differences.

Homophily

Homophily, the tendency for individuals to interact with those who have similar attributes such as race, gender, religion, or values, is one of the most common measurements of network composition and has been a particular focus of attention for gender researchers. Several early studies demonstrated the pervasiveness of gender homophily in the workplace and its harmful impact on women. Specifically, in his study of non-supervisory employees of a newspaper publishing company, Brass found that while women were slightly more central within the organization overall, two sex-segregated networks were underlying this pattern (Brass, 1985). As a result of women's low degree of interaction with men, they were excluded from the entirely male "dominant coalition" in the organization, and thus were less influential and less likely to be promoted than men. South and colleagues, in their study of female employees of a large federal bureaucracy, found a similar association between gender homophily and negative outcomes for women; as the number of women in the organization increased, the degree of homophily increased, resulting in less interaction between women and men and less social support provided to women by men (South et al., 1982).

While the prior studies tended to focus on individual preferences for homophily (the "preference perspective"), a number of other studies argue that it is the availability of same-sex contacts within a given social context or organization that largely influences gender differences in network homophily (the "structural perspective"). This structural perspective was popularized by Blau, who argued that "social associations depend on opportunities for social contact" (Blau, 1977, p. 281). In other words, the network relationships that individuals choose to form are highly constrained by the composition and dynamics of the social context in which they are embedded. Consistent with this argument, a number of studies have shown that the availability of same-sex contacts, as well as the relative status of those contacts, affects the degree of homophily of individuals' social networks. In their 1987 study of homophily in voluntary organizations, McPherson and Smith-Lovin coined the terms "choice homophily" which is the type of homophily produced by individual choices and "induced homophily" which is the result of constraints imposed by group composition (McPherson & Smith-Lovin, 1987). Not surprisingly, they found evidence of both types; however, for age, sex, and occupation attributes, induced homophily was the more powerful factor.

Several years later, Ibarra extended this research in a study of professional and semi-professional employees of a regional advertising firm by empirically testing the competing hypotheses from the preference and structural perspectives to determine whether the degree of network homophily is driven by individual *preferences* for same-sex ties or by the *structurally determined opportunity* for forming homophilous ties (Ibarra, 1992). Further, the paper offered a theoretical argument integrating the two perspectives. Although individuals in general have a tendency toward gender homophily, since women in work organizations are often at a disadvantage to men with respect to status and access to resources, women may rationally perceive interaction with men as a more effective strategy to achieve influence, status and power. As a result, "preferences for homophily and status will tend to coincide for men and exist in competition for women" (Ibarra, 1992, p. 425) and therefore, women will pursue a differentiated strategy to obtain friendship, social support, and emotional mentoring from women while attempting to access more instrumental information, advice and influence through relationships with men. To test this proposition, Ibarra distinguished between "instrumental networks" which are comprised of relationships that "arise in the course of work role performance and involve the exchange of job-related resources, including information, expertise, professional advice, political access, and material resources" and "expressive networks" which are comprised of relationships that "involve the exchange of friendship and social support and are characterized by higher levels of closeness and trust than those that are exclusively instrumental" (Ibarra, 1993, p. 59). As predicted, the study's findings supported Ibarra's interpretation that men and women pursue different network strategies; men demonstrated a high degree of homophily across all networks, while women had more heterophilous ties within their instrumental networks and more homophilous ties in their expressive networks (Ibarra, 1992).

Ibarra further extended this research by linking homophily to performance outcomes for men and women in a 1997 study of mid-level managers in four Fortune 500 companies (Ibarra, 1997). In a pattern suggestive of induced homophily, men had more homophilous information and career contacts than women. However, high-performing women had more homophilous information and career ties than non-high-performing women and in fact, not a single non-high-performing woman reported seeking out instrumental ties with other women. While this finding is contrary to previous arguments that homophily is detrimental to women (Brass, 1985; South et al., 1982), Ibarra argued that it is evidence of choice homophily on the part of high-performing women and may demonstrate the important role that same-sex relationships can have in providing support and advice, including on topics such as how to attract organizational sponsors and enhance one's perceived credibility (Ibarra, 1997; Kram, 1988).

Mostly recently, Mehra and colleagues demonstrated evidence of homophily in friendship networks, in this instance in the context of a nationally ranked MBA program (Mehra et al., 1998). While prior studies were primarily conducted in hierarchical organizations, this study found that friendship networks within the context of a "de-layered" environment still showed a strong pattern of gender homophily. Interestingly, for women, this homophily may have been largely induced, as the lower status of women rendered them less attractive as network partners. The findings were supportive of this explanation, indicating that "the marginalization of women resulted more from exclusionary pressures than from their preferences for women friends" (Mehra et al., 1998, p. 447).

In summary, homophily has been shown to be both an important dimension upon which the social networks of men and women differ and a noteworthy determinant of women's perceived credibility and career advancement. While both choice and induced homophily were observed, induced homophily appears to play a greater role within work environments and instrumental networks. Further, within the workplace, women tend to have less homophilous networks than men because they employ a differentiated strategy, seeking out heterophilous instrumental ties and homophilous expressive ties. Finally, homophily has been shown to have both detrimental and beneficial effects on women's careers. On the one hand, greater homophily may limit women's access to the halls of power in organizations, in particular, making it less likely that they will receive the support of high-status organizational sponsors which are crucial to closing the gender credibility gap. In addition, homophilous networks are likely to contribute to men and women having access to different types of information about jobs and promotions, with women potentially being less aware of high-status opportunities than men. On the other hand, relationships with other women in similar situations may provide valuable and needed social support and advice.

Tie Strength

Tie strength indicates "the amount of time, the emotional intensity, the intimacy (mutual confiding), and reciprocal services which characterize the tie" (Granovetter, 1973, p. 1361). As such, strong ties are generally associated with being closer, more stable and reciprocal, and characterized by more frequent interaction, while weak ties are characterized by relationships that are more distant in nature, involve infrequent communication and less emotional investment (Ibarra, 1993).

In a landmark work, Granovetter demonstrated that weak ties, as important avenues for accessing non-redundant information, ideas, and opportunities, can be more valuable than strong ties for instrumental purposes such as finding a job (Granovetter, 1973). Inversely, strong ties, which tend to be more homogeneous and therefore more redundant in information, may be less instrumentally productive, but provide other types of benefits such as greater opportunities for influence and persuasion, a higher likelihood of help in a crisis (Granovetter, 1982; Krackhardt, 1992), and a greater degree of sponsorship and legitimacy within and across organizations (Burt, 1992, 1998). Recognizing the different benefits of strong and weak ties, several researchers have argued that the most effective networks will be relatively well balanced between the two (Brass, 1984; Granovetter, 1982).

However, the relative value of strong and weak ties may differ for women, in particular for instrumental purposes. In her 1997 study of managerial networks, Ibarra found that high-performing women relied more heavily on strong ties than non-high-performing women and all men. While the traditional notion that women prefer close, intimate relationships might have explained the difference with men, it did not explain the difference between high and non-high-performing women. Thus, Ibarra proposed the alternative explanation that strong ties are more instrumentally effective for women than weak ties because they "help women to counteract the effect of bias, gender-typed expectations, and contested legitimacy" (Ibarra, 1997, p. 99). In a similar vein, Burt reported that women who relied on a high-status organizational sponsor to form their social networks were promoted earlier than women who directly built their own networks (Burt, 1998). He attributed this finding to women's lack of legitimacy within the focal organization of the study.

In summary, strong ties may be particularly crucial for women to establish credibility, as it is the partners in these intimate, intense, and reciprocal relationships who are most likely to act as organizational sponsors and advocate for their career advancement. It is equally important, however, that women form strong ties with the "right" people; specifically, with high-status, typically male individuals. Unfortunately, given individuals' preference for homophily, it may be difficult for women to form strong ties with high-status men. Exacerbating this difficulty even more may be prescriptive social norms which define and limit the level of closeness which is appropriate in a male–female work relationship. Further, women's necessary focus on developing strong ties in order to successfully recruit legitimating organizational sponsors may limit their access to the same level of information about opportunities for development, promotion, or hire which men have as a result of maintaining broader networks of weak ties.

Multiplexity

A network concept closely related to tie strength, multiplexity is the number of relationship dimensions associated with each individual tie. For example, a tie that is characterized by a workplace relationship, a friendship relationship, and an extended family relationship would be considered one of high multiplexity, while a tie that is characterized by only a workplace relationship would not. Ties that are higher in multiplexity are generally considered to be stronger, closer, more stable, and more likely to be reciprocal (Granovetter, 1973; Ibarra, 1992).

In her 1992 paper, Ibarra argued that one potential but perhaps less obvious implication of the differentiated strategy that women use in developing workplace contacts is to decrease the degree of multiplexity of women's social networks relative to men's (Ibarra, 1992). The findings in support of this argument were mixed; while unexpectedly, men and women had a similar overall number of multiplex ties, the results indicated that homophily was highly correlated with multiplexity for women, but not for men. In other words, women's multiplex relationships were generally homophilous, suggesting that once again, women may be at a disadvantage in forming strong multiplex relationships with the highest status (i.e. male) individuals in the organization. Further, common sense suggests individuals would be more likely to use their own social capital to assist a person with whom they have a multi-faceted relationship (i.e. a friend as well as a colleague) than someone with whom they only have a single relationship. Thus, women's lack of multiplex relationships with men may once again work to disadvantage them with respect to developing important high-status sponsors and ultimately, to developing the credibility necessary for advancement to the executive suite.

Range

Range refers to the breadth and diversity of ties within a network, and has been measured in several ways, including the number of contacts within a network, the diversity of types of contacts within a network, and the degree to which ties are situated within or across organizational workgroups. Diversity can be based upon a wide variety of attributes including the nature of the relationship (kin, coworker, friend, etc.), the ascribed attributes of the contact (gender, race, age, etc.), the organizational membership of the contact, or the status of the contact. A broad range of network ties, comprised of both strong and weak relationships with a diverse group of individuals has often been associated with access to greater instrumental resources (Campbell, 1988; Campbell et al., 1986; Marsden, 1987).

Several studies have explored whether the range of men's and women's networks differs. Of note, Moore found that men's and women's network composition differed substantially, with men's networks including fewer kin ties and more non-kin ties such as coworkers, friends, and advisors (Moore, 1990). Women's networks included more kin overall and more different types of kin ties, but fewer non-kin ties and types than men. However, after controlling for structural variables such as age, education, employment, marital status, and children, women's and men's networks were largely similar; the only significant remaining difference was that women continued to have more kin ties than men. These findings strongly support the conclusion that "most gender differences in networks were due to opportunities and constraints arising out of women's and men's different locations in the social structure" (Moore, 1990, p. 734). Looking at network range exclusively in the workplace, another study found that high-performing women had wider ranging networks than high-performing men, including a substantial number of ties to higher or equal-status women across other organizations (Ibarra, 1997). Because of the constraints imposed by organizational demographics (i.e. few opportunities for high-status intra-organizational ties to other women), women were forced to choose "between dispersed homophilous contacts and within-group cross-gender ties;" in this study, the most effective strategy appeared to be to cultivate wide-ranging homophilous ties and strong within-group cross-gender ties (Ibarra, 1997, p. 100).

There are several ways to interpret this strategy. First, it may be that women are aware of their "legitimacy problem" and thus recognize the need to develop strong relationships with high-status men within their organizations. Consequently, they actively attempt to augment their structurally prescribed instrumental relationships with such men with other types of ties. By focusing their resources internally, generating the credibility that emerges from strong relationships, and demonstrating indisputable levels of competence and ability (Pugh & Wahrman, 1983), women may ultimately be successful in advancing within their organizations. However, outside their organizations where opportunities to display competence and to strengthen relationships are less frequent, these same women may be perceived as lower status and thus less likely to be sought out as network partners by high-status males. Additionally, both men and women are often careful of initiating cross-gender relationships outside the context of work because of the potential of having their intentions misconstrued. In contrast, less encumbered are women's opportunities to forge relationships with same- and higher-status women with whom they come in contact in their extra-organizational interactions. Further, higher status women may seek to mentor and advise lower status women in other organizations with whom they come in contact. Differentially mentoring women within their own organizations might be perceived of as favoritism; however, across organizational lines it is less observable and subject to scrutiny. As a result of these numerous dynamics, women's wider-ranging network ties tend to be with other women.

An alternative, but not mutually exclusive interpretation is that women are status conscious in forming instrumental ties within organization, but in forming their expressive ties look for homophilous relationships wherever they can find them. Since there are simply fewer women proximally available with whom to form relationships, women's same-sex relationships are necessarily wider ranged. The result of either mechanism is that the broader range of high performing women's networks seems to serve them well, but the absence of wide-ranging and multiplex cross-gender ties may still limit their ability to generate credibility outside of their own organizations and gain consideration for external career advancement opportunities.

Network Centrality

Generally speaking, network centrality is a measure of the prominence or visibility of an individual actor within a network. Thus, an individual with "high centrality" is typically well integrated in the network with extensive access to other actors. There are a variety of types and specific measures of centrality: the number of direct ties that an individual has to others in the network ("degree centrality"); the extent to which an individual is close to others in the network (i.e. connected through short paths with very few links) ("closeness centrality"); the extent to which an individual acts as an intermediary in the network, linking other individuals who are not already connected to each other ("betweenness centrality"); and the amount of information contained in all of the network paths to which an individual is connected ("information centrality") (Wasserman & Faust, 1994). Despite the fairly common usage of these specific centrality measures, within the gender literature, the term "centrality" is often used quite broadly and vaguely as a general measure of the degree to which a group or individual is integrated within a network with access to the resources, status, power, and influence shown to be associated with centrality (Ibarra, 1992).

In 1979, Lincoln and Miller carried out one of the first studies to investigate the influence of ascribed attributes on network centrality (Lincoln & Miller, 1979). The study measured path distance (the smallest number of links required to connect to individuals in a network), a typical measure of closeness centrality, for employees in five professional and semi-professional organizations and used this measure to determine the degree to which gender, race, education, and authority influenced network position. With very few exceptions across the organizations, the findings showed that these four attributes "operate on network structure by determining which persons will occupy central locations and which persons will find themselves at the margin of an organization's social system;" specifically, "white males with high education in formal positions of authority have high probabilities of occupying the most central locations in the network space" (Lincoln & Miller, 1979, p. 193). Consistent with these findings, a later study also using path distance as a measure of centrality found that while women were equally central in the organization overall, they were much less central in men's networks and the dominant power coalition in the firm (Brass, 1985). Further, both influence and promotion were strongly associated with access to these groups. As a result, within the organization, women were perceived as less influential and received fewer promotions than men.

In contrast, another empirical work has reported somewhat more complex findings around the effects of gender on network centrality. A study of social and work networks within six federally sponsored agencies found that gender and race were not meaningful predictors in explaining network centrality (also measured using path distance) (Miller et al., 1981). However, an analysis of the interaction effects between gender and measures of achieved status such as authority (formal rank), education, and professional experience showed that women were much less able than men to translate investments in education, experience, or authority into a more central organizational position. Specifically, women's authority was associated with network centrality, but much less so than for men; education did not indicate any clear payoff for women; and experience was found to be "virtually irrelevant" (Miller et al., 1981).

Ibarra reported similar results using a somewhat more sophisticated measure of centrality, aggregate prominence, which "indexes individual centrality as a function of the centrality of those to whom one is connected through direct and indirect links" (Ibarra, 1992, p. 432). According to this formulation of centrality, an individual is considered to be more central when linked to other individuals with high centrality themselves. While the study findings indicated than men had higher network centrality than women, these differences were entirely explained by differences between men and women in rank, department, education, tenure with the organization, prestige of past work, and professional activity. However, in consistence with Miller et al. (1981), the findings also showed that women were less able to convert achieved rank and professional activity into network centrality. In other words, investments by women to achieve the typical bureaucratic symbols of success resulted in lower returns than the same investments by men.

One logical explanation of this finding is again, the aura of illegitimacy that hangs over the achieved successes of women in organizations and even more broadly, across society. Because women are perceived as less professionally credible than men, their accomplishments such as educational attainment, achieved rank, and experience on the job may be suspect and therefore, less likely to be translated into the status, power, and opportunities for advancement that come with being central to an organization. Thus, women may be caught in a Catch-22 where in order to be considered professionally credible, they must be highly accomplished, but in order for these accomplishments to be valued and recognized, they must first be considered credible. While no single factor will provide a solution to this conundrum, we argue that this pattern again suggests that women may particularly benefit from the endorsement of an organizationally central, high-status professional sponsor.

Network Constraint

Network constraint is an inverse measure of an individual's social capital (i.e. social capital increases as network constraint decreases) and is a function of the number of ties in a network (size), the degree to which the ties know each other (density), and the extent to which the contacts in a network are indirectly connected through a central individual (hierarchy) (Burt, 1998). As a network becomes smaller in size, more dense, and more hierarchical, constraint increases (and social capital decreases) as in each instance, the number of available contact alternatives decreases. This measure was developed and used by Burt (1998) to show that the association between having greater social capital and early promotion can operate very differently for men and women. Specifically, for men, network constraint was negatively correlated with early promotion while for women, the opposite pattern was seen; i.e. greater network constraint and lower social capital translated into earlier promotion, contrary to what might be expected.

To explain these unexpected findings, Burt first considered and rejected the notion that women are more successful with dense, clique networks. The data showed that women had larger networks and no more dense ones than men. Thus, Burt concluded that "women have no less access than men do to the information and control benefits of structural holes that advance men's careers. They differ in how the firm reacts to their access" (Burt, 1998, p. 19).

Second, while both men and women exhibited homophily, this homophily did not cause women to have more constrained networks and early promotion was not related to a preference for networking with women. Finally, based on a comparison between two women with similar network constraint but very different promotion timing, Burt concluded that the observed pattern was due to women's lack of legitimacy in the organization. Because of this lack of legitimacy, women who built their own networks directly were much less successful than women who "borrowed" social capital from a high-status organizational sponsor and thus had more hierarchical and constrained networks. This finding once again illustrates that the path of career advancement is somewhat different for women than that for men. While credibility and organizational sponsorship can be helpful to any executive, for women, these factors are not just helpful; instead, they are virtually requirements to success, the absence of which may prove to be substantial roadblocks to their upward career mobility.

CONCLUSIONS AND IMPLICATIONS FOR FUTURE RESEARCH

In this chapter, we sought to understand the ways in which the different social networks in which female and male candidates are embedded strengthens or undermines the credibility they accumulate and are able to leverage in their attempts to reach the executive suite. Existing literature provides us with a quite rich understanding of the ways in which the social networks of men and women differ with respect to qualities such as homophily, tie strength, multiplexity, range, centrality, and network constraint, and the ways in which those differences are detrimental to women's influence, status, access to information, likelihood of promotion and hire, and career mobility. It is also instructive in identifying some of the systematic barriers that women face in translating rational investments in themselves into tangible benefits. The more recent social network investigations are also prescriptive in highlighting the increased importance for women of strategically managing their social networks to garner sponsorship from key individuals who provide access to opportunities which they otherwise would not be able to avail themselves. To a lesser degree, existing research can inform our investigation of what societal and organizational factors cause these gender differences in social networks. Clearly, it indicates that the gender composition of the organization and the relative status of men and women in that organization should be significant factors. However, with respect to other potentially influential factors, the existing social networks literature is largely silent.

While the social networks research conducted to date has been invaluable, clearly additional work is needed to specifically investigate the role of sponsorship in hiring and promotion processes. We echo and extend Ibarra's (1993) call for research at multiple levels, including work to understand both the societal and organizational level antecedents of gender differences in social networks, identification of actual differences, and examination of the outcomes of such differences, specifically as they relate to executive advancement. Research on the antecedents of dissimilarity in the social networks of men and women should first be situated within the broader context of our society, in particular paying attention to our overall gender belief system, which conceptualizes women as lower status, less competent, less powerful, and generally less attractive as network contacts. Understanding how this gender system operates on organizations in general, as well as on the individuals who make up those organizations, is a critical first step to embarking upon research investigating the organizational antecedents of gender differences in advancement. In other words, to correctly identify organizational influences, we must first understand how, why and when the broader system of gender beliefs is operating.

At the organizational level, research focused on understanding currently unexplored factors on the creation and maintenance of social networks such as the reliance of individuals and organizations on gender stereotypes; the relative turnover and mobility of men and women; the age, overall size, and growth of the organization; the gender of organizational leadership; the gendering of occupations within organizations; and the existence or absence of diversity or mentoring policies would likely provide a meaningful advance in our understanding of the processes that lead to the differential representation of women and men in the executive suites of organizations. At the individual level, we need research that investigates differences in men's and women's social networks over time. This work would allow us to understand issues such as how networks are created and subsequently decay over time, and how men's and women's relative mix of weak and strong ties influences the ability to maintain and leverage their networks over time. Also potentially fruitful would be research that explores whether men and women use dissimilar strategies for building and using their social networks and whether these strategies advantage men or women in their attempts for advancement. Finally, with a firmer grasp on the causes and realities of gender differences in social networks, the strategies for building, maintaining and using these networks, and the ways in which networks change over time, we must also take a more systematic and careful look at the consequences of any disparities on the gender-based demography of organizations.

We know that social networks matter. We also know that one of the most significant barriers to women's successful career progression is their exclusion from these systems of social interaction where who gets what – power, status, money, and influence – is so often decided. As we already discussed, over the last two decades a core group of researchers have advanced our understanding of how the social networks of men and women differ, and why we should care. However, if we desire to address these differences in an effort to create a more equitable representation of men and women in high-power organizational positions, we must better understand their causes, consequences, and the dynamic processes in between. We hope that a future program of research along the lines suggested above will prove to be a step toward extending our knowledge about the social networks of men and women, elucidating the processes by which "opportunity structures" are created and destroyed, and equalizing the suitability and risk assessments that are so critical to generating greater equality in the representation of men and women at the helm of organizations (Cabrera & Thomas-Hunt, 2006).

ACKNOWLEDGMENT

We would like to thank Shelley Correll for her helpful suggestions on earlier drafts of this chapter.

REFERENCES

Barnes, J. (1954). Class and committees in a Norwegian island parish. *Human Relations, 7*, 39–58.

Bartol, K. M. (1978). The sex structuring of organizations: A search for possible causes. *Academy of Management Review, 3*, 805–815.

Blau, P. M. (1977). *Inequality and heterogeneity: A primitive theory of social structure.* New York, NY: Free Press.

Brass, D. J. (1984). Being in the right place – a structural-analysis of individual influence in an organization. *Administrative Science Quarterly, 29*(4), 518–539.

Brass, D. J. (1985). Men's and women's networks – a study of interaction patterns and influence in an organization. *Academy of Management Journal, 28*(2), 327–343.

Burt, R. S. (1992). *Structural holes: The social structure of competition.* Cambridge, MA: Harvard University Press.

Burt, R. S. (1998). The gender of social capital. *Rationality and Society*, *10*(1), 5–46.
Cabrera, S. F., & Thomas-Hunt, M. C. (2006). *Risky business: A theoretical framework for the advancement of executive women*. Manuscript in preparation.
Campbell, K. E. (1988). Gender differences in job-related networks. *Work and Occupations*, *15*(2), 179–200.
Campbell, K. E., Marsden, P. V., & Hurlbert, J. S. (1986). Social resources and socioeconomic-status. *Social Networks*, *8*(1), 97–117.
Carli, L. L. (2001). Gender and social influence. *Journal of Social Issues*, *57*(4), 725–741.
Carroll, G. R., & Teo, A. C. (1996). On the social networks of managers. *Academy of Management Journal*, *39*(2), 421–440.
Catalyst. (2006). *2005 Catalyst census of women corporate officers and top earners of the Fortune 500*. New York, NY: Catalyst.
Corrigan, M. E. (2002). *The American college president: 2002 edition*. Washington: American Council on Education.
DeMatteo, J. S., Dobbins, G. H., Myers, S. D., & Facteau, C. L. (1996). Evaluations of leadership in preferential and merit-based leader selection situations. *Leadership Quarterly*, *7*(1), 41–62.
van Emmerik, I. J. H. (2006). Gender differences in the creation of different types of social capital: A multilevel study. *Social Networks*, *28*(1), 24–37.
Fortune. (2006). Women CEOs for Fortune 500 companies. Retrieved August 30, 2006, from http://money.cnn.com/magazines/fortune/fortune500/womenceos/
Granovetter, M. S. (1973). Strength of weak ties. *American Journal of Sociology*, *78*(6), 1360–1380.
Granovetter, M. S. (1974). *Getting a job: a study of contacts and careers*. Cambridge, MA: Harvard University Press.
Granovetter, M. S. (1982). The strength of weak ties: A network theory revisited. In: P. V. Marsden & N. Lin (Eds), *Social structure and network analysis* (pp. 105–130). Beverly Hills, CA: Sage Publications.
Hogue, M. B., Yoder, J. D., & Ludwig, J. (2002). Increasing initial leadership effectiveness: Assisting both women and men. *Sex Roles*, *46*(11–12), 377–384.
Hollander, E. (1992). The essential interdependence of leadership and followership. *Current Directions in Psychological Science*, *1*, 71–75.
House, J. S., Landis, K. R., & Umberson, D. (1988). Social relationships and health. *Science*, *241*(4865), 540–545.
Ibarra, H. (1992). Homophily and differential returns – sex-differences in network structure and access in an advertising firm. *Administrative Science Quarterly*, *37*(3), 422–447.
Ibarra, H. (1993). Personal networks of women and minorities in management – a conceptual-framework. *Academy of Management Review*, *18*(1), 56–87.
Ibarra, H. (1997). Paving an alternative route: Gender differences in managerial networks. *Social Psychology Quarterly*, *60*(1), 91–102.
Kanter, R. M. (1977). *Men and women of the corporation*. New York, NY: Basic Books.
Krackhardt, D. (1992). The strength of strong ties: The importance of philos in organizations. In: N. Nohria & R. G. Eccles (Eds), *Networks and organizations: Structure, form, and action*. Boston, MA: Harvard Business School Press.
Kram, K. E. (1988). *Mentoring at work: Developmental relationships in organizational life*. Lanham, MD: University Press of America.
Lin, N., Ensel, W. M., & Vaughn, J. C. (1981). Social resources and strength of ties – structural factors in occupational-status attainment. *American Sociological Review*, *46*(4), 393–403.

Lincoln, J. R., & Miller, J. (1979). Work and friendship ties in organizations – comparative analysis of relational networks. *Administrative Science Quarterly, 24*(2), 181–199.

Marsden, P. V. (1987). Core discussion networks of Americans. *American Sociological Review, 52*(1), 122–131.

McPherson, J. M., & Smith-Lovin, L. (1987). Homophily in voluntary organizations – status distance and the composition of face-to-face groups. *American Sociological Review, 52*(3), 370–379.

McPherson, J. M., Smith-Lovin, L., & Cook, J. M. (2001). Birds of a feather: Homophily in social networks. *Annual Review of Sociology, 27*, 415–444.

Mehra, A., Kilduff, M., & Brass, D. J. (1998). At the margins: A distinctiveness approach to the social identity and social networks of underrepresented groups. *Academy of Management Journal, 41*(4), 441–452.

Miller, J. (1986). *Pathways in the workplace: The effects of gender and race on access to organizational resources*. Cambridge [Cambridgeshire], NY: Cambridge University Press.

Miller, J., Labovitz, S., & Fry, L. (1975). Inequities in organizational experiences of women and men. *Social Forces, 54*(2), 365–381.

Miller, J., Lincoln, J. R., & Olson, J. (1981). Rationality and equity in professional networks – gender and race as factors in the stratification of interorganizational systems. *American Journal of Sociology, 87*(2), 308–335.

Moen, P., Dempster-McClain, D., & Williams, R. M. (1989). Social integration and longevity – an event history analysis of women's roles and resilience. *American Sociological Review, 54*(4), 635–647.

Moore, G. (1990). Structural determinants of men's and women's personal networks. *American Sociological Review, 55*(5), 726–735.

Podolny, J. M., & Baron, J. N. (1997). Resources and relationships: Social networks and mobility in the workplace. *American Sociological Review, 62*(5), 673–693.

Pugh, M. D., & Wahrman, R. (1983). Neutralizing sexism in mixed-sex groups – do women have to be better than men? *American Journal of Sociology, 88*(4), 746–762.

Ridgeway, C. L. (2001). Gender, status, and leadership. *Journal of Social Issues, 57*(4), 637–655.

Rutgers University, Eagleton Institute of Politics, Center for American Women and Politics. (2006). *Facts on women candidates and elected officials*. Retrieved August 26, 2006, from http://www.cawp.rutgers.edu/Facts.html#elective

Smith-Lovin, L., & McPherson, J. M. (1992). You are who you know: A network approach to gender. In: P. England (Ed.), *Theory on gender/feminism on theory* (pp. 223–251). New York, NY: Aldine.

South, S. J., Bonjean, C. M., Markham, W. T., & Corder, J. (1982). Social-structure and intergroup interaction – men and women of the federal bureaucracy. *American Sociological Review, 47*(5), 587–599.

Steinpreis, R. E., Anders, K. A., & Ritzke, D. (1999). The impact of gender on the review of the curricula vitae of job applicants and tenure candidates: A national empirical study. *Sex Roles, 41*(7–8), 509–528.

U.S. Census Bureau, Population Division. (2006). *Annual estimates of the population by sex and five-year age groups for the United States: April 1, 2000 to July 1, 2005* (NC-EST2005-01). Retrieved August 15, 2006, from http://www.census.gov/popest/national/asrh/NC-EST2005/NC-EST2005-01.xls

Valian, V. (1998). *Why so slow? The advancement of women*. Cambridge, MA: MIT Press.

Wasserman, S., & Faust, K. (1994). *Social network analysis: Methods and applications*. Cambridge, NY: Cambridge University Press.

Watts, D. J. (2003). *Six degrees: The science of a connected age* (1st ed.). New York, NY: Norton.

Yoder, J. D. (2001). Making leadership work more effectively for women. *Journal of Social Issues, 57*(4), 815–828.

Yoder, J. D., Schleicher, T. L., & McDonald, T. W. (1998). Empowering token women leaders – the importance of organizationally legitimated credibility. *Psychology of Women Quarterly, 22*(2), 209–222.

FEELING INJUSTICE, EXPRESSING INJUSTICE: HOW GENDER AND CONTEXT MATTER

Cathryn Johnson, Karen A. Hegtvedt,
Leslie M. Brody and Krysia Wrobel Waldron

ABSTRACT

Although cultural beliefs about gender differences in emotional experience and expression are pervasive, empirical evidence does not always bear out those beliefs. This disjuncture has led scholars to argue for the examination of specific emotions in specific contexts in order to understand more clearly the conditions under which gender differences emerge. Heeding this call, we focus on the justice context, reviewing and investigating men's and women's feelings about and emotional displays regarding distributive justice. Using a vignette study, we specifically examine how gender and the contextual factors of procedural justice, legitimacy of the decision-maker, and gender of the decision-maker affect emotional responses of injustice victims. We argue that a focus on the gender combination of actors in a situation moves the study of gender and emotions beyond the assumption that gender-specific cultural beliefs dictate individual's feelings across situations. Our findings show few gender differences in the experience and expression of anger, resentment, and satisfaction. Rather, contextual factors, including the gender of the decision-maker, had stronger effects on emotional responses than gender of the victim. In our justice situation, then, context matters more than gender in understanding emotional responses.

Cultural beliefs in the U.S. about gender and emotion assume that men and women differ in their experience and expression of some emotions. For example, men are believed to experience and express anger more frequently than women in general, while women are thought to experience sadness and anxiety more frequently (Stearns & Stearns, 1986; Cancian & Gordon, 1988). These cultural beliefs influence individuals' interpretations of and responses to everyday interactions, whether these interactions involve conflict or cooperation. Key theoretical perspectives in the sociology of emotions offer varying explanations for these taken-for-granted beliefs about gender differences in emotions. Yet only some of the empirical evidence suggests that actual experiences and expressions of emotions are consistent with what cultural beliefs imply. This disjuncture between cultural beliefs and empirical evidence provides a basis for explicitly considering how contextual factors, alone or in conjunction with gender, impact men's and women's experience and expression of specific emotions.

Within the interactionist approach to emotions (see Smith-Lovin, 1995), some scholars focus on the cultural vocabulary and rules that shape individuals' emotional experiences and expressions while others examine the sources and meanings of actors' emotions. Hochschild's (1975, 1983) approach to emotion management entails a cultural approach. She argues that cultural beliefs affect individuals' emotional responses through norms dictating how people should feel and what they should express in particular situations. Feeling rules represent cultural standards pertaining to what people ought to feel – in terms of the type, intensity, and duration of an emotion – in a given situation. Display or expression rules define often unarticulated norms regarding what individuals may express in social interaction, which may circumscribe displays of feelings. Brody (2000) details how parents and caregivers teach these rules to ensure that children engage in acceptable and appropriate behavior. Individuals learn general and gender-specific cultural beliefs about emotions as they mature and take on various social roles (see Alexander & Wood, 2000). Thus given cultural assumptions suggesting that women are more emotional and should be more emotional than men, gender differences may arise in people's reports about how they actually feel. Similarly, insofar as cultural norms deem it appropriate in various contexts for women to express sadness more than men and for men to express anger more than women, gender differences are likely to emerge in observed expressions of emotions.[1]

Interactionists who focus more on the causes of emotional responses rather than cultural rules tend to focus on the role of social identities in stimulating emotional experiences. Affect control theory (e.g., Heise, 1977; Robinson & Smith-Lovin, 2006; Smith-Lovin, 1990; Smith-Lovin & Heise, 1998) introduces emotions as a signal for the extent to which events confirm or disconfirm an identity. The meanings evoked by identities and actions, given contextual factors, are critical in this perspective. With regard to gender differences, meanings are associated with specific gendered identities (e.g., mother, father), which are associated with emotions that map on to the positivity of the role. Insofar as situational factors may influence the interpretation of the actions by those occupying the gendered identities, the perspective implies a bit more flexibility than the scripts implied by cultural rules.

A structural approach to emotions (Kemper, 1978, 1990, 1991) also implies potential deviation from strict gender-specific cultural rules. Kemper argues that structural factors, such as an individual's social position relative to others, affect emotional responses in situations. A number of studies take a structural approach to understanding emotional responses in situations (e.g., Hegtvedt, 1990; Lovaglia & Hauser, 1996; Lawler & Yoon, 1993, 1998; Molm, 1991; Ridgeway & Johnson, 1990). Specifically, the two fundamental dimensions of relationships – status and power – elicit specific emotions during interaction. Individuals with higher status and power in a situation are more likely to experience positive emotions (such as happiness and satisfaction) than individuals with lower status and power, who are more likely to experience negative emotions. According to this argument, gender differences in emotions may emerge because women are more likely than men to have less status and power in situations in general (in the U.S.). Thus women may be more likely to experience negative emotions, such as sadness, fear, and anger, and men are more likely to experience positive emotions, on average. These general gender differences, however, may dissipate in specific situations that provide women with greater status or power.

Although cultural rules, identities, and structural positions suggest why gender differences in emotions may emerge, empirical investigations are only loosely, if at all, shaped by specific theoretical frameworks. And, more surprisingly, empirical evidence regarding the presumed pattern of gender differences is inconsistent. As reviewed in more detail below, some studies show gender differences in self-reported frequencies and expressions of emotions, although not always in the direction suggested by cultural beliefs, and other studies find no gender differences (see e.g., Brody & Hall, 1993; Lively & Powell, 2006; Simon & Nath, 2004). A generally consistent finding, however, is that women report greater feelings of intensity in some emotions (including anger) than do men (see Simon & Nath, 2004). The contradictory evidence has led some scholars to suggest examination of specific emotions in specific contexts.

Following this suggestion, here we specifically examine how contextual factors affect the emotional responses of men and women to injustice. The experience of emotion is a key feature of the justice process and, therefore, our focus on the justice context is an appropriate situation to shed light on when to expect gendered patterns of feelings and emotional expressions. We attend closely to three specific emotions – satisfaction, anger, and resentment – which constitute key responses to injustice.

Following a general overview of empirical patterns of gender differences in emotion, we review emotional reactions to distributive injustice. We then narrow our focus to the relationship between gender and such responses. By doing so, we compare general patterns of gender differences in emotions to those in justice studies. We note that in both the general and the justice studies, the gender of the individual has an effect on the reported intensity of a felt emotion. This effect remains regardless of the additional impact of a wide array of structural or contextual factors (e.g., the relative power or status levels; the fairness of decision-making rules (i.e., procedural justice); the legitimacy of the decision-maker). Gender, however, has a much weaker effect on the expression of these emotions when taking into account contextual factors.

We further examine the influence of gender and emotions in a justice situation by reporting on the results of a recent vignette study that includes the gender of the decision-maker as well as that of the perceiver. We investigate whether this contextual factor independently or in conjunction with the fairness of the decision-making procedures (i.e., procedural justice) and the legitimacy of the decision-maker affects perceivers' emotional experiences and expressions in response to receiving an unjust outcome. Consideration of the *gender combination* of actors in a situation moves the study of gender and emotions beyond the assumption that gender-specific cultural beliefs dictate individuals' feelings across situations, demonstrating the need for a nuanced understanding of the complex genesis of emotions in a situation.

GENDER DIFFERENCES IN EXPERIENCE AND EXPRESSION OF EMOTIONS

We define the experience of emotions as, "a relatively short term evaluative response essentially positive or negative in nature involving distinct somatic (and often cognitive) components" (Kemper, 1978, p. 47). Emotion thus refers to the actual experience of feeling in a situation, such as feeling angry, resentful, satisfied, or guilty. Emotions vary considerably in intensity and duration. In addition, studies show variation in expression – people hide or express feelings to others, depending on the context (Erickson & Ritter, 2001; Thoits, 1990).

Our review focuses heavily on satisfaction, anger, and resentment because they are most commonly studied across a number of studies on gender differences in emotions. Similar to previous literature, satisfaction refers to feeling pleased. In addition, anger represents a feeling of displeasure, while resentment is a feeling of indignation at the violation of entitlement to certain rewards (Hegtvedt, 1990; Hegtvedt & Killian, 1999). Empirical assessments of satisfaction, anger, and resentment in terms of the dimensions of evaluation, potency, and activity stemming from affect control theory investigations demonstrate their distinctiveness. Morgan and Heise (1988) show that satisfaction is a very positive, powerful, and lively emotion. Anger and resentment are similar on the evaluation dimension (good/bad), but anger is rated more active and significantly more powerful than resentment. In addition to examining the experience of these emotions, we pay particular attention to a central aspect of emotional display: an individual's expression of the emotion toward the person (target) responsible for generating the situation that stimulated the emotional response.

In surveying the literature, we find that the results on gender differences in both experience and expression of emotions are largely inconclusive (see e.g., Brody, 1985; Brody & Hall, 1993, 2000; Erickson & Ritter, 2001; Lively & Heise, 2004; Lively & Powell, 2006; Simon & Nath, 2004). Some studies show that gender does shape emotional experiences and expressions in the pattern suggested by gender-specific cultural beliefs and norms. Yet other studies find that gender, as an individual characteristic associated with cultural meanings, fails to predict emotional responses when situational factors are taken into account.

For example, with regard to the experience of emotion, Brody and Hall (2000) summarize research that shows that women feel joy, empathy, sadness, shame, and embarrassment (to name a few) more frequently and intensely in general than men, while men feel more contempt and pride than women. Also, women often describe themselves as more emotional than men, in both frequency and intensity (e.g., Grossman & Wood, 1993; Kring, Smith, & Neale, 1994; Sprecher & Sedikides, 1993). To some extent, such patterns confirm cultural beliefs about gender differences in emotions. Simon and Nath (2004), however, only partially confirm this pattern. Using the 1996 General Social Survey emotions module, they fail to find gender differences in the frequency of emotion in general, but do show that women report a greater intensity of feelings than do men. In addition, their findings indicate that men report feeling more positive emotions than women in general, even when socio-demographic variables and status characteristics are considered. Also, women report feeling more negative emotions than men, but these differences disappear when socio-demographic variables such as household income are taken into account. In contrast to the results of Simon and Nath (2004) and Kemper's expectations, Alexander and Wood (2000) show that women feel positive emotions more intensely than men. Specifically, they review studies that report gender differences in joy and happiness that are related to establishing and maintaining relations with others. Based on self-reports of emotions, women report more intense experiences of joy and happiness than do men (e.g., Brody, 1996; Larsen, Diener, & Emmons, 1986).

Mixed results also emerge with regard to the expression of emotion. Simon and Nath (2004) and others (e.g., Alexander & Wood, 2000; Brody & Hall, 1993; Rosenfield, 1999; Simon, 2002) find that women report that they are more likely to express their emotions in general than men. Women are more likely than men to disagree with the statements that they keep their emotions to themselves and that they try not to worry anyone else when they feel anxious. Other studies, however, indicate that the likelihood of expressing emotions is similar for men and women. Results from Erickson and Ritter (2001) show that men and women's emotional expressions (except for feelings of agitation) at work are similar. And, Lively and Powell (2006) find the same in both the home and at work when relative status is controlled. Thus gender of the individual is not a significant predictor of the expression of emotions (toward the target or to others) when social domain and relative status are taken into account.

In some studies focusing on the specific emotion of anger, findings suggest that men are more likely to report experiencing and expressing it, as would be consistent with cultural beliefs (e.g., Ross & Van Willigen, 1996). Yet results from other studies fail to affirm cultural beliefs, showing instead no gender differences in the frequency of anger and an unexpected pattern of women characterizing their anger as more intense and of longer duration than men describe their anger (Simon & Nath, 2004). Women also report that they are more likely to talk with others, including the target of the emotion, about their angry feelings than are men. In contrast, men report coping with their feelings of anger by drinking and taking pills – internalizing behaviors believed to be more likely among women. In a review of the literature on gender and anger, Kring (2000) suggests that "... men and women's anger may differ *depending on the situation*, and this may explain the divergence in findings" (p. 222). She argues that gender differences in anger are most often found within the context of interpersonal relationships. Women report more anger than men following betrayal, unwarranted criticism, or negligence, whereas men report more anger when their partner is moody or self-absorbed.

These mixed results on gender and emotions may stem, in part, from the measurement of self-reports of emotions and the extent to which analysis takes into account contextual factors. For example, LaFrance and Banaji (1992) find that gender differences in reported experience of emotions were much more likely when people make judgments of their global emotionality (i.e., the global experiences of positive and negative emotions not tied to specific events/situations) rather than make judgments on their particular emotional states. Cultural norms about how men and women are supposed to experience and express emotions may be likely to affect global emotionality. And, rating emotional experience during or immediately after a specific event appears to decrease gender effects on reported emotional experience (Shields, 1991). In such instances, environmental cues may be more important in determining emotional responses than underlying beliefs about gender and emotion (Feldman Barrett, 1998). As Feldman Barrett (1998) states, "... the data suggest that the answer to whether sex differences really exist depends primarily on how we ask the question and to some degree on the context in which the question is asked" (p. 572) (Kring, 2000 offers a similar view). These studies highlight the importance of focusing on the contextual factors that affect emotional responses to situations.

Indeed, many scholars emphasize how crucial the social context is for understanding specific emotional responses in given situations (e.g., Schachter & Singer, 1962; Smith-Lovin, 1995; Lively & Powell, 2006; Thoits, 1989, 1990). In their call for future studies that examine more carefully the meaning, significance, antecedents, and consequences of emotions for women and men, Simon and Nath (2004) emphasize the importance of understanding how both cultural beliefs and contextual factors affect emotional experience and expression. And as a result of their findings that individuals' experience and management of emotion are variable across a wide array of the short list than a male applicant but was less likely to be hired (though these effects were evident only among participants exposed to a female experimenter). This finding of greater short listing but lesser hiring of a female applicant was replicated in a second experiment in which participants viewed a pool of applicants, instead of just one applicant. Participants selected 3 applicants from a pool of 14 to short list and, from the short-listed applicants, selected 1 to hire. Among the female participants, a female applicant was significantly less likely to be hired than placed on the short list. Among the male participants, a female applicant was over-hired relative to the representation of females on the short list. Across all participants, the rate at which a female was hired decreased when participants were made to feel accountable for their decisions.

Taken together, the results of these studies suggest that women are not immune to bias against other women. While we have no definitive explanation for women's harshness toward other women, it may reflect a disdain for self-promoting women (Rudman, 1998), a tendency to view other women as competitors in what is considered a zero-sum game (Staines, Travis, & Jayaratne, 1974), or an expectation that their own credibility will be questioned if they do not judge other women according to strict standards (Broder, 1993).

Probation and Firing Study

While the short listing and hiring studies showed that more evidence of competence was needed to hire a woman than a man, it is also worthwhile to examine how minimum and confirmatory standards affect decisions relevant to diagnosing incompetence. In the short listing and hiring studies, we asked participants how much evidence of competence was needed to confirm that women have ability. We may also ask the obverse: how much evidence of *in*competence is needed to confirm that women *lack* ability? For example, when an individual is employed and that individual's work performance begins to suffer, what kind of evidence is needed before a termination decision is made?

Our prediction here is the mirror opposite of our prediction regarding inferring competence: persons will set *higher minimum* but *lower confirmatory* standards for judging lack of task competence in women relative to men. Poor performance may not be surprising if one expects it. Thus, it may take more evidence of poor performance by a woman than a man to set off alarms or arouse concern. Nevertheless, the amount of evidence needed to

A number of studies confirm the predictions of the classic models of distributive justice regarding the feelings experienced in an unjust situation. Early work on emotional responses using global measures of distress and occasionally employing physiological measures observes higher levels of distress among those suffering injustice (see Hegtvedt & Markovsky, 1995). Later work compares the distinct emotions experienced by those whose outcomes represent under-reward, over-reward, or just rewards. Research on both personal (e.g., Sprecher, 1992) and impersonal (e.g., Hegtvedt, 1990) relationships shows that people suffering disadvantageous injustice feel greater anger and far less satisfaction than those who are fairly rewarded. Results are more ambiguous regarding feelings of guilt among those receiving higher than expected outcomes. As Homans (1974) noted, unless the over-benefit is at another's expense in an interdependent relationship (e.g., Sprecher, 1992; Kuijer, Buunk, Yberma, & Wobbes, 2002), guilt levels rarely vary systematically across reward levels or vary at such low levels to be relatively meaningless (Hegtvedt, 1990).

Recent studies (Krehbiel & Cropanzano, 2000; Weiss, Suckow, & Cropanzano, 1999) show, not surprisingly, that individuals are likely to report higher levels of happiness when they receive favorable versus unfavorable outcomes, regardless of the level of perceived procedural justice characterizing the decision-making process. They also indicate feeling the most anger when they receive an unfavorable outcome as a result of an unfair procedure.[2]

Most of the research on emotional reactions to unjust outcomes involves reports from the individuals who receive the outcome. Several studies, however, pertain to *observers*' perceptions and emotional reactions to another's unfair outcome. Hegtvedt and Killian (1999) examine emotional responses to perceptions of distributive (and procedural) justice in an experimental bargaining situation. Their results support the typical pattern of negative feelings in response to distributive (and procedural) injustices pertaining to one's own situation and also show that such negative responses are less evident with regard to others' injustices. But, subjects who judge the outcome to their partners as unfair report higher levels of guilt. Such a finding is consistent with Homans' theorizing about when people are likely to feel guilty in response to over-reward.

Peters, van den Bos, and Bobocel (2004) show that observers are likely to believe that others are more satisfied with over-reward than they themselves are. This "moral superiority" of observers may account, in part, for the generally low levels of guilt experienced by those who are overpaid. But, by focusing only on projections about how satisfied another actor might be with his or her outcomes, the study does not directly address observers' actual emotional reactions to another's unjust situation. Thus, while these two distinct studies make inroads in the study of emotional responses to injustice, specific extensions on what observers feel and express about unfair outcomes received by others remain warranted.

Gender Differences in Emotional Experiences and Expression in Unjust Situations

Most of the studies that focus on specific emotions in unjust situations typically ignore or control for gender effects while examining the relationship between various contextual factors and emotional experiences and expressions. Researchers control for gender effects because they recognize that the impact of gender on emotional reactions may stem from differences in socialization practices or in expectations regarding intensity and expression of emotions based on stereotypes and/or feeling and display rules (Brody & Hall, 1993; Heise & Calhan, 1995; Thoits, 1989). As a consequence, there is very little theorizing regarding the conditions under which gender differences in emotions may or may not occur as a result of unfair outcomes. In this section, we review the empirical patterns that emerge in the few studies that include gender in addition to the effects of contextual factors on individuals' and observers' experienced and/or expressed emotions in response to their own or another group member's unfair outcomes.

Justice researchers typically focus only on the feelings individuals report in response to an unjust situation, without a comparison to the likelihood of expressing those feelings. Hegtvedt and Killian (1999), in their study of emotional experiences in a bargaining situation, find that men report more intense negative feelings (based on a composite of disappointment, anger, and resentment) and less satisfaction about the final outcome distribution than do women, taking into account situational factors such as group reward level, performance levels of the negotiators, and the bargaining process. Stets (2003), in her study of justice, emotion, and identity, shows that women report more intense feelings of resentment than males when under-rewarded. In addition, when women were persistently under-rewarded, their anger became less intense whereas the intensity of anger experienced by men remained constant over this persistence. There was no gender difference in the experience of satisfaction. And, Sprecher (1986, 1992) demonstrates that women expect to become generally more distressed (measured by subtracting contentment and happiness from anger and depression) and specifically more angry and depressed than men in response to an imaginary disadvantageous inequity in a romantic relationship. She argues that women may be taught from an early age to be sensitive to imbalances in their relationships. As a result, women feel more angry and depressed when there are inequities in their relationships.

In the few studies that compare both the experience and expression of emotion as a result of an unjust outcome, gender is again a control rather than a focal factor. A clear pattern, however, emerges: gender differences arise largely in regard to the intensity of the felt emotion rather than in the expression of the emotion. For example, Johnson, Ford, and Kaufman (2000), in their vignette study of a subordinate/superior conflict in the workplace over pay raise, find that women report anticipating feeling more intense anger, and men report feeling stronger satisfaction with the conflict (even though both men and women feel little satisfaction in the situation), regardless of the dependence relation between the subordinate and the superior and the legitimacy of the superior based on support and endorsement from subordinates. These factors, however, affect the likelihood that both men and women would express their emotions to their superior. Regardless of gender, subordinates who were more dependent upon the superior because they had fewer available alternatives or who had highly endorsed superiors tend to be less likely to express anger and resentment compared to subordinates who were less dependent. Johnson et al. (2000) note that perhaps women anticipated feeling more anger and less satisfaction in this conflict because women may feel that they have fewer opportunities and resources in the workplace than men in general. Similar to Kemper (1990), women in general have less power and status in society than men, and this, along with specific contextual factors, may affect their emotional reactions in the workplace.

In addition, Hegtvedt, Johnson, and Morgan (forthcoming) examine the influence of procedural justice, interpersonal ties, and endorsement of the group decision-maker on observers' emotional experiences and expressions of an unjust outcome, as described in a vignette of a volunteer organization. Taking into account these contextual factors, results show that women report anticipating more anger and resentment and less satisfaction than men in response to an unfair outcome received by another group member. In contrast, with regard to expressing anger and resentment toward the decision-maker, no differences emerge between men and women, controlling for the situational factors. Women, however, express more satisfaction when the decision-maker uses fair rather than unfair procedures whereas men's expression of satisfaction remains independent of procedural justice.

Similarly, Brody (2006), in a vignette study of the effects of gender of victim, procedural justice, and friendship finds that female observers report anticipating feeling less satisfied in response to another's injustice than do male observers. Results also indicate that friendship with a male victim heightens women's reports of anger and resentment whereas for men feelings of anger are most intense when the victim is a female friend rather than a female acquaintance. Thus gender differences arise in the experience of emotion, given various configurations of contextual factors. But, men and women are equally likely to express anger and resentment.

The patterns of results that emerge from these studies indicate overall gender differences in the reported and anticipated intensity of anger, resentment, and satisfaction in unfair situations, regardless of the impact of contextual factors, but very few gender differences in the reported or anticipated expression of these emotions toward the target of the injustice. Both men and women respond similarly to the context when considering the expression of emotions.

Comparing Gender Differences in Emotion: General versus Justice Studies

Clear consistencies emerge from a comparison of findings from general studies on gender differences in reported emotional experience and expression and specific studies focusing on responses to injustice. First, even when taking into account contextual factors, the intensity of reported emotions (in this case, anger, resentment, and satisfaction) varies for men and women. Moreover, these patterns correspond to gender differences in the intensity of emotional experience. Much of the recent research in both general and justice specific studies shows that women are more likely to report greater intensity in anger and resentment, while men are more likely to report more intense positive emotion. Even given this consistency, it is important to recognize that the pattern is, to some extent, subject to the influence of situational factors (Kring, 2000). For example, in the bargaining situation created by Hegtvedt and Killian (1999), men reported experiencing more intense anger than did women.

And, second, it appears that contextual factors often override gender effects on the expression of emotions. Power dependence, legitimacy of the decision-maker, relative status and other factors have a greater impact on emotional expression than does gender per se. Gender-specific cultural beliefs about emotional expressions have less bearing than the specific norms in the situation, typically dictated by salient contextual features.

Interestingly, with the exception of Brody (2006), rarely have either general studies or justice studies considered the effects of the gender combination of the interacting dyad or group members. Theories relying on cultural beliefs about gender and emotions assert patterns based only on the gender of the person experiencing the emotions. And, while Kemper (1978) focuses on the influence of status and power levels for the experience of positive and negative emotions, at least implicitly, he assumes that interacting partners vary in terms of status levels, which may impact feelings. Moreover, the multiple statuses that actors hold may be consistent – like when males occupy authority positions – or inconsistent – such as when females occupy authority positions. In addition, he recognizes that in any situation the actual interaction may create gains or losses in status or power, which also produce emotions. In effect, consideration of the gender of others in a given situation constitutes an additional contextual factor. The emotions that a man or woman experiences in response to the behavior of a gender similar individual (and in that sense, a status equal) may be different from what he or she feels in response to a gender dissimilar person. With regard to the expression of emotions, given cultural beliefs, women may be more likely to display their emotions to other women who are likely to understand feeling intense emotions. And because men may be less familiar with feeling intense emotions and given their assumed status, women may be less likely to express emotions around men. The opposite may be true for men who find it more comfortable to express their emotions around women than around men. Thus the gender similarity or difference between the person experiencing the emotion and the interaction partner whose behavior stimulates the emotion (i.e., the target) requires systematic investigation.

Here we offer such an investigation in the hope of extending the literature in justice and emotions by examining how the gender of the person making the decision about a distribution of outcomes affects gender differences in felt and expressed emotion. Specifically, in addition to key situational factors examined in previous studies (i.e., procedural justice and legitimacy), we explore how gender of the decision-maker and gender similarity or dissimilarity between the decision-maker and the perceiver impact emotional responses to injustice. We draw upon gender-specific cultural beliefs, arguments regarding the effects of structural factors on emotion, and empirical patterns of gender effects to speculate about the impact of both factors on emotional responses.

The Role of Gender of the Decision-Maker in Emotional Responses to Distributive Injustice

As much of the research reviewed above notes, contextual factors matter tremendously in terms of the expression of emotions in response to unjust situations. And those factors also sometimes shape, in conjunction with perceiver's gender, the experience of emotions in such situations. In our prior work (Hegtvedt et. al., forthcoming), we examine how three contextual factors – procedural justice, interpersonal ties, and the legitimacy of the decision-maker – affect male and female observers' emotional responses to an unfair outcome received by a group member. As noted above and described in more depth below, gender effects, along with contextual effects, emerge for the experience of both negative and positive emotions but contextual factors alone affect the expression of negative emotions.

In extending this work, we again examine procedural justice and legitimacy, but we make two additional significant changes. First, we shift our focus from the emotional responses of observers to those of victims. Some research indicates that personal experiences with injustice, rather than simply observations of injustice, produce stronger perceptions of injustice (Kray & Lind, 2002). Emotional responses, as a consequence, are likely to be more intense if people experience the injustice themselves. Second, we include both the gender of the victim of injustice and the gender of the decision-maker. Given stereotypical beliefs about whether men or women are most suited for authority positions, the gender of the decision-maker alone may affect what individuals believe they should feel or express in response to unfair outcomes. In addition, the genders of both the victim and the decision-maker together create combinations of status similarity/ difference or presumed consistency/inconsistency in actors' cultural beliefs about emotions. These combinations form a contextual backdrop that may shape what individuals report feeling toward the decision-maker. Below we briefly define procedural justice and legitimacy, and then we analyze how the gender of the victim and the decision-maker are likely to influence emotional responses to injustice.

Procedural Justice and Legitimacy: Factors Shaping Emotional Responses to Injustice

Procedural justice and the legitimacy of the decision-maker are group-oriented contextual factors (see Hegtvedt, Clay-Warner, & Johnson, 2003; Hegtvedt et al., forthcoming). Procedural justice refers to fairness in the rules underlying decision-making or in the treatment of group members. Leventhal, Karuza, and Fry (1980) suggest that fair decision-making rules involve consistency, the suppression of bias and arbitrariness, the accuracy of information, the potential to make corrections for bad decisions, and the representativeness or "voice" of individuals affected by the decision. Tyler and Lind (1992) also indicate that procedurally fair treatment includes demonstration of respect, neutrality, and trust. The use of fair procedures communicates to individuals that they are valued members of the group, and that communication bolsters the self-esteem that group members seek. A further implication of fair procedures is the emergence of group pride and, in the long run, maintenance of the integrity of the group. Such social rewards may compensate for outcomes that fall short of expectations, leading actors to judge the fairness of their outcomes less severely.

As a consequence of this "fair process effect" (van den Bos, Lind, & Wilke, 2001; van den Bos, 2005), individuals adjust their reactions to the outcome injustice accordingly. Hegtvedt et al. (forthcoming) find that when procedures are fair, observers' feelings and expressions of satisfaction are higher than when procedures are unfair. In contrast, observers' feelings of anger decrease when the decision-maker uses fair procedures. Other studies suggest similar findings with regard to satisfaction and negative emotions (Cohen-Charash & Spector, 2001; Krehbiel & Cropanzano, 2000). Assuming victims experience their unfair outcomes more intensely than observers, we would thus expect that in this study, procedural justice would lead to higher levels of felt and expressed satisfaction but would dampen the experience and expression of negative emotions.

Legitimacy involves people's recognition that they must obey the operating rules of the group, regardless of whether or not they personally believe them to be appropriate (Weber [1924] 1978). Zelditch and Walker (1984, 2000) argue that the views of others in the group enhance the legitimacy of the rules. They identify two collective sources of legitimacy: (1) authorization, which exists when support for the rules comes from people who occupy higher positions within a group; and (2) endorsement, which represents support from individuals of equal or lower status than the focal person. Research shows that endorsement generally has stronger effects than authorization on justice perceptions and emotional reactions within groups (Johnson et al., 2000; Mueller & Landsman, 2004).

Although legitimate decision-makers may receive the benefit of the doubt in situations in which their behavior is inconsistent with what group members might expect, there are also higher expectations for their behavior. To have achieved endorsement indicates that the decision-maker had, in the past, acted in a manner to win the respect, trust, and support of group members. Failure to continue to act in such ways may be met with surprise and disdain. The use of fair procedures is consistent with behavioral expectations and reinforces reasons for why the decision-maker is endorsed.

In contrast, the use of unfair procedures is likely to be surprising and met with irritation. Individuals are likely to wonder why this unexpected behavior occurred (van den Bos, Bruins, Wilke, & Dronkert, 1999) and may readily imagine other possible procedures that the decision-maker could have used (Folger, 1986). Such wondering may create a backlash against the decision-maker, which intensifies negative emotions. And, ironically, lack of endorsement coupled with the use of unfair procedures may be met with less concern because expectations of trust and respect are weaker.

Findings from Hegtvedt et al. (forthcoming) show that observers feel the most resentment and frustration and the least satisfaction when endorsed decision-makers use unfair procedures and produces unfair outcomes. Such conditions also elicit the greatest expression of anger, resentment, and frustration in response to another group member's injustice. Negative emotions are the least intense, in contrast, when an endorsed decision-maker uses fair procedures and thereby meets behavioral expectations. We expect that the emotional experiences of individuals who personally suffer injustice are likely to be similarly shaped by the joint effects of procedural justice and endorsement, with an endorsed authority who uses unfair procedures eliciting the most negative feelings and one who uses fair procedures attenuating those reactions. Although in Hegtvedt et al. (forthcoming) observers' emotional displays follow the same pattern as their experiences, the same may not be so for victims of injustice. As noted below, situational factors may increase what the victim perceives as social costs for expressing negative emotions. For example, despite feeling angry toward an endorsed decision-maker who uses unfair procedures, individuals who directly experience unfair outcomes may fear repercussions from peers if they voice their anger.

As noted above, in the study reported here we focus on whether the gender of the injustice victim and the gender of the decision-maker independently or jointly affect the feelings and expressions of those experiencing distributive injustice. The gender of the decision-maker, alone or in combination with the gender of the victim, constitutes an additional contextual factor that may interact with the group-oriented factors of procedural justice and legitimacy.

The Effects of Gender on Emotional Responses to Injustice

We circumscribe our hypotheses to the following conditions. First, the situation pertains to interaction that takes place in a hierarchical organization. Second, the focal instance involves a distributive disadvantage, which may be described objectively as unfair to the perceiver. Third, the individual is embedded in the group and thus would expect continuing relationships with other group members, both peers and authorities. And fourth, the distributive disadvantage created by the authority is the first instance of such behavior on the authority's part.

Emotional Experiences

Consistent with the literature on gender and emotions and previous findings (e.g., Hegtvedt et al., forthcoming; Johnson et al., 2000), we anticipate that women compared to men will report more intense anticipated feelings of anger and resentment, and less intense satisfaction, when controlling for the situational factors. Hypothesis 1 captures this main effect of gender:

Hypothesis 1. Women are more likely than men to anticipate experiencing more intense anger, resentment, and dissatisfaction in response to the distributive injustice.

In addition, given the presumed connection between procedures and outcomes, we argue that the use of fair procedures is likely to be more salient than other situational factors. This suggests that when fair procedures are used, there will be no effect of gender of the decision-maker alone or in conjunction with endorsement on emotions. As in past research, the use of fair procedures should attenuate negative emotions and enhance positive ones (see Cohen-Charash & Spector, 2001). Thus we predict a main effect for procedural justice on emotional experiences:

Hypothesis 2. Procedural justice will be negatively related to an individual's experience of negative emotions and positively related to the experience of positive emotions in response to a distributive injustice.

Assuming that procedural justice exerts the predicted effects, individuals are less likely to feel irritated or distressed, which may inhibit any further contemplation of the situation. In contrast, when procedures are unfair, people may be more likely to consider why the decision-maker acted in an unexpected manner, and one which resulted in unfair outcomes to the perceiver him- or herself. It is under the condition of *unfair procedures*, that the effects of endorsement and gender of the decision-maker on emotions are likely to be most pronounced. Those effects, moreover, may stem from the extent to which the decision-maker's behavior appears to be consistent with expectations for men and women in authority positions.

Hegtvedt et al. (forthcoming) demonstrate the impact of the coupling of endorsement and unfair procedures. An endorsed decision-maker who uses unfair procedures produces the greatest resentment and the least satisfaction among observers, compared to all other combinations of the factors. The use of unfair procedures is inconsistent with what is expected of legitimate authorities and thus the combination results in strong emotions. Consideration of gender of the decision-maker adds another layer of expectations to be met by the authority.

Specifically, we note that the gender of the decision-maker carries with it expectations for behavior. Although women have made inroads into managerial positions, men (particularly white men) still have greater access to authority positions in organizations and wider span of control in their positions (McGuire & Reskin, 1993; Reskin & McBrier, 2000; Reskin & Padavic, 1994; Smith, 2002). Thus, in general, group members may feel more familiar with having a man as the decision-maker. Expectations for how the male authority will behave in terms of enacting his role obligations are likely to be clearer than for how a female authority will behave. In addition, male authorities may be perceived as more likely to be endorsed than female authorities. Thus expectations are likely to be strongest for an endorsed, male decision-maker compared to other combinations of the gender of the decision-maker and his or her legitimacy. When an endorsed male decision-maker throws into disarray expectations by using unfair procedures, individuals are likely to be both surprised and irritated. In contrast, given that expectations are less clear for female decision-makers in general and endorsed ones in particular, the violation of expectations to use fair procedures may have weaker effects. In effect, the backlash in terms of emotional responses is greater for endorsed male than female authorities. Thus we predict that under conditions of unfair procedures, there will be a gender of the decision-maker by endorsement interaction effect.

Hypothesis 3a. Under conditions of procedural injustice, when the decision-maker is a man, endorsement will be positively related to the individual's experience of anger and resentment and negatively related to satisfaction in response to the distributive injustice.

Hypothesis 3b. Under conditions of procedural injustice, when the decision-maker is a woman, endorsement will be negatively related to an individual's experience of anger and resentment and positively related to satisfaction.

In addition, the combination of the gender of the decision-maker and that of the victim of injustice may affect emotional experiences – at least when unfair procedures are used. Again, the fairness of the procedures is likely to be a more salient consideration than the gender match between the decision-maker and the victim. When a decision-maker acts in a procedurally just way, whether one detects similarity to the authority is a moot issue.

In contrast, *when procedures are unfair*, victims' responses may be affected by the extent to which they perceive themselves as similar to the decision-maker. When the individual is similar to the decision-maker in regard to gender, his or her feelings may reflect their shared cultural assumptions about how men and women should feel. This may be particularly true for women for whom cultural expectations suggest more intense feelings. The gender similarity may also lead to expectations of similar behavior and trust. If a similar decision-maker distributes outcomes unfairly, using unfair procedures, victims of the injustice may feel "slighted" because of the violations of their expectations, leading to an erosion of trust and behavioral expectations. In such cases, clearly the decision-maker has failed to act in a manner consistent with what the perceiver anticipates. As a consequence individuals who are similar to the decision-maker will feel more intense anger and resentment and less satisfaction than when the decision-maker is dissimilar in terms of gender. Ironically, failure by a dissimilar other to use fair procedures may be attributed to the dissimilarity, which corresponds with weaker expectations of trust and less informed behavioral expectations. Thus we predict an interaction effect between the gender of the decision-maker and the gender of the injustice victim under the condition of procedural injustice such that:

Hypothesis 4. When the decision-maker uses unfair procedures, gender similarity between the decision-maker and the victim of the distributive injustice will exacerbate the individual's intensity of anger and resentment and weaken the intensity of satisfaction, whereas gender dissimilarity will attenuate emotional experiences.

Emotional Expressions
Even if individuals experience emotions in response to receiving an unfair outcome, they may not show those feelings. Many work situations discourage the display of negative emotions in particular (Heise & Calhan, 1995). Situational circumstances are likely to dictate the social costs associated with the expression of these emotions. To the extent that individuals fear social repercussions or sanctions if they express their feelings of anger or

resentment, they are more likely to suppress displaying those emotions. Because few social costs accompany expressions of satisfaction with an unfair outcome, situational factors are unlikely to shape those expressions. In addition, we suggest that situational factors (and their relation to associated costs) outweigh the importance of the gender of the victim in their effects on emotional expressions, which may account for the findings from previous studies demonstrating that, unlike the situational factors, gender of the victim exerts no effects on the likelihood of expressing satisfaction, anger, and resentment (e.g., Hegtvedt et al., forthcoming; Johnson et al., 2000). Our hypotheses below thus pertain only to contextual factors – procedural justice and the legitimacy and gender of the decision-maker – that may be linked to social costs associated with the expression of anger or resentment.

As noted above, the use of fair procedures is a key mechanism by which authorities convey to other group members that they are valued members of the group (Tyler & Lind, 1992). Those feelings help to maintain individual self-esteem as well as group pride, which may underlie group integrity. Authorities who use fair procedures cement the integrity of the group, which individuals may be wary of disrupting through the expression of negative emotions about their outcomes. In contrast, the failure of an authority to use fair procedures undermines group integrity. Individuals may be more likely to express their disdain for their unfair outcomes if the authority has already acted in a manner that threatens the group's well-being. In effect, expression of negative emotions carries greater costs when the decision-maker has employed fair procedures than when he or she has used unfair procedures. Thus we predict a main effect of procedural justice:

Hypothesis 5. Procedural justice will be negatively related to an individual's expression of negative emotions.

Endorsement of the decision-maker suggests attitudinal similarity among group members. The costs associated with expressing negative emotions when procedural justice exists may overwhelm any potential impact of endorsement on emotional expressions. But when the decision-maker uses unfair procedures, the legitimacy of the decision-maker may bring into play consideration of additional issues. Johnson et al. (2000) show that in a work situation, subordinates were less likely to express negative emotions when the authority was endorsed than when the authority was not endorsed. The lack of endorsement may have minimized fear of sanctions from peers. Hegtvedt et al. (forthcoming), however, demonstrate that observers express greater anger (and resentment) when an endorsed decision-maker in a voluntary group uses unfair procedures. Observers seemed to view the inconsistency between support for a decision-maker and the decision-maker's use of unfair procedures as an affront that needs to be addressed. Failure to use fair procedures in the long run affects the functioning of the group – and the rewards that others might obtain from it. As a result, victims of injustice may believe that other group members would be less likely to exert sanctions on them when they express negative emotions because to have a legitimated authority act in an unfair manner is also not in their interests. Victims of injustice, then, may be compelled to let the decision-maker know how they feel in order to protect others from future costs. Thus, predicting a procedural justice by endorsement interaction effect, we suggest:

Hypothesis 6. When the decision-maker uses fair procedures, endorsement will have no effect on the expression of negative emotions. When the decision-maker uses unfair procedures, endorsement has a positive effect on the expression of negative emotions.

Finally, the gender of the decision-maker may condition whether individuals display their anger or resentment. To the extent that individuals presume women to be more skilled at handling other people's emotions owing to their empathetic and nurturing tendencies (e.g., Feingold, 1994; Zammuner, 2000), injustice victims may not worry about suffering repercussions for expressing their emotions. Indeed expectations are less clear for the behavior of female authorities and people are likely to have had less experience with them. The empathetic nature of women and the weaker expectations reduce the potential costs of expressing negative emotions. In contrast, to display negative emotions toward a male authority figure may engender greater costs, largely owing to expectations associated with male authorities, as discussed above. Thus we predict a main effect for the gender of the decision-maker:

Hypothesis 7. Individuals are more likely to express negative emotions when the decision-maker is a woman than when the decision-maker is a man.

STUDY METHODS

Overview

To test our hypotheses, we created a set of vignettes about a distributively unjust situation. The vignettes describe a decision-making situation in a fictitious volunteer organization (National Coalition to End Cancer or NCEC). We asked subjects to imagine themselves as NCEC volunteers. From the vignette, the subjects learn that the decision-maker fails to choose them, despite their qualifications, to be on a prestigious fundraising committee. Thus the subject assumes the role of the "victim" of the unjust decision.

Using a 2 × 2 × 2 factorial design, we manipulated the decision-maker's gender (Joanne/Jim), use of fair/unfair decision-making procedures, and level of endorsement for the decision-maker (high versus low). We expected that these variables would directly, or in combination with one another, impact subjects' emotional reactions to this unfair situation.

Subjects

Subjects were recruited from introductory and other lower division sociology classes at a large southeastern university. They were told that the purpose of the study was to investigate organizational dynamics. They were asked to spend 15–20 min reading a one-page story and answering questions regarding their perceptions and potential responses to the situation as well as the manipulation checks. Subjects were assured that participation was strictly voluntary and was not tied to their grade for the course. One hundred thirty-eight students (74 males, 54 females) completed one of the eight randomly distributed vignettes. Cell sizes ranged 14–19.

Vignette Manipulations

We manipulated the decision-maker's gender by indicating in half of the vignettes that Jim was the decision-maker and in the remaining vignettes that Joanne held that position. Gender appropriate pronouns were used throughout the vignette.

Procedural justice was operationalized through the contents of an email sent to the subject from the decision-maker. In the email, Jim (Joanne) explained how he (she) chose members for the fundraising committee. The procedures varied in terms of consistency, bias suppression, and informational accuracy (Leventhal et al., 1980). In the high procedural justice condition, the decision-maker wrote "I know that Directors in the past have followed NCEC guidelines, so I did too. I read all of the applications thoroughly. I created a checklist so I could accurately compare the applicants. Ultimately, I based my decision on this information, not what I already knew about the applicants. I hope you try again next year." In contrast, in the low procedural justice condition, the decision-maker says "I know that Directors in the past have followed NCEC guidelines. This year, however, I did something different. I read some applications thoroughly and skimmed others. I created a checklist so I could compare the applicants but, ultimately, I based my decision on what I already knew about them. You can try again next year."

To manipulate endorsement, we indicated whether or not other group members believed the decision-maker to be the right (or appropriate) person for the job and whether they supported him (her) in the role (Johnson & Ford, 1996). Thus, subjects in the high endorsement condition read "The other volunteers think Jim (Joanne) is the right person for the job and fully support him (her) as the Director of Fundraising." In contrast, low endorsement was conveyed by "The other volunteers question whether Jim (Joanne) is the right person for the job and don't fully support him (her) as Director of Fundraising."

Questionnaire Measures

To assess the extent to which subjects felt satisfaction, anger, and resentment after hearing that they were not selected for the committee, we asked subjects to indicate on a scale ranging from 1 (not at all) to 9 (a great deal) how much they felt these emotions.

We measured emotional expressions in a similar manner. Subjects were asked "How likely would you be to express [to the decision-maker] the following emotions about the situation?" Again, satisfaction, anger, and resentment were assessed. Answers ranged from 1 (not at all likely) to 9 (very likely). Table 1 provides the means for these feelings and expressions.

Other questions constituted manipulation checks for procedural justice and endorsement. To test the adequacy of our procedural justice manipulation, we asked subjects to rate on 1 (not at all) to 9 (a great deal) point scales how arbitrary, biased, and inconsistent the decision-maker seemed in the selection of the committee members. To examine the endorsement manipulation, subjects indicated on similar 1–9 point scales whether or not other volunteers agreed that the decision-maker was the right person for the job and whether or not they supported him or her as the Director of

Table 1. Means and Standard Deviations of Emotional Experiences and the Likelihood of Emotional Expressions.

Dependent Variable	Mean	Standard Deviation
Emotional experiences		
Feel satisfied	2.47	1.52
Feel angry	5.90	2.09
Feel resentful	5.92	2.11
Emotional expressions		
Express satisfaction	1.98	1.42
Express anger	4.73	2.41
Express resentment	4.63	2.52

Notes: $N = 132$. Scales range from 1 to 9.

Fundraising. Analyses confirm the success of the manipulations by indicating that only the corresponding condition produced a significant effect.

In addition, we checked to make sure that subjects thought of themselves as qualified for the committee, assuming that such a belief was necessary in order to conceive of not being selected as distributively unjust. On average, subjects rated themselves as qualified ($M = 7.96$ on a 9 point scale). And, finally, several questions with 1–9 point response scales allowed us to assess the success of the role-play method. Most subjects found the situation easy to understand ($M = 3.11$, where 1 = very easy), felt somewhat involved ($M = 5.53$), perceived the situation as realistic ($M = 7.19$), and were confident that their responses reflected how they would be likely to respond emotionally ($M = 7.33$).

Analyses

We used analysis of variance (ANOVA) to test our hypotheses regarding the effects of gender and the contextual factors on reported experiences and likelihood of the expressions of emotions. For significant interaction effects, we used simple means effects to determine the patterns of the interactions (Keppel & Wickens, 2004).[3]

RESULTS

Emotional Experiences

Hypotheses 1–4 predict varying effects for gender and contextual factors on anticipated emotional experiences. Table 2 shows the pattern of results

Table 2. F-Statistics for ANOVA Results of the Effects of Procedural Justice (PJ), Endorsement (E), Gender of Decision-Maker (GenderDM), and Gender of Respondent (GenderRes) on the Experience of Satisfaction, Anger, and Resentment.

	Satisfaction	Anger	Resentment
PJ	12.14***	3.65*	.52
	(.0007)	(.0587)	(.4717)
E	0.00	.24	.26
	(.9864)	(.6282)	(.6105)
GenderDM	0.00	.00	.00
	(.9770)	(.9451)	(.9695)
GenderRes	1.11	.04	.75
	(.2944)	(.8426)	(.3893)
PJ × E	1.95	1.12	.19
	(.1656)	(.2918)	(.6654)
PJ × GenderDM	0.24	5.80**	1.24
	(.6260)	(.0177)	(.2673)
PJ × GenderRes	0.46	.00	.87
	(.5006)	(.9779)	(.3519)
E × GenderDM	0.20	1.28	.20
	(.6557)	(.2608)	(.6590)
E × GenderRes	4.71*	1.38	.03
	(.0321)	(.2429)	(.8675)
GenderDM × GenderRes	0.72	.02	.18
	(.3969)	(.8975)	(.6712)
E × PJ × GenderDM	6.37**	.62	.10
	(.0130)	(.4345)	(.7523)
E × PJ × GenderRes	7.05**	.60	1.40
	(.0090)	(.4394)	(.2395)
E × PJ × GenderDM × GenderRes	.19	.18	.03
	(.9030)	(.9088)	(.9929)
R^2	.2288	.1040	.0544
N	131	130	130

Notes: Numbers in parentheses are *p*-values. Gender is coded: 0 = male, 1 = female.
*$p \leq .05$ (Two-tailed tests).
**$p \leq .01$ (Two-tailed tests).
***$p \leq .001$ (Two-tailed tests).

bearing upon these hypotheses. Hypothesis 1 suggests that women are more likely than men to anticipate feeling anger, resentment, and satisfaction in response to distributive injustice. No main effect for gender of the respondent emerges to confirm this hypothesis. Two unpredicted interaction effects, however, emerge involving gender of the respondent and other situational factors.

The two-way interaction effect between respondent's gender and endorsement shows no effect of gender when the decision-maker is endorsed, and an effect opposite to that expected when the decision-maker lacks endorsement. Table 3 illustrates that male subjects feel more satisfaction ($M=2.82$) than female subjects ($M=2.03$) when the decision-maker lacks endorsement ($F=4.82$, $<.05$). A three-way interaction effect with procedural justice, however, qualifies this effect. Table 4 shows that the effects of endorsement and procedural justice differ for male and female respondents. For males the effects of procedural justice are strongest when the decision-maker lacks endorsement ($M=2.26$ for low procedural justice and $M=3.35$ for high procedural justice; $F=4.34$, $p<.05$). For females, the effects of procedural justice are strongest when the decision-maker is endorsed ($M=1.47$ for low procedural justice and $M=3.54$ for high procedural justice; $F=15.87$, $p<.001$). In addition, endorsement seems to enhance women's feelings of satisfaction when decision-makers use fair procedures ($M=2.06$ for low endorsement and $M=3.54$ for high endorsement; $p<.05$). For female

Table 3. Means for Endorsement × Gender of Respondent Interaction Effect on the Experience of Satisfaction.

Endorsement	Gender of Respondent	
	Male	Female
Low	2.82	2.03
High	2.49	2.43

Table 4. Means for Endorsement × Procedural Justice × Gender of Respondent Interaction Effect on the Experience of Satisfaction.

Endorsement	Procedural Justice and Gender of Respondent			
	Male		Female	
	Low PJ	High PJ	Low PJ	High PJ
Low	2.26	3.35	2	2.06
High	2.31	2.59	1.47	3.54

respondents, then, it is the combination of procedural justice and legitimacy that increases feelings of satisfaction thereby buffering the negative feelings that could result from an unfair outcome. For males, fair procedures enhance satisfaction only when the decision-maker lacks legitimacy.

Procedural justice, as predicted by Hypothesis 2, exerts a direct effect on feelings of satisfaction and anger. As expected, when the decision-maker uses fair procedures, feelings of anger are attenuated ($M = 5.59$) and feelings of satisfaction are enhanced ($M = 2.84$), compared to when the decision-maker uses unfair procedures ($M = 6.28$ for anger and $M = 2.03$ for satisfaction). Procedural justice, however, does not affect anticipated feelings of resentment.

The effects of gender of the decision-maker and endorsement are more complex, predicted to occur only under conditions of procedural injustice. Hypotheses 3a and 3b focus on the interaction between gender of the decision-maker and the legitimacy of the decision-maker when unfair procedures are used. Hypothesis 3a predicts that endorsement will be positively related to the experience of negative emotions and negatively related to satisfaction in response to distributive injustice when the decision-maker is a man whereas Hypothesis 3b predicts the opposite pattern for when the decision-maker is a woman. Results, however, do not confirm the predicted three-way interaction. Although a few significant effects emerge, the pattern of findings varies by the emotion. No factor, however, affects anticipated feelings of resentment.

For anger, no effects of endorsement are evident. Rather, a two-way interaction between gender of the decision-maker and procedural justice is significant. Results in Table 5 indicate that for male decision-makers, procedural justice indeed buffers feelings of anger. The significant simple main effect indicates that respondents get more angry at a male decision-maker who uses unfair procedures ($M = 6.71$) compared to one who uses fair procedures ($M = 5.18$; $F = 9.68$, $p < .01$). In contrast, for female

Table 5. Means for Procedural Justice × Gender of Decision-Maker Interaction Effect on the Experience of Anger.

Procedural Justice	Gender of Decision-Maker	
	Male	Female
Low	6.71	5.90
High	5.18	6.00

Table 6. Means for Endorsement × Procedural Justice × Gender of Decision-Maker Interaction Effect on the Experience of Satisfaction.

Endorsement	Procedural Justice and Gender of Decision-Maker			
	Male		Female	
	Low PJ	High PJ	Low PJ	High PJ
Low	2.5	2.5	2	3
High	1.4	3.21	2.29	2.59

decision-makers, victims anticipate feeling the same level of anger, regardless of the fairness of the procedures used.

For satisfaction, some results (Table 6) confirm the pattern expected in Hypothesis 3a regarding the backlash effect of having an endorsed male decision-maker use unfair procedures. When the decision-maker is male, victims feel the least satisfaction under conditions of high endorsement and low procedural justice ($M = 1.4$) and the most satisfaction when the endorsed decision-maker uses fair procedures ($M = 3.21$). The simple main effect of procedural justice within high endorsement is significant ($F = 11.16, p < .01$). The lack of endorsement tempers feelings of dissatisfaction resulting when procedures are unfair. The simple main effect of endorsement within low procedural justice is also significant ($F = 8.13, p < .01$). In contrast, results regarding female decision-makers do not demonstrate the backlash effect and thus provide some support, albeit weak, for Hypothesis 3b. The pattern of means in Table 6 shows that endorsement does not affect the intensity of anticipated feelings of satisfaction when unfair procedures are used by the female decision-maker. The means do suggest, however, that the use of fair procedures enhances satisfaction when the female decision-maker lacks endorsement. The means for feelings of satisfaction across levels of procedural justice ($M = 2.0$ for low procedural justice and $M = 3.0$ for high procedural justice) when the female decision-maker lacks endorsement produce a significant simple main effect ($F = 4.04, p = .05$).

To test Hypothesis 4, we created a factor that combined male–male dyads with female–female dyads to represent gender similarity and combined opposite gender dyads (i.e., male decision-maker and female victim with female decision-maker and male victim) to indicate gender dissimilarity. We predicted that when procedures were unfair, gender similarity would exacerbate negative feelings and intensify satisfaction. Results, however, indicate no significant effects for the gender combinations variable, alone or in conjunction with other contextual factors.

Emotional Expressions

Table 7 presents findings pertaining to the likelihood that subjects would express their emotions to the decision-maker. No effects emerge for gender

Table 7. *F*-Statistics for ANOVA Results of the Effects of Procedural Justice (PJ), Endorsement (E), Gender of Decision-Maker (GenderDM), and Gender of Respondent (GenderRes) on the Expression of Satisfaction, Anger, and Resentment.

	Satisfaction	Anger	Resentment
PJ	5.75*	5.01*	3.85*
	(.0181)	(.0271)	(.0522)
E	.01	.02	.40
	(.9053)	(.8953)	(.5292)
GenderDM	.13	.08	.15
	(.7197)	(.7734)	(.7018)
GenderRes	1.51	2.20	.24
	(.2221)	(.1409)	(.6252)
PJ × E	.07	.32	.22
	(.7991)	(.5735)	(.6409)
PJ × GenderDM	.72	4.02*	1.92
	(.3983)	(.0473)	(.1691)
PJ × GenderRes	.23	1.86	.82
	(.6346)	(.1752)	(.3660)
E × GenderDM	.62	.00	.01
	(.4342)	(.9687)	(.9222)
E × GenderRes	.01	1.91	1.03
	(.9181)	(.1699)	(.3130)
GenderDM × GenderRes	.58	.01	1.47
	(.4469)	(.9265)	(.2275)
E × PJ × GenderDM	2.76	.00	.48
	(.0992)	(.9911)	(.4907)
E × PJ × GenderRes	.03	.20	.34
	(.8705)	(.6582)	(.5602)
E × PJ × GenderDM × GenderRes	.42	.33	.35
	(.7415)	(.8011)	(.7922)
R^2	.0987	.1159	.0934
N	131	131	130

Notes: Numbers in parentheses are *p*-values. Gender is coded: 0 = male, 1 = female.
*$p < .05$ (Two-tailed tests).

Table 8. Means for Procedural Justice × Gender of Decision-Maker Interaction Effect on the Expression of Anger.

Procedural Justice	Gender of Decision-Maker	
	Male	Female
Low	5.75	4.66
High	4.08	4.66

of the respondent, as expected. Hypothesis 5 predicts a main effect for procedural justice, which the results confirm. When the decision-maker uses fair procedures, in response to distributive injustice individuals express more satisfaction ($M = 2.27$) and less anger ($M = 4.36$) and resentment ($M = 4.27$) compared to when the decision-maker uses unfair procedures ($M = 1.63$ for satisfaction, 5.17 for anger, and 5.07 for resentment).

Hypothesis 6 suggests a procedural justice by endorsement interaction effect. The expected pattern indicates that when unfair procedures are used, endorsement will have no effect but when fair procedures are used, individuals will be more likely to express negative emotions when the decision-maker is endorsed. Results, however, fail to confirm the prediction. In fact, endorsement of the decision-maker has no effect at all, in combination with any other factor, on the likelihood of expressing emotions.

Similarly, the predicted main effect for the gender of the decision-maker (Hypothesis 7) is also non-significant. What does emerge, however, is an interaction effect between procedural justice and the gender of the decision-maker on the expression of anger. Means in Table 8 show that the likelihood of expressing anger toward female decision-makers does not vary at all by the fairness of the procedures. In contrast, fair procedures has a significant simple main effect on the expression of anger toward male decision-makers ($F = 9.38$, $p < .01$), with means indicating that victims express the least anger toward a male decision-maker who uses fair procedures ($M = 4.08$) and the greatest anger toward the male decision-maker who uses unfair procedures ($M = 5.75$).

DISCUSSION

Overall, in both general studies of gender and emotion and in specific justice studies, gender of the individual is more likely to affect the reported intensity of emotions than the expression of these emotions. Similar to these studies, our study shows that gender of the respondent, in conjunction with several of the contextual factors, affects one of the emotional experiences, and exerts no significant effect on the likelihood of the expression of the emotions. Specifically, gender of the respondent, procedural justice, and endorsement had complex effects on the experience of satisfaction as a result of an unjust outcome. For men, procedural justice influences experience of satisfaction only when the decision-maker is not endorsed. They feel most satisfied when the decision-maker is not endorsed, but uses fair procedures and the least satisfied when he or she is not endorsed and uses unfair procedures. For women, procedural justice impacts satisfaction only under the condition of high endorsement. They feel more satisfied when the decision-maker is endorsed and uses fair procedures than when he or she uses unfair procedures. Gender of the respondent, however, does not affect the likelihood of the expression of satisfaction toward the decision-maker – only procedural justice has a significant effect. Also similar to many previous studies on gender and emotional expression, gender of the respondent did not affect expression of the negative emotions – only contextual factors have an impact on their likelihood of expression.

Inconsistent with previous research in justice and some of the general studies, however, gender did not impact the experience of anger. In previous justice studies, women reported more intense feelings of anger than men, regardless of the contextual factors. This inconsistency may be a result of the addition of the contextual factor – gender of the decision-maker. Both men and women reported more angry feelings toward a male decision-maker who uses unfair procedures than toward one who uses fair procedures. They also reported the same level of anger toward the female decision-maker regardless of whether or not she used fair or unfair procedures. A similar pattern emerges for the expression of anger. Victims, regardless of gender, reported that they would be likely to express the most anger toward a male decision-maker who uses unfair procedures and the least anger toward a male decision-maker who uses fair procedures. In this case, procedural justice seems to matter more when the decision-maker is a man than when the decision-maker is a woman.

Gender of the decision-maker also has a complex effect on experience of satisfaction. With male decision-makers, victims feel the least satisfied when the decision-maker is endorsed yet uses unfair procedures, thereby violating expectations of endorsed authorities, and the most satisfied when he is endorsed and uses fair procedures. With female decision-makers, victims are most satisfied when the decision-maker is not endorsed but uses fair procedures, and the least satisfied when she is not endorsed and uses unfair procedures. Clearly, gender of the decision-maker matters for respondents' reported experience of satisfaction and anger. But admittedly, its effect is not entirely clear when looking at both emotions. We address this issue in the conclusion.

We also examined whether gender similarity between the victim and the decision-maker affects emotional experiences, but this contextual variable had no effect on any emotional reaction. Gender of decision-maker and gender of the victim had separate effects, but not the gender combination of actors in a situation. We are cautious about our lack of significant results, however, because this is a first attempt to examine this contextual variable.

CONCLUSION

Our findings show that the gender of the decision-maker (a contextual variable) has a greater effect on emotional experiences and expressions than the gender of the victim, at least in this study. Specifically, gender of the decision-maker, in conjunction with procedural justice, affects the experience and expression of anger and, in conjunction with procedural justice and endorsement, affects the experience of satisfaction. Gender of the victim, in conjunction with procedural justice and endorsement, only affects the experience of satisfaction.

Importantly, however, our reasoning about how and why the gender of the decision-maker affects these emotional responses needs further study. Our most surprising result is that victims report the likelihood of feeling the same level of anger in response to receiving an unjust outcome from a female decision-maker, *regardless of the fairness of procedures used.* On the other hand, when the decision-maker is a man, victims feel less angry when the decision-maker uses fair than unfair procedures. Procedural justice buffers somewhat the feelings of anger, but only for male decision-makers. And this same pattern holds for the likelihood of expressing anger toward the decision-maker. The fair process effect suggests that social rewards gained by the use of fair procedures compensate for outcomes that fall short of expectations, leading actors to judge the fairness of their outcomes less severely. Based on this effect, we would assume that victims of an unjust outcome will be less angry when fair procedures are used than when unfair procedures are used, regardless of the gender of the decision-maker, but this did not occur. Perhaps respondents expected male decision-makers to be more likely to use fair rather than unfair procedures because they are more likely to occupy positions of authority, compared to female decision-makers. As a result, when these expectations were not met, procedural justice had a greater impact on feelings of anger.

Future studies should continue to examine the effects of gender of the victim and the gender of the decision-maker on emotional responses in specific contexts. Following up on this study in which victims respond to an unfair outcome (failing to be appointed to a prestigious committee), one future investigation might compare emotional reactions to such an injustice in volunteer and for-profit business settings. It could be that perceptions of the value of the outcome may vary by men and women across contexts. Men may be more likely than women to value outcomes in a business setting where the claims for status may be higher than in a volunteer setting. Volunteer work is optional and therefore may be associated with lower status than paid work in for-profit settings where workers are paid for their labor. Women, on the other hand, may perceive the appointment as equally valuable across contexts because women may be expected to work in volunteer settings on average more so than men and also value the work equally in both contexts, regardless of compensation. As a result, this may affect emotional reactions to unfair outcomes. Emotional experiences in specific contexts may vary by gender if the value of the unfair outcome also varies by gender.

A second avenue for further study is to examine the effect of contextual factors and gender on emotional reactions to different types of outcomes (e.g., pay versus appointments) within the same organizational setting. Once again, the value of the outcome may vary for men and women that in turn may affect the experience of emotions. Consistent with previous research, however, we also suggest that expression of these emotions will not be affected by the gender of the victim, but rather the contextual variables of procedural justice and endorsement.

Third, given that gender of the decision-maker is important to emotions in our study, we need to further explore the effects of this contextual variable, along with gender of the victim, in contexts where we vary the type of outcome (pay versus appointment) and the type of organization (volunteer versus for-profit). We could examine whether the same interaction pattern between gender of the decision-maker and procedural justice holds in contexts in which the outcome is pay in a business setting versus an outcome of an appointment in a volunteer setting. For reasons similar to those stated above, this pattern may vary, given the possible gender differences in perceived value of the unfair outcome and the organizational setting.

Given the inconsistency between cultural beliefs about gender differences in emotional experiences and expressions and the empirical evidence found in general studies of emotion, our study, like other recent studies, heeds the call to examine specific emotions in specific contexts. In our study we find that gender differences in the experience and expression of the specific emotions of anger, resentment, and satisfaction in our particular justice situation are very few. Rather, contextual factors, including the gender of the decision-maker, have stronger effects on emotional responses than gender. Similar to scholars in emotions, we believe that further examination of specific emotions in specific contexts will further the understanding of the conditions under which gender differences in emotions will emerge.

NOTES

1. Hochschild (1979) argues that these rules underlie emotional management. When individuals feel something different than that expected on the basis of feeling rules, they may engage in behaviors to create a more appropriate feeling or change in degree the emotion that they are feeling. Research demonstrates the strategies people use to bring their feelings in line with the appropriate feeling and expression rules and the consequences of such strategies for well-being, especially in work situations (e.g., Erickson & Ritter, 2001; Hochschild, 1983; Smith & Kleinman, 1989).

2. See Vermunt and Steensma (2005) for a discussion of the relationship between justice and stress in the organizational justice literature. The authors touch on emotional reactions (e.g., stress and depression) to distributive (and procedural) justice. They, however, do not focus nor do they note any gender differences in emotional experiences.

3. Tables of means based on the full factorial design for each emotional experience and expression is available from the authors upon request.

ACKNOWLEDGMENTS

We thank the editor, Shelley Correll, for her insightful comments on an earlier version. We are also indebted to Nancy Bliwise for her helpful advice regarding the analyses. Finally, we are grateful to Lynn Chen, Kyle Valenti, Angela Choi, and Monica Yau for their invaluable assistance on the development of the vignette study.

REFERENCES

Adams, J. S. (1965). Inequity in social exchange. *Advances in Experimental Social Psychology*, 2, 267-299.

Alexander, M. G., & Wood, W. (2000). Women, men and positive emotions: A social role interpretation. In: A. H. Fischer (Ed.), *Gender and emotion: Social psychological perspectives* (pp. 189–210). New York: Cambridge University Press.

van den Bos, K. (2005). What is responsible for the fair process effect? In: J. Greenberg & J. A. Colquitt (Eds), *Handbook of organizational justice* (pp. 273–300). London: Lawrence Erlbaum Associates.

van den Bos, K., Bruins, J., Wilke, H. A. M., & Dronkert, E. (1999). Sometimes procedures have nice aspects: On the psychology of the fair process effect. *Journal of Personality and Social Psychology, 77,* 324–336.

van den Bos, K., Lind, E. A., & Wilke, H. A. M. (2001). The psychology of procedural and distributive justice viewed from the perspective of Fairness Heuristic Theory. In: R. Cropanzano (Ed.), *Justice in the workplace* (pp. 49–66). Mahwah, NJ: Lawrence Erlbaum.

Brody, L. M. (2006). *Justice for all: Perceptions of and responses to others' experiences of injustice.* Unpublished manuscript, Emory University, Atlanta.

Brody, L. R. (1985). Gender differences in emotional development: A review of theories and research. *Journal of Personality, 53,* 102–149.

Brody, L. R. (1996). Gender, emotional expression, and parent-child boundaries. In: R. D. Ablon, D. Brown, E. Khantzina & J. Mack (Eds), *Emotion: Interdisciplinary perspectives* (pp. 139–170). Mahwah, NJ: Lawrence Erlbaum.

Brody, L. R. (2000). The socialization of gender differences in emotional expression: Display rules, infant temperament, and differentiation. In: A. H. Fischer (Ed.), *Gender and emotions: Social psychological perspectives* (pp. 24–47). Cambridge: Cambridge University Press.

Brody, L. R., & Hall, J. A. (1993). Gender and emotion. In: M. Lewis & J. Haviland (Eds), *Handbook of emotions* (pp. 447–460). New York: Guilford Press.

Brody, L. R., & Hall, J. A. (2000). Gender, emotion, and expression. In: M. Lewis & J. Haviland-Jones (Eds), *Handbook of emotions* (pp. 338–349). New York: Guilford Press.

Cancian, F. M., & Gordon, S. L. (1988). Changing norms in marriage: Love and anger in U.S. women's magazines since 1900. *Gender and Society, 2,* 308–342.

Cohen-Charash, Y., & Spector, P. E. (2001). The role of justice in organizations: A meta-analysis. *Organizational Behavior and Human Decision Processes, 86,* 278–321.

Erickson, R. J., & Ritter, C. (2001). Emotional labor, burnout, and inauthenticity: Does gender matter? *Social Psychology Quarterly, 64,* 146–163.

Feingold, A. (1994). Gender differences in personality: A meta-analysis. *Psychological Bulletin, 116,* 429–456.

Feldman, L. B. (1998). Discrete emotions or dimensions? The role of valence focus and arousal focus. *Cognition and Emotion, 12,* 579–599.

Folger, R. (1986). Re-thinking equity theory: A referent cognitions model. In: H. Bierhoff, R. L. Cohen & J. Greenberg (Eds), *Justice in social relations* (pp. 145–163). New York: Plenum Press.

Grossman, M., & Wood, W. (1993). Sex differences in intensity of emotional experience: A social role interpretation. *Journal of Personality and Social Psychology, 65,* 1010–1022.

Hegtvedt, K. A. (1990). The effects of relationship structure on emotional responses to inequity. *Social Psychology Quarterly, 53,* 214–228.

Hegtvedt, K. A., Clay-Warner, J., & Johnson, C. (2003). The social context of responses to injustice: Considering the indirect and direct effects of group level factors. *Social Justice Research, 16,* 343–366.

Hegtvedt, K. A., Johnson, C., & Morgan, N. (forthcoming). Expressing emotional responses to the injustice of others: It's not just what you feel. In: D. T. Robinson & J. Clay-Warner (Eds), *Social Structure and Emotions*. Amsterdam: Elsevier Press.

Hegtvedt, K. A., & Killian, C. (1999). Fairness and emotions: Reactions to the process and outcomes of negotiation. *Social Forces, 78*, 269–303.

Hegtvedt, K. A., & Markovsky, B. (1995). Justice and injustice. In: K. S. Cook, G. A. Fine & J. S. House (Eds), *Sociological perspectives in social psychology* (pp. 257–280). Boston, MA: Allyn & Bacon.

Heider, F. (1958). *The psychology of interpersonal relationships*. New York: Wiley.

Heise, D. R. (1977). Social action as the control of affect. *Behavioral Sciences, 22*, 163–177.

Heise, D. R., & Calhan, C. (1995). Emotion norms in interpersonal events. *Social Psychology Quarterly, 58*, 233–240.

Hochschild, A. (1975). The sociology of feeling and emotion: Selected possibilities. In: M. Millman & R. M. Kanter (Eds), *Another voice: Feminist perspectives on social life and social science* (pp. 280–307). New York: Anchor.

Hochschild, A. (1979). Emotion work, feeling rules, and social structure. *American Journal of Sociology, 85*, 551–575.

Hochschild, A. (1983). *The managed heart: Commercialization of human feeling*. Berkeley, CA: University of California Press.

Homans, G. C. (1974). *Social behavior: Its elementary forms*. New York: Hartcourt Brace Jovanovich.

Johnson, C., & Ford, R. (1996). Dependence power, legitimacy, and tactical choice. *Social Psychology Quarterly, 59*, 126–139.

Johnson, C., Ford, R., & Kaufman, J. (2000). Emotional reactions to conflict: Do dependence and legitimacy matter? *Social Forces, 79*, 107–137.

Kemper, T. D. (1978). *A social interactional theory of emotions*. New York: Wiley.

Kemper, T. D. (1990). *Research agendas in the sociology of emotions*. Albany, NY: SUNY Press.

Kemper, T. D. (1991). Predicting emotions from social relations. *Social Psychology Quarterly, 54*, 330–342.

Keppel, G., & Wickens, T. D. (2004). *Design and analysis: A researcher's handbook*. Englewood Cliffs, NJ: Prentice Hall.

Kray, L., & Lind, E. A. (2002). The injustices of others: Social reports and the integration of others' experiences in organizational justice judgments. *Organizational and Human Decision Processes, 89*, 906–924.

Krehbiel, P. J., & Cropanzano, R. (2000). Procedural justice, outcome favorability, and emotion. *Social Justice Research, 13*, 339–360.

Kring, A. M. (2000). Gender and anger. In: A. H. Fischer (Ed.), *Gender and emotion: Social psychological perspectives* (pp. 211–232). New York: Cambridge University Press.

Kring, A. M., Smith, D. A., & Neale, J. M. (1994). Individual differences in dispositional expressiveness: Development and validation of the expressiveness scale. *Journal of Personality and Social Psychology, 66*, 934–949.

Kuijer, R. G., Buunk, B. P., Ybcrma, J. F., & Wobbes, T. (2002). The relation between perceived inequity, marital satisfaction and emotions among couples facing cancer. *British Journal of Social Psychology, 41*, 39–56.

LaFrance, M., & Banaji, M. (1992). Towards a reconsideration of the gender–emotion relationship. In: M. S. Clark (Ed.), *Emotion and social behavior: Review of personality and social psychology* (Vol. 14, pp. 178–201). Newbury Park, CA: Sage.

Larsen, R. J., Diener, E., & Emmons, R. A. (1986). Affect intensity and reactions to daily life events. *Journal of Personality and Social Psychology, 51,* 803–814.
Lawler, E. J., & Yoon, J. (1993). Power and the emergence of commitment behavior in negotiated exchange. *American Sociological Review, 58,* 465–481.
Lawler, E. J., & Yoon, J. (1998). Network structure and emotion in exchange relations. *American Sociological Review, 63,* 871–894.
Leventhal, G. S., Karuza, J., & Fry, W. R. (1980). Beyond fairness: A theory of allocation preferences. In: G. Mikula (Ed.), *Justice and social interaction* (pp. 167–218). New York: Springer-Verlag.
Lively, K. J., & Heise, D. R. (2004). Sociological realms of emotional experience. *American Journal of Sociology, 109,* 1109–1136.
Lively, K. J., & Powell, B. (2006). Emotional expression at work and at home: Domain, status, or individual characteristics? *Social Psychology Quarterly, 69,* 17–38.
Lovaglia, M. J., & Hauser, J. A. (1996). Emotional reactions to status in groups. *American Sociological Review, 61,* 867–883.
McGuire, G. M., & Reskin, B. F. (1993). Authority hierarchies at work: The impacts of race and sex. *Gender and Society, 7,* 487–506.
Molm, L. (1991). Affect and social exchange: Satisfaction in power-dependence relations. *American Sociological Review, 56,* 475–493.
Morgan, R., & Heise, D. R. (1988). Structure of emotions. *Social Psychology Quarterly, 51,* 19–31.
Mueller, C. W., & Landsman, M. J. (2004). Legitimacy and justice perceptions. *Social Psychology Quarterly, 67,* 189–202.
Peters, S. L., van den Bos, K., & Bobocel, D. R. (2004). The moral superiority effect: Self versus other differences in satisfaction with being overpaid. *Social Justice Research, 17,* 257–274.
Reskin, B. F., & McBrier, D. B. (2000). Why not ascription? Organizations' employment of male and female managers. *American Sociological Review, 65,* 210–233.
Reskin, B. F., & Padavic, I. (1994). *Women and men at work.* Thousand Oaks, CA: Sage.
Ridgeway, C. L., & Johnson, C. (1990). What is the relationship between task socioemotional behavior and status in task groups? *American Journal of Sociology, 95,* 1189–1212.
Robinson, D. T., & Smith-Lovin, L. (2006). Affect control theory. In: P. J. Burke (Ed.), *Contemporary social psychology theories* (pp. 137–164). Stanford, CA: Stanford University Press.
Rosenfield, S. (1999). Gender and mental health: Do women have more psychopathology, men more, or both the same (and why)? In: A. V. Horwitz & T. L. Scheid (Eds), *Handbook for the study of mental health: Social contexts, theories, and systems* (pp. 349–360). Cambridge: Cambridge University Press.
Ross, C. E., & Van Willigen, M. (1996). Gender, parenthood, and anger. *Journal of Marriage and the Family, 58,* 572–584.
Schachter, S., & Singer, J. E. (1962). Cognitive, social and physiological determinants of emotional state. *Psychological Review, 69,* 370–399.
Shields, S. A. (1991). Gender in the psychology of emotion: A selective research review. In: K. T. Strongman (Ed.), *International review of studies on emotion* (pp. 227–245). New York: Wiley.
Simon, R. (2002). Revisiting the relationship among gender, marital status, and mental health. *American Journal of Sociology, 107,* 1065–1096.
Simon, R. W., & Nath, L. E. (2004). Gender and emotion in the United States: Do men and women differ in self-reports of feelings and expressive behavior? *American Journal of Sociology, 109,* 1137–1176.

Smith, R. A. (2002). Race, gender, and authority in the workplace: Theory and research. *Annual Review of Sociology, 28,* 509–542.

Smith, A., & Kleinman, S. (1989). Managing emotions in medical school: Students' contacts with the living and the dead. *Social Psychology Quarterly, 52,* 59–69.

Smith-Lovin, L. (1990). Emotion as the confirmation and disconfirmation of identity: An affect control model. In: T. D. Kemper (Ed.), *Research agendas in the sociology of emotions* (pp. 238–270). Albany, NY: State University of New York Press.

Smith-Lovin, L. (1995). The sociology of affect and emotion. In: K. S. Cook, G. A. Fine & J. S. House (Eds), *Sociological perspectives on social psychology* (pp. 118–148). Boston, MA: Allyn and Bacon.

Smith-Lovin, L., & Heise, D. R. (1998). *Analyzing social interaction: Advances in affect control theory.* New York: Gordon and Breach.

Sprecher, S. (1986). The relationship between inequality and emotions in close relationships. *Social Psychology Quarterly, 49,* 309–321.

Sprecher, S. (1992). How men and women expect to feel and behave in response to inequity in close relations. *Social Psychology Quarterly, 55,* 57–69.

Sprecher, S., & Sedikides, C. (1993). Gender differences in perceptions of emotionality: The case of close heterosexual relationships. *Sex Roles, 28,* 511–530.

Stearns, C. Z., & Stearns, P. N. (1986). *Anger: The struggle for emotional control in America's history.* Chicago, IL: The University of Chicago Press.

Stets, J. (2003). Emotions and sentiment. In: J. Delamater (Ed.), *The handbook of social psychology* (pp. 309–335). New York: Plenum.

Thoits, P. A. (1989). The sociology of emotions. *Annual Review of Sociology, 15,* 317–342.

Thoits, P. A. (1990). Emotional deviance: Research agendas. In: T. D. Kemper (Ed.), *Research agendas in the sociology of emotions* (pp. 180–206). Albany, NY: State University of New York Press.

Tyler, T. R., Boeckmann, R. J., Smith, H. J., & Huo, Y. J. (1997). *Social justice in a diverse society.* Boulder, CO: Westview Press.

Tyler, T. R., & Lind, E. A. (1992). A relational model of authority in groups. *Advances in Experimental Social Psychology, 25,* 115–191.

Vermunt, R., & Steensma, H. (2005). How can justice be used to manage stress in organizations? In: J. Greenberg & J. A. Colquitt (Eds), *Handbook of organizational justice* (pp. 383–410). London: Lawrence Erlbaum Associates.

Walster, E., Walster, G. W., & Bersheid, E. (1978). *Equity: Theory and research.* Boston, MA: Allyn & Bacon.

Weber, M. [1924] (1978). *Economy and society: An outline of interpretive sociology* (Vol. 1–2). In: G. Roth, & C. Wittich (Eds). Berkeley, CA: University of California Press.

Weiss, H. M., Suckow, K., & Cropanzano, R. (1999). Effects of justice conditions on discrete emotions. *Journal of Applied Psychology, 84,* 786–794.

Zammuner, V. L. (2000). Men's and women's lay theories of emotions. In: A. H. Fischer (Ed.), *Gender and emotion: Social psychological perspectives* (pp. 48–70). New York: Cambridge University Press.

Zelditch, M., & Walker, H. (1984). Legitimacy and the stability of authority. *Advances in Group Processes, 1,* 1–25.

Zelditch, M., & Walker, H. (2000). The normative regulation of power. *Advances in Group Processes, 17,* 155–178.

THE DEVIL MADE HER DO IT? EVALUATING RISK PREFERENCE AS AN EXPLANATION OF SEX DIFFERENCES IN RELIGIOUSNESS

Jeremy Freese and James D. Montgomery

ABSTRACT

Risk preference theory posits that females are more religious than males because they are more risk averse and are thus more motivated by the threat of afterlife punishment. We evaluate the theory formally and empirically. Formally, we show that the rational choice reasoning implied by the theory leads to unexpected conclusions if one considers belief in eternal rewards as well as eternal punishment. Empirically, we examine cross-cultural data and find that, across many populations, sex differences in religiosity are no smaller among those who do not believe in hell. We conclude by arguing that psychological characteristics are almost certainly crucial to understanding the difference, just not risk preference.

Females tend to be more religious than males, both in the United States and most other nations that have been studied (see reviews in Francis, 1997; Walter & Davie, 1998; Stark, 2002). For example, females are more likely to express certainty about the existence of God, more likely to assess themselves as being "religious" or "extremely religious" persons, and more often attend church, pray, and participate in other religious activities (Stark, 2002). Given increasing recognition of the importance of religion for, among other things, social participation, political orientation, psychological well-being, and health, understanding causes of social cleavages in religiosity may contribute in better understanding of some of the reasons for cleavages in its apparent consequences. Importantly, debates about the causes of the difference provide an intriguing example of the more general question about the extent to which differences in male and female behavior are the result of males and females facing different choice problems with similar psychology (whether between the sex differences in circumstances or the implications of the choices provided to them), versus facing similar choice problems with different psychology (regardless of how those psychological differences happen to be caused). Although we have reason to expect individual differences in religiousness to be the result of a complex array of psychological and social factors, which among these are specifically responsible for the observed sex difference?[1]

A recent, creative line of reasoning in the sociology of religion proposes that sex differences in religiousness are largely the result of sex differences in risk preference (Miller & Hoffmann, 1995; Stark, 2002; Miller & Stark, 2002). The reasoning is consonant with a larger movement toward explanations that present decisions regarding religion in rational-choice or quasi-rational-choice terms. Adopting a decision-theoretic perspective, Miller and Hoffmann (1995) posit irreligiousness to be a form of subjectively risky behavior insofar as it exposes the individual to the risk of eternal punishment. Given psychological and economic evidence suggesting that females are more risk averse than males, it would seem to follow that if being religious is the less risky choice, females should be more religious than males.

Going further, Miller and Stark (2002) (see also Stark, 2002) suggest that the sex difference in risk preference is "physiological," and they counterpose the theory that risk preference explains the sex difference in religiosity against the long-held, if amorphous, idea that "differential socialization" is responsible for the difference. Evolutionary psychology has already provided scenarios under which psychological differences in risk preference between males and females would have been selected for in the environments of our ancestral past (Wilson & Daly, 1985; Kanazawa & Still, 2000). The difference in the conceptual level at which the "risk preference" and "socialization" proposals are pitched, however, must be kept clear. Even though Miller and Stark often pose "risk" and "gender socialization" as if they are naturally opposing possibilities (e.g., Miller & Stark, 2002, p. 1415), risk preference could explain the sex difference in religiosity, but yet the difference in preferences could be the result of differential socialization. Conversely, an innate psychological (or "physiological") difference between males and females could explain differences in religiousness, and yet reflect something other than risk preference. In either case, such proposals would stand opposed to explanations that imagine differences as resulting entirely from differences in immediate circumstances, as in theories that have focused on sex differences in work or other time obligations that have found little empirical support (e.g., Iannaccone, 1990). They would also be opposed to explanations that attribute the difference to females disproportionately occupying social roles in which incumbents are expected to exhibit more religiousness, or that females' subordinate position leads to the escapist or otherwise therapeutic benefits of religion to be greater on average for females than that for males (see reviews in Francis, 1997; Miller & Stark, 2002).

As an explanation based on psychological differences, subsequent work has revealed the distinct fronts on which the risk preference thesis can be engaged. Sullins (2006) offers evidence he interprets as undermining claims about the "universality" of greater female religiosity upon which the putative need for an innatist explanation is based. Roth and Kroll (2007) do not dispute a tendency for females to be more religious, but they present evidence that beliefs about hell seem unable to explain this sex difference, regardless of the developmental origins of the difference. Freese (2004) shows that the empirical measure of risk preference used elsewhere by Miller (2002) fails to account for the observed sex difference in religiosity. Lizardo and Collett (2005), on the other hand, seem willing to grant the possible importance of risk preference for explaining sex differences in religiosity, but offer evidence they regard as indicating that the relevant sex differences in risk preference may be more due to socialization than any innate differences.

We set aside the enticement of debates that pit "biology" against "the social" in determining human behavior. Instead, our purpose here is to provide more formal and detailed scrutiny of the logically prior proposal that risk preferences – whatever their etiology – provide the appropriate focus for understanding sex differences in religiousness. In attempting to engage the theory, one runs immediately into the problem that "risk" is a vernacular word that has been appropriated by different literatures in different ways; indeed, the concept has not been used consistently by those who see risk as central to sex differences in religion. However, in its reasoning and its employment of phrases like "risk preference" and "risk aversion," Miller and Stark (2002) seem to be seeking to incorporate the well-developed tools of orthodox economics for discussing and deriving predictions regarding risk.

Given this orientation, we begin by attempting to specify the risk preference theory in more formal terms familiar to economists. Doing so leads to a somewhat different set of conclusions than those presented by Miller and Stark. We then seek to address matters empirically in analyses of the World Value Surveys (WVS) and the International Social Survey Program (ISSP) surveys. Our approach is similar to that taken by Roth and Kroll (2007), and our more formal arguments are bolstered by the findings of their empirical analyses, which use the WVS and the General Social Survey (GSS) and arrive at empirical conclusions broadly consistent with ours. We subsequently conduct further analyses that anticipate some objections to our initial formulation. Taken together, these analyses lead us to doubt that risk preference figures importantly as a cause of the observed sex differences in religiousness. We conclude with a discussion about what might be more productive avenues to explore in trying to resolve this standing puzzle in the sociology of religion.

RELIGIOUS BEHAVIOR AS CHOICE UNDER UNCERTAINTY

In this section, we formally consider the predictions that orthodox economic reasoning might seem to imply about the relationship between afterlife beliefs and religious behavior. In brief, the conclusion of this effort is that the proposition that being irreligious is more risky than being religious is not as straightforward as it may seem. Given an exclusive emphasis on afterlife punishment, religious behavior might correctly be viewed as a form of insurance against hell, and we might expect risk-averse individuals (disproportionately females) to be more likely to engage in such behavior. However, traditional Christian teaching, for example, emphasizes the existence of both extreme afterlife punishments for the faithless (i.e., hell) and extreme afterlife rewards for the faithful (i.e., heaven). If one emphasized only the possibility of an afterlife *reward*, religious behavior might be seen as more akin to buying a lottery ticket – a sure cost borne now for a chance at a large prize to be claimed later – that risk takers (disproportionately males) would find more appealing. Among those who believe in both heaven and hell, then, the predicted implications of an individual's risk attitudes for the choice between religiousness and irreligiousness is indeed ambiguous.

Making this argument formally requires us first to review briefly the standard economic perspective on choice under uncertainty (see Pindyck

Risk Preference as an Explanation of Sex Differences in Religiousness

& Rubinfeld, 2001 for further discussion; Kreps, 1990; Hirshleifer & Riley, 1992 offer more advanced treatments). Given a set of possible actions, an individual chooses the action that provides the highest expected utility. More formally, for each possible action, the individual first computes the expected utility

$$\text{EU(action)} = \sum_{i \in I} p_i U(v_i) \tag{1}$$

where E is the expectation operator, I the set of possible (mutually exclusive) outcomes, p_i the probability that outcome i occurs given the action, v_i the payoff associated with outcome i, and $U(v_i)$ the subjective level of utility generated by this payoff. Having determined the expected utility for each possible action, the individual then prefers action A to action B if

$$\text{EU(action } A) \geq \text{EU(action } B) \tag{2}$$

Within this framework, risk preferences are reflected by the shape of the utility function. The individual is risk averse if utility is a concave function of payoffs, risk neutral if the utility function is linear, and risk loving if the utility function is convex.

More concretely, suppose that an individual is given a choice to gamble or not gamble as depicted by the decision-tree diagram below:

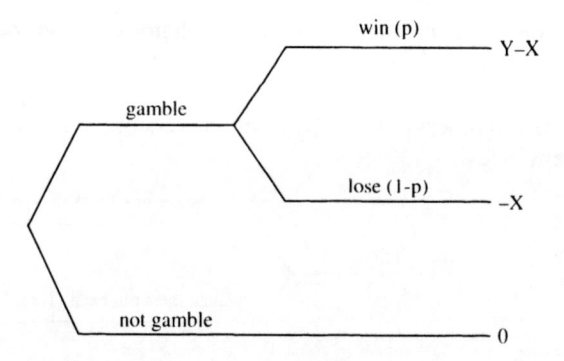

If the individual does not gamble, she receives payoff 0 for sure. If the individual does gamble, she pays the amount X (for, say, a lottery ticket). The individual then wins the prize Y with probability p. Thus, the expected utility of each action is

$$\text{EU(gamble)} = pU(Y - X) + (1 - p)U(-X)$$
$$\text{EU(not gamble)} = U(0) \tag{3}$$

and the individual prefers to gamble if

$$pU(Y - X) + (1 - p)U(-X) \geq U(0) \quad (4)$$

Obviously, gambling becomes more attractive (increasing the left-hand side of this inequality relative to the right-hand side) as the probability p rises, the prize Y rises, or the cost X falls. However, holding these variables constant, the decision to gamble also depends on the individual's risk preferences – that is, on the shape of the utility function.

To illustrate the role of risk preferences, suppose that $p = 1/2$ and $Y = 2X$. Note that this gamble is "fair" in the sense that expected winnings are equal to the cost of the gamble ($pY = (1/2)(2X) = X$). Further normalizing the utility function so that $U(0) = 0$, inequality (4) now implies that the individual will gamble if

$$U(X) \geq -U(-X) \quad (5)$$

In words, the individual chooses to gamble if the subjective pleasure associated with winning X exceeds the subjective pain associated with losing X. Comparing the utility functions in Fig. 1, it is obvious that this condition will be satisfied for risk-loving individuals (with convex utility functions) but not satisfied for risk-averse individuals (with concave utility functions).[2]

Given that brief review of the economic approach, we now consider religious choice. The classic discussion of religious behavior as choice under uncertainty is Pascal's Wager (Pascal, 1966 [1670]; see also Durkin & Greeley, 1991). Reflection on this decision problem suggests many possible specifications (see Montgomery, 1992). One simple version is given by the decision-tree diagram below.

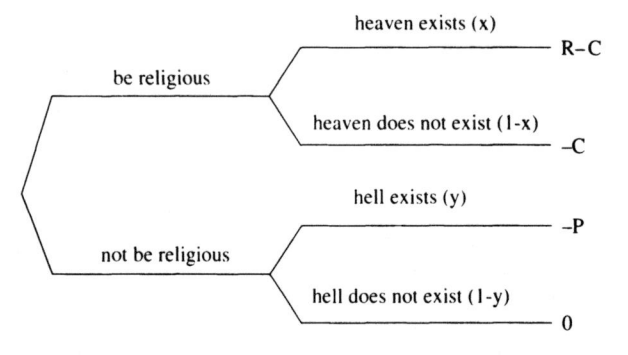

```
                          heaven exists (x)
                         ─────────────────── R-C
           be religious ╱
                        ╲
                         ─────────────────── -C
                          heaven does not exist (1-x)

                          hell exists (y)
                         ─────────────────── -P
        not be religious ╱
                         ╲
                          ─────────────────── 0
                          hell does not exist (1-y)
```

In this version of Pascal's Wager, the individual is faced with the choice to be religious or not religious. (Anticipating the GSS and WVS data, this

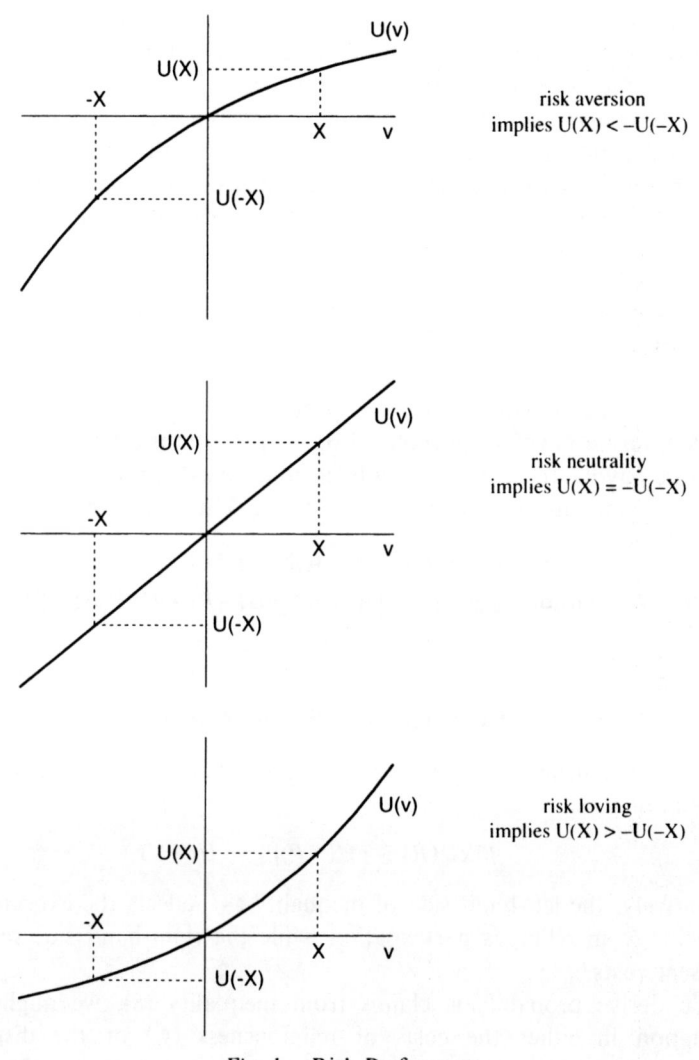

Fig. 1. Risk Preferences.

- risk aversion implies $U(X) < -U(-X)$
- risk neutrality implies $U(X) = -U(-X)$
- risk loving implies $U(X) > -U(-X)$

choice might be reflected either in church attendance or in the more general claim to be "a religious person.") We assume that religiousness imposes some cost C. If heaven exists (probability x) and the individual was religious, she receives an afterlife reward R. If hell exists (probability y)

and the individual was not religious, she receives an afterlife punishment P. Otherwise, the individual receives an afterlife payoff of zero.[3]

Given the ordering of payoffs ($R-C>0>-C>-P$), inspection of the decision tree immediately reveals that either choice could be the riskier option depending on the probabilities x and y. If the individual is certain that heaven does not exist ($x=0$) but unsure about hell ($0<y<1$) then religiousness provides insurance against an afterlife punishment. If the individual is certain that hell does not exist ($y=0$) but unsure about heaven ($0<x<1$) then religiousness becomes a gamble on an afterlife reward. In the more general case where both heaven and hell are uncertain ($0<x<1$ and $0<y<1$), both choices entail risk.[4]

To compute expected utilities, we need to recognize the time dimension implicit in the individual's decision problem: costs are borne in the present while afterlife payoffs are received only in the future. Formally, we allow afterlife payoffs to be discounted by a subjective discount factor β, between 0 and 1 (compare Azzi & Ehrenberg, 1975). Thus, expected utilities are

$$\begin{aligned} \text{EU(religious)} &= U(-C) + \beta[xU(R) + (1-x)U(0)] \\ \text{EU(not religious)} &= U(0) + \beta[yU(-P) + (1-y)U(0)] \end{aligned} \quad (6)$$

and the individual chooses to be religious if

$$\text{EU(religious)} \geq \text{EU(not religious)} \quad (7)$$

Again normalizing the utility function so that $U(0)=0$, we obtain the condition

$$\beta[xU(R) - yU(-P)] \geq -U(-C) \quad (8)$$

Intuitively, the left-hand side of inequality (8) reflects the expected future benefits from religious participation while the right-hand side reflects the present costs.

To derive probabilistic claims from inequality (8), we might assume variation in either the costs of religiousness (C) or the disutility of religiousness ($-U(-C)$) across individuals.[5] Conceptualizing the disutility $-U(-C)$ as a random variable ε, the probability of religiousness equals

$$\text{prob}\{\varepsilon \leq \beta[xU(R) - yU(-P)]\} \quad (9)$$

Recognizing that ε might sometimes be negative – religiousness might generate this-worldly benefits rather than costs – it becomes possible to rationalize religious participation by some individuals who completely discount future outcomes ($\beta = 0$) or do not believe in an afterlife ($x = y = 0$).

To explain sex differences in religiousness, sociologists have often emphasized differential socialization (see Miller & Stark, 2002) while economists might emphasize differences in wages and hence the value of time (see Azzi & Ehrenberg, 1975). Essentially, both arguments focus on sex differences in the present costs of religiousness (the right-hand side of inequality 8). Equivalently, these arguments implicitly assert that the distribution of ε differs across sexes, presumably having a lower mean for females than males. In contrast, rejecting these conventional explanations for sex differences, Miller and Stark emphasize differences in the expected future benefits of religiousness (the left-hand side of inequality (8)). To develop a test of the risk preference argument, we thus maintain the assumption that the distribution of ε does not vary by sex.

Focusing now on the expected future benefits of religious participation, we might first consider whether sex differences in the discount factor β are responsible for differential religiousness. While Miller and Stark (2002) and Miller and Hoffmann (1995) clearly emphasize sex differences in risk preferences, Stark (2002) seems to conflate male "risk taking" with an inability to delay gratification. If males tend to have lower subjective discount factors than females, it is obvious from (9) that males will tend to be less religious than females. But the evolutionary rationale for male impatience is unclear, at least with respect to the rational-choice reasoning employed by Miller and Hoffmann (1995). Indeed, extreme male impatience would seem inconsistent with evolutionary arguments for differential risk preferences which emphasize male willingness to incur *present* costs to obtain *future* mating opportunities. Thus, we will presume here that the discount factor does not vary systematically by sex, and we emphasize that a theory that turns on sex differences in *time* preference (discount factor) is not a theory of differential *risk* preference. We will return to the difference between time preference and risk preference in the conclusion.

We might next consider whether sex differences in risk assessment – beliefs in the existence of heaven and hell reflected in the probabilities x and y – are responsible for differential religiousness. We discuss this topic further below. For now, while Miller and Stark (2002) sometimes seem to conflate these two concepts as well, it is important to maintain the distinction between risk *preferences* (reflected in the shape of the utility function) and risk *assessment* (reflected in subjective probabilities). As discussed above, differences in risk preferences may cause two individuals with the *same* subjective beliefs to make different choices. Thus, in our test of the risk preference argument, we compare those males and females who make similar assessments of risk. That is, we examine rates of religiousness among those with similar beliefs about the existence of heaven and hell.

Having addressed the other potential sources of sex differences in religiousness, we now suppose (following Miller and Stark) that these differences are driven by sex differences in risk preferences. As discussed above, risk preferences are reflected in the subjective utilities associated with gains and loses. Recognizing that utility scales are arbitrary, direct comparison of subjective utility levels across individuals might seem problematic. However, assuming that all males have the utility function $U_M(v)$, that all females have the utility function $U_F(v)$, and normalizing these functions to have the same level and slope at the origin so that $U_M(0) = U_F(0) = 0$ and $U_M'(0) = U_F'(0)$, some straightforward comparisons become possible. If males are more risk loving than females (so that U_M is more convex than U_F), then males will receive higher subjective utility from heaven but lower subjective utility from hell. More formally, we obtain the inequalities

$$U_M(R) > U_F(R) \text{ and } -U_M(-P) < -U_F(-P) \qquad (10)$$

which are illustrated in Fig. 2.[6] Several of our key empirical predictions derive solely from the inequalities in (10). However, if we further assume symmetry

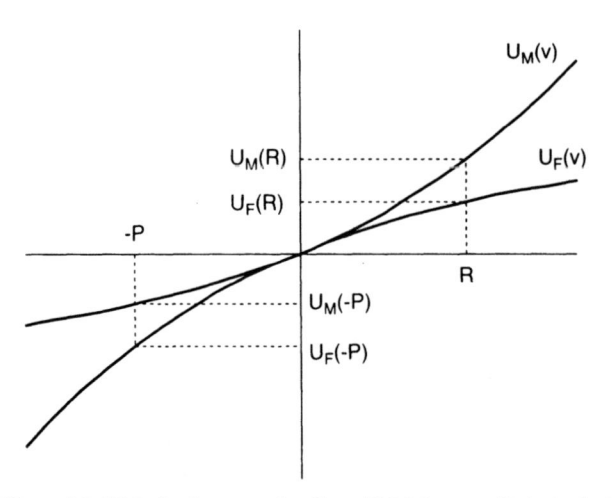

Fig. 2. Differential Risk Preferences by Sex. If Males are Relatively More Risk-Loving than Females, then $U_M(R) > U_F(R)$ and $-U_F(-P) > -U_M(-P)$.

in the afterlife rewards and punishments (so that $R=P$) and impose an "inverted" symmetry in the utility functions (so that $U_M(v) = -U_F(-v)$ for all v), we obtain the stronger result

$$U_M(R) = -U_F(-P) > -U_M(-P) = U_F(R) \qquad (11)$$

allowing us to more clearly rank subjective utilities both within and between sexes.

Given Eq. (9), the proportion of individuals of sex g ($=$ M for male or F for female) with afterlife beliefs x and y who choose to be religious may be written

$$\text{pr(religious}|g, x, y) = \text{prob}\{\varepsilon < \beta[xU_g(R) - yU_g(-P)]\} \qquad (12)$$

For individuals who believe in neither heaven nor hell ($x=y=0$), the bracketed term $[xU_g(R) - yU_g(-P)]$ reduces to zero. Thus, among these individuals, the model predicts that the rate of religiousness will not vary by sex. Formally,

$$\text{pr(religious}|M, 0, 0) = \text{pr(religious}|F, 0, 0) = \text{prob}\{\varepsilon < 0\} \qquad (13)$$

Intuitively, because these males and females expect no future benefits, the proportion who choose to be religious will be low regardless of sex.

For individuals who believe in heaven but not hell ($x=1$, $y=0$), the bracketed term $[xU_g(R) - yU_g(-P)]$ reduces to $U_g(R)$. Given inequality (10), this subjective utility level is larger for males than females. Thus, among these individuals, the model predicts that males will be more religious. Formally,

$$\begin{aligned}\text{pr(religious}|M, 1, 0) &= \text{prob}\{\varepsilon < \beta U_M(R)\} \\ > \text{pr(religious}|F, 1, 0) &= \text{prob}\{\varepsilon < \beta U_F(R)\}\end{aligned} \qquad (14)$$

As the afterlife reward generates more subjective pleasure for risk-loving males than risk-averse females, males have a stronger incentive to become religious. For individuals who believe in hell but not heaven ($x=0$, $y=1$), the bracketed term $[xU_g(R) - yU_g(-P)]$ reduces to $-U_g(-P)$. Given inequality (10), this subjective utility level is larger for females than for males. Thus, among these individuals, the model predicts that females will be more religious:

$$\begin{aligned}\text{pr(religious}|F, 0, 1) &= \text{prob}\{\varepsilon < \beta[-U_F(-P)]\} \\ > \text{pr(religious}|M, 0, 1) &= \text{prob}\{\varepsilon < \beta[-U_M(-P)]\}\end{aligned} \qquad (15)$$

Intuitively, because the afterlife punishment generates more subjective pain for risk-averse females than risk-loving males, females have a stronger incentive to become religious.

Finally, for individuals who believe in both heaven and hell ($x = y = 1$), the bracketed expression becomes $[U_g(R) - U_g(-P)]$. Given only inequality (10), the sign of the expression

$$[U_M(R) - U_M(-P)] \gtreqless [U_F(R) - U_F(-P)] \quad (16)$$

remains ambiguous. However, we might anticipate that the difference between these bracketed expressions (and hence the sex differential in religiousness) would be small in absolute value. Indeed, imposing the stronger symmetry assumptions that led to inequality (11), the model predicts no differences by sex:

$$\begin{aligned} \text{pr(religious}|M, 1, 1) &= \text{prob}\{\varepsilon < \beta[U_M(R) - U_M(-P)]\} \\ &= \text{pr(religious}|F, 1, 1) \\ &= \text{prob}\{\varepsilon < \beta[U_F(R) - U_F(-P)]\} \quad (17) \end{aligned}$$

Given belief in both heaven and hell, both males and females have a strong incentive for religious participation. But differential risk preferences would not generate differential religiousness because the greater subjective utility that males place on heaven is balanced by the greater subjective disutility that females place on hell.

Having emphasized the empirical predictions of the model for religiousness by sex controlling for afterlife beliefs, it may also be worth noting that the model generates intuitive predictions for differences in religiousness within sex across belief classes. In particular, simply using the fact that the terms $U_g(R)$ and $-U_g(-P)$ are all positive, the model predicts

$$\begin{aligned} \text{pr}(g, 0, 0) &= \text{prob}\{\varepsilon < 0\} \\ < \text{pr}(g, 1, 0) &= \text{prob}\{\varepsilon < \beta U_g(R)\} \\ < \text{pr}(g, 1, 1) &= \text{prob}\{\varepsilon < \beta[U_g(R) - U_g(-P)]\} \quad (18) \end{aligned}$$

$$\begin{aligned} \text{pr}(g, 0, 0) &= \text{prob}\{\varepsilon < 0\} \\ < \text{pr}(g, 0, 1) &= \text{prob}\{\varepsilon < \beta[-U_g(-P)]\} \\ < \text{pr}(g, 1, 1) &= \text{prob}\{\varepsilon < \beta[U_g(R) - U_g(-P)]\} \end{aligned}$$

for both sexes $g \in \{M, F\}$. Incentives for religiousness grow with belief in both heaven and hell. Thus, those who believe in neither ($x = y = 0$) have less incentive to become religious than those who believe in one or the other (either $x=1$ or $y=1$), while those who believe in both ($x=y=1$) have the largest incentive. Given the stronger assumptions underlying inequality (11), we obtain

$$\text{pr}(M,0,0) = \text{pr}(F,0,0)$$
$$< \text{pr}(M,0,1) = \text{pr}(F,1,0)$$
$$< \text{pr}(M,1,0) = \text{pr}(F,0,1)$$
$$< \text{pr}(M,1,1) = \text{pr}(F,1,1) \qquad (19)$$

Intuitively, this ordering reflects the fact that risk-loving males are more motivated by heaven than hell, while risk-averse females are more motivated by hell than heaven.

PREDICTIONS

At this point, our attempt to pursue formally the implications of Miller and Starks's argument yields both specific empirical predictions and a quandary. The implications are presented again as Prediction Set A of Table 1. When we divide populations into four subgroups based on their belief in heaven and in hell, the only group for which we are led unambiguously to predict greater religiousness among females than males is those who believe in hell but not in heaven. As it happens, this combination of beliefs is quite rare in all of the countries that have participated in either the WVS or the ISSP surveys, as we discuss further below. For the three subgroups that together represent the overwhelming majority of survey respondents, the predicted sex difference in religiousness is either ambiguous (and expectedly small) or of a greater religiousness among *males*. What makes this a quandary is that Miller and Hoffmann (1995) embarked on risk preference theory in an effort to explain the widely observed greater religiousness of females. In other words, a formal examination of the argument leads us to be skeptical of whether Miller and Hoffman's broadest explanans – that females often tend to be more religious than males – actually follows from their key suppositions that: (1) religiousness is a rational choice based on an "expected utility model;" (2) males are more risk-loving than females; and (3) this is the important psychological difference responsible for any sex difference in religiousness. While below we will examine whether these predictions are consistent with available data, we can anticipate negative results.

Table 1. Predicted Sex Differences in Religion Derived from Alternative Specifications of the Risk Preference Theory.

For Those who Believe in	Predicted Sex Difference
Prediction Set A (sex difference influenced by rewards and punishments)	
Both heaven and hell [1,1]	Ambiguous; expectedly small
Hell but not heaven [0,1]	Females more religious
Heaven but not hell [1,0]	Males more religious
Neither heaven nor hell [0,0]	No gender difference
Prediction Set B (sex difference influenced by punishments only)	
Both heaven and hell [1,1]	Females more religious
Hell but not heaven [0,1]	Females more religious
Heaven but not hell [1,0]	No gender difference
Neither heaven nor hell [0,0]	No gender difference
Prediction Set C (sex influenced by punishment and non-afterlife considerations)	
Both heaven and hell [1,1]	Females more religious: larger difference
Hell but not heaven [1,0]	Females more religious: larger difference
Heaven but not hell [0,1]	Females more religious: smaller difference
Neither heaven nor hell [0,0]	Females more religious: smaller difference

One might consider it unfair, however, to regard such findings as inconsistent with risk preference theory. We, not they, asserted that explaining religious choice in terms of afterlife beliefs would seem to require consideration of the influence of possible afterlife rewards as well as possible afterlife punishment. An alternative, perhaps, would be to maintain that risk attitudes do serve as the crucial psychological variable for understanding sex differences in religious choice, but to posit that only the prospect of afterlife punishment – *not* the prospect of heavenly rewards – figures (or figures importantly) in religious choice. In other words, one can posit that the prospect of hell is a sufficient deterrent to irreligiousness for many people, but the prospect of heaven is not sufficiently rewarding to provoke religiousness.

This leads to the second set of predictions presented in Table 2. If the sex difference in religiousness really is to be explained by the application of differential risk attitudes to the aversion of hell, then it seems reasonable to conclude that one would not expect to observe sex differences among those persons who do not believe in hell (and regardless of whether or not those persons believe in heaven). A greater religiousness among females, however, would be expected for those who do believe in hell, and thus, if belief in hell

Table 2. Summary of Sex Differences in Religiosity, 1998 ISSP and 1990 & 1995 WVS Samples.

	1998 ISSP				1990 and 1995 WVS			
	Regard self as religious person		Attendance at religious services		Importance of religion in life		Attendance at religious services	
Which gender is more religious?	Females	Males	Females	Males	Females	Males	Females	Males
Overall	24	0	24	0	47	1	48	0
	(100)	(0)	(100)	(0)	(98)	(2)	(100)	(0)
No. of sig. ($p<.05$)	22	0	20	0	47	0	43	0
	(92)	(0)	(83)	(0)	(98)	(0)	(89)	(0)
Believes in heaven and hell	18	6	18	6	47	1	42	6
	(75)	(25)	(75)	(25)	(98)	(2)	(88)	
	8	0	6	0	35	1	31	0
	(33)	(0)	(25)	(0)	(73)	(2)	(65)	(0)
Believes in neither	23	1	22	2	47	1	47	1
	(96)	(4)	(96)	(8)	(98)	(2)	(98)	(2)
No. of sig. ($p<.05$)	15	0	14	0	34	0	38	0
	(63)	(0)	(58)	(0)	(71)	(0)	(79)	(0)
Believes in heaven, not hell	12	12	14	10	43	5	41	7
	(50)	(50)	(58)	(42)	(89)	(10)	(85)	(15)
No. of sig.	2	0	5	1	21	1	19	1
($p<.05$)	(8)	(0)	(21)	(4)	(44)	(2)	(40)	(2)
Is gender difference smaller among nonbelievers in hell?	Yes	No	Yes	No	Yes	No	Yes	No
All	19	5	17	6	34	14	34	14
	(79)	(21)	(74)	(26)	(71)	(29)	(71)	(29)
No. of sig. ($p<.05$)	0	0	0	0	10	1	10	1
	(0)	(0)	(0)	(0)	(21)	(2)	(21)	(2)

predominates among members of a population, then we would expect to observe a greater religiousness among females than males overall (see Roth & Kroll [2007] for similar reasoning).

We can obtain a still different set of predictions if we weaken the supposed causal potency of the theory to an assertion that different risk attitudes contribute importantly to sex differences in religiousness, rather than being the only or dominant determinant of these differences. That is, one could posit that other, unspecified factors also figure into the greater religiousness of females, but that, without the (putatively "physiological") difference in risk preferences, the greater religiousness of females would be less than it otherwise is. Accordingly, then, when we look among those who do not believe in hell, we would be unsurprised if females were more religious than males, but we would expect the difference in religiosity to be less than that among those who do believe in hell.

EMPIRICAL RESULTS

Given the highly general nature of Miller and Stark's theory, we sought to include data from many different countries in our empirical investigations. Toward this end, we used two different cross-national data sources: the 1990 and 1995 WVS (combined when possible); and the 1998 ISSP. The WVS attempts representative, comparable surveys of values and attitudes for a large number of populations; we use 48 populations that ask pertinent items and have sufficient sample size. The ISSP conducts topical modules in what are typically larger surveys in their host countries (in the United States, the ISSP is conducted as part of the GSS), and 24 populations include the relevant questions from the 1998 module on religion and have sufficient sample size for use here. Tables for later analyses list the populations used in both sources (Table 3 for WVS and Table 5 for ISSP); following others' practice, we will hereafter refer to the populations as "nations" or "countries" even though not all of them are.

Both the WVS and the participating surveys in the 1998 ISSP ask respondents about their beliefs in the existence of heaven and hell. The WVS asks about belief simply as a "yes" or "no" question, while the ISSP provides four response categories by adding "definitely" and "probably" to both the "yes" and "no" alternatives. Taken together, these data offer considerable leverage to examine whether the sex difference in religiousness varies depending on respondent's beliefs about the existence in heaven and hell.

Ideally, for our purposes, respondents in many countries would be distributed in at least modest quantities across all permutations of belief in heaven and hell. Instead, as already noted, inspection of the data reveals that there is virtually no one, in all the places surveyed, who believes in the existence of hell but not heaven. Across the 73 countries surveyed in any wave of the WVS, the percentage of the population who believe in hell but not heaven was below 1% in 61 countries, below 2% in all but three countries, and had a maximum of 3.3% (Taiwan). Among those who believe in hell, the probability of belief in heaven exceeded 95% in all but five countries, and was never lower than 91.3% (Latvia).[7] Consequently, we

Table 3. Bivariate Ordered Probit for Importance of Religion in One's Life by Belief in Hell, Combined 1990–1995 World Values Survey.

	% Belief in Hell	Believes in Hell	Does not Believe in Hell	Difference	N
Nigeria	73.5	.438	.470*	−.032	3,616
USA	73.2	.395***	.315***	.080	3,053
Puerto Rico	72.7	.356	.399*	−.043	1,089
Peru	64.2	.617*	.317**	.300*	1,066
South Africa	63.6	.514***	.240***	.274***	4,959
Lithuania	59.1	.182*	.509*	−.327	673
Georgia	56.5	.202***	.273***	−.071	2,137
Poland	55.4	.263	.043	.219	462
Venezuela	55.1	.331**	.242**	.089	1,101
Mexico	53.7	.229***	.220***	.009	2,683
Ireland	53.6	.318**	.246*	.072	924
Chile	49.2	.500***	.287***	.214*	2,348
India	46.1	.130***	.051***	.079	4,187
Moldova	45.4	.164**	.244	−.080	735
Argentina	45.1	.408***	.387***	.022	1,896
Romania	43.3	.433**	.140*	.292*	922
Brazil	42.9	.347***	.208***	.138	2,806
Croatia	42.5	.090**	.334*	−.245	1,037
Canada	42.2	.387***	.325**	.062	1,550
Australia	42.1	.350***	.191***	.159	1,837
Andalusia	42.0	.624***	.630**	−.007	1,538
Italy	41.0	.405***	.251*	.154	1,634
Colombia	40.5	.452***	.206***	.246**	2,904
Armenia	36.4	.222***	.561**	−.338**	1,520
Finland	34.9	.393***	.305*	.088	1,216
Spain	32.0	.445***	.440***	.005	4,425
Belarus	30.9	.292***	.350**	−.058	2,252
Great Britain	30.1	.621***	.185*	.437**	1,275
Portugal	29.2	.387**	.801	−.414	955
Japan	27.8	.281**	.040	.241	1,134
Galicia	26.9	.439***	.279	.160	1,036
Uruguay	24.8	.460**	.066	.394*	923
Basque	24.3	.377***	.296*	.081	1,819
Switzerland	23.9	.477***	.188**	.290*	2,133
Russia	23.7	.454***	.347**	.107	2,906
Slovenia	22.2	.182***	.374*	−.192	1,682
Austria	21.5	.291***	.392	−.101	1,131
Norway	20.1	.451***	.409*	.041	2,112
Bulgaria	17.8	.339***	.315	.024	1,571
France	17.7	.078***	.404	−.327	881
Belgium	16.9	.286***	.173*	.113	2,420

Table 3. (Continued)

	% Belief in Hell	Believes in Hell	Does not Believe in Hell	Difference	N
Hungary	16.6	.342***	.492	−.149	877
West Germany	16.5	.428***	.353*	.075	2,528
Netherlands	15.2	.142*	−.503	.645*	889
Iceland	13.0	.327**	.739	−.412	607
Sweden	10.4	.559***	.116	.442*	1,696
Denmark	8.1	.461***	.221	.240	919
East Germany	7.7	.218***	.183	.035	2,134

Note: Listwise deletion for missing data.
*$p < .05$.
**$p < .01$.
***$p < .001$.

exclude this category from our analyses; we also exclude countries that do not have at least 50 persons in each of the three other permutations (belief in heaven and hell, belief in heaven but not hell, and belief in neither).

For both samples, we focus here on results regarding one relatively objective measure of religious participation (self-reported church attendance) and one more subjective measure. In the WVS, the subjective measure we use is "How important is God in your life?" with responses on a 10-point scale with endpoints labeled "Not at all" and "Very." In the ISSP, the subjective measure we use is, "Would you describe yourself as ...?" with seven options ranging from "extremely religious" to "extremely non-religious." We choose these subjective measures because they seemed most consistent with Stark's reasoning about the best subjective measure of the construct of interest (Stark, 2002; Stark & Glock, 1968). The analyses we present are based on simple ordered probit models with only sex as a regressor, although substantively the results are not affected by the inclusion of controls and are consistent with alternative specifications trying other measures of observed religiosity. We present the results briefly because they are also broadly consistent with the analysis of the WVS by Roth and Kroll (2007), although their analytic strategy and measures differ somewhat.[8]

Table 2 provides a summary of the relevant results for the predictions presented above, in terms of both the direction of results and their statistical significance. We can see that, consistent with other work, females overall are more religious than males on at least one of the religious measures in all of the WVS and ISSP samples, and these results are statistically significant in the vast majority of instances. Although we showed above that applying a decision-theoretic perspective to those who believe in both heaven and hell might predict ambiguous and small results, there is a clear pattern for females to be more religious than males, thus refuting Prediction Set A of Table 1 as expected.

If we look at results conditional on belief in heaven and hell, we do not observe any pattern in which the sex difference in religiosity is confined to only those whose belief in the afterlife includes hell. Indeed, a larger number of countries observe results in the expected direction when analyses are restricted to those who believe in neither heaven nor hell than those who believe in both heaven and hell. Results are more mixed when considering the group that believes in heaven but not hell, but this group is smaller than either of the two others. Overwhelmingly, in all groups, when significant results are observed, it is in the direction of females being more religious than males. These results would also seem to refute Prediction Set B of Table 1 and thus the idea that aversion to hell may be the dominant explanation for the sex difference in religion.

We can then turn to the Prediction Set C of Table 1, which specifies just that if aversion to eternal punishment was important for understanding sex differences in religion then these differences ought to be largest for those who believe in hell. Here, looking first at the ISSP, we can see that sex differences are more often larger among believers in hell than nonbelievers, although nowhere is the difference significant. In the WVS, sex differences are also more often larger among believers in hell than nonbelievers, and here for 10 of the 48 countries surveyed the differences for females are significantly larger (at the $p<.05$ level) than for males. Consequently, while results seemed to flatly contradict the first two sets of predictions, the weaker third set is not as inconsistent with the data. It would still seem quite wishful to regard these results as positive support of a weaker version of the risk preference hypothesis, especially given Freese's (2004) finding that a more direct (according to Miller, 2002) risk preference measure did not much attenuate observed sex differences in the WVS data.

Table 3 provides country-by-country results for the combined 1990 and 1995 WVS. The nations for which a significantly greater sex difference among believers in hell is observed – Peru, South Africa, Chile, Romania, Colombia, Great Britain, Uruguay, Switzerland, the Netherlands, and Sweden – do not share any discernible characteristics that would explain why they are more consistent with the weaker risk preference theory than others.[9] Given that significant differences between coefficients are especially hard to evaluate for nonlinear regression models in which the baseline value for the dependent variable varies between groups (i.e., nonbelievers in hell regarding religion as less important on average than believers), these results should be regarded as weak. Notable also in Table 3 is that the United States is second of all nations in the percentage who believe in hell (73.2%). There might seem some irony in American researchers making hell the basis of a general theory of sex differences in religiosity when hell is so much more popular in America than elsewhere (and much less ubiquitous than the sex difference itself).

RISK ASSESSMENT

The foregoing test of the risk preference argument was built upon the standard economic conception of choice under uncertainty. On that view, risk preferences (risk-aversion, risk-neutrality, or risk-lovingness) are reflected in the shape of the utility function (concave, linear, or convex) and are conceptually distinct from risk assessment (i.e., the process by which individuals form subjective judgments about the likelihood of future outcomes). Our test for sex differences in risk preferences thus examined sex differences in religiousness conditional on beliefs. But moving outside economics, discussions of "risk taking" in sociology and psychology often seem to conflate risk preferences and risk assessment. Arguably, a male propensity for "risk taking" might be reflected more in their denial of an afterlife – males might assign lower subjective probability to heaven or hell – than in their subjective utility levels associated with those outcomes. Given a sex differential in risk assessment, some version of Miller and Stark's argument (one understood as an argument about risk assessment rather than risk preferences) might seem to survive our preceding test.

Standard economic theory would seem to provide little help explaining systematic sex differences in religious beliefs (Montgomery, 1996). Within orthodox economics, beliefs are not chosen and hence do not reflect an actor's interests. Consequently, Pascal's Wager should be considered as a choice between action and inaction given a fixed belief, rather a choice between belief and non-belief (Montgomery, 1992). As such, within standard economic theory it would make no sense to suggest that beliefs are chosen on the basis of risk preferences (against Miller & Stark, 2002, p. 1418). Of course, economic theory recognizes that beliefs can be updated (using Bayes' Rule) in light of new information. Thus, sex differences in afterlife beliefs might stem from asymmetric information (assuming that females are more likely than males to receive "signals" implying that heaven and hell truly exist). Arguably, if information flows through social networks with a sex-based homophily bias, economic models of "herd behavior" (Bikhchandani, Hirshleifer, & Welch, 1998) might provide some part of the explanation for persistent sex differentials. But these models incorporate strong restrictions on information flow that might seem implausible in a religious context: females and males do talk, often, and so one would expect any credible "signal" to quickly become common knowledge.[10]

Non-standard economic theories might provide more leverage. Akerlof and Dickens (1982) and Akerlof (1989) developed theoretical models in which actors did not hold those beliefs that are most accurate (based on the information they possess) but rather those beliefs with which they felt most comfortable. That the most discomfiting configuration of afterlife beliefs (no heaven, but hell) is by far the least common might seem consonant with this perspective. Against orthodox economic theory, the perspective would allow beliefs to be driven by interests (including risk preferences). Attempting to take seriously the Miller and Stark's suggestion that sex differences in beliefs are driven by differential risk preferences, Appendix C contains a simple model of self-serving bias in belief formation. The intuition from this model is that beliefs in heaven and hell are biased upwards (downwards) conditional on the choice to be religious (irreligious), and that males (females) have a greater incentive to distort their beliefs in heaven (hell). In other words, among those who are religious, we might expect that males are more likely to believe in heaven than females, while females are more likely to believe in hell, with the opposite to be the case for those who are not religious. Note that this model would seem to reverse the direction of causation maintained within the rest of Miller and Stark's argument: actions now determine beliefs, rather than vice versa. In the attempt to explain religious beliefs, we lose the explanation for religious behavior.

Recall our observation that, from anywhere included in WVS or ISSP, if someone believes in hell, they almost certainly believe in heaven; in contrast, there are many more people who believe in heaven but do not believe in hell. The preceding logic implies the prediction that we might expect the category of believers in heaven but not hell to be disproportionately appealing to religious males and to nonreligious females. As before, this prediction can be weakened to allow for the possibility of a general tendency for females to endorse beliefs in heaven and hell overall. In this case, we might still expect the specific belief in heaven and not hell to be increasingly popular among males relative to females as religiosity increases. Table 4 summarizes these predictions.

For simplicity, we consider only results from the 1998 ISSP. Before considering the specific model results, we looked first at just the bivariate relationship between sex and joint belief in heaven and hell. Not surprisingly,

Table 4. Predicted Sex Differences in Risk Assessment.

	Religious	Non-religious
Prediction Set D		
$\dfrac{Pr(heaven, hell)}{Pr(heaven, \sim hell)}$	Greater for females	Greater for males
$\dfrac{Pr(heaven, \sim hell)}{Pr(\sim heaven, \sim hell)}$	Greater for males	Greater for females
Prediction Set E		
$\dfrac{Pr(heaven, hell)}{Pr(heaven, \sim hell)}$	Relative odds for females increases as religiosity increases	
$\dfrac{Pr(heaven, \sim hell)}{Pr(\sim heaven, \sim hell)}$	Relative odds for males increases as religiosity increases	

in all ISSP countries, males are less likely than females to believe in the existence of both heaven and hell, and in most cases the relationship was significant (20 of 24 countries significantly at $p<.05$; not shown). Less obviously, however, in a majority of countries, females were also relatively more likely than males to believe in heaven without hell than heaven and hell (18 of 24 countries, but only 3 significantly at $p<.05$). Given that risk preference theory would make the clearest predictions for a cosmology with hell but not heaven, it is intriguing that observed beliefs actually might show a slightly greater attraction of females toward its opposite.

Table 5 tests the pertinent interaction terms for our attempt to respecify the theory in formal terms of risk assessment. We use attendance at services as our measure of religious behavior, which again is measured as a six category variable ranging from "never" ($=0$) to "once a week or more" ($=5$). We estimate a multinomial logit with coefficients presented using belief in heaven but not hell as the base category. Prediction Set E of Table 4 proposes that as religiosity increases, the relative odds of believing in heaven and hell versus heaven but not hell should increase for females. This corresponds to positive coefficients for "female × attendance" in the left panel of Table 5. Prediction Set E of Table 4 also proposes that increased religiosity is associated with increases in the relative odds of believing in neither heaven nor hell versus heaven but not hell for males. This corresponds to negative coefficients for the interaction term in the right panel of Table 5.

We can see that in neither case are many interaction terms significant nor are they consistently in one direction or the other. For the comparisons among believers in heaven, 12 of 24 coefficients are in the predicted

Table 5. Coefficients from Multinomial Logit Model for Interaction of Sex and Participation in Religious Services, 1998 ISSP.

	Believes in Heaven and Hell			Believes in neither Heaven nor Hell			N
	Female	Attendance	Female × Attendance	Female	Attendance	Female × Attendance	
West Germany	−.186	.240	.076	−.650	−.481***	.170	851
East Germany	.312	.370**	−.032	.090	−.433***	−.466*	872
Great Britain	−.278	.177	−.044	−.993**	−.384**	.167	568
No. Ireland	.201	.099	−.025	−.024*	−.679***	.321	640
USA	.680*	.278***	−.301**	−.183	−.476***	−.050	1,104
Austria	−.020	.265*	−.036	−.336	−.334**	.065	823
Hungary	.058	.150	.007	−.994*	−.664***	.201	976
Italy	−.901	.078	.139	−.360**	−.522***	.182	861
Ireland	−.456	.033	.138	−.337	−.518***	−.124	904
Netherlands	−.193	.239***	.042	−.713***	−.591***	.236**	1,561
Norway	−.122***	.265**	.392**	−.312***	−.137***	.282	1,123
Sweden	−.304	.402**	−.034	−.953**	−.685***	.047	918
Czech Republic	.201	.340*	.032	−.929*	−.838***	.412*	1,124
Poland	.285	.368**	−.373*	.674	−.386**	−.269	860
New Zealand	−.421	.411***	−.063	−.016***	−.588***	.149	828
Canada	−.380	.174*	−.091	−.195***	−.467***	−.006	667
Japan	.450	.136	−.246	−.073	.040	−.265	894
Spain	.182	.149**	−.074	−.473*	−.408***	.000	2,070
Slovak Rep.	−.656	.362***	.116	−.610	−.696***	.089	1,139
France	−.319	.028	.119	−.948**	−.036***	.301	928
Portugal	−.373	.132	−.028	−.971*	−.548***	.124	1,129
Chile	−.331	−.030	.117	−.392	−.340***	.003	1,421
Denmark	−.331***	.221	.244	−.236***	−.454***	.250	1,022
Switzerland	−.324*	−.067	.259	−.005***	−.351***	.326**	817

Note: Listwise deletion for missing data.
*p < .05.
**p < .01.
***p < .001.

direction, and only 1 is significant and in the predicted direction. For the comparisons among nonbelievers in hell, only 6 of 24 interactions are in the predicted direction, and again only 1 is significantly so. Because Prediction Set E of Table 4 is a weaker version of Prediction Set D of Table 4, the failure to find support for E is a failure for D as well. In sum, these results do not support our attempted modification of the theory, indicating that this way of thinking about the possible relationship between sex differences in risk assessment and religiosity is not a promising avenue for explaining sex differences in religiosity.

IF NOT RISK PREFERENCE, THEN WHAT?

Confronted with the risk preference argument, many sociologists might immediately reject its rational-choice premise that religious behavior can be understood as the product of expected utility maximization given subjective beliefs about the afterlife. On this view, survey responses to questions about belief in heaven and hell should not be interpreted as subjective probability assessments. And even if these responses could be understood in this way, it would seem implausible that these probabilities are then entered into a decision calculus governing the choice to be or not to be religious. Opponents of the rational-choice perspective might further emphasize the difficulty of specifying Pascal's Wager as a decision problem given the manifold conceptions of God and hence many conceivable mappings from religious behavior into afterlife outcomes.[11] If an economic theorist is unsure precisely how to specify Pascal's Wager as a decision-theory problem, it is hard to imagine that every individual has given the problem a clear personal specification (much less derived the optimal solution).[12]

Nevertheless, we have attempted in this paper to evaluate the risk preference theory as articulated by Miller and Hoffmann (1995) and Miller and Stark (2002) on its own terms, deriving empirical predictions from a formal decision-theoretic model. Given the standard economic conception of risk preferences, one problem with the risk preference argument becomes immediately obvious: being irreligious is not necessarily a riskier choice than being religious. Hence, even if females are more risk averse than males, the risk preference argument does not necessarily imply that females will choose to be more religious than males. Our formalization of the risk preference argument thus yields predictions that are conditional upon the individual's belief in heaven and hell. However, we join Roth and Kroll (2007) in finding little empirical reason to believe that afterlife beliefs explain much of the sex difference in religiosity, and Freese (2004) found earlier that an apparent measure of risk preference itself does little to resolve observed sex differences. Our exploration of modifying the theory to focus on risk assessment instead of risk preference proved likewise fruitless. For these reasons, we conclude that sex differences in "risk preference" or "risk assessment" with regard to the afterlife evince little promise of explaining the sex difference in religion.

Miller and Stark (2002) and Stark (2002) formulate their argument as a matter of "biological" versus "social" causes, or more specifically innatist "physiology" versus "socialization." We think this was an unfortunate framing decision, except that by invoking the specter of innate causes the theory has almost certainly drawn more attention to the underlying theoretical problem than it otherwise would have (regarding the particular provocation of "biology" to sociologists, see Freese, Li, & Wade, 2003). The logically prior question for this literature, we think, is the degree to which psychological traits, of the sort collected by "personality" broadly conceived, explain sex differences in religiosity. An alternative would be to imagine the difference as pertaining entirely to differences in immediate circumstances, as in the empirically discredited explanations that focused on sex differences in work or other time obligations. Others would be that females occupy social roles in which incumbents are expected to exhibit more religiousness, or that females' subordinate position leads the escapist or otherwise therapeutic benefits of religion to be greater on average for females than males (see Francis, 1997; Miller & Stark, 2002 for review of theories). As noted, the question is to what extent males and females face different religious choice problems with the same psychology (different choice problems because of systematic sex differences in circumstances or the implications for males and females of religious content) and to what extent males and females respond to similar religious choice problems with different psychology (regardless of the origins of these differences).

Francis (1997) and Miller and Stark (2002) amply summarize reasons to be skeptical of the possibility of an explanation of the sex difference that focuses exclusively on immediate situational differences and does not articulate some reference to more immediate psychological factors. In concluding their own disconfirmation of risk preference theories, Roth and Kroll (2007) seem to advocate returning to explanations that minimize the role of intervening psychology, which we think conflicts with the balance of available evidence and thus would be a mistake. In our view, psychological differences seem almost certain to figure in understanding the sex difference. We need to understand with specificity what these psychological differences are that figure centrally in the observed religious difference, and only then will we be able conduct a more fruitful assessment of the relative contribution of genes and environments (including, but not limited to, "socialization") in the development of these psychological differences. Miller and Stark's blurring together of two fundamentally distinct questions – *Is the sex difference "biological?" Is the sex difference the result of differences in risk preferences?* – only invites confusion in an area for which clear thinking is sorely needed.

In this respect, discussions of male "risk taking" also conflate a variety of claims about preferences, beliefs, and actions that should remain conceptually distinct. The confusion seems to stem from "risk-taking behaviors" having causes that are not preference for risk per se, so seeing commonalities between "risk-taking" and irreligiousness do not imply that preference regarding risk per se is the pertinent commonality. In particular, male "risk taking" in risk preference theory is sometimes equated with claims about (a) risk preference (that males are more risk loving than females), (b) risk assessment (that males assign lower probabilities to bad outcomes), (c) time preference (discount factors; that males are less willing to delay gratification), or (d) rebelliousness (that males are less willing to obey social norms). In drawing upon evolutionary psychology, Miller and Stark alternate between these claims. Generally, Miller and Stark seem to be making claim (a), though occasionally veer toward claims (b) and (d), especially in their discussion of Japan (Miller & Stark, 2002. pp. 1416–1418).[13] In contrast, Stark (2002, p. 496) clearly emphasizes claim (c), saying that "male irreligiousness ... [is] rooted in the fact that far more males than females have an underdeveloped ability to inhibit their impulses, especially those involving gratification and thrills."

More generally, the effort to identify psychological variables pertinent to understanding sex differences in religiosity is a task complicated by the lack of good psychological measurement in prominent social survey data that include measures of religion. Indeed, it may well be that the pertinent intervening psychological variables for the sex difference in religiousness are already well enough understood, and it is more that the datasets used by sociologists in this area have not allowed them to repeat the feat. In studies that contain measures of so-called "masculinity" and (especially) "femininity" but with limited non-population samples, these measures of personality – despite their limitations (discussed below) – explain most or all of the variation that would otherwise be attributed to respondents' sex (Thompson, 1991; Francis & Wilcox, 1996, 1998; Thompson & Remmes, 2002; Francis, 2005). Ideally, comparable measures would be available in the ISSP and WVS, and plausibly they might explain much or even all of the sex difference that the failure of risk preference theory leaves still mysterious.

Miller and Stark (2002) consider matters instead in terms of the extent to which individuals are "socialized" into "traditional gender roles," which can then be put into operation by social attitude questions about the proper place of males and females that are familiar to researchers who have worked with GSS or WVS data. What cannot be emphasized enough is that these attitude questions are not personality characteristics, and the failure of these attitude items (or changes in sex-associated societal roles) to account for sex differences in religiosity does not at all speak to the relevance of psychological characteristics associated with "masculinity," "femininity," or any other aspect of personality. Without clearer understanding of the specific psychology involved, these data are also poor for drawing any conclusions about the relative importance of genetics and environments. Large-scale cross-sectional surveys allow sociologists to imagine the possibility of doing developmental psychology on the cheap, but the resulting inferences here are too often convoluted and confused, especially when the pertinent psychological characteristics are not even attemptedly measured.

Indeed, the implications of deficient data are perhaps exacerbated by the unfortunate identification of the "psychological" with "biological" and the opportunity for this to be pitted against the "social" by researchers whose disciplines are strongly inclined to favor "social" explanations at every turn (indeed, may see the relevance of their discipline hinging on the success of "social" explanations).[14] Sullins (2006), for example, concludes from his analysis of the GSS that "non-social factors are independently generally less powerful than social factors" in explaining either subjective or behavioral indicators of religiosity. On the side of "non-social factors" are some survey items that are far from direct or thorough measures of psychological constructs already demonstrated to be important for religiosity. The item measuring "tender-mindedness," which might seem closest to the "femininity" measures of other studies, asks respondents whether "I would describe myself as a pretty-soft hearted" person, while risk "tolerance" is measured by how fearful respondents report being to walk alone at night.[15] The "social factors" side, meanwhile, includes variables posing such obvious endogeneity problems for estimating causal effects as the percentage of friends who belong to one's religious congregation (termed a "network" measure) and the relative fundamentalism of one's religious affiliation (considered a "demographic" measure), as well as an earlier measure of one's own religiosity (attendance at age 12, termed a "socialization" measure).

While "data duels" between binary competitors may be a favorite trope of quantitative sociology, contests between "psychological" and "social" are generally wanting in the absence of some conceptualization of whether social factors are thought to be working by affecting circumstances or by shaping subsequent psychology. Experienced social differences are thought to operate precisely by affecting more immediate psychological causes – this is the fundamental logic of "socialization" explanations (with specific reference to sex differences in religion, see Francis, 1997). In other words, socializing experiences are posited to have psychological effects that in turn influence later behavior, and so pitting "psychology" against "socialization" makes it unclear how an analyst believes the later influence of socialization works. Analyses that define earlier measures and likely effects of the outcome as "social factors" and weak and indirect measures of psychology as "non-social factors" can be counted upon to produce results in which the "social factors" prevail, but what exactly has been won remains unclear. Ultimately, such work might contribute more to assuaging the chronic insecurities of sociologists than to elaborating our understanding of how psychology, social experiences, and present social circumstances interact dynamically to produce differences among social groups.

Existing work gives ample reason to think that measures attempting to tap "femininity" are central to explaining the sex difference, but theory lags behind in trying to determine precisely what about these measures leads to differential attraction of the more "feminine" to religion. With respect to whatever psychological trait(s) prove important for describing the proximate psychology, Sullins's work provides an extremely important clue for researchers interested in articulating theory that links this psychology to religiousness. He shows that sex differences are larger for "affective" rather than "active" measures of religiosity, and that differences seem especially pronounced for reported frequency of prayer. More importantly, though, we can modify and extend part of Sullins's analyses for the GSS to all ISSP countries. Table 6 compares the bivariate difference in the two measures considered above with the bivariate difference net of reported frequency of prayer.[16] Overall, the results suggest that sex differences in church attendance and religious self-concept may be entirely explained over these countries by the difference in frequency of prayer.[17] To us, the implication is that the task of explaining the sex difference in various religious measures may be usefully replaced (at least for the time being and for the mostly predominantly Christian countries included in the 1998 ISSP) to a concentration on explaining the observed sex differences in prayer. Despite our inclination toward observable behaviors like service attendance, this finding leads us to urge researchers to think more about developing theories orienting toward explaining the difference in frequency of prayer.[18] Whether a rational choice perspective will be useful for developing such theories is an open question.

Analysis of the prayer item in the ISSP also makes plain the limitations of differences in content of belief for understanding sex differences in religiousness, at least within the Christian religious tradition in which prayer is commonly a private, personal act. Table 7 considers how the sex difference in prayer is influenced by beliefs in the existence of God (measured with a six category nominal variable that allows characterization as atheist, agnostic, believing in a "higher power," having wavering beliefs, having some doubts, or having no doubts), beliefs in the veridicality of the Bible (a four category nominal-level variable in which the Bible is characterized

Table 6. Ordered Probit Coefficients for Sex Difference in Religiosity with and without Controls for Frequency of Prayer, 1998 ISSP.

Country	Regards Self as Religious Person			Attendance at Religious Services			N
	Bivariate	Adding prayer	% decrease	Bivariate	Adding prayer	% decrease	
West Germany	.276***	.029	89.5	.273***	.073	73.2	967
East Germany	.294***	.025	91.4	.212*	−.190	189.8	955
Great Britain	.383***	−.013	103.3	.423***	.050	88.1	676
Northern Ireland	.183*	−.061	133.0	.175*	−.031	117.8	731
USA	.278***	−.033	111.9	.242***	−.033	113.7	1,186
Austria	.379***	.020	94.9	.264***	−.085	132.3	968
Hungary	.415***	−.259***	162.5	.352***	−.347***	198.6	993
Italy	.350***	−.035	109.9	.289***	−.135	146.7	996
Ireland	.341***	.153*	55.2	.192*	−.070	136.5	966
Netherlands	.203***	.037	81.6	.121*	−.056	146.2	1,841
Norway	.286***	.011	96.1	.193***	−.060	131.3	1,447
Sweden	.257***	.044	82.8	.320***	.158*	50.8	1,086
Czech Republic	.249***	.006	97.5	.200**	−.055	127.6	1,136
Poland	.348***	−.035	110.0	.443***	.089	79.9	1,089
New Zealand	.297***	−.038	112.8	.246***	−.102	141.6	922
Canada	.229**	−.060	126.3	.130	−.213*	263.1	743
Japan	.121*	−.042	134.8	.079	−.086	208.4	1,243
Spain	.545***	.128**	76.5	.531***	.092	82.6	2,325
Slovak Rep	.408***	.023	94.4	.430***	−.002	100.6	1,277
France	.083	−.128	254.0	.064	−.176*	376.1	1,062
Portugal	.327***	−.111	133.9	.502***	−.077	115.4	1,184
Chile	.320***	.033	89.8	.418***	.107	74.4	1,471
Denmark	.278***	.048	82.6	.176**	−.009	105.1	1,037
Switzerland	.133*	−.182**	236.4	.177*	.071	59.7	980
Combined	.274***	−.010	103.8	.245***	−.053***	108.8	27,281

Note: Models use listwise deletion on sex, prayer, or either dependent variable.
*p<.05.
**p<.01.
***p<.001.

either as the actual word of God, inspired by God, an ancient book of man, or not applying to the respondent). Given the use of questions about the Bible, we look only at predominantly Christian nations (i.e., excluding Japan in addition to Israel) and exclude respondents who report growing up in a non-Christian religious household. Looking down the list, one can see that the degree of attenuation varies and that afterlife beliefs per se contribute relatively little to the overall attenuation. On the whole, though, these

Table 7. Attenuation of Sex Difference in Prayer by Measures of Religious Belief, Predominantly Christian Nations in 1998 ISSP.

Country	Bivariate	Adding Beliefs about God and Bible	Adding Afterlife Beliefs	% Attenuation	N
West Germany	.379***	.167*	.168*	55.7	731
East Germany	.382***	.426***	.422***	−10.5	719
Great Britain	.554***	.416***	.344***	38.0	546
Northern Ireland	.387***	.173	.161	58.4	575
USA	.490***	.389***	.380***	22.6	957
Austria	.532***	.421***	.395***	25.7	729
Hungary	.813***	.728***	.748***	7.9	924
Italy	.650***	.565***	.541***	16.8	741
Ireland	.412***	.240**	.193*	53.3	803
Netherlands	.220***	.121	.055	75.0	1,381
Norway	.389***	.195*	.143	63.2	959
Sweden	.398***	.247**	.183*	54.0	834
Czech Republic	.409***	.398***	.326***	20.2	965
Poland	.683***	.502***	.524***	23.2	696
New Zealand	.371***	.312***	.248**	33.2	752
Canada	.387***	.337***	.204*	47.3	531
Spain	.704***	.500***	.484***	31.2	1,835
Slovak Rep	.543***	.393***	.411***	24.2	1,072
France	.164*	.224**	.150	8.4	817
Portugal	.748***	.721***	.679***	9.3	1,055
Chile	.608***	.562***	.537***	11.8	1,363
Denmark	.358***	.246**	.229**	36.1	946
Switzerland	.469***	.539***	.438***	6.7	804
Combined	.437***	.349***	.322***	26.4	21,384

Note: Listwise deletion for missing data.
*$p < .05$.
**$p < .01$.
***$p < .001$.

various belief measures together only account for about a quarter of the sex difference in frequency of prayer. Most of the sex difference, then, is not about differences in basic beliefs about the existence of God, veridicality of the Bible, or existence of an afterlife, but the religiosity of males and females with similar beliefs.

Risk preference theorists thus seem to have been on the right track in their focus on a psychological characteristic whose relevance is independent of belief formation, even if risk preference itself does not work. As noted, we think a promising avenue of future work is to engage the measures of "femininity" and "masculinity" that have already been shown repeatedly to be very important – indeed, often *sufficient* – for explaining the sex difference in religiosity in select samples. Many scholars have long been skeptical of "masculinity" and "femininity" scales as such, for good reasons (e.g., Pedhazur & Tetenbaum, 1979), including the lack of psychological coherence for the individual measures comprising such scales. For our purposes, the labels given to the measures are not important, and ambiguity about the meaning of the scales is precisely what provides the puzzle for analysts. If these scales do in fact resolve observed sex differences in affective religiousness, then we need to understand what it is about what is measured by those scales yields differential religiousness. If one had the primary data from these studies, the obvious next step would be to look at which scale items contributed to resolving the differences and which did not. As things stand, whether the pertinence of masculinity and femininity seem ultimately to turn on "impulsivity," "nonconformity" "aggressiveness" (three constructs raised at varying points by Stark, 2002 which would all be best left conceptually distinct) or something else entirely, is a matter for future research. The point worth repeating is that any empirical demonstration that some psychological characteristic(s) resolves the sex difference in religiosity demands theoretical work toward explaining why the characteristic(s) influences religiosity – work that is separate and likely more tractable than the question of why males and females differ in the characteristic(s) in the first place. The work is more difficult in the present case because the scales of "masculinity" and "femininity" themselves need to be scrutinized to figure out what parts of these scales resolve the differences and how these parts might be usefully conceptualized in genuinely explanatory terms (rather than terms that just reify existing interpretations of "masculinity" and "femininity").

At this point, we think more can be gained from large-scale survey data that has extensive psychological measures on a single population rather than weak measures on many populations. Cross-population variation in the magnitude of a sex difference in an outcome like religiousness can provide important clues to the intervening (psychological or other) mechanisms, as one might infer why the way the outcome is realized in different societies would make specific factors more important for some populations than others. Miller and Stark (2002) attempted to do this deductively with the afterlife beliefs of different countries and religious groups, but their conclusions from this exercise are not supported when individual-level data on belief are used (Roth & Kroll, 2007).[19] Whether cross-population variation can be productively used to generate explanations of the sex difference in religiousness that withstand empirical scrutiny remains to be seen. Because religion is so heterogeneous within and across populations, variation in the sex difference does not at all speak to how traits relevant to religiousness in any population are determined. In sum, we think existing evidence suggests much promise for the effort to construct an explanation of the intervening psychology of the observed sex difference in religiousness. At the same time, we believe sociologists ultimately hinder themselves in this effort when they succumb to the illusion that the same data will provide decisive insight into how sex differences in this intervening psychology originates.

NOTES

1. We use "sex" instead of "gender" in the main text because some literature on this topic draws much on this distinction (e.g., Thompson, 1991), and following language there, the observed difference to be explained would seem better characterized as respondent's "sex." Our usage is not intended to engage any other or larger debates about the meaning of "sex" and "gender" and the propriety of using one or the other in a particular context. For the same reason, we use "male" and "female" instead of "men" and "women" throughout.

2. More generally, the rejection of fair bets by risk-averse individuals and the acceptance of fair bets by risk-loving individuals follows from Jensen's inequality (see Hirshleifer & Riley, 1992). This result states that, given a random variable v and utility function U, the utility of the expected payoff $U(Ev)$ is greater than the expected utility $EU(v)$ if U is concave, while $U(Ev)$ is less than $EU(v)$ if U is convex. In the present example, given any fair bet such that $X = pY$, we obtain $EU(v) = pU((1-p)Y) + (1-p)U(-pY)$, and $U(Ev) = U(p(1-p)Y + (1-p)(-pY)) = U(0)$. Thus, inequality (4) holds if U is convex (i.e., the individual is risk loving) but does not hold if U is concave (i.e., the individual is risk-averse). Risk-neutral individuals possess linear utility functions of the form $U(v) = \lambda v$ which implies that $U(Ev) = \lambda Ev = E(\lambda v) = EU(v)$. Thus, risk-neutral individuals are indifferent to fair bets.

3. In Pascal's (1966 [1670]) original argument, he asserts that R is infinite and thus obtains the result that religiousness is the optimal choice if there is any possibility of heaven (i.e., any $x > 0$ implies EU(religious) > EU(not religious)). Here, we presume that both the afterlife reward R and punishment P are finite. Azzi and Ehrenberg (1975) defend this assumption by noting that even an infinite (never-ending) stream of payoffs will have a finite present discounted value.

4. Given this (very simple) version of Pascal's Wager, individuals who are certain that heaven and hell exist (and thus hold the subjective probabilities $x = y = 1$) would face no risk. But given a more elaborate model with probabilistic links between present behavior and afterlife payoffs, risk persists even for these individuals. In Appendix 1, we develop a more general version of Pascal's Wager, demonstrating that the predictions drawn from the simpler model remain valid.

5. Given that both assumptions generate similar empirical predictions, the latter assumption is developed here, while analysis of the former assumption (which

requires introduction of the economic concept of "certainty equivalents") is presented as Appendix 2.

6. While Fig. 2 assumes that males are risk loving while females are risk averse, note that the inequalities $U_M(R) > U_F(R)$ and $-U_M(-P) < -U_F(-P)$ merely require females to be *relatively* more risk averse than males (so that, in an absolute sense, both sexes could be risk averse or both could be risk loving).

7. It is worth emphasizing that the combination of hell but no heaven does not seem a *logical* impossibility. Indeed, belief patterns that would seem logically necessary fare less well in survey data. For instance, in the United States sample of the WVS, conditional on believing in heaven, only 86% of respondents report believing in life after death. Thus, non-trivial numbers of Americans appear to believe in heaven but not an afterlife, a belief pattern precluded by the skip pattern on some surveys (e.g., the 1996 Religion and Politics Survey). One possible reaction to this result would be to exclude respondents who say no to the life after death question but express belief in heaven or hell; doing so does not produce results substantively different from those presented here. We do not exclude them in the presented analyses because of the possibility that many of the seemingly inconsistent responses could reflect a belief that what is being asked about in a question of "life after death" is something different (e.g., reincarnation) than the fate of the spirit after physical death.

8. Importantly, although Roth and Kroll's (2007) main results separate respondents by belief in hell, they also conduct analyses in which belief in hell is included as a covariate, and seem to believe that risk preference theory would be supported by changes in the sex difference with the inclusion of belief as a control. In any case, if A and B are binary variables (e.g., sex and belief in hell) and the relationship between A and an outcome is strong when $B = 0$ and nothing when $B = 1$, this is properly estimated by stratifying analyses by B or by including the interaction term $A \times B$. Only if A and B are correlated will the coefficient for the effect of A on Y be affected by the inclusion of B in the model, which is irrelevant to whether there is an interaction. As we argue, risk preference theory does not require a correlation between gender and belief. In short, those parts of Roth and Kroll's analyses that use belief in hell as a covariate do not actually test the risk preference argument but rather an argument that turns on risk assessment.

9. More correctly, one would look at the countries that have the largest gender differences regardless of significance, to avoid conflating sample size with substantive characteristics of countries, but the overlap between the two lists is considerable and looking at nations with nontrivial gender differences but small WVS samples (e.g., Japan, Denmark) does not provide any additional information suggestive of similarity among countries with larger differences.

10. Moreover, any serious attempt within orthodox economics to explain gender differentials in religious belief would need to grapple with the theoretical results that rational actors cannot agree to disagree (Aumann, 1976) and that common knowledge about actions negates asymmetric information about events (Geneakoplos, 1992).

11. Beyond the complications introduced in Appendix 1, a more complete specification of Pascal's Wager would need to incorporate the possibility of multiple *types* of Gods, each of whom might require a different form of religious behavior

and might (or might not) look kindly upon behavior directed toward other Gods (see Montgomery, 1992).

12. In response, an economist might assert that individuals need not be conscious of decision problems, but merely behave as if they were solving such problems (see Becker, 1976). However, this "as if" defense becomes less compelling when there is no possibility of learning through trial and error. Obviously, in the present context, individuals make one-time choices (whether or not to lead a religious life) that cannot be reversed following success or failure (which becomes apparent only after death).

13. Importantly, Roth and Kroll (2007) report being unable to reproduce Miller and Stark's empirical findings regarding Japan.

14. The epistemic double standard at work is illustrated by how Stark, the advocate of the biological position, feels compelled to articulate at the outset how reaching this conclusion "was not done eagerly or even very willingly" and to add that he regards current work in evolutionary psychology to be "mostly worthless" (Stark, 2002, p. 496).

15. "Tender-mindedness" in this respect also calls attention to the trait of "agreeableness" from the Five Factor Model of personality, which is known to be associated with religiousness and with measures of femininity (Saroglou, 2002).

16. While the Philippines had complete data on the relevant variables, the prayer measure for the Philippines seemed to produce anomalous data relative to even other highly religious countries in the ISSP, so it is excluded from the analyses.

17. Following an analytic strategy with which we disagree, Sullins (2006) suggests his results show that the prayer measure evinces substantial gender bias in self-report, with females apparently over-reporting their real frequency of prayer to a greater degree than males. Regardless of the truth of the proposition, we note that the result that prayer resolves the other gender differences in measures suggests that whatever psychology is behind the reporting differences would seem importantly implicated in the other differences as well. In other words, one cannot simultaneously attribute the gender difference in prayer substantially to self-report biases and regard measures of attendance at services as an "objective" measure (or at least one not similarly biased), as this would be inconsistent with prayer resolving the gender difference in attendance at services.

18. We do not wish to overstate this, as certainly there are findings about gender differences in religion for which we have no empirical reason to believe can be explained by differences in private prayer, and seemingly reason to expect this is not the case. As one notable example, Stark (2002) begins by discussing the difference in the success of new religious movements at recruiting females. In addition, we should emphasize that what we are calling for is not necessarily theories of prayer per se, but theories that recognize that some cause(s) of variation in prayer seems central to understanding of sex differences in a broader set of measures of religiosity.

19. Indeed, in this regard, religion provides a site for demonstration of the deeply sociological point that social contexts (in this case the structure, content, and practice of different religious traditions) influence the degree to which psychological difference between persons (however caused) end up being relevant for different domains of their lives.

20. See Aronson (1988) for discussion of dissonance as a consequence of decision-making. Developing a related model in which post-decision dissonance alters utility

parameters, Montgomery (1994) interprets dissonance reduction as a subconscious phenomenon. Thus, even within this non-orthodox perspective, we might continue to assert that beliefs are not (consciously) chosen.

ACKNOWLEDGMENTS

We thank Louise Marie Roth, Brian Powell, and Shelley Correll for helpful discussions.

REFERENCES

Akerlof, G. A. (1989). The economics of illusion. *Economics and Politics, 1*, 1–15.
Akerlof, G. A., & Dickens, W. T. (1982). The economic consequences of cognitive dissonance. *American Economic Review, 72*, 307–319.
Aronson, E. (1988). *The social animal*. New York: Freeman.
Aumann, R. J. (1976). Agreeing to disagree. *Annals of Statistics, 4*, 1236–1239.
Azzi, C., & Ehrenberg, R. (1975). Household allocation of time and church attendance. *Journal of Political Economy, 83*, 27–56.
Becker, G. S. (1976). *The economic approach to human behavior*. Chicago, IL: University of Chicago Press.
Bikhchandani, S., Hirshleifer, D., & Welch, I. (1998). Learning from the behavior of others: Conformity, fads, and informational cascades. *Journal of Economic Perspectives, 12*, 151–170.
Durkin, J. T., Jr., & Greeley, A. M. (1991). A model of religious choice under uncertainty: On responding rationally to the non-rational. *Rationality and Society, 3*, 178–196.
Francis, L. J. (1997). The psychology of gender differences in religion: A review of empirical research. *Religion, 27*, 81–96.
Francis, L. J. (2005). Gender role orientation and attitude toward christianity: A study among older men and women in the United Kingdom. *Journal of Psychology and Theology, 33*, 179–186.
Francis, L. J., & Wilcox, C. (1996). Religion and gender orientation. *Personality and Individual Differences, 20*, 119–121.
Francis, L. J., & Wilcox, C. (1998). Religiosity and femininity: Do females really hold a more positive attitude toward Christianity? *Journal for the Scientific Study of Religion, 37*, 462–469.
Freese, J. (2004). Risk preferences and gender differences in religiousness: Evidence from the World Values Survey. *Review of Religious Research, 46*, 88–91.
Freese, J., Li, J. C. A., & Wade, L. D. (2003). The potential relevances of biology to social inquiry. *Annual Review of Sociology, 29*, 233–256.
Geneakoplos, J. (1992). Common knowledge. *Journal of Economic Perspectives, 6*, 53–82.
Hirshleifer, J., & Riley, J. G. (1992). *The analytics of uncertainty and information*. New York: Cambridge University Press.

Iannaccone, L. R. (1990). Religious practice: A human capital approach. *Journal for the Scientific Study of Religion, 3,* 297–314.
Kanazawa, S., & Still, M. C. (2000). Why males commit crimes (and why they desist). *Sociological Theory, 18,* 434–447.
Kreps, D. M. (1990). *A course in microeconomic theory.* Princeton, NJ: Princeton University Press.
Lizardo, O. & Collett, J. L. (2005). *Why biology is not (religious) destiny: A second look at gender differences in religiosity.* American Sociological Association Annual Meetings, Philadelphia.
Miller, A. S. (2002). Going to hell in Asia: The relationship between risk and religion in a cross cultural setting. *Review of Religious Research, 42,* 5–18.
Miller, A. S., & Hoffmann, J. P. (1995). Risk and religion: An explanation of gender differences in religiosity. *Journal for the Scientific Study of Religion, 34,* 63–75.
Miller, A. S., & Stark, R. (2002). Gender and religiousness: Can socialization explanations be saved? *American Journal of Sociology, 107,* 1399–1423.
Montgomery, J. D. (1992). Pascal's Wager and the limits of Rational Choice: A comment on Durkin and Greeley. *Rationality and Society, 4,* 117–121.
Montgomery, J. D. (1994). Revisiting Tally's Corner: Mainstream norms, cognitive dissonance, and underclass behavior. *Rationality and Society, 6,* 462–488.
Montgomery, J. D. (1996). Contemplations on the economic approach to religious behavior. *American Economic Review, 86,* 443–447.
Pascal, B. (1966 [1670]). *Pensées.* New York: Penguin.
Pedhazur, E., & Tetenbaum. T. J. (1979). Bem Sex Role Inventory: A theoretical and methodological critique. *Journal of Personality and Social Psychology, 37,* 996–1016.
Pindyck, R. S., & Rubinfeld, D. L. (2001). *Microeconomics.* Upper Saddle River, NJ: Prentice Hall.
Rabin, M. (1994). Cognitive dissonance and social change. *Journal of Economic Behavior and Organization, 23,* 177–194.
Roth, L. M. & Kroll, J. C. (2007). Risky business: Assessing risk-preference explanations for gender differences in religiosity. *American Sociological Review, 16,* 205–220.
Saroglou, V. (2002). Religion and the five factors of personality: A meta-analytic review. *Personality and Individual Differences, 32,* 15–25.
Stark, R. (2002). Physiology and faith: Addressing the 'universal' gender difference in religious commitment. *Journal for the Scientific Study of Religion, 41,* 495–507.
Stark, R., & Glock, C. Y. (1968). *American piety.* Berkeley, CA: University of California Press.
Sullins, D. P. (2006). Gender and religion: Deconstructing universality, constructing complexity. *American Journal of Sociology, 112,* 838–880.
Thompson, E. H. (1991). Beneath the status characteristic: Gender variations in religiousness. *Journal for the Scientific Study of Religion, 30,* 381–394.
Thompson, E. H., & Remmes, K. R. (2002). Does masculinity thwart being religious? An examination of older males' religiousness. *Journal for the Scientific Study of Religion, 41,* 521–532.
Walter, T., & Davie, G. (1998). The religiosity of females in the modern West. *British Journal of Sociology, 49,* 640–660.
Wilson, M., & Daly, M. (1985). Competitiveness, risk taking, and violence: The young male syndrome. *Ethology and Sociobiology, 6,* 59–73.

APPENDIX A. A MORE GENERAL SPECIFICATION OF PASCAL'S WAGER

There are many possible conceptions of God, implying many different mappings from religious behavior to afterlife payoffs. Thus, there are many possible specifications of Pascal's Wager. In the text, we developed a simple version that was chosen in light of existing survey questions on religious belief. Here, we consider a more general version to explore the robustness of our empirical test of the risk preference argument.

Again suppose that an individual can choose to be religious or not religious. In either case, there are four possible contingencies: only heaven exists (probability x'); only hell exists (probability y'); both heaven and hell exist (probability z'); and neither exist (probability $1-x'-y'-z'$).

Suppose that the individual chooses to be religious. If only heaven exists, she receives R with probability t and 0 with probability $(1-t)$. If only hell exists, she receives 0 with probability t and $-P$ with probability $(1-t)$. If both heaven and hell exists, she receives R with probability t and $-P$ with probability $(1-t)$. If neither exists, she receives 0 for sure. Intuitively, t is the probability that God demonstrates "trustworthiness" by not allowing bad things (a non-rewarded afterlife) to happen to good people (individuals choosing to be religious). Alternatively, assuming that God is not omniscient, t might be interpreted as the probability that God makes a Type I error.

Suppose that the individual chooses not to be religious. If only heaven exists, she receives R with probability m and 0 with probability $(1-m)$. If only hell exists, she receives 0 with probability m and $-P$ with probability $(1-m)$. If both heaven and hell exists, she receives R with probability m and $-P$ with probability $(1-m)$. If neither exists, she receives 0 for sure. Intuitively, m is the probability that God demonstrates "mercifulness" by allowing good things (a non-punished afterlife) to happen to bad people (individuals choosing not to be religious). Alternatively, m might be interpreted as the probability that God makes a Type II error.

Computing the expected utility generated by each action, we obtain

$$EU(\text{religious}) = U(-C) + \beta\{x'tU(R) + y'(1-t)U(-P) + z'[tU(R) + (1-t)U(-P)]\} \quad (A.1)$$

$$EU(\text{not religious}) = \beta\{x'mU(R) + y'(1-m)U(-P) + z'[mU(R) + (1-m)U(-P)]\} \quad (A.2)$$

The individual chooses to be religious if

$$EU(\text{religious}) \geq EU(\text{not religious}) \quad (A.3)$$

which implies

$$\beta(t - m)[(x' + z')U(R) - (y' + z')U(-P)] \geq -U(-C) \quad (A.4)$$

Given $x' + z' = x$ (the probability that heaven exists with or without hell) and $y' + z' = y$ (the probability that hell exists with or without heaven), inequality (A.4) becomes identical to inequality (9) with the exception of the $(t-m)$ term on the left-hand side of (A.4). Intuitively, this term reveals that the incentive for religious behavior decreases as God's mercy becomes more likely relative to God's trustworthiness. In the special case where $t = m$, the probabilities of receiving afterlife payoffs are not conditional on the individual's chosen action, so there is no expected net benefit from religious behavior.

Our simpler model implicitly assumed that, conditional upon the existence of heaven or hell, God is definitely trustworthy ($t = 1$) and definitely not merciful ($m = 0$). However, our empirical tests of Miller and Stark's argument (summarized in Table 1) would remain valid under the weaker conditions that $(t-m)$ is positive and does not vary by sex. Ideally, given survey questions that probed beliefs not merely about the existence of heaven and hell (assessments of probabilities x and y) but also about the link from actions to afterlife payoffs (assessments of probabilities t and m), we could control for the latter beliefs in the same manner that we controlled for the former.

APPENDIX B. AN ALTERNATIVE DERIVATION OF EMPIRICAL PREDICTIONS

To derive probabilistic claims from inequality (8), we assume in the text that the disutility of religiousness $-U(-C)$ is stochastic, given by the random variable ε, with the same distribution of ε for males and females. Here, we make the alternative assumption that the cost of religiousness C is stochastic, given by the random variable ϕ, with the same distribution of ϕ for males and females. In place of Eq. (12), we now obtain

$$\text{pr}(\text{religious}|g, x, y) = \text{prob}\{\phi \leq -U_g^{-1}(-\beta[xU_g(R) - yU_g(-P)])\} \quad (B.1)$$

where U_g^{-1} denotes the inverse function of U_g. Adopting economic terminology, the term $-U_g^{-1}(-\beta[xU_g(R) - yU_g(-P)])$ is a "certainty equivalent" that converts lottery outcomes into a monetary benefit that be compared directly to monetary costs (see Kreps, 1990, p. 83). In the case where the individual is risk neutral (so that $U_g(v) = \lambda v$ and $U_g^{-1}(u) = u/\lambda$), this certainty equivalent reduces simply to $\beta[xR + yP]$. The certainty equivalent is lower than $\beta[xR + yP]$ if the individual is risk averse, and higher than $\beta[xR + yP]$ if she is risk loving.

We may now use (B.1) to compare the probability of religiousness for males and females. Conditioning on the subjective probabilities x and y, religiousness is more likely among males when

$$-U_M^{-1}(-\beta[xU_M(R) - yU_M(-P)]) > -U_F^{-1}(-\beta[xU_F(R) - yU_F(-P)]) \quad (B.2)$$

Conversely, religiousness is more likely among females when inequality (B.2) is reversed so that the female certainty-equivalent exceeds the male certainty-equivalent.

To simplify our analysis, we assume that females are risk averse while males are risk neutral. (Our results extend immediately to the case where males are risk loving, and the analysis could be extended to cover the case where males are risk averse in absolute terms but still relatively less risk averse than females.) Formally, this implies that $U_M(v)$ is linear (i.e., $U_M(v) = \lambda v$) while $U_F(v)$ is concave (i.e., $U_F'(v) > 0$ and $U_F''(v) < 0$ for all v). Following our assumptions in the text, we normalize the utility functions (without loss of generality) so that $U_M(0) = U_F(0) = 0$ and $U_M'(0) = U_F'(0) = \lambda$.

We may now consider the sex differential in religiousness given the four possible combinations of belief in heaven and hell. Given belief in neither heaven nor hell ($x = y = 0$), both certainty equivalents (i.e., both sides of inequality B.2) become zero. Thus, both males and females would become religious with prob$\{\phi \leq 0\}$ and there would be no sex differential in religiousness. Intuitively, in the absence of afterlife considerations, religious behavior is rational only if it generates this-worldly benefits.

Given belief in heaven but not hell ($x = 1$, $y = 0$), the male certainty-equivalent reduces to βR while the female certainty-equivalent reduces to $-U_F^{-1}(-\beta U_F(R))$. Concavity of the female utility function implies that $U_F(v) < \lambda v$ for all $v \neq 0$ and that $U_F^{-1}(u) > u/\lambda$ for all $u \neq 0$. Hence, given a positive discount factor ($\beta > 0$), we obtain

$$\beta R > \frac{\beta U_F(R)}{\lambda} > -U_F^{-1}(-\beta U_F(R)) \quad (B.3)$$

Thus, males are more likely than females to become religious. Intuitively, given the concavity of the female utility function, even relatively small costs of religious participation would impose large disutility. Thus, while males are willing to incur costs up to βR, females are not willing to incur costs that high.

Given belief in hell but not heaven ($x=0$, $y=1$), the male certainty-equivalent reduces to βP while the female certainty-equivalent reduces to $-U_F^{-1}(\beta U_F(-P))$. Given the concavity of the female utility function, Jensen's inequality implies that

$$(1 - \beta)U_F(0) + \beta U_F(-P) < U_F(-\beta P) \tag{B.4}$$

if the discount factor is bounded so that $0 < \beta < 1$. Given $U_F(0) = 0$, this implies

$$-U_F^{-1}(\beta U_F(-P)) > -U_F^{-1}(U_F(-\beta P)) = \beta P \tag{B.5}$$

Thus, females are willing to incur higher costs than males and are hence more likely to be religious. Note that, if individuals did not discount future payoffs ($\beta = 1$), both certainty-equivalents would reduce simply to P. In this case, both males and females become religious with prob$\{\phi < P\}$ and there would be no sex differential in religiousness. From a formal perspective, the discount factor acts like a probability: individuals evaluate the decision problem as though there was a probability β of going to hell conditional on irreligiousness. Hence, even if hell is a certain outcome for the irreligious, risk-averse females have more incentive than risk-neutral males to choose religiousness.

Finally, given belief in both heaven and hell ($x = y = 1$), the male certainty-equivalent reduces to $\beta[R + P]$ while the female certainty-equivalent reduces to $-U_F^{-1}(-\beta[U_F(R) - U_F(-P)])$. Because these terms cannot be ordered unambiguously, the religiousness rate could be higher among either males or females (depending on parameter values). But further analysis reveals that, in many cases, males would be more likely than females to be religious. In the special case with no time discounting ($\beta = 1$), the male-certainty equivalent always exceeds the female certainty-equivalent. To see this, note that

$$-U_F^{-1}(-[U_F(R - z) - U_F(-P - z)]) \tag{B.6}$$

is equal to the female certainty-equivalent when $z = 0$, equal to the male certainty-equivalent when $z = R$, and (differentiating B.6 with respect to z) monotonically increasing in z (given that $U_F'(-P-z) > U_F'(R-z)$ for any z). Thus, we obtain

$$R + P > -U_F^{-1}(-[U_F(R) - U_F(-P)]) \tag{B.7}$$

which implies that males are more likely than females to be religious. To consider the more general case ($\beta \le 1$), define λ' such that $\lambda'[R+P] = U_F(R) - U_F(-P)$. (Graphically, λ' is the slope of the chord connecting the points $\{-P, U_F(-P)\}$ and $\{R, U_F(R)\}$.) The female certainty-equivalent becomes $-U_F^{-1}(-\beta\lambda'[R+P])$ which is less than $(\lambda'/\lambda)\beta[R+P]$. Thus, if $\lambda' < \lambda$, the female certainty-equivalent is less than the male certainty-equivalent (and hence fewer females will be religious) for all β. If $\lambda' > \lambda$, the female certainty-equivalent will exceed the male certainty-equivalent (and hence more females will be religious) given β sufficiently small.

APPENDIX C. A SIMPLE MODEL OF SELF-SERVING BIAS IN BELIEF FORMATION

Miller and Stark (2002, p. 1418) suggest that sex differences in religious beliefs are driven by differential risk preferences. From the perspective of orthodox economic theory, beliefs are not volitional and hence this claim is nonsensical. But drawing upon non-orthodox economic perspectives (Akerlof & Dickens, 1982; Akerlof, 1989; Montgomery, 1994; Rabin, 1994), we develop a simple model of biased belief formation in order to determine the empirical implications of the Miller and Stark's suggestion.

Following Akerlof and Dickens (1982), we assume that beliefs are chosen to minimize the cognitive dissonance that occurs following a decision.[20] Assuming that an individual has chosen to be religious, she would thus wish to alter beliefs to increase the difference

$$[EU(\text{religious}) - EU(\text{not religious})] = U(-C) + \beta[xU(R) - yU(-P)] \quad (C.1)$$

and hence strengthen the apparent wisdom of her choice. If the individual could simply choose any beliefs x and y (subject to the restriction that x and y are between 0 and 1), she would obviously choose to set $x = y = 1$ (given that $U(R)$ and $-U(-P)$ are positive). But under the presumption that beliefs are not completely malleable, we might posit a "loss function" capturing the dissonance generated when subjective beliefs diverge from objective beliefs. Formally, suppose that the objective probabilities of heaven and hell (based on a non-biased assessment of available information) are given by x_0 and y_0. Further suppose that the loss function is equal to

$$\alpha[(x - x_0)^2 + (y - y_0)^2] \quad (C.2)$$

where x and y are subjective (chosen) beliefs and α is an exogenous parameter. Thus, dissonance costs are proportional to the square of the differences between subjective and objective beliefs. Combining (C.1) and (C.2), we now suppose that the individual chooses subjective beliefs to maximize

$$[EU(\text{religious}) - EU(\text{not religious})] - \alpha[(x - x_0)^2 + (y - y_0)^2] \quad (C.3)$$

which captures both the dissonance from decision making (inversely related to the first term) and the dissonance from distorted beliefs (directly related to the second term).

Differentiating (C.3) with respect to x and y, we obtain the optimal subjective beliefs in heaven (x^*) and hell (y^*):

$$x^* = x_0 + \left[\frac{\beta}{(2\alpha)}\right] U(R) \quad (C.4)$$

$$y^* = y_0 + \left[\frac{\beta}{(2\alpha)}\right] [-U(-P)] \quad (C.5)$$

(We might further add the restriction that x^* and y^* must remain between 0 and 1, or else assume α is large enough that this constraint is not binding.) Given the ordering of subjective utilities from Eq. (10) in the text, we obtain the following orderings of subjective probabilities:

$$x_M^* > x_F^* > x_0 \text{ and } y_F^* > y_M^* > y_0 \quad (C.6)$$

In words, for individuals who have chosen to be religious, we should expect males to have a stronger belief than females in heaven. Intuitively, given that males place a higher subjective utility on heaven, they have more incentive to distort their belief in heaven, increasing x^* further above x_0. Analogously, we should expect females to have a stronger belief than males in hell.

Note that our analysis has been conditioned on the choice to be religious. If the individual had instead chosen not to be religious, expression (C.3) becomes

$$[EU(\text{not religious}) - EU(\text{religious})] - \alpha[(x - x_0)^2 + (y - y_0)^2] \quad (C.7)$$

Eqs. (B.4) and (B.5) become

$$x^* = x_0 - \left[\frac{\beta}{(2\alpha)}\right] U(R) \tag{C.8}$$

$$y^* = y_0 - \left[\frac{\beta}{(2\alpha)}\right][-U(-P)] \tag{C.9}$$

and (C.6) becomes

$$x_0 > x_F^* > x_M^* \text{ and } y_0 > y_M^* > y_F^* \tag{C.10}$$

Intuitively, for individuals who have chosen not to be religious, beliefs in heaven and hell are now distorted downward. But again we find distortion of beliefs about heaven greatest among males, and distortion of beliefs about hell greatest among females.

THE SEXUAL SOCIALIZATION OF YOUNG CHILDREN: SETTING THE AGENDA FOR RESEARCH

Karin A. Martin, Katherine P. Luke and Lynn Verduzco-Baker

ABSTRACT

In this chapter we reinvigorate socialization as a theoretical framework for studying gender and sexuality, and we do so by focusing attention on the sexual socialization of young children. We provide an overview of the literature on the sexual socialization of young children. We discuss why researchers should be interested in childhood sexuality, and the role of parents, peers and schools, and the media in sexual socialization. We also address three overarching issues: methodology, the hegemony of heterosexuality, and child sexual abuse. Throughout, we suggest and organize some of the empirical questions that form a research agenda for those interested in this topic.

INTRODUCTION

Feminists, social psychologists, and others have intensely studied gender socialization for several decades. However, socialization is no longer the theoretical favorite for explaining gender and gender inequality that it once was. While in the 1970s and early 1980s many feminists used a combination of sex-role theory and socialization for understanding gender, by the mid-1980s role theory had met with much critique for being ahistorical and failing to conceptualize power (see Connell, 1987). Similarly, socialization's lack of a structural account and an on-the-ground political sense that attempts at gender-neutral socialization that had not begun to radically transform gender, led to gender being seen as a more complex phenomenon in need of multiple theoretical explanations. Socialization has also been challenged by sociologists of childhood because of its exaggerated view of children as unagentic, blank slates studied only in the process of their becoming adults and not as social actors participating in and creating the social world (Thorne, 1993; Waksler, 1991).

However, in our view, socialization has been too completely abandoned by researchers interested in the construction of gender and gender inequality. While sociologists have theorized that gender has multiple locations, in identity, interaction, social structure, and discourse, we argue that it is through socialization (and the management, negotiation, and resistance of it) that children learn how to operate in these multiple locations of gender. Through socialization children learn the rules of gendered interaction and that they are accountable for such doings of gender (West & Zimmerman, 1987). Through socialization children learn their gender (and race and class and sexual) location in social structure (Lorber, 1994). Through processes of socialization children learn a multitude of discourses and how to employ some of them. They learn the repetitive stylized performances of gender (Butler, 1990). Thus, the many theories of gender and gender inequality that contemporary scholars make use of do not render socialization a stagnant theoretical perspective. Rather, socialization can provide important and complementary insight into these other domains of gendered social life. Socialization can help us understand the processes through which social actors, especially children, come to be in and understand these various domains of gendered social life. Again, we emphasize that in our view of socialization, children are not blank slates who are merely in the process of becoming adult social actors. Rather, socialization is a process through which children begin to make meaning from the many pieces of culture they absorb from the social world, while they simultaneously alter, resist, and manage the many conflicting meanings of various pieces of culture, discourse, interaction, and social structures around them.

In this chapter, however, we not only want to reinvigorate socialization as one lens for examining gender and gender inequality in childhood, but we want to widen the lens and ask what we might learn if we examine the sexual socialization of young children. We know much about how gender is constructed through the processes of socialization, including that it begins in infancy and that early childhood is an important and intense period of socialization. Yet, despite the fact that many feminists have theorized close theoretical links between gender and sexuality, the sexual socialization of young children has been virtually ignored. Thus, we provide an overview of the literature on the sexual socialization of young children (approximately age 2–10 and when possible with an emphasis on the lower end of the range). First, we ask why researchers should be interested in childhood sexuality. We then examine the extant literature on the role of parents, peers and schools, and the media and finally turn to several overarching issues that shape this literature: methodology, the hegemony of heterosexuality, and child sexual abuse. Throughout, we suggest and organize some of the empirical questions that form a research agenda for those interested in this topic.

We also note that unfortunately, most research that has been conducted does not examine sexuality as it operates across differences of race, ethnicity, class, parents' sexual orientation, or family structure (although, analysis involving differences between middle and working class children can be found in Renold, 2005; Skelton, 2001; Thorne, 1993). White middle class children with two (presumptively) heterosexual parents make up the sample in most studies. Future research that includes analyses of the intersections of sexuality/sexual socialization, race, ethnicity, and class is needed and will certainly complicate what we know.

UNDERSTANDING CHILDREN AND SEXUALITY

The little theoretical and empirical work there is about young children's sexuality either focuses on incest and sexual abuse of children (Angelides, 2004) or describes young children's sexuality using a developmental frame on the way to examining adolescents in more detail (i.e., Shibley Hyde & Jaffee, 2000). In these latter accounts, young children's sexuality is frequently described in psychoanlaytic terms (as Freuds' (1962 [1910]) is perhaps the most prominent and well-developed theory of childhood sexuality), or such work naturalizes young children's sexuality, describing very young children as "naturally" curious about examining their bodies and about the bodies of others (Frayser, 1994; Martinson, 1994). Sometimes such work considers social components of very young sexuality, such as how societies restrict such behavior. However, this work rarely uses socialization as a frame for understanding sexuality in young children. Neither does it ask how children learn about (adult) sexuality, what meanings they make out of the information they receive from others, how they navigate through various partial and potentially conflicting sources of meaning, how they understand and interpret the structures of sexuality in society, how these issues might vary across and within different socio-cultural contexts, nor even what young children understand or might actually "know" about sexuality – their own or others (Robinson, 2005). Rather, children are reduced to innately curious beings examining their physical bodies. The socially constructed natures of the child and of sexuality are implicitly denied.

Gagnon and Simon (2004 [1973]), social constructionist pioneers of the sociology of sexuality, provide an exception to this account. Gagnon and Simon, although considering early childhood only briefly, are emphatic about the role of social learning for sexuality during this early period. They emphasize three points that are important to us. First, that while we owe a debt to Freud for recognizing how a range of emotions in infancy become attached to embodied experiences of pleasure and comfort, we should see in infancy not the emergence of a natural sexuality, but a period when "the groundwork for the potential complexity of the sexual is established" (p. 22). Second, they attend to how parents use adult sexual scripts to interpret young children's behavior, for whom the meaning of such behavior – even when apparently sexual – may be very different. The interaction between parents and children is, as for all social behaviors, critical for how children learn about sexuality. Third, sexuality is only one aspect of social life about which young children are learning. Many others, especially gender, are profoundly important for children's sexual learning.

While very few researchers use social constructionism or a framework of socialization in understanding sexuality in childhood, there is a rich literature on the sexual socialization of older children, particularly adolescents (Ward, 2003; Tolman, 2002; Thompson, 1995; Martin, 1996; Schooler, Ward, Merriwether, & Caruthers, 2005). Social scientists of many stripes are interested in how adolescents acquire their knowledge, attitudes, expectations, values, and sense of norms about sexuality. This interest in adolescent sexual socialization may not extend to young children because young children are culturally understood to be innocent and asexual, which in turn presents many research hurdles (see below). Further, this work may be seen as less important than work on adolescent sexuality as it is not linked to social problems. Clearly, teen pregnancy, sexually transmitted diseases

(STDs), and other such risks motivate much adolescent research and such issues are seen as unconnected to the sexual socialization of young children. The vast majority of the extant research on sexuality and early childhood *is* tied to a social problem – childhood sexual abuse – while other aspects of sexuality in childhood are completely ignored (see below).

While childhood sexual abuse is an important and pressing issue, we ought to be interested in the sexual socialization of young children for other reasons as well. First, young children are beginning to build a "cultural toolkit" for sexuality and sexual action (Swidler, 1986). Although by adolescence and adulthood they may discard some of the "tools" they acquire in early childhood, it is likely they keep some as well (Fine, 2004). Sexuality does not begin in adolescence, nor, as some adolescent researchers claim, on exposure to a sexualized culture (Kuik, 2003). The discourses, meanings, strategies, feelings, and motivations of adolescents are built with the cultural toolkits of childhood. What young children understand about romance, kissing, heterosexuality, where babies come from, menstruation, masturbation, and many other things all inform the first strategies of actions that adolescents employ as they navigate their way to sexual adulthood. How many stories have researchers heard from young adolescents about what causes (kissing, menstruation) and prevents (jumping up and down, menstruation) pregnancy (Martin, 1996; Thompson, 1995)? How many stories have we heard from adolescents about the shame of masturbation, menstruation, homosexuality, and sexual abuse (Martin, 1996; Schooler et al., 2005)? Certainly, these stories and feelings are at least partially built from childhood understandings of sexuality and reproduction.

Second, examining the sexual socialization of young children opens up the possibility of contributing to several broad research areas. To the vibrant work in sexuality it will contribute more evidence that sexuality is a social phenomenon as well as describing how particular constructions of sexuality come to be and perhaps how they intersect with other social identity categories. It may further allow childhood researchers to see children as social beings and actors, and not merely natural creatures whose development unfolds from within, and whose sexuality naturally emerges as a force to be reckoned with only at adolescence. For queer scholarship in particular, it will help to address questions of how heterosexuality comes to be understood as hegemonic. That is, it will contribute more data to theoretical and historical work on how heterosexuality is constructed. (Katz, 1995; Rich, 1980; Sedgwick, 1993) To scholars of gender and gender socialization it will provide links to how gender and sexuality are constructed together.

THREE DOMAINS OF SEXUAL SOCIALIZATION: PARENTS, PEERS, AND THE MEDIA

While sexual socialization is an intricate, on-going process, researchers in this field typically identify parents (Raffaelli, Smart, Horn, Hohbein, & Al, 1999; Somers & Canivez, 2003; Taris & Semin, 1997), peers (Maxwell, 2002), and media (Ward, 2003) as the main socializing agents. We first examine these domains of socialization that are primary in work on adolescents.

Parents

Parents are a highly influential force in the socialization of young children, and sexual socialization is no exception (Cossman, 2004; Finan, 1997; Frankham, 2006; Larsson & Svedin, 2002). While only a handful of studies have examined the parental sexual socialization of young children (Frankham, 2006; Geasler, Dannison, & Edlund, 1995; Ward & Wyatt, 1994; Weaver, Byers, Sears, Cohen, & Randall, 2002), the existing research does tell us a few important things, particularly regarding intentional sex/sexuality education. One third of parents think sex education in school should begin in kindergarten (Weaver et al., 2002) or elementary school and two topic areas are of particular importance for these parents; both at school and at home parents are primarily concerned that young children learn about "personal safety" (how to avoid sexual abuse) and the correct names for genitals (Weaver et al., 2002). Additionally, gender matters in the intentional sexual socialization of children. Mothers discuss such topics with children more than fathers (Downie & Coates, 1999; Nolin & Petersen, 1992), fathers tend to hold more relaxed views of sexual behavior (particularly masturbation) among children than mothers (Larsson & Svedin, 2002) and the specific topics that are discussed vary by the gender of the child (Geasler et al., 1995).

Research also consistently reports that parents hope to do better than their own parents in providing information and education about sexuality to their children (Geasler et al., 1995, Frankham, 2006; Wilson, 2004). In an interview-based qualitative study of parents regarding the sexuality education of their young children, Frankham (2006) found that today's parents have strong memories of receiving too little information or shaming information about sexuality that negatively impacted their adult sexuality and sexual experiences. Parents report their memories of these experiences as a motivating force for being better sexuality educators for their own children.

Despite these hopes for better educating their children about sexuality, parents have a high degree of uncertainty and tension about what, when, and how to tell their children about sexuality (Frankham, 2006; Geasler et al., 1995; Heiman, Leiblum, Cohen Esquilin & Melence-Pallitto, 1998; Larsson & Svedin, 2002; Wilson, 2004). Given this lack of certainty, parents often do what many experts recommend (Martin, 2005) and let their children's questions be the guide to their sexuality education (Brilleslijper-Kater & Baartman, 2000; Frankham, 2006). In their study on parents' and teachers' views of the sexual behavior of 3–6 years old children, Larsson and Svedin (2002) wrote, "It is not common that they [parents] speak to the children on sexual issues other than on request from the children themselves" (p. 263). This puts the responsibility for sexuality education on very young children who have extremely limited knowledge about sexuality (Brilleslijper-Kater & Baartman, 2000) and thus a small knowledge base from which to draw questions.

Children's initial questions to their parents about sexuality generally fall into three categories: (1) where did I [or do babies] come from? (2) sex/gender differences in body parts, and (3) explanations for sexually-related words (Geasler et al., 1995; Larsson & Svedin, 2002; Sandweg, 2005). Some research suggests that children also ask questions about genital or sexual exploration play, but that parents more often provide answers to the "nuts and bolts" questions about reproduction and body parts (Sandweg, 2005). Further, these initial questions asked by children and their parents' answers provide the lens through which future information is processed (Ward & Wyatt, 1994). For example, one of the first questions children ask is about differences in body parts between men and women. When parents explain those differences in terms of genitalia, gender is naturalized for children. Similarly, when initial questions from children circulate around reproduction, sexuality is constructed for children as being heterosexual, vaginal/penetrative, procreative, and without pleasure. Letting children's questions about sexuality guide the discussion limits the amount and type of information they receive. Thus, despite parents' goals of being better sexuality educators than their parents, they often (re)construct a view of sexuality that is similarly narrow to that constructed for them by their parents.

Part of the reason parents provide such a limited vision of sexuality to their young children is that they are concerned about providing their children with "too much" information, or information that is not age appropriate (Heiman et al., 1998; Frankham, 2006; Geasler et al., 1995). Parents, according to Frankham (2006) believe that children do not ask more questions about sexuality because they are not "ready" for the information as opposed to because they do not have enough information to know what to ask. Both Frankham (2006) and Heiman et al. (1998) suggest that parents' hesitance about giving their children "too much" information about sexuality stems partly from the cultural assumption of children as *pure* and sexuality as *dirty* or *polluting*. To preserve this image of purity, parents limit the potentially polluting information about sexuality and deny the reality of children's sexuality.

In the end, Frankham (2006) suggests parents are so concerned with providing too much information about sexuality to their children that they give vague, euphemistic, and confusing answers to requests for factual information; for example "babies come from mommies' tummies because daddies put them there." Such responses have the potential of conveying to children that parents are uncomfortable answering their questions and eventually may lead them to ask fewer questions or seek sexuality information elsewhere.

Again, most of what we know about parents' sexual socialization of young children is about their intentional socialization or attempts at sex education. There are many research trajectories still to be explored in parents' intentional sexual socialization of young children: how, when, and which parents *initiate* conversations about sexuality; gender, race, religious, and class differences in parental sexual socialization; how family structure (single mothers, two mothers, two fathers, etc.) may shape sexual socialization (Stacey & Biblarz, 2001); and more detailed information on which sexual topics parents talk about with children and how and why they do and how this changes with a child's age. Future research should also explore a diverse range of parents' implicit or unintentional sexual socialization of their children, perhaps building upon Ward and Wyatt's (1994) finding that adult recall of verbal messages about sexuality received from parents as children was negative while non-verbal (and thus implicit) messages were more positive or instructional.

Peers and Schools

Peer interaction, especially within the institution of school, is an important site of socialization, both in general and in terms of sexuality. Although Raphaela Best's (1983) *We've All Got Scars*, documented a hidden curriculum of peer-to-peer sex education which children themselves created, peer sexual socialization has been explored by very few researchers. Perhaps one reason for this neglect is that play between children has often been seen as the mimicking of adults or as naively childish behavior without social significance (Thorne, 1993), and therefore play is dismissed as unimportant in understanding the socialization of and between children. This misconception is aggravated by the desire to see children as pure and asexual. Children themselves use the discourse of play to obscure the seriousness of their behavior, for instance by defending verbal (often homophobic) insults as "just playing" (Epstein, 1996; Renold, 2005; Thorne, 1993). Many researchers now acknowledge the sociological importance of "serious play" (Baker, 2004), and contemporary ethnographies of children have made it increasingly apparent that children construct and reproduce, as well as practice and teach, gender and sexual norms through play (Blaise, 2005; Epstein, 1996; Renold, 2005; Thorne, 1993).

The belief that schools (as well as children) are asexual has served to obscure how schools (staff, curriculum, culture) encourage and even "teach" (hetero)sexuality to children (Wallis & VanEvery, 2000). Formal sex education in U.S. schools is controversial for both staff and parents (Luker, 2006; Moran, 2000). In general, schools debate what information to give to children and when, and typically offer minimal education in early grades and often the information is offered later than children would like to receive it (Best, 1983; Martin, 1996).

Informally, however, sexuality is "pervasive" in early schooling. Heterosexual gender constitutes the key matrix through which children's play and narratives are constructed (Blaise, 2005; Epstein, 1996). School cultures encourage particular (i.e., heterosexual) constructions of masculinity and femininity through their classroom and playground management practices (Martin, 1998; Skelton, 2001). For example, teachers of young children often overtly praise proper feminine gender behavior (e.g., telling girls their barrettes are pretty or their dresses make them beautiful (Blaise, 2005)) and covertly support expected masculine behavior (ignoring boys' subordination of girls (Epstein, 1996; Wallis & VanEvery, 2000)). Girls' sexuality is particularly policed: both girls (Martin, 1998) and boys (Wallis & VanEvery, 2000) tell girls to sit properly (especially if they have dresses on and their underwear is exposed), girls and teachers tell girls when their outfits are too sexy (Renold, 2005; Thorne, 1993). Adults and children seem to feel it is appropriate (and perhaps even important) to monitor the kind and amount of sexuality girls exhibit. Research on children in later elementary school reveals an anxiety felt by many girls to appear attractive to boys but not so sexy that sanctions are imposed by peers and adults, or, as Renold (2005) phrased it: "tarty, but not too tarty" (p. 49).

The games children play are also rich sites of sexual socialization. Children as young as 5-years-old construct (e.g., through artwork, rhymes, and games) narratives about themselves and each other which revolve around their roles as future heterosexual adults (Blaise, 2005; Epstein, 1996). Chasing games and "cooties," which are originally caught by boys from girls, making boys and girls distinct groups, imply that cross sex contact is not only contaminating but possibly sexual and that girls are the source of contamination because they are defined on more sexual terms (Thorne & Luria, 1986). A particular kind of heterosexuality is the subtext of these games. Some studies have documented overtly sexual play between same sex friends, most often experienced while role-playing heterosexual sexual scenarios (Institute for Sex Research & Kinsey, 1953; Lamb, 2004; Martinson, 1994; Renold, 2005). Studies also show that boys become aroused and excited during group (all boys) play involving rule transgressions, especially those which involve sexual meanings (such as a MadLib game involving sexually explicit words) (Renold, 2000, 2005; Thorne & Luria, 1986). More research is needed in and out of school as well as across a wide range of sociodemographic communities to understand the prevalence and significance of sexual play and peer interactions for sexual socialization.

Children, especially as they move through elementary school, become preoccupied with pairings of opposite sex classmates, whether they actually participate in "dating" or not (Epstein, 1996; Renold, 2005; Thorne, 1993). Boys who perform hegemonic masculinity best (often through physical aggression and athletic prowess) are most often the ones who become "boyfriends" and are then able to access a wider range of behaviors, i.e., cross gender boundaries, while simultaneously maintaining and reinforcing their hegemonic masculine status (Epstein, 1996; Renold, 2003; Skelton, 2001; Swain, 2000). Several ethnographies have found an alarming tendency for primary school "romance" and sexual harassment to occur in conjunction and for teachers and staff to fail to respond to the harassing behavior appropriately (Renold, 2003; Skelton, 2001).

Bullying and teasing with sexual overtones are commonly found in peer interactions between children. Sexual harassment and homophobic insults aimed at peers who fail or refuse to meet heterosexual gender norms are commonly observed in qualitative studies of school children (Renold, 2002a, 2002b, 2005; Thorne & Luria, 1986; Epstein, 1996; Skelton & Francis, 2003; Skelton, 2001). Additionally, teasing which links peers romantically (e.g., "Sue *likes* Joe") is always heterosexual and often keeps boys and girls from simply being friends within school (Renold, 2003, 2005; Thorne & Luria, 1986), as do the chasing games (boys chasing girls or vice versa) frequently found in primary schools (Thorne & Luria, 1986; Thorne, 1993). More research needs to be conducted on bullying and how children use bullying to gain, teach, and enforce heterosexual (and perhaps racialized) gender norms.

Media

The world of media has been rapidly expanding for young children, and young children are fully ensconced in the technology that has made that possible. For example, 30% of children under 3-year-old and 43% of children 4–6 years old have a television in their bedrooms. More than one quarter of children under six have a VCR or DVD player and one in ten have a video game console in their bedrooms (Rideout, Vandewater, & Wartella, 2003). Children under 6 use this technology and media with about half being able to load DVD players and VCRs themselves and over half owning at least 20 videos (Rideout et al., 2003). Further, while young children watch educational videos, they are also absorbed in mass popular culture. In a 2006 survey of 600 mothers of children from 3–6 years old, Martin found that from a list of 21 children's movies making 100 million dollars or more from 1990 to 2005, only 1% of the children had not seen any of these movies and half had seen 13 or more. For example, 87% had seen *Shrek*; 81% had seen *Shrek 2*; and 66% (88% of girls) had seen *Beauty and the Beast*.

Policy advocates, pediatricians, and researchers all have an intense interest in the consumption of media by young children. However, to date most of this interest has been focused on the amounts of media consumption that are "healthy" and the age at which very young children or babies should be exposed to particular types of media (Clemetson, 2006; Lewin, 2005). Some work has examined the impact of educational programming (i.e., Anderson et al., 2000; Wright et al., 2001), gender and race stereotypes (Mo & Shen, 2000; Pewewardy, 1996; Witt, 2000), and violence (see review in Kaiser Family Foundation, 2005) in young children's programming. For slightly older children – "tweens" or preadolescents and adolescents – there is much research on the media as a force of sexual socialization (see review, Ward, 2003). However, there is little work on any type of media as a force of sexual socialization for young children. Again, this may be due to cultural understandings of young children as asexual. However, as we argue throughout this chapter, children are learning about sexuality in a variety of ways from the time they are very young. What and how might various media contribute to the sexual socialization of young children?

Television, Movies, Videos

Although there is scant attention to the media as a socializing force with respect to sexuality for young children, there is attention to gender (i.e., Tobin, 2000; Witt, 2000). Some of the research on sexuality may be embedded in, or subsumed by, research on gender. That is, work that looks at gender construction in the media sometimes includes analysis of heterosexuality and romantic love (see for example, Do Rozario, 2004). These are places where both boys and girls learn about sexuality, about the hegemony of heterosexuality, and about the link between romance, love, and physicality. Think of a Disney movie: it has all these qualities. Disney movies teach children the tropes of romance (candle light, songs, longing looks, beautiful clothes, man and woman), and link these to love, monogamy, happily-ever-after, and goodness (after all a villain/evil is always defeated on the way to "True Love"). Such movies also begin, just begin, to link love to physicality and pleasure – to a kiss. We need further work on which discourses about sexuality are contained in children's movies and television programming, video games, and other such media. One specific path for future research in this area is the examination of how young girls' early (Disneyified) understandings of romance, love, and heterosexuality shape the narratives of romantic love and relationship that (pre)adolescents construct about early boyfriends (Martin, 1996; Thompson, 1995).

We also need to examine empirically what and how children absorb cultural tools from these media. Children often do not watch movies the way adults, or even adolescents, do. Rather, many young children watch movies over and over again and their comprehension of the material expands with repeated viewing (Crawley, Anderson, Wilder, Williams, & Santomero, 1999). The discourses about sexuality that adult researchers identify within such media may or may not be the same as what young children take away from them, and what children learn from them may vary according to many factors like the child's own social context, age, class, race, gender, and even the number of times within which she/he sees the movie. Further we know that young children view (passively or actively) some adult media including movies intended for teens and adults, or adult television programming (everything from sports to soap operas to nighttime dramas) including commercials, all of which may provide multiple discourses on sexuality from which children learn (Rideout & Hamel, 2006; Roberts, Foehr, Rideout, & Brodie, 1999).

Books
What might young children learn from print media about sexuality? We know very little about what children's books convey about sexuality. Although a virtual research industry on the depiction of gender in children's books has continued to flourish since Weitzman, Eifler, Hokada, & Ross (1972) classic work, none of it examines sexuality (Clark, 2002; Clark, Guilmain, Saucier, & Tavarez, 2003; Clark, Lennon, & Morris, 1993;

Diekman & Murnen, 2004; Evans & Davies, 2000; Gooden & Gooden, 2001; Tepper & Cassidy, 1999; Turner-Bowker, 1996). Is this because (explicit references to) sexuality is so absent in children's books? Or because heterosexuality is so entirely hegemonic that it is invisible? What might we learn if we examined the growing list of books for and about children with LGBT (lesbian, gay, bisexual, transgender) parents? What do children take away from these books? How is that related to their family structure, their age, religion, or the context (school, home, friends' home) in which they hear/read the book?

There is also now a plethora of books to help parents answer children's questions about "*The Birds and the Bees*" and "*Where Did I Come From?*" Yet there are few empirical investigations of these (one exception, Moore, 2003). Martin's (2006) study found that of 600 mothers of 3–6 year olds only 10% reported using a book to talk with their child about these issues. The continued publication of such books suggests there is a market for them. Is it for older children? What do these books say about sexuality to children? Moore's (2003) examination of the construction of sperm within and across 18 children's books about reproduction finds that these seemingly "biological" stories told to children, even those that "strive to be feminist," are really "normative guidelines for gender display, sexual orientation and citizenship" (p. 300). We do not know how or when such books are used by parents and children, how utilization patterns vary across and within race/ethnicity, class, and other social identity categories, or how children make meaning from them.

Popular Music
Children may also add to their cultural toolkit on sexuality from popular music. Again, while there is much work on adolescents and preadolescents there is little on younger children. However, there is reason to think that young children listen to and make sense from the music they hear and such music often contains (gendered) accounts of sexuality (Baker, 2004). Parenting magazines and Internet discussion boards, for instance, are full of anecdotal accounts of parents' horror and amusement at young girls singing provocative lyrics they may or may not understand. (For example, "My 3-year-old stands in front of the mirror and belts out words from a Britney Spears song – 'I'm not that inn-o-cent ...'" (Hales, 2001).) However, we have virtually no research on how and what very young children learn or understand from listening to popular music. How might such music contribute to their developing understandings of gender and sexuality?

New Media
Finally, it would be useful to turn our empirical attention to other forms of media and technology that may also contribute to the sexual socialization of young children. Of course the Internet, IPods, and computer and video games are relatively recent developments that are marketed to children and that more young children have access to, both at home and in preschool/elementary school, and which may have sexual content that children discover, absorb, navigate, and even produce. Again, there is virtually no work/empirical research on how such media contribute to young children's sexual socialization.

However, we also have in mind here "new" personal media like photographs and videos. Babies born today routinely have their pictures taken before they are born in the form of a sonogram. Anecdotal evidence suggests that parents frequently show these pictures to their children (the child him/herself when she/he is older or a sibling before the birth). Further, many births, especially for middle and upper class parents, are photographed or video-taped. Parents may show these to their young children. Children may also learn about birth from a group of new television shows that take the videoed birth a step further and puts it on television. "A Baby Story" on the cable channel TLC and others offer (often repeated) 30 min daytime doses of narratives of dating, romance, love, marriage, birth preparation, and birth and images of a variety of types of births (c-section, home, water, hospital, etc.). In open-ended survey questions asking mothers about talking to their children about sexuality and reproduction, about 5% volunteered that they had used these shows to educate their child (Martin, 2006). Certainly, such images have meanings for children that contribute to their understandings of sexuality and reproduction. Such images were much less available only a generation ago and have likely changed, if not increased, children's understandings of "where babies come from." Finally, the varying use of media and technologies across socio-economic communities is likely an additional site of differential experiences of sexual socialization among children.

ISSUES IN THE SEXUAL SOCIALIZATION OF YOUNG CHILDREN

Abuse

Childhood sexual abuse is disturbingly pervasive and widely understood to be a major social and public health problem (Finkelhor and Browne, 1985;

Finkelhor, 1994; Putnam, 2003). It is often acknowledged as one of parents' greatest fears for their children, and a primary motivator for talking to children about sexuality. As such, by far the majority of research on childhood sexuality is about sexual abuse. Thus, understanding the cultural and empirical terrain of childhood sexual abuse is important for understanding and developing research on the sexual socialization of young children.

In the late 1970s, the combination of interest in interpersonal and family violence from feminists and social science researchers (see, for example, Haaken & Lamb, 2000; Mildred, 2003; Straus, Gelles, & Steinmetz, 1980) brought the issue of childhood sexual abuse to the attention of the American public. This interest brought about a profound change in the cultural understanding of childhood sexuality. What had previously been constructed as an activity in which, "flirtatious and sexually precocious" (Angelides, 2004) girls seduced (or at least actively cooperated with) adult men was now understood as an abuse of male power over (female) children. While it is true that this cultural change may have had the effect, to paraphrase Angelides, of expanding the discourse of child sexual abuse at the expense of the discourse of child sexuality and thus shaping the research that can be done on both child sexuality and childhood sexual abuse, it also brought important professional and public attention to the phenomena of child sexual abuse and its many consequences.

So what have we learned about childhood sexual abuse from all of this attention? And based on what we know about childhood sexual abuse, how might it shape sexual socialization? Given the complexity of child sexual abuse, including its secretive nature, stigma, and age of victims, accurate and definitive information on the incidence and prevalence of it are not available (Finkelhor, 1994). This is particularly true for non-retrospective studies of the victimization of young children. Most data on victimization come from three sources: (1) surveys (ranging from nationally representative to small scale, clinical, or community samples) which ask caregivers about their children's experience of sexual abuse; (2) official data from child welfare or criminal justice systems, which has an overrepresentation of those more often under the supervision of regulating authorities (largely poor people of color); and (3) adult retrospective studies of abuse experienced in childhood. The latter is the favored source of data, though not without its problems.[1] Available data suggest at least 20% of women and 5–10% of men in the US experienced some form of sexual abuse in childhood. Approximately 25% of childhood sexual abuse victims were abused before the age of 7. Most often (70–90% of the time) abusers are known to the child, with between one-third and one-half of abusers of female victims and 10–20% of abusers of male victims being family members (Finkelhor, 1994). This is consistent with other reviews of the research that puts adjusted prevalence rates at 16.8% for women and 7.9% for men (Putnam, 2003). Given the issues with gathering reliable data on childhood sexual abuse, these numbers are mostly likely an underestimate.

Childhood sexual abuse is widely understood to have implications for multiple facets of identity development and a range of deleterious consequences including mental illness, substance abuse, juvenile delinquency, sexual offending and "risky" sexual behavior, etc. (Cinq-Mars, Wright, Cyr, & McDuff, 2004; Goodkind, Ng, & Sarri, 2006; Kendall-Tackett et al., 1993; Noll, Trickett, & Putnam, 2003). Finkelhor and Browne (1985), in their landmark article on the traumatic effects of childhood sexual abuse, suggested four "traumagenic" dynamics associated with experiencing childhood sexual abuse, betrayal, stigmatization, powerlessness, and traumatic sexualization. Although all have implications for gender and sexual socialization, for the purposes of this chapter we focus on traumatic sexualization. Finkelhor and Browne describe traumatic sexualization as resulting from "premature and inappropriate exposure to sexuality" that prevents "normal" sexuality from developing in children and often is observed in "inappropriate and dysfunctional" sexual behavior. Causal factors related to childhood sexual abuse and associated with experiencing traumatic sexualization include perpetrators of such abuse rewarding children for sexual behavior, which in turn can cause sexually abused children to seek rewards for themselves through sexual behavior. Perpetrators also explicitly teach children to enact specific sexual behaviors that shape children's conception of what sexual activity is, as well as both their own embodied sense of pleasure and their ability to give pleasure to others. Perpetrators also provide children with ideas about sexuality that can be confusing and frightening.

In addition to experiencing childhood sexual abuse themselves, childhood sexual abuse shapes the sexuality of children through their parents' experiences with it. Mothers (and likely fathers too, but the literature focuses on mothers) who are survivors of childhood sexual abuse have additional stressors on their parenting experience. These often begin with traumatic body memories during pregnancy and manifest themselves in caring for young children in a variety of ways. In Fopma-Loy, Wright, and Sebastian (2006) multi-method study of survivor mothers, mothers reported particular difficulty with diapering and toilet training their children, experienced hypervigilance and concern for their children when they were at the age the mothers themselves were abused, and worried about how they would handle their children's questions about sexuality – a dynamic which is not often taken into consideration when parents report distress about talking with their children about sexuality.

Given the well-documented connections between childhood sexual abuse and a multitude of poor outcomes for children, much effort has gone into developing sexual abuse prevention programs. Through school/preschool curricula, community education workshops, and public awareness campaigns, these efforts have focused primarily on educating children about ways to identify and avoid sexual abuse (Gilbert, 1988) or helping parents and teachers to identify and help children avoid it. Much controversy has surrounded these prevention efforts which primarily centers in three areas: (1) how to simultaneously teach children about sexual abuse and preserve their innocence; (2) unclear definitions of what kinds of touching qualifies as abusive; (3) the suggestion that focusing prevention efforts on children constructs the victims as responsible for the abuse perpetrated against them.

Clearly the experience of sexual abuse plays both a direct and indirect role in the sexual socialization of children. Future research would benefit from studying the impact of social institutions (family, community, reporting agencies such as child protection services and police, and treatment programs) on how children understand sexual abuse and how these experiences both shape and are shaped by different intersections of race/ethnicity, class, and other such categories. Efforts at childhood sexual abuse prevention and their effect on gender and sexuality socialization are also deserving of further study. Specifically, it would be worthwhile to explore the potential link between the early childhood focus on teaching young children to protect themselves from being sexually victimized and college students (at whom much sexual violence prevention is also aimed) believing they are the only ones who should be responsible for keeping them safe from sexual violence.

Research and Methodology

There are many issues unique to studying children sociologically (Fine & Sandstrom, 1988) and many hurdles to studying sexuality (Laumann, Gagnon, Michael, & Michaels, 1994). Research on the sexual socialization of children is complicated by both sets of these issues, and especially by: the presumed asexuality of children, fears of adult exploitation of children, the power adults have over children, and the (presumed) limited ability of children to communicate their thoughts and experiences directly, especially those regarding sexuality. Further, cultural fears of any connection between children and sexuality result in difficulty finding funding (Laumann et al., 1994) and difficulties of access via parents, schools, and human subject review boards. Thus, the extant research on the sexual socialization of young children often suffers from: small, unsystematic samples (Frankham, 2006; Geasler et al., 1995; Moore, 2003); a focus on adolescents even in research that includes young children (Downie & Coates, 1999; Weaver et al., 2002); and data that is second hand or retrospective (Ward & Wyatt, 1994).

Given the cultural difficulty of studying children and sexuality, it is easy to understand how these methodological issues arise, and thus why, especially with young children, researchers often resort to asking adults about children's sexuality. That is, researchers may resort to asking young adults to provide retrospective information from their own experiences with childhood sexuality (Institute for Sex Research & Kinsey, 1953; Lamb, 2004; Ward & Wyatt, 1994), or using clinical samples, or asking parents or teachers about young children's sexuality (e.g., Friedrich, Fisher, Broughton, Houston, & Shafran, 1998). These approaches, while providing some insight, have limitations. First, retrospective accounts, even from adolescents, are shaped by memory, current and intervening understandings, experiences, contexts, and identities. Thus, while they are a window into childhood sexuality, as researchers we need to assess how they are constructed by both memory and current social contexts.

Second, much of what we know about childhood sexuality comes from clinical research and the reports of adult therapists, psychologists, and physicians. Clinical data can be useful, especially for understanding the effects of (some experiences of) childhood sexual abuse. However, even this is a secondhand account of childhood experience, and of course is based on an atypical (in treatment), and not general, population (Friedrich et al., 1998).

Third, adults, often parents and teachers, who report to researchers about children's sexuality, may not be fully aware of their children's sexual behaviors. They certainly are not fully apprised of what meanings their children may attach to such behaviors. Children are aware of the discomfort most adults feel about childhood sexuality (Baker, 2004) and often express their reluctance to be honest with adults about these issues (Best, 1983). For instance, boys using "dirty" words while playing MadLibs asked the researcher not to observe the game (the children later allowed her to interview them about the game) (Thorne & Luria, 1986). Young women interviewed about arousal during play with their girl friends expressed shame at their arousal during sexual play, labeling it "wrong" and expressed the need to hide it from parents (Lamb, 2004). Girls, in particular, know that adults closely monitor them for signs of "too much" sexuality at too young an age. These factors limit the information parents and teachers can provide about childhood sexuality. However, they may be better conduits for information about their own (intentional) sexual socialization of children. That is, adults can better recount what they have purposefully told and withheld from children with regard to sexuality and how they handled sexual behavior, words, information, and questions children presented to them.

We must also remember that researchers are adults as well, and the above dynamics can also affect the information children share directly with researchers. Some researchers are using interviews, focus groups, and ethnographies designed to better access (slightly older) children's experiences as directly as possible (Renold, 2000, 2002a, 2002b, 2005; Thorne, 1985, 1993). However, gathering data directly from children (e.g., observation, interviews, participant observation) is also complicated by society's concern that adults not introduce ideas about sex and sexuality to children before they are "ready" as well as the concern that the presence of an adult researcher will change the behavior and discourse of the children, thereby affecting the data collected. Informed consent may also be difficult to navigate because of power imbalance. When children discover the researcher is an adult who is trustworthy and willing to take them seriously, they may share information which is far more sensitive than they or the researcher expected, and they may not be aware of the potential impact of telling such information (Duncan, 1999).

Further, as in all research, researchers of childhood sexual socialization must be aware of how their own social locations may shape the findings. Especially when researching sexuality issues, the race, gender, and sexuality of the researcher may shape the data gathered as well as the analysis and findings (Thorne, 1993; Thorne & Luria, 1986; Duncan, 1999). Furthermore, the answers to children's questions which relate to sexuality ("are you married?" "do you have a girlfriend?") and the questions asked *of* the children ("why aren't there any families with two moms?") also construct their perspectives and the data.

Finally, even when the researcher observes with as little intervention as possible, others may be resistant to such findings given the assumptions of asexuality and the lack of agency in children (e.g., "they're *just* playing – it doesn't mean anything") (Frankham, 2006; Thorne, 1993). Studying sexuality and the sexual socialization of children forces the researcher to confront the dilemma of what to do when she sees sexuality in childhood, and whether children's sexual behavior requires action on the part of adults. Most obviously, researchers must think carefully (and human subjects review boards require them to do so) about what is to be done if a child reveals sexual abuse (either victimization or perpetration) during interviews.

However, there are other "revelations" of sexuality that researchers are bound to encounter in studying childhood sexual socialization. For instance, who, if anyone, should the researcher tell of the observation of children, seemingly consensually, pretending to kiss or even to have sex in the "house" area of a preschool (Best, 1983)? Is this behavior that the teacher should know about? Should stop? Should the parents be told? And what happens when it appears in the researcher's report? Thinking seriously about such issues when negotiating access to children, parents, and schools can reduce the complexity of such issues when they arise.

Heterosexuality/Homosexuality

Virtually all models of, and research on, sexual socialization assume heterosexuality. This is particularly the case when the work is about young children. Heterosexuality is hegemonic in our society and that makes it and its construction invisible. It is also compulsory. Compulsory heterosexuality, classically defined by Rich (1980) over a quarter of a century ago, suggests that heterosexuality is not only normative but is managed, learned, instituted, and structured. This suggests a rich terrain for those interested in sexual socialization. How is heterosexuality managed, learned, instituted, and structured? Feminists who have theorized compulsory heterosexuality have primarily focused on the macro forces that make heterosexuality required rather than on the everyday practices and processes of socialization that occur within and contribute to such forces (Rich, 1980; Ingraham, 1994; Sedgwick, 1990; Butler, 1990).

Some research does examine the path to heterosexual adulthood and to bisexual, and gay and lesbian adulthood (Bem, 1996; Carver, Egan, & Perry, 2004; Diamond, 1998, 2003; Shibley Hyde and Jaffe, 2000; Savin-Williams, 2005; Savin-Williams & Diamond, 2000). However these paths, perhaps being the terrain of psychologists, are less focused on the compulsory, managed, and constructed (socialized) aspects of heterosexuality or the marginalized and stigmatized ones of homosexuality, and more on their social and psychological unfolding. Further, they typically start no earlier than adolescence and primarily study middle/upper middle class, white populations. A full scale rendering of how children become gay and what social forces might contribute to building a gay identity is well beyond the scope of this chapter. Rather, here we want to call attention to the everyday processes and contexts through which young children might learn about heterosexuality and homosexuality.

First, schools have been designated by researchers as one of the places where heterosexuality is constructed as normative and homosexuality is stigmatized (Wallis & VanEvery, 2000). As discussed above, there are several sociological, ethnographic accounts of elementary-school children (e.g., Best, 1983; Renold, 2005; Thorne, 1993, 1985) that demonstrate that elementary-age children clearly understand the compulsory nature of heterosexuality. These ethnographies give us accounts of how children employ heterosexuality and how it is linked with gender in elementary school. Skelton (2001), for instance, finds that male primary school teachers sometimes use heterosexuality in their interactions with students in order to position themselves and the boys as properly masculine. For instance, Skelton observed the use of sexual humor, flirtation, and a distinctively male-centered passion for soccer by male teachers to emphasize their own and male students' heterosexual masculinity while positioning the girls as outsiders or as feminine subjects. Some of the girls in the study did not passively accept these behaviors, however, and were seen to challenge the teacher "by reversing the male gaze and positioning him as 'not a proper teacher'" (p. 162). This, of course, has implications for boys who are learning about masculinities and girls who are being positioned not as students but as females subjected to the heterosexual masculine gaze. In another study, Blaise (2005) suggests boys and girls co-construct their gender roles within the school's heterosexual matrix through cross-gender interactions that center on the expected (and encouraged) (hetero) masculine and feminine behaviors. Such constructions of heterosexuality are seen throughout primary school. Even preschool and kindergarten children are well acquainted with the expected heterosexual gender roles and know when they are challenging the norms (Blaise, 2005; Danby, 1998).

Yet most research on very young children does not center on heterosexuality as the object of study. We know from decades of previous research (Lorber, 1994; Martin, 1998) that gender socialization is difficult to see if it is not looked for systematically, and since we know early childhood is an intense period for gender socialization and gender and sexuality are quite linked (Martin, 2005), we think systematic investigation of the construction of heterosexuality in early childhood would be fruitful and revealing. Through our own anecdotal data from a variety of preschool research settings, we know some preschools that have as part of their curricular materials for children a "wedding prop box," and that others make use of traditional fairy tales that teach about gender and sexuality, and that holiday celebrations, like Valentine's Day, make use of heterosexual imagery in describing love to preschoolers, and that very young children pick up the vocabulary of "boyfriend-girlfriend." More research of these every day constructions of heterosexuality that young children engage in, interpret, and navigate within and across different social locations would add to our understanding of children's sexual socialization.

Second, young children also learn about homosexuality, despite many adults' fears. Parents and policy makers often want to "protect" children from learning about homosexuality. In the last decade (1990–1999) *Daddie's Roommate* (#2) and *Heather Has Two Mommies* (#11) were at the top of the American Library Association's list of the Top 100 Challenged books (outranking, for example, *Sex* by Madonna). In 2005 many PBS television stations pulled an episode of "Postcards from Buster" from the air. This seemingly innocuous children's television show about a rabbit who visits children across the globe was pulled after the Secretary for Education denounced the episode about maple sugaring in Vermont because it included two pairs of lesbian mothers. Many commentators criticized the programming for introducing sexuality (despite the virtual invisibility of it in this episode) to children at such a young age. The debate and commentary that waged in the media for several weeks ignored the many contexts (including other media) in which young children might regularly learn about homosexuality.

Deborah Chasnoff's film, *It's Elementary: Talking About Gay Issues in School* (1999), provides clear evidence that children as young as second grade know something about what homosexuality is and already carry with them iconic stereotypes of gays and lesbians from parents and especially from the media. Other researchers have documented well how elementary school children use homophobic taunts to enforce gender and how (hetero)sexist harassment becomes everyday fare (Renold, 2002b, 2003, 2005) and by middle school and high school "that's so gay" and "fag" are unquestioned insults thrown around freely (Duncan, 1999; Pascoe, 2007). Clearly such issues have implications for children with LGBT parents and children who might themselves be on their way to an LGBT identity (Epstein, 1994).

In recent years several large school districts have fought battles over whether or not to include a variety of aspects about LGBT identity and life in various curriculums. These fights included not only high school sex education curriculums, but also the family curriculums taught to young children. Schools often celebrate heterosexual milestones, particularly marriage, through curriculum and discussions of staff marriages and family dynamics (Wallis & VanEvery, 2000). At the same time, the families of LGBT people in general and teachers at the school in particular are made invisible (Wallis & VanEvery, 2000). Curriculums used in schools rarely include non-heterosexual families (Casper, Cuffaro, Schultz, Silin, & Wickens, 1998), although they sometimes include other alternative family arrangements such as single parents, adoptive parents, and grandparents as caretakers. Some early childhood educators have investigated how to include homosexuality in curriculums for young children (Gilbert, 1988; Lesser, Burt, & Gelnaw, 2005). More systematic research on these issues – diversity curriculums that include LGBT issues (particularly as they intersect or not with other diversity issues of other), homophobia in elementary school, the differences for children of LGBT parents, gender non-conforming children, and protogay children – will further our understandings of the sexual socialization of all children.

CONCLUSION

The sexual socialization of young children is a broad, multifaceted research area with important potential links to gender socialization and to the sexual socialization of adolescents. Despite this, the area has been sorely understudied, likely due to many of the themes that emerged in this chapter, including a cultural presumption/image of children as asexual and *pure* and sex/sexuality as dirty and polluting, a social problems approach that has focused for important reasons on childhood sexual abuse, and methodological challenges to studying sexuality in any context, but particularly with young children.

It is clear from the research that sexual socialization, particularly heterosexual socialization, is pervasive in children's lives and that children are active agents in their own (and their peers') sexual socialization. Building on this frequent finding, we suggest that many of the limitations previously believed to be inherent in socialization theory can be addressed by theorizing agency as an integral aspect of socialization. Through the conceptualization of social actors (in this case, children) as active agents in shaping the social contexts that they are socialized by, and through a focus on everyday practices and processes, employing the framework of socialization can yield important insights into the construction of both gender/gendered inequality and sexuality in childhood. Finally, and generally, we argue that a broader focus on childhood sexuality would contribute importantly to our understandings of socialization, inequality, gender, children, and sexuality. We are hopeful that our examination and analysis of the extant literature and its significant gaps, particularly around childhood sexuality as it intersects with race, ethnicity, class, and other important social identity and behavior categories, provides both an impetus for researchers to focus on the sexual socialization of young children and some direction in which to do so.

NOTE

1. Though beyond the scope of this chapter, a major source of controversy surrounding childhood sexual abuse is the issue of forgotten or repressed memories. Additional concerns with adult retrospective data are the quality and specificity of memory over many years, the stigma of sexual abuse including victim-blaming, and varied definitions about what constitutes abuse.

REFERENCES

Anderson, D. R., Bryant, J., Wilder, A., Santomero, A., Williams, M., & Crawley, A. M. (2000). Researching *Blues Clues*: Viewing behavior and impact. *Media Psychology*, 2(2), 179–194.

Angelides, S. (2004). Feminism, child sexual abuse, and the erasure of child sexuality. *GLQ*, 10(2), 141.

Baker, S. (2004). 'It's not about candy': Music, sexiness and girls' serious play in after school care. *International Journal of Cultural Studies*, 7(2), 197–212.

Bem, D. J. (1996). Exotic becomes erotic: A developmental theory of sexual orientation. *Psychological Review*, 103(2), 320–335.

Best, R. (1983). *We've all got scars: What boys and girls learn in elementary school.* Bloomington, IN: Indiana University Press.

Blaise, M. (2005). A feminist poststructuralist study of children "doing" gender in an urban kindergarten classroom. *Childhood Research Quarterly*, 20, 85–108.

Brilleslijper-Kater, S. N., & Baartman, H. E. M. (2000). What do young children know about sex? Research on the sexual knowledge of children between the ages of 2 and 6 years. *Child Abuse Review: Journal of the British Association for the Study and Prevention of Child Abuse and Neglect*, 9(Part 3), 166–182.

Butler, J. P. (1990). *Gender trouble: Feminism and the subversion of identity.* New York: Routledge.

Carver, P. R., Egan, S. K., & Perry, D. G. (2004). Children who question their heterosexuality. *Developmental Psychology*, 40(1), 43–53.

Casper, V., Cuffaro, H. K., Schultz, S., Silin, J. G., & Wickens, E. (1998). Toward a most thorough understanding of the world: Sexual orientation and early childhood education. In: N. Yelland (Ed.), *Gender in early childhood* (pp. 72–97). New York: Routledge.

Cinq-Mars, C., Wright, J., Cyr, M., & McDuff, P. (2004). Sexual at-risk behaviors of sexually abused adolescent girls. *Journal of Child Sexual Abuse*, 12(2), 1–18.

Clark, R. (2002). Why all the counting? Feminist social science research on children's literature. *Children's Literature in Education*, 33(4), 285–295.

Clark, R., Guilmain, J., Saucier, P. K., & Tavarez, J. (2003). Two steps forward, one step back: The presence of female characters and gender stereotyping in award-winning picture books between the 1930s and the 1960s. *Sex Roles*, 49(9/10), 439.

Clark, R., Lennon, R., & Morris, L. (1993). Of caldecotts and kings: Gendered images in recent American children's books by black and non-black illustrators. *Gender and Society*, 7(2), 227–245.

Clemetson, L. (2006). *The New York Times: Parents making use of TV despite risks.* New York: The New York Times Company.

Connell, R. W. (1987). *Gender and power*. Palo Alto, CA: Stanford University Press.
Cossman, J. (2004). Parents' heterosexism and children's attitudes toward people with AIDS. *Sociological Spectrum, 24*(3), 319–339.
Crawley, A. M., Anderson, D. R., Wilder, A., Williams, M., & Santomero, A. (1999). Effects of repeated exposures to a single episode of the television program *Blue's Clues* on the viewing behaviors and comprehension of preschool children. *Journal of Educational Psychology, 91*(4), 630–637.
Danby, S. (1998). The serious and playful work of gender: Talk and social order in a preschool classroom. In: N. Yelland (Ed.), *Gender in early childhood* (pp. 175–205). New York: Routledge.
Diamond, L. (1998). The development of sexual orientation among adolescent and young adult women. *Developmental Psychology, 34*, 1085–1095.
Diamond, L. (2003). Was it a phase? Young women's relinquishment of lesbian/bisexual identities over a five-year period. *Journal of Personality and Social Psychology, 84*, 352–364.
Diekman, A. B., & Murnen, S. K. (2004). Learning to be little women and little men: The inequitable gender equality of nonsexist children's literature. *Sex Roles, 50*(5/6), 373.
Do Rozario, R. C. (2004). The princess and the magic kingdom: Beyond nostalgia, the function of the disney princess. *Women's Studies in Communication, 27*(1), 34.
Downie, J., & Coates, R. (1999). The impact of gender on parent–child communication: Has anything changed? *Sexual and Marital Therapy, 14*(2), 109–121.
Duncan, N. (1999). *Sexual bullying: Gender conflict and pupil culture in secondary schools*. New York: Routledge.
Epstein, D. (1994). *Challenging lesbian and gay inequalities in education*. Buckingham [England]: Open University Press.
Epstein, D. (1996). *Cultures of schooling, cultures of sexuality*. New York, NY: American Educational Research Association.
Evans, L., & Davies, K. (2000). No sissy boys here: A content analysis of the representation of masculinity in elementary school reading textbooks. *Sex Roles, 41*(3/4), 255.
Finan, S. (1997). Promoting healthy sexuality: Guidelines for infancy through preschool. *The Nurse Practitioner, 22*(10), 79.
Fine, G. A. (2004). Adolescence as cultural toolkit: High school debate and the repertoires of childhood and adulthood. *The Sociological Quarterly, 45*(1), 1–20.
Fine, G. A., & Sandstrom, K. L. (1988). *Knowing children: Participant observation with minors*. Newbury Park, CA: Sage Publications.
Finkelhor, D. (1994). Current information on the scope and nature of child sexual abuse. *The Future of Children, 4*(2), 31.
Finkelhor, D., & Browne, A. (1985). The traumatic impact of child sexual abuse: A conceptualization. *American Journal of Orthopsychiatry, 55*(4), 530–541.
Fopma-Loy, J., Wright, M. O., & Sebastian, K. (July 11, 2006). *Mothering as a survivor: A grounded theory analysis*. Portsmouth, NH: International Family Violence and Child Victimization Research Converence.
Frankham, J. (2006). Sexual antimonies and parent/child sex education: Learning from foreclosure. *Sexualities, 9*(2), 236–254.
Frayser, S. G. (1994). Defining normal childhood sexuality: An anthropological approach. *Annual Review of Sex Research, 5*, 173–217.
Freud, S. (1962[1910]). *Three essays on the theory of sexuality*. New York: Basic Books.

Friedrich, W. N., Fisher, J., Broughton, D., Houston, M., & Shafran, C. R. (1998). Normative sexual behavior in children: A contemporary sample. *Pediatrics*, *101*(4), e9.
Gagnon, J. H., & Simon, W. (2004 [1973]). *Sexual conduct: The social sources of human sexuality*. New York: Aldine de Gruyter.
Geasler, M. J., Dannison, L. L., & Edlund, C. J. (1995). Sexuality education of young children: Parental concerns. *Family Relations*, *44*, 184–188.
Gilbert, N. (1988). Teaching children to prevent sexual abuse. *The Public Interest*, (93), 3.
Gooden, A. M., & Gooden, M. A. (2001). Gender representation in notable children's picture books: 1995–1999. *Sex Roles*, *45*(1/2), 89.
Goodkind, S., Ng, I., & Sarri, R. (2006). The impact of sexual abuse in the lives of young women involved or at risk of involvement with the juvenile justice system. *Violence Against Women*, *12*(5), 456–477.
Haaken, J., & Lamb, S. (2000). The politics of child sexual abuse research. *Society*, *37*(4), 7.
Hales, D. (2001). *Raising kids in an R-rated culture*. Parents.com, http://www.parents.com/parents/story.jhtml?storyid=/templatedata/parents/story/data/3105.xml
Heiman, M. L., Leiblum, S., Cohen Esquilin, S., & Melendez Pallitto, L. (1998/4). A comparative survey of beliefs about "Normal" childhood sexual behaviors. *Child Abuse and Neglect*, *22*(4), 289–304.
Ingraham, C. (1994). The heterosexual imaginary: Feminist sociology and theories of gender. *Sociological Theory*, *12*(2), 203–219.
Institute for Sex Research, & Kinsey, A. C. (1953). *Sexual behavior in the human female*. Philadelphia, PA: Saunders.
Kaiser Family Foundation. (2005). *The effects of electronic media on children ages zero to six: A history of research*. Menlo Park, CA: The Henry J. Kaiser Family Foundation.
Katz, J. (1995). *The invention of heterosexuality*. New York: Dutton.
Kendall-Tackett, K. A., Williams, L. M., & Finkelhor, D. (1993). Impact of sexual abuse on children: A review and synthesis of recent empirical studies. *Psychological Bulletin*, *113*(1), 164–180.
Kuik, S. (2003). Leaving childhood: Sexuality and how children become adolescents. *The Netherlands' Journal of Social Sciences*, *39*(1), 11–22.
Lamb, S. (2004). Sexual tensions in girls' friendships. *Feminism and Psychology*, *14*(3), 376–382.
Larsson, I. B., & Svedin, C. G. (2002/3). Teachers' and parents' reports on 3- to 6-year-old children's sexual behavior: A comparison. *Child Abuse and Neglect*, *26*(3), 247–266.
Laumann, E. O., Gagnon, J. H., Michael, R. T., & Michaels, S. (1994). *The social organization of sexuality: Sexual practices in the United States*. Chicago, IL: University of Chicago Press.
Lesser, L. K., Burt, T., & Gelnaw, A. (2005). *Making room in the circle: Lesbian, gay, bisexual and transgender families in early childhood settings*. San Rafael, CA: Parent Services Project.
Lewin, T. (2005). *The New York Times: See baby touch a screen. But does baby get it?* New York: The New York Times Company, National Desk.
Lorber, J. (1994). *Paradoxes of gender*. New Haven, CT: Yale University Press.
Luker, K. (2006). *When sex goes to school: Warring views on sex – and sex education – since the sixties*. New York: W.W. Norton.
Martin, K. (1996). *Puberty, sexuality, and the self: Girls and boys at adolescence*. New York: Routledge.
Martin, K. (1998). Becoming a gendered body: Practices of preschools. *American Sociological Review*, *25*(3), 123–222.

Martin, K. A. (2005). William wants a doll. Can he have one?: Feminists, child care advisors, and gender-neutral child rearing. *Gender and Society, 19*(4), 456–479.

Martin, K. A. (2006). *The ABCs of the birds and the bees: Parents sexual socialization of three to six year olds.* Unpublished.

Martinson, F. M. (1994). *The sexual life of children.* Westport, CT: Bergin & Garvey.

Maxwell, K. A. (2002). Friends: The role of peer influence across adolescent risk behaviors. *Journal of Youth and Adolescence, 31*(4), 267.

Mildred, J. (2003). Claimsmakers in the child sexual abuse "wars": Who are they and what do they want? *Social Work, 48*(4), 492.

Mo, W., & Shen, W. (2000). A mean wink at authenticity: Chinese images in Disney's "Mulan". *New Advocate, 13*(2), 129–142.

Moore, L. J. (2003). 'Billy, the sad sperm with no tail': Representations of sperm in children's books. *Sexualities, 6*(3/4), 277–300.

Moran, J. P. (2000). *Teaching sex: The shaping of adolescence in the 20th century.* Cambridge, MA: Harvard University Press.

Nolin, M., & Petersen, K. (1992). Gender differences in parent-child communication about sexuality: An exploratory study. *Journal of Adolescent Research, 7*(1), 59–79.

Noll, J. G., Trickett, P. K., & Putnam, F. W. (2003). A prospective investigation of the impact of childhood sexual abuse on the development of sexuality. *Journal of Consulting and Clinical Psychology, 71*(3), 575–586.

Pascoe, C. J. (2007). *Hey dude, you're a fag.* Berkeley, CA: University of California Press. (forthcoming, June).

Pewewardy, C. (1996). The Pocahontas paradox: A cautionary tale for educators. *Journal of Navajo Education, 14*(1–2), 20–25.

Putnam, F. W. (2003). Ten-year research update review: Child sexual abuse. *Journal of the American Academy of Child and Adolescent Psychiatry, 42*(3), 269(10).

Raffaelli, M., Smart, L. A., Horn, S. C. V., Hohbein, A. D., & Al, E. (1999). Do mothers and teens disagree about sexual communication? A methodological reappraisal. *Journal of Youth and Adolescence, 28*(3), 395.

Renold, E. (2000). 'Coming out': Gender, (hetero)sexuality and the primary school. *Gender and Education, 12*(3), 309.

Renold, E. (2002a). Close encounters of the third kind: Researching children's sexual cultures in the primary school. In: G. Walford (Ed.), *Doing a doctorate in educational ethnography: Studies in educational ethnography 7* (pp. 29–43). Oxford: JAI Press.

Renold, E. (2002b). Presumed innocence: (Hetero)Sexual, heterosexist and homophobic harassment among primary school girls and boys. *Childhood, 9*(4), 415–434.

Renold, E. (2003). "If you don't kiss me, you're dumped": Boys, boyfriends and heterosexualized masculinities in the primary school. *Educational Review, 55*(2), 179–194.

Renold, E. (2005). *Girls, boys and junior sexualities: Exploring children's gender and sexual relations in the primary school.* New York: RoutledgeFalmer.

Rich, A. (1980). Compulsory heterosexuality and lesbian existence. *Signs, 5*(4, Women: Sex and Sexuality), 631–660.

Rideout, V., & Hamel, E. (2006). *The media family: Electronic media in the lives of infants, toddlers, preschoolers and their parents.* Menlo Park, CA: Kaiser Family Foundation.

Rideout, V., Vandewater, E. A., & Wartella, E. A. (2003). *Zero to six: Electronic media in the lives of infants, toddlers, and preschoolers.* Menlo Park, CA: Kaiser Family Foundation.

Roberts, D. F., Foehr, U. G., Rideout, V., & Brodie, M. (1999). *Kids and media at the new millennium*. Menlo Park, CA: The Henry J. Kaiser Family Foundation.

Robinson, K. (2005). Childhood and sexuality: Adult constructions and silenced children. In: J. Mason & T. Fattore (Eds), *Children taken seriously: In theory, policy and practice* (pp. 66–78). London: Jessica Kingsley Publishers.

Sandweg, G. (2005). Masters of Science: Utah State University. *Masters Abstracts International*, 43(01), 114.

Savin-Williams, R. C. (2005). *The new gay teenager*. Cambridge, MA: Harvard University Press.

Savin-Williams, R. C., & Diamond, L. M. (2000). Sexual identity trajectories among sexual-minority youths: Gender comparisons. *Archives of Sexual Behavior*, 29(6), 607–627.

Schooler, D., Ward, M., Merriwether, A., & Caruthers, A. (2005). Cycles of shame: Menstrual shame, body shame, and sexual decision making. *Journal of Sex Research*, 42(4), 324–334.

Sedgwick, E. K. (1990). *Epistemology of the closet*. Berkeley, CA: University of California Press.

Sedgwick, E. K. (1993). *Tendencies*. Durham: Duke University Press.

Shibley Hyde, J., & Jaffee, S. R. (2000). Becoming a heterosexual adult: The experiences of young women. *Journal of Social Issues*, 56(2), 283–296.

Skelton, C. (2001). *Schooling the boys: Masculinities and primary education*. Philadelphia, PA: Open University Press.

Skelton, C., & Francis, B. (Eds). (2003). *Boys and girls in the primary school*. Berkshire: Open University Press.

Somers, C. L., & Canivez, G. L. (2003). The sexual communication scale: A measure of frequency of sexual communication between parents and adolescents. *Adolescence*, 38(149), 43.

Stacey, J., & Biblarz, T. J. (2001). (How) Does the sexual orientation of parents matter? *American Sociological Review*, 66(2), 159–183.

Straus, M. A., Gelles, R. J., & Steinmetz, S. K. (1980). *Behind closed doors: Violence in the American family*. Garden City, NY: Anchor Press/Doubleday.

Swain, J. (2000). 'The money's good, the fame's good, the girls are good': The role of playground football in the construction of young boys' masculinity in a junior school. *British Journal of Sociology of Education*, 21(1), 95–109.

Swidler, A. (1986). Culture in action: Symbols and strategies. *American Sociological Review*, 51, 273–286.

Taris, T. W., & Semin, G. R. (1997). Parent-child interaction during adolescence, and the adolescent's sexual experience: Control, closeness, and conflict. *Journal of Youth and Adolescence*, 26(4), 373.

Tepper, C. A., & Cassidy, K. W. (1999). Gender differences in emotional language in children's picture books. *Sex Roles*, 40(3/4), 265.

Thompson, S. (1995). *Going all the way*. New York: Farrar, Straus, Giroux.

Thorne, B. (1993). *Gender play: Girls and boys in school*. New Jersey: Rutgers University Press.

Thorne, B., & Luria, Z. (1986). Sexuality and gender in children's daily worlds. *Social Problems*, 33, 176–190.

Tobin, J. J. (2000). *"Good guys don't wear hats": Children's talk about the media*. New York: Teachers College Press.

Tolman, D. L. (2002). *Dilemmas of desire: Teenage girls talk about sexuality*. Cambridge, MA: Harvard University Press.

Turner-Bowker, D. M. (1996). Gender stereotyped descriptors in children's picture books: Does "curious Jane" exist in the literature? *Sex Roles*, 35(7–8), 461.

Waksler, F. C. (1991). *Studying the social worlds of children: Sociological readings*. London: Falmer Press.

Wallis, A., & VanEvery, J. (2000). Sexuality in the primary school. *Sexualities, 3*(4), 409–423.

Ward, L. M. (2003). Understanding the role of entertainment media in the sexual socialization of American youth: A review of empirical research. *Developmental Review, 23*, 347–388.

Ward, L. M., & Wyatt, G. (1994). The effects of childhood sexual messages on African American and white women's adolescent sexual behavior. *Psychology of Women Quarterly, 18*, 183–201.

Weaver, A. D., Byers, E. S., Sears, H. A., Cohen, J. N., & Randall, H. E. S. (2002). Sexual health education at school and at home: Attitudes and experiences of New Brunswick parents. *The Canadian Journal of Human Sexuality, 11*(1), 19.

Weitzman, L. J., Eifler, D., Hokada, E., & Ross, C. (1972). Sex-role socialization in picture books for preschool children. *American Journal of Sociology, 77*(6), 1125–1150.

West, C., & Zimmerman, D. (1987). Doing gender. *Gender and Society, 1*(2), 125–151.

Wilson, P. (2004). Forty years of encouragement: SIECUS on family communication about sexuality. *SIECUS Report, 32*(2), 6.

Witt, S. D. (2000). The influence of television on children's gender role socialization. *Childhood Education, 76*(5), 322.

Wright, J. C., Huston, A. C., Murphy, K. C., St.Peters, M., Pinon, M., & Scantlin, R. (2001). The relations of early television viewing to school readiness and vocabulary of children from low income families: The early window project. *Child Development, 72*(5), 1347–1366.

STATUS PROCESSES AND GENDER DIFFERENCES IN SELF-HANDICAPPING

Jeffrey W. Lucas, Heather Ridolfo, Reef Youngreen, Christabel L. Rogalin, Shane D. Soboroff, Layana Navarre-Jackson and Michael J. Lovaglia

ABSTRACT

Two studies investigate gender and status effects on self-handicapping: selecting actions that can impair future performances, perhaps to protect self-image. Gender socialization and status processes suggest two potential explanations for the consistent finding that men self-handicap more than women. If status differences contribute to the tendency to self-handicap, then holding gender constant, those with high status on other characteristics would self-handicap more than those with low status. In Study 1, men assigned to high-status positions selected less study time (and thus self-handicapped more) than did men assigned to low-status positions. Women assigned high status, however, self-handicapped no more than did women assigned low status. Because study time as a measure of self-handicapping may be confounded with confidence or motivation, a second study assigned status and measured self-handicapping by the selection of performance-enhancing or -detracting music. Study 2 also found that high status increased self-handicapping among men but not among women. Both gender socialization and status processes may play roles in self-handicapping.

INTRODUCTION

Individuals *self-handicap* when they select alternatives that they expect will impair their future performances (Berglas & Jones, 1978). Such behavior may have the goal of deflecting attention away from one's personal ability and toward situational causes (Urdan, Midgley, & Anderman, 1998). Research consistently finds that men are more likely to self-handicap than women across a variety of age groups and settings (see, for example, Arkin et al., 1998; Dietrich, 1995; Kimble, Kimble, & Croy, 1998; Kimble & Hirt, 2005; Migdley & Urdan, 1995; Rhodewalt & Hill, 1995; Shepperd & Arkin, 1989). Understanding the gender difference in self-handicapping is important in part because it may shed light on gender differences in academic performance. High self-handicapping is associated with lower performance in academic settings (Keller, 2002; Martin, Marsh, & Williamson, 2003; Montgomery, Haemmerlie, & Zoellner, 1996; Urdan & Midgley, 2001). Men self-handicap more than women. And, females outperform males on average on almost all measures at every level of education, from grade school through college (Freeman, 2004; Lemke, et al., 2002; Pomerantz, Altermatt, & Saxon, 2002). Gender differences in self-handicapping may contribute to gender differences in academic performance, and a better understanding of the gender difference in self-handicapping can potentially contribute to applied efforts to improve the performance of boys in academic settings.

One potential explanation for the gender difference in self-handicapping is that boys and girls experience differences in socialization, leading men to be more competitive (Garza & Borchert, 1990) and thus more concerned with the evaluative outcomes of poor performances. Alternatively, status processes may account for gender differences in self-handicapping. When high-status individuals perform poorly, they face potential status loss – a concern less salient for low-status individuals. Because men are higher in status than women, they may see more value in self-handicapping than do women.

Experimental tests can investigate these explanations by holding gender constant and systematically varying the status of men and women. After examining previous self-handicapping research and developing the two explanations for the gender difference in self-handicapping, we test predictions from the theories in two controlled laboratory studies.

RELEVANT SELF-HANDICAPPING RESEARCH

Self-handicapping may protect a self-image of personal competence. By self-handicapping, individuals can avoid attributing anticipated poor performances to low ability and instead attribute failure to external factors (Berglas & Jones, 1978). Yet self-handicapping also interferes with performance when, for example, individuals opt to take drugs they believe will hamper performance rather than drugs they believe will enhance their performance (Kolditz & Arkin, 1982).

Self-handicapping applies to individuals at a wide range of ability levels, not just perennial failures. For example, Shepperd and Arkin (1989) informed college students that they would be taking a test that was a predictor of college success. Students then were given the option of listening to music that would facilitate their performance on the task or music that would worsen it. In the study, *most* students self-handicapped by selecting the performance hampering music.

A problem with preparing excuses in advance is that the excuses can hamper performance, making self-handicapping an important research area (Markus, 1989, Urdan et al., 1998).

Gender Differences in Self-Handicapping

Men self-handicap more than women across a variety of age groups and settings. Examples include elementary school boys self-handicapping more than elementary school girls (Kimble et al., 1998) and adult men self-handicapping more than adult women (Shepperd & Arkin, 1989). Men also have been found to self-handicap more than women at a variety of tasks, from athletic competitions to academic tests (Martin, 2004; Migdley & Urdan, 1995; Rhodewalt & Hill, 1995; Shepperd & Arkin, 1989; Urdan et al., 1998).

Although the gender effect on self-handicapping is robust, explaining it is problematic. For example, Dietrich (1995) proposed that men would self-handicap more when the task is indicative of academic ability but women would self-handicap more when the task is indicative of social ability. Results, however, showed that men self-handicapped more than women regardless of the social or academic implications of the task. Other attempts to determine the causes of gender differences in self-handicapping have also met with limited success (Rhodewalt & Hill, 1995; Harris & Snyder, 1986).

The following sections develop two theories to explain self-handicapping that may help determine why men self-handicap more than do women. The goal is important. High self-handicappers perform less well academically than do low self-handicappers (Migdley & Urdan, 1995). Self-handicapping also results in poorer academic adjustment over time (Urdan et al., 1998). Thus, self-handicapping may partially account for boys struggling in school more than girls (Burke, 1989; Richardson, 1981). More generally, understanding why people self-handicap could lead to interventions that help them optimize their performance.

SOCIALIZATION THEORIES

Theories of gender socialization may explain the gender difference in self-handicapping. According to socialization theories male children are socialized to be more competitive than female children (Balswick, 1988; Garza & Borchert, 1990; Humphreys & Smith, 1987; Hunt, 1980; Kilmartin, 1994; Miller, 1987). Because of their competitiveness, men may be more concerned with the outcomes of performances than women. Men have a greater socialized tendency to compare themselves with others than women (Gross, 1992; Messner, 1992; O'Neil, 1990). Further, the traditional male role demands an orientation toward task outcomes (Kilmartin, 1994). Thus, it may be that the potential outcomes of positive and negative performances are more salient to men than to women.

Men may also have more incentive to be concerned with performance outcomes than women. For example, boys receive more positive and more negative attention in the classroom than girls (Cherry, 1975; Fagot, 1984; Sadker & Sadker, 1985). Boys also receive more praise and more punishment from parents than girls (Block, 1984; Lytton & Romney, 1991; Maccoby & Jacklin, 1974). Boys, then, in comparison to girls, can expect more positive outcomes to result from successful performances and more negative outcomes to result from unsuccessful performances. Research finds that boys learn a greater orientation toward winning than girls (Pasick, 1990; Messner, 1992; Skovholt & Hansen, 1980; Block, 1984; Leafgren, 1990; Fogel & Paludi, 1984; Derlega & Chaikin, 1976; Lewis & McCarthy, 1988). Thus, men may be more concerned with the positive consequences of a strong performance and the negative consequences of a poor performance than women.

To the extent that self-handicapping results from a desire to protect a competent self-image, self-handicapping may be more likely in individuals who are competitive and concerned with task outcomes. Men, having been socialized to be more competitive and more concerned with success and failure, would be expected to self-handicap more than women.

A related explanation focuses on differences in status between men and women. It may be that men self-handicap more because they are higher in status than women, rather than because they have been socialized to compete and seek higher status.

STATUS CHARACTERISTICS THEORY

Status characteristics theory may explain gender differences in self-handicapping because performances have status implications. It may be that high-status individuals expect greater negative consequences to result from a poor performance than do low-status individuals. If a high-status individual fails when working on an important task, then her or his high-status position may be challenged, unless the failure is attributed to something other than personal competence. Gender is a status characteristic in many societies, with men more highly valued and esteemed than women (Pugh & Wahrman, 1983). Thus men may self-handicap more than women to protect expectations for personal competence.

Status characteristics theory (Berger, Cohen, & Zelditch, 1966, 1972; Berger, Fisek, Norman, & Zelditch, 1977) explains how status rank in groups is acquired, based on inequalities that exist in society at large. The theory argues that group members develop expectations (often unconscious) for the competence of themselves and other group members, and that these expectations act to form status hierarchies. According to the theory, high-status group members, in comparison to low-status group members (1) are given more opportunities to perform in the group, (2) perform more, (3) have their performances evaluated more highly, and (4) have more influence over group decisions.

Status characteristics theory addresses the processes in which expectations formed from the characteristics of group members lead to inequalities in group interaction (Berger, Wagner, & Zelditch, 1985). The scope of status characteristics theory is limited to groups working on a valued and collective task (Berger, Fisek, & Norman, 1989). A status characteristic is any feature of individuals around which expectations and beliefs come to be organized (Berger et al., 1989). One category of a status characteristic is considered to be more desirable and highly esteemed than another. A status characteristic is *diffuse* if it carries with it expectations for competence in a wide variety of situations. Gender, race, and education are examples of diffuse characteristics. A characteristic is *specific* if it carries expectations for competence in a narrow range of situations, such as high school grade point average. Both diffuse and specific status characteristics contribute to determining group members' relative status – whether or not the characteristic is directly relevant to the task – by altering expectations for competence that members hold for one another (Berger, Norman, Balkwell, & Smith, 1992).

Gender as a Diffuse Status Characteristic

Gender is a diffuse characteristic because it carries expectations for performance in a wide range of situations. In the United States, men are expected to perform better than women on many important tasks. Thus, status characteristics theory proposes that men as compared to women have more opportunities to perform, perform more, receive higher performance evaluations, and have more influence over group decisions.

Tests of status characteristics theory indicate that gender acts as a diffuse status characteristic in the United States, with men being more highly valued than women (Berger, Rosenholtz, & Zelditch, 1980; Carli, 1991; Pugh & Wahrman, 1983; Ridgeway & Diekema, 1989). Research shows that men have more influence than women on tasks that would appear to be gender neutral, that men tend to receive higher evaluations for their performances than women, and that it is illegitimate for women to occupy positions of high status (Eagly, Makhijani, & Klonsky, 1992; Fennell, Barchas, Cohen, McMahon, & Hilderbrand, 1978; Lucas, 2003). Thus, men enjoy higher positions than women in the status hierarchies of groups.

Using Status Characteristics Theory to Explain Gender Differences in Self-Handicapping

Men may self-handicap in an attempt to protect their high status. Status characteristics theory establishes that men have higher status in task groups than women. That is, because of their high status, men are expected to perform better and make the most valuable contributions. Thus men may feel increased pressure to perform well and self-handicap to protect expectations of competence.

High- and low-status group members can expect different consequences to result from a poor performance. When low-status group members fail, they may expect few negative consequences – they are already in low-status positions. In contrast, when high-status members fail, their status positions may be challenged. Thus, high-status group members can use self-handicapping to offset the negative consequences that may result from a poor performance. We propose that, if self-handicapping is used as an image-protecting mechanism, then high-status group members are more likely to self-handicap than low-status group members, explaining why men self-handicap more than women.

The status explanation also implies that status differences in characteristics other than gender will produce a similar self-handicapping effect, those with higher status self-handicapping more than those with lower status. Race is a diffuse status characteristic with European-Americans valued more highly than members of other racial (and ethnic) groups in the United States (Webster & Driskell, 1978). If status has an effect on self-handicapping, then we would predict that European-American participants will self-handicap more than members of other racial and ethnic groups, similar to the way that men self-handicap more than women.

Lucas and Lovaglia (2005) carried out a study in which they told participants that they would complete an ability test and then meet in focus groups to discuss members' performances and issues related to the test. Instructions informed participants that study time is one factor that affects performances on tests and that they could select how much time they would like to study for the test. Lucas and Lovaglia (2005) found higher self-handicapping among men than among women. They also found that for both men and women, European-Americans selected less study time (and thus self-handicapped more) than did members of all other represented racial and ethnic groups.

The results of the Lucas and Lovaglia (2005) study provide tentative support for the status account of gender differences in self-handicapping. European-Americans self-handicapped similar to the way that the men do. Results, however, would be more conclusive had it been possible to assign participants randomly to racial or gender categories. Factors other than status vary with race and gender. Some factor other than status differences could have produced the observed differences in self-handicapping.

We created status differences in the laboratory and randomly assigned experimental participants to high- or low-status conditions to determine whether status processes can *produce* differences in self-handicapping.

RESEARCH DESIGN: STUDY 1

To investigate independent effects of status processes and gender on self-handicapping, we created four conditions in a 2 × 2 design varying the gender and status of participants. Study conditions varied by the gender of the participant and the characteristics of the partner. The study had four conditions as follows:

Condition 1. Male participants assigned to low status compared to their partner.

Condition 2. Male participants assigned to high status compared to their partner.

Condition 3. Female participants assigned to low status compared to their partner.

Condition 4. Female participants assigned to high status compared to their partner.

Participants were assigned high or low status by giving them information about their future partner. Participants assigned low status were informed that the partner had a higher level of education and a higher grade point average than the participant; participants assigned high status were informed that the partner had lower levels on these status characteristics. The partner was always the same gender as the participant.

According to socialization theories, men are more likely than women to be concerned with the evaluative consequences of performances and thus will be more likely to self-handicap. Further, research has shown that men are more likely than women to self-handicap. Thus, in line with socialization theories, we make the following prediction:

Hypothesis 1 from Socialization Theories. Male participants (Conditions 1 and 2 combined) will be more likely to self-handicap than female participants (Conditions 3 and 4 combined).

Although support for Hypothesis 1 would be consistent with theories of gender socialization, it would not allow us to foreclose explanations for the difference other than socialization, such as arguments based on perceptions of masculinity and femininity. The design does allow us to measure whether status processes impact self-handicapping. Residual gender effects beyond status effects may be the result of a variety of processes, including but not limited to socialization. Because we are primarily concerned with how status processes affect self-handicapping behavior, and also to acknowledge other potential explanations without comprehensive treatments of each, we group these explanations under the general label "Socialization Theories."

Because higher performances are expected from high-status group members, it may be that high-status individuals self-handicap in an attempt to protect their status positions from the negative consequences that can result from a poor performance. Thus, in line with status characteristics theory, we make the following prediction:

Hypothesis 2 from Status Characteristics Theory. High-status participants (Conditions 2 and 4 combined) will be more likely to self-handicap than low-status participants (Conditions 1 and 3 combined).

Prior theory and research has addressed how low status acts to constrain performance (Steele, 1997; Steele & Aronson, 1995; Lovaglia, Lucas, Houser, Thye, & Markovsky, 1998). We predict that high-status test takers will perform actions that constrain their performances, a seeming contradiction. Many factors, however, influence test performance (see the review in Lovaglia et al., 1998). We do not propose that high-status individuals will score lower overall than low-status individuals; only that high-status individuals are more likely to self-handicap than low-status individuals.

METHODS: STUDY 1

To investigate independent effects of status processes and gender on self-handicapping, we created four conditions in a 2×2 design varying the gender and status of participants. Study participants were undergraduate students at a large midwestern university who were told that they would complete a standard ability test and then work as part of a focus group with a partner to discuss issues related to the test.

Computer instructions had participants enter information about themselves including their highest education levels completed and grade point averages. Participants then received the information entered by their future focus group partners. Partners were in fact fictitious, and the information participants received about their partners varied by experimental condition. Education and grade point average are status characteristics. In Condition 1, male participants learned that they had a male partner who was a 4th year graduate student with a 4.0 grade point average (GPA). In Condition 2, male participants learned that they had a male partner who was a high school freshman with a 1.8 GPA. In Condition 3, female participants learned that they had a female partner who was a 4th year graduate student with a 4.0 GPA. And, in Condition 4, female participants learned that they had a female partner who was a high school freshman with a 1.8 GPA. Thus a participant was assigned high status when the partner had less education and a lower GPA. A participant was assigned low status when the partner had more education and a higher GPA.[1]

After learning characteristics of their partners, and before taking the test, participants were told that study time is a factor that influences test scores and that increased study time improves performance. They were then asked to select how much time they wanted to study for the test, between 5 and 20 min. We required 5 min as a minimum amount of study time so that all participants would at least be familiar with the test materials and thus produce valid scores on the ability test. Beyond 5 min, positive effects on test score directly resulting from study time should be negligible. Instructions made clear to participants that their partners would know both the amount of study time they selected and their score on the test.

After selecting the amount of study time, participants studied using the Standard Raven Progressive Matrices test. Then they took the Advanced Raven Progressive Matrices, a standard mental ability test for individuals with IQ in the top 15% of the population.[2] The Raven is considered one of the least biased and most accurate tests of general intelligence (Raven, Court, & Raven, 1992; Jensen, 1992). Each item on both the Standard and Advanced Raven Progressive Matrices consists of a large pattern of geometric shapes that is missing a piece. The test taker must determine what the missing piece should look like and identify it from several options in a multiple-choice format. The tests are similar except that questions on the advanced test are more difficult. After studying, participants were given as much time as they needed to complete the Advanced Raven Progressive Matrices.

Our measure of self-handicapping was the amount of study time that the participant chose, a standard measure of self-handicapping (Deppe & Harackiewicz, 1996; Eronen, Nurmi, & Salmela-Aro, 1998; Ferrari & Tice, 2000; Urdan et al., 1998). Participants who selected a small amount of study time self-handicapped more than participants who selected a larger amount.

RESULTS: STUDY 1

We analyzed data from 30 participants in each of our four experiment conditions. Data from an additional 13 participants were not analyzed due to experimenter error, suspicion that the group was not real, or having a GPA outside the target range. There were 24 non-European-American participants in Study 1.

Table 1. Study 1: Mean Levels of Selected Study Time (Standard Deviations) by Gender and Assigned Status of Participants.

	Men	Women
Assigned high status	7.97 (3.39)	12.17 (5.02)
Assigned low status	11.37 (4.19)	12.00 (5.09)

Note: $N = 30$ per condition.

As in the Lucas and Lovaglia (2005) study, non-European-Americans ($N = 24$, $M = 11.33$, $SD = 5.87$) selected more study time than European-Americans ($N = 96$, $M = 10.76$, $SD = 4.44$) although the difference is not significant ($t = 0.528$, $p = 0.300$).[3]

Table 1 displays mean levels of study time selected by participants across conditions.

Hypothesis 1 from socialization theories predicted that male participants would select less study time (and thus self-handicap more) than female participants. The mean study time selected by male participants was 9.67 ($SD = 4.15$) min. The mean study time selected by female participants was 12.08 ($SD = 5.01$) min. The difference in study time for men and women is in the predicted direction and significant ($t = 2.88$, one-tailed $p = 0.003$); men were more likely to self-handicap than women.

Hypothesis 2 developed using status characteristics theory predicted that participants assigned high status are more likely to self-handicap than participants assigned low status. The mean study time selected by high-status participants (Conditions 2 and 4 combined) was 10.07 ($SD = 4.74$) min. The mean study time selected by low-status participants (Conditions 1 and 3 combined) was 11.68 ($SD = 4.63$) min. This difference is in the predicted direction and significant ($t = 1.89$, one-tailed $p = 0.031$). Thus, as predicted, high-status participants were more likely to self-handicap than low-status participants.

Mean levels of study time selected by men and women assigned to high or low status (see Table 1) suggest that status processes may explain self-handicapping in men but not in women. The mean study time selected by high-status male participants was 7.97 min, while low-status male participants selected 11.37 min, a significant difference ($t = 3.46$, one-tailed $p < 0.001$). Thus, high-status men self-handicapped more than low-status men. High-status women selected 12.17 min of study time, however, slightly *more* than low-status women who selected 12.00 min. Women assigned high-status self-handicapped no more than women assigned low status.[4]

Table 2. Study 1: Analysis of Variance for Gender and Status Effects on Selected Study Time.

Source of Variation	df	MS	F	p
Gender	1	175.21	8.75	0.004
Status	1	78.41	3.91	0.050
Gender × status	1	95.41	4.76	0.031

The one-way ANOVA results in Table 2 generally confirm bivariate analyses. The main effect for gender ($F = 8.75$, $p = 0.004$) is significant and for assigned status ($F = 3.914$, $p = 0.050$) approaches significance, indicating that men and those assigned high-status self-handicapped more than did others. The interaction of gender and assigned status is also significant ($F = 4.762$, $p = 0.031$), indicating that status processes may predict self-handicapping behavior in men but not women.

DISCUSSION: STUDY 1

Predictions from socialization theories and status characteristics theory about gender differences in self-handicapping received some support. Overall, men were more likely to self-handicap than women and participants assigned high status were more likely to self-handicap than those assigned low status. However, a test of the gender and status interaction showed that status processes may explain self-handicapping for men but not women.

Results of the Lucas and Lovaglia (2005) study that investigated self-handicapping effects of the naturally occurring diffuse status characteristics race and gender were consistent with a status explanation. For both men and women, European-Americans self-handicapped more than did non-European-Americans. Study 1 presented here, however, created status differences based on education and GPA and found status differences in self-handicapping only for men.

There are several possible explanations for these results. They could be due to an idiosyncratic sample, especially for the naturally occurring diffuse status characteristics. Or, some attribute of race or gender unrelated to status, such as different socialization experiences specific to race or gender, may have produced differences in self-handicapping between European-American and non-European-American women found in Lucas and Lovaglia (2005), whereas women assigned high status and low status in Study 1 self-handicapped at similar low levels. The inconclusive nature of the results suggests the need for replication.

RESEARCH DESIGN: STUDY 2

One puzzling aspect of self-handicapping is that motivation to succeed does not reduce self-handicapping (Rhodewalt, 1990) and in some contexts may increase it. Shepperd and Arkin (1989) found that students more often self-handicapped before taking a test that was more important. In another study, men more concerned with the prospect of failure on a test chose less study time than men less concerned with the prospect of failure (Hirt et al., 2000). Stone (2002) gave athletic participants the option of choosing the amount of practice time they wanted before an athletic contest. He found that participants who were motivated and engaged in the contest self-handicapped at least as much as those who were unmotivated and disengaged.

Although research has failed to identify a connection between high motivation and low self-handicapping, we cannot rule out motivation as a potential explanation for our findings in Study 1, or for the Lucas and Lovaglia (2005) findings. It may be that men (particularly high-status men) and European-Americans were less motivated or more confident in their abilities, and that they selected less study time for these reasons rather than as self-handicapping strategies.

To replicate Study 1, and in an effort to rule out confidence or motivation as alternative explanations for Study 1 results, we ran a new study with the same conditions and procedures as Study 1, but with a different dependent measure of self-handicapping. In Study 2, participants selected music to listen to while taking an ability test that they believed would impair or improve their test performance. Although a non-motivated or highly confident person might select less study time, perhaps in the hope of finishing more quickly, there is little apparent benefit for a non-motivated person to select performance hampering music unless the goal is to self-handicap. In other words, self-handicapping exists only in the presence of an anticipatory motive to self-protect. A non-motivated person might select a low amount of study time for reasons other than self-protection. It is difficult to conceive of a reason for selecting performance-hampering music, however, other than self-protection.

The conditions in Study 2 were identical to those in Study 1. We also make the same predictions as in Study 1:

Hypothesis 1 from Socialization Theories. Male participants (Conditions 1 and 2 combined) will be more likely to self-handicap than female participants (Conditions 3 and 4 combined).

Hypothesis 2 from Status Characteristics Theory. High-status participants (Conditions 2 and 4 combined) will be more likely to self-handicap than low-status participants (Conditions 1 and 3 combined).

METHODS: STUDY 2

As in Study 1, we created four conditions in a 2 × 2 design varying the gender and status of participants to investigate independent effects of status processes and gender on self-handicapping. Study participants were undergraduate students at a large university on the East Coast who were told that they would complete a standard ability test and then work as part of a focus group with a partner to discuss issues related to the test.

Procedures in Study 2 were identical to those in Study 1 with the following changes. After learning characteristics of their partners, instructions informed participants that a number of factors can affect performances on tests and that music is one such factor. Instructions asked participants to select music to listen to while taking the test. Participants made selections on a scale of 1 to 5, with 1 indicating extremely performance-enhancing music and 5 indicating extremely performance-detracting music. Participants in Study 2 did not take the ability test. After they made their music selection, the study was complete, and they were debriefed and paid.

RESULTS: STUDY 2

We analyzed data from 175 participants in Study 2. These included 61 women assigned low status, 28 men assigned low status, 49 women assigned high status, and 37 men assigned high status. Data from an additional 11 participants were not analyzed due to experimenter error, suspicion that the group was not real, or having a GPA outside the target range. Unlike Study 1, we had unequal number of participants across conditions in Study 2. In Study 1, we randomly assigned participants to conditions until a condition had reached 30 participants. We then randomly assigned participants to

Table 3. Study 2: Mean Music Selections (Standard Deviations, N) by Gender and Assigned Status of Participants.

	Men	Women
Assigned high status	3.78 (1.53, 37)	2.35 (1.32, 49)
Assigned low status	3.00 (1.72, 28)	2.48 (1.56, 61)

Note: 5 = Extremely performance-detracting music.

remaining conditions, closing each condition when it had reached 30 participants. In Study 2, we randomly assigned participants to conditions through the completion of the study.

Table 3 displays mean music selections by participants across experimental conditions. A selection of "1" indicates a choice for extremely performance-enhancing music. A selection of "5" indicates a choice of extremely performance-detracting music. A selection of "3" indicates a choice for music that neither enhances nor detracts from performance.

Hypothesis 1, drawn from theories of socialization, predicted that male participants would select more performance-detracting music than female participants. The mean music selection for male participants was 3.45 (SD = 1.65). The mean music selection for female participants was 2.42 (SD = 1.45). The difference in music selection for men and women is in the predicted direction and significant, $t = 4.31$, one-tailed $p < 0.001$; men were more likely to self-handicap than women.

Hypothesis 2 from status characteristics theory predicted that participants assigned high status would be more likely to self-handicap than participants assigned low status. The mean music selection for high-status participants (Conditions 2 and 4 combined) was 2.97 (SD = 1.58). The mean music selection for low-status participants (Conditions 1 and 3 combined) was 2.64 (SD = 1.62). This difference, while in the predicted direction, is not significant ($t = 1.35$, one-tailed $p = 0.09$).

An examination of music selections by men and women assigned to high- and low-status positions reveals results remarkably consistent with Study 1, again indicating that status processes may explain self-handicapping in men but not in women. The mean music selection by high-status male participants was 3.78 (SD = 1.53). The mean selection for low-status male participants was 3.00 (SD = 1.72). This difference is in the direction of high-status men selecting more performance-detracting music (and thus self-handicapping more) than low-status men and is significant ($t = 1.938$, one-tailed $p = 0.029$). The mean music selection by high-status women was 2.35 (SD = 1.32) and by

Table 4. Study 2: Analysis of Variance for Gender and Status Effects on Music Selection.

Source of Variation	df	MS	F	p
Gender	1	38.65	16.83	<0.001
Status	1	4.31	1.88	0.172
Gender × status	1	8.36	3.64	0.058

low-status women was 2.48 (SD = 1.56). This difference is in the direction of high-status women self-handicapping less than low-status women but is not significant ($t = 0.461$, two-tailed $p = 0.323$). These findings by gender and status show an identical pattern to findings in Study 1 – high-status men self-handicapped more than low-status women, while high-status women self-handicapped no more (although not significant, slightly less in both studies) than low-status women.

One-way ANOVA results for Study 2 are presented in Table 4. Gender ($F = 16.83$, $p < 0.001$) but not assigned status ($F = 1.88$, $p = 0.172$) significantly predicts music selection. The interaction between gender and status approaches significance ($F = 3.64$, $p = 0.058$).

DISCUSSION: STUDY 2

Results of Study 2 using an alternative measure of self-handicapping were very similar to results from Study 1. Although we did not find the main effect for status that emerged in Study 1, we found a pattern of results by gender and status that was identical to Study 1, with high-status men self-handicapping more than low-status men but high-status women self-handicapping no more than low-status women. The consistency of these findings across two studies with different samples and dependent variables and carried out at different universities gives weight to the possibility that status processes may produce self-handicapping in men but not women.

CONCLUSION

Our results suggest that there is a role for both socialization and status explanations of gender differences in self-handicapping. Individuals may self-handicap who feel that they can afford the reduction in performance that self-handicapping might produce. Men, having been socialized to value high status more than women, perhaps unconsciously self-handicap to protect their status. In contrast, women may disregard status and focus on performance.

It also may be that competitiveness plays a role in the differential impact of status processes in predicting self-handicapping behavior between women and men. The task in our studies was described as one in which the participant would work as part of a group to discuss issues that might influence performances on standardized tests. Socialization research indicates that men would be likely to see this task as more competitive and women as more cooperative. If women did not see the task as competitive, then they likely had little fear of failure, and would not have needed to self-handicap in order to protect their status positions.

In support of the proposition that self-handicapping results from the desire to protect a status advantage, we found status effects on self-handicapping in both studies. In line with socialization theories, we found that status processes explained self-handicapping behavior in men but not in women when participants were assigned randomly to a status position. Future research could test predictions in explicitly competitive situations demonstrated to favor women. How would status processes impact the self-handicapping of men and women when women are expected to be superior at a task? Self-handicapping may occur when protecting a status position but outweighs the drop in performance that self-handicapping might produce.

NOTES

1. In order to ensure that GPA is salient in the experimental situation, all participants have been removed from analyses who have GPAs that may not be seen as noticeably different from those of their partners. Thus, we only include data on participants with GPAs at or higher than 2.0 and at or lower than 3.8.

2. Because participants work alone to complete a test, it may appear that our experimental situation violates the scope condition of status characteristics theory that group members be collectively oriented. Researchers, however, have extended status characteristics theory to apply to individual tasks, especially those, like standardized tests, that have implications for an individual's future status rank. See Jemmott and Gonzalez (1989), Lucas (1999), Lovaglia et al. (1998).

3. Random assignment of participants to conditions in Study 1 produced the following distribution of non-European-Americans in the study: 2 in Condition 1; 7 in Condition 2; 6 in Condition 3; and 9 in Condition 4.

4. Analysis excluding data from non-European Americans produces similar results. High status men selected less study time ($N=23$, $M=8.35$, $SD=3.60$) than

did low status men ($N=28$, $M=11.64$, $SD=4.15$), $t=2.99$, $p=0.002$. High status women selected slightly more study time ($N=21$, $M=11.67$, $SD=4.81$) than did low status women ($N=24$, $M=11.25$, $SD=4.59$). Excluding non-European Americans from the ANOVA in Table 2 also produces comparable results.

REFERENCES

Arkin, R. M., Oleson, K. C., Shaver, K. G., & Schneider, D. J. (1998). Self-handicapping. In: J. M. Darley & J. Cooper (Eds), *Attribution and social interaction: The legacy of Edward E. Jones* (pp. 317–371). Washington, DC: American Psychological Association.

Balswick, J. (1988). *The inexpressive male*. Lexington, MA: D.C. Heath.

Berger, J., Cohen, B. P., & Zelditch, M., Jr. (1966). Status characteristics and expectation states. In: J. Berger, M. Zelditch, Jr. & B. Anderson (Eds), *Sociological theories in progress* (Vol. 1, pp. 29–46). Boston, MA: Houghton Mifflin.

Berger, J., Cohen, B. P., & Zelditch, M., Jr. (1972). Status characteristics and social interaction. *American Sociological Review, 37*, 241–255.

Berger, J., Fisek, M. H., & Norman, R. Z. (1989). The evolution of status expectations: A theoretical extension. In: J. Berger, M. Zelditch, Jr. & B. Anderson (Eds), *Sociological theories in progress: New formulations* (pp. 100–130). Newbury Park, CA: Sage.

Berger, J. M., Fisek, H., Norman, R. Z., & Zelditch, M., Jr. (1977). *Status characteristics and social interaction: An expectation states approach*. New York, NY: Elsevier.

Berger, J., Norman, R. Z., Balkwell, J., & Smith, R. F. (1992). Status inconsistency in task situations: A test of four status processing principles. *American Sociological Review, 57*, 843–855.

Berger, J., Rosenholtz, S. J., & Zelditch, M., Jr. (1980). Status organizing processes. *Annual Review of Sociology, 6*, 477–508.

Berger, J., Wagner, D. G., & Zelditch, M., Jr. (1985). Introduction: Expectation states theory – Review and assessment. In: J. Berger & M. Zelditch, Jr. (Eds), *Status, rewards, and influence* (pp. 1–72). San Francisco, CA: Jossey-Bass.

Berglas, S., & Jones, E. E. (1978). Drug choice as self-handicapping strategy in response to success. *Journal of Personality and Social Psychology, 36*, 405–417.

Block, J. H. (1984). *Sex role identity and ego development*. San Francisco, CA: Jossey-Bass.

Burke, P. J. (1989). Gender, identity, sex, and school performance. *Social Psychology Quarterly, 52*(2), 159–169.

Carli, L. L. (1991). Gender, status, and influence In: E. J. Lawler, B. Markovsky, C. Ridgeway & H. Walker (Eds), *Advances in group processes* (Vol. 8, pp. 89–114). Greenwich, CT: JAI Press.

Cherry, L. (1975). Teacher-child verbal interaction: An approach to the study of sex differences. In: B. Thorne & N. Henley (Eds), *Language and sex: Differences in dominance* (pp. 172–183). Rowley, MA: Newbury House.

Deppe, R. K., & Harackiewicz, J. M. (1996). Self-handicapping and intrinsic motivation from the threat of failure. *Journal of Personality and Social Psychology, 70*(4), 868–876.

Derlega, V. J., & Chaikin, A. L. (1976). Norms affecting self-disclosure in men and women. *Journal of Consulting and Clinical Psychology, 44*, 376–380.

Dietrich, D. (1995). Gender differences in self-handicapping – Regardless of academic or social competence implications. *Social Behavior and Personality*, *23*(4), 403–410.

Eagly, A. H., Makhijani, M. G., & Klonsky, B. G. (1992). Gender and the evaluation of leaders: A meta-analysis. *Psychological Bulletin*, *111*, 3–22.

Eronen, S., Nurmi, J., & Salmela-Aro, K. (1998). Optimistic, defensive-pessimistic, impulsive, and self-handicapping strategies in the university environments. *Learning and Instruction*, *8*(2), 159–177.

Fagot, B. I. (1984). Teacher and peer reactions to boys' and girls' play styles. *Sex Roles*, *11*, 691–702.

Fennell, M. L., Barchas, P. R., Cohen, E. G., McMahon, A. M., & Hilderbrand, P. (1978). An alternative perspective on sex differences in organizational settings: The process of legitimation. *Sex Roles*, *4*, 589–604.

Ferrari, J. R., & Tice, D. M. (2000). Procrastination as a self-handicap for men and women: A task-avoidance strategy in a laboratory Setting. *Journal of Research in Personality*, *34*(1), 73–83.

Fogel, R., & Paludi, M. A. (1984). Fear of success and failure, or norms for achievement? *Sex Roles*, *10*, 431–443.

Freeman, C. E. (2004). Trends in educational equity of girls and women: 2004. *Education Statistics Quarterly* (U.S. Department of Education) *6*(4), http://nces.ed.gov/programs/quarterly/vol_6/6_4/8_1.asp

Garza, R. T., & Borchert, J. E. (1990). Maintaining social identity in a mixed-gender setting: Minority/majority status and cooperative/competitive feedback. *Sex Roles*, *22*, 679–691.

Gross, A. F. (1992). The male role and heterosexual behavior. In: M. A. Kimmel & M. A. Messner (Eds), *Men's lives* 2nd ed., pp. 424–432). New York, NY: Macmillan.

Harris, R. N., & Snyder, C. R. (1986). The role of uncertain self-esteem in self-handicapping. *Journal of Personality and Social Psychology*, *51*(2), 451–458.

Hirt, E. R., McCrea, S. M., & Kimble, C. E. (2000). Public self-focus and sex differences in behavioral self-handicapping: Does increasing self-threat still make it "Just a man's game?" *Personality and Social Psychology Bulletin*, *26*, 1131–1141.

Humphreys, A. P., & Smith, P. K. (1987). Rough and tumble friendship and dominance in school children: Evidence for continuity and change in middle childhood. *Child Development*, *58*, 201–212.

Hunt, J. S. (1980). Sex stratification and male biography: From deprivation to ascendance. *The Sociological Quarterly*, *21*(2), 143–156.

Jemmott, J. B., III, & Gonzalez, E. (1989). Social status, the status distribution, and performance in small groups. *Journal of Applied Social Psychology*, *19*, 584–598.

Jensen, A. R. (1992). Spearman's hypothesis: Methodology and evidence. *Multivariate Behavioral Research*, *27*, 225–233.

Keller, J. (2002). Blatant stereotype threat and women's math performance: Self-handicapping as a strategic means to cope with obtrusive negative performance expectations. *Sex Roles*, *47*, 193–198.

Kilmartin, C. T. (1994). *The masculine self*. New York, NY: Macmillan.

Kimble, C. E., & Hirt, E. R. (2005). Self-focus, gender, and habitual self-handicapping: Do they make a difference in behavioral self-handicapping? *Social Behavior and Personality*, *33*, 43–55.

Kimble, C. E., Kimble, E. A., & Croy, N. A. (1998). Development of self-handicapping tendencies. *Journal of Social Psychology*, *138*(4), 524–534.

Kolditz, T. A., & Arkin, R. M. (1982). An impression management interpretation of the self-handicapping strategy. *Journal of Personality and Social Psychology*, *43*(3), 492–502.

Leafgren, F. (1990). Men on a journey. In: D. Moore & F. Leafgren (Eds), *Problem solving strategies and interventions for men in conflict* (pp. 3–10). Alexandria, VA: American Association for Counseling and Development.

Lemke, M., Calsyn, C., Lippman, L., Jocelyn, L., Kastberg, D., Liu, Y., Roey, S., Williams, T., & Bairu, G. (2002). *Outcomes of learning: Results from the 2000 program for international student assessment of 15 year olds in reading, mathematics, and science literacy* (NCES 2002-115). U.S. Department of Education, National Center for Education Statistics. Washington, DC: U.S. Government Printing Office.

Lewis, E. T., & McCarthy, P. R. (1988). Perceptions of self-disclosure as a function of gender-linked variables. *Sex Roles*, *19*, 47–56.

Lovaglia, M. J., Lucas, J. W., Houser, J. A., Thye, S. R., & Markovsky, B. (1998). Status processes and mental ability test scores. *American Journal of Sociology*, *104*, 195–228.

Lucas, J. W. (1999). Behavioral and emotional outcomes of leadership in task groups. *Social Forces*, *78*(2), 747–778.

Lucas, J. W. (2003). Status processes and the institutionalization of women as leaders. *American Sociological Review*, *68*, 464–480.

Lucas, J. W., & Lovaglia, M. J. (2005). Self-handicapping: Gender, race, and status. *Current Research in Social Psychology*, *10*(16), 234–249.

Lytton, H., & Romney, D. M. (1991). Parents' differential socialization of boys and girls: A meta-analysis. *Psychological Bulletin*, *109*, 267–296.

Maccoby, E. M., & Jacklin, C. N. (1974). *The psychology of sex differences*. Stanford, NY: Stanford University Press.

Markus, A. (1989). Performance and self-reflexive indicators in problem-solving. *Studia Psychologica*, *31*(3), 237–239.

Martin, A. J. (2004). School motivation of boys and girls: Differences of degree, differences of kind, or both? *Australian Journal of Psychology*, *56*, 133–146.

Martin, A. J., Marsh, H. W., & Williamson, A. (2003). Self-handicapping, defensive pessimism, and goal orientation: A qualitative study of university students. *Journal of Educational Psychology*, *95*, 617–628.

Messner, M. A. (1992). Boyhood, organized sports, and the construction of masculinity. In: M. A. Kimmel & M. A. Messner (Eds), *Men's lives* 2nd ed., pp. 161–176). New York, NY: Macmillan.

Migdley, C., & Urdan, T. C. (1995). Predictors of middle-school students' use of self-handicapping strategies. *Journal of Early Adolescence*, *15*(4), 389–411.

Miller, C. L. (1987). Qualitative differences among gender-stereotyped toys: Implications for cognitive and social development in girls and boys. *Sex Roles*, *16*, 473–487.

Montgomery, R. L., Haemmerlie, F. M., & Zoellner, S. (1996). The "imaginary audience," self-handicapping, and drinking patterns among college students. *Psychological Reports*, *79*, 783–786.

O'Neil, J. M. (1990). Assessing men's gender role conflict. In: D. Moore & F. Leafgren (Eds), *Problem solving strategies and interventions for men in conflict* (pp. 23–38). Alexandria, VA: American Association for Counseling and Development.

Pasick, R. S. (1990). Raised to work. In: R. L. Meth & R. S. Pasick (Eds), *Men in therapy: The challenge of change* (pp. 35–53). New York, NY: Guilford.

Pomerantz, E. M., Altermatt, E. R., & Saxon, J. L. (2002). Making the grade but feeling distressed: Gender differences in academic performance and internal distress. *Journal of Educational Psychology, 94,* 396–404.

Pugh, M. D., & Wahrman, R. (1983). Neutralizing sexism in mixed-sex groups: Do women have to be better than men? *American Journal of Sociology, 88,* 746–762.

Raven, J. C., Court, J. H., & Raven, J. (1992). Standard progressive matrices. *Raven Manual: Section 3.* Oxford, England: Oxford Psychologists Press.

Rhodewalt, F. (1990). Self-handicappers: Individual differences in the preference for anticipatory, self-protective acts. In: R. L. Higgins, C. R. Snyder & S. Berglas (Eds), *Self-handicapping: The paradox that Isn't* (pp. 69–106). New York: Plenum.

Rhodewalt, F., & Hill, K. S. (1995). Self-handicapping in the classroom: The effects of claimed self-handicaps on responses to academic failure. *Basic and Applied Social Psychology, 16*(4), 397–416.

Richardson, L. R. (1981). *The dynamics of sex and gender: A sociological perspective* (2nd ed.). Boston, MA: Houghton-Mifflin.

Ridgeway, C. L., & Diekema, D. (1989). Dominance and collective hierarchy formation in male and female task groups. *American Sociological Review, 54,* 79–93.

Sadker, M., & Sadker, D. (1985). Sexism in the schoolroom of the '80s. *Psychology Today, 3,* 54–57.

Shepperd, J. A., & Arkin, R. M. (1989). Self-handicapping: The moderating roles of public self-consciousness and task importance. *Personality and Social Psychology Bulletin, 15*(2), 252–265.

Skovholt, T. M., & Hansen, A. (1980). Men's development: A perspective and some themes. In: T. M. Skovholt, P. G. Schauble & R. Davis (Eds), *Counseling men* (pp. 1–39). Monterey, CA: Brooks/Cole.

Steele, C. M. (1997). A threat in the air: How stereotypes shape intellectual identity and performance. *American Psychologist, 52,* 613–629.

Steele, C. M., & Aronson, J. (1995). Stereotype threat and the intellectual test performance of African-Americans. *Journal of Personality and Social Psychology, 69,* 797–811.

Stone, J. (2002). Battling doubt by avoiding practice: The effects of stereotype threat on self-handicapping in white athletes. *Personality and Social Psychology Bulletin, 28,* 1667–1678.

Urdan, T., & Midgley, C. (2001). Academic self-handicapping: What we know, what more there is to learn. *Psychological Review, 13,* 115–138.

Urdan, T. C., Midgley, C., & Anderman, E. M. (1998). The role of classroom goal structure in students' use of self-handicapping strategies. *American Educational Research Journal, 35*(1), 101–122.

Webster, M., Jr., & Driskell, J. E., Jr. (1978). Status generalization: A review and some new data. *American Sociological Review, 43,* 220–236.

WOMEN'S PREDOMINANCE IN COLLEGE ENROLLMENTS: LABOR MARKET AND GENDER IDENTITY EXPLANATIONS

Kevin T. Leicht, Douglas Thompkins,
Tina Wildhagen, Christabel L. Rogalin,
Shane D. Soboroff, Christopher P. Kelley,
Charisse Long and Michael J. Lovaglia

ABSTRACT

Beginning in 1982, the majority of college students have been women and that majority has increased since. Explanations for the predominance of women in college enrollments and completion include a variety of labor-market factors that might now advantage men less than in the past. A variety of labor-market analyses show that, while some recent developments may have reduced incentives for men to enroll in college, labor-market explanations alone cannot account for the predominance of women in college. Some of the reduced incentives for male college enrollment point to gender identities typical of young men and women as an important explanation for the predominance of women in college. Preliminary evidence for the gender identity explanation is offered. More controlled studies capable of testing and exploring the implications of the gender identity explanation are proposed.

INTRODUCTION

The United States and other developed nations have experienced an important demographic shift in the gender distribution of students at 4-year colleges and universities from a predominantly male to a predominantly and increasingly female student body (Buchmann & DiPrete, 2006). This trend is occurring in a context where college enrollments for both men and women are rising, but at different rates (see Fig. 1). In 1960, 65% of bachelor's degrees in the United States went to men; by 1982, 50% of bachelor's degrees went to women, rising to 58% in 2004. The gender gap for African Americans is wider with 67% of bachelors degrees awarded to women. Now that entry into top-tier occupations depends heavily on performance in college, the trend foreshadows a major shift in the gender-composition of professional occupations as well.

Perhaps most interesting for researchers is that no one seems to have predicted women's predominance in higher education, while the prediction that women will soon predominate in at least the lower ranks of most professional occupations remains hard to visualize. Common sense tells us

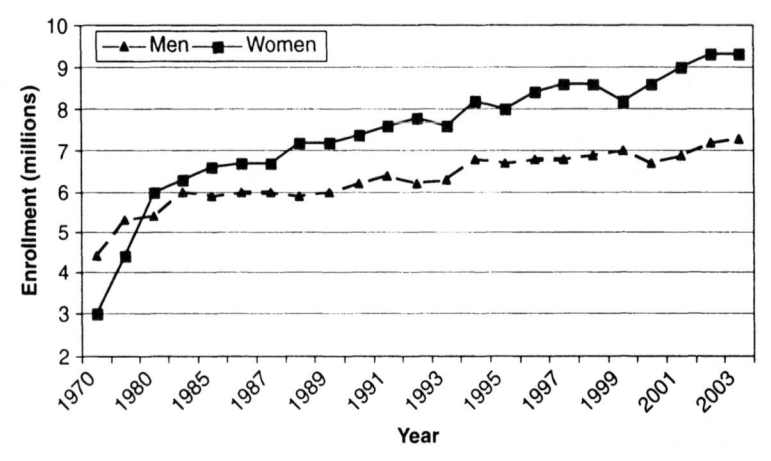

Fig. 1. Men and Women Students Enrolled (in Millions) in Colleges and Universities, 1970–2003. *Source:* Statistical Abstract of the United States, 2006.

that as barriers to women's higher education fell, the percentage of women in higher education would rise to 50%, but why would it go higher than that? Jacob (2002) credits women's advantage in "noncognitive" skills for their success, including the ability to pay attention, work with others, organize and monitor tasks and materials, and seek help. While these skills are labeled "noncognitive," they seem to be advantageous for success in the highly cognitive work of professional occupations. If women are more capable than men in ways that count most for success in higher education and later life, then the prediction that women will soon predominate in most professional occupations seems reasonable.

Sociologists generally resist explanations for broad social trends that rely on innate differences among individuals. If women are not innately more capable than men, then social forces likely explain much of their success in higher education. Diprete and Buchmann (2006) attribute women's growing predominance in colleges and universities as the result of more rapidly rising returns from education for women compared to men. That explanation, however, covers only the pattern up to 1982 when women passed the 50% mark in college graduation rates. If men continue to enjoy high returns for education, then those returns cannot account for women's recent predominance in it.

In our presentation we examine several labor-market mechanisms that may account for the current predominance of women in college. We then propose a new explanation for the predominance of women in higher education: The role of student in general and the role of college student in particular are more consonant with a feminine identity and in considerable conflict with a masculine identity. We identify the social forces that contribute to this dichotomy, describe the results of research that partially support our gender identity explanation, and propose an experimental investigation to test our developing theory that gender identity plays a substantial role in the gender gap in higher education.

LABOR-MARKET ALTERNATIVES, RETURNS TO EDUCATION, AND COLLEGE ENROLLMENT

There are several labor-market-based explanations for the growing predominance of women as students in colleges and universities. These explanations all suggest that either (a) there are declining returns to college education for men and/or growing returns to college education for women, (b) men who do not attend college have attractive alternative job opportunities compared to women who make the same choice, or (c) trends in the recruitment of students into higher education over the post-World War II era, perhaps in tandem with rising college costs, have discouraged men from specific socioeconomic backgrounds from pursuing higher education without producing similar deterrents to women's performance.

Trends in College Earnings Premia for Men and Women: Evidence within Groups

The evidence surrounding changing returns to college education by gender does not suggest that the male college-graduate earnings advantage is eroding. If anything, it suggests exactly the opposite (Fig. 2).

Male college graduates and men with some graduate education continue to out-earn their less educated counterparts in real-dollar terms. The differences are more exaggerated in nominal-dollar terms. More telling from the standpoint of a labor-market argument for the relative attractiveness of a college education are the *very real declines in the relative*

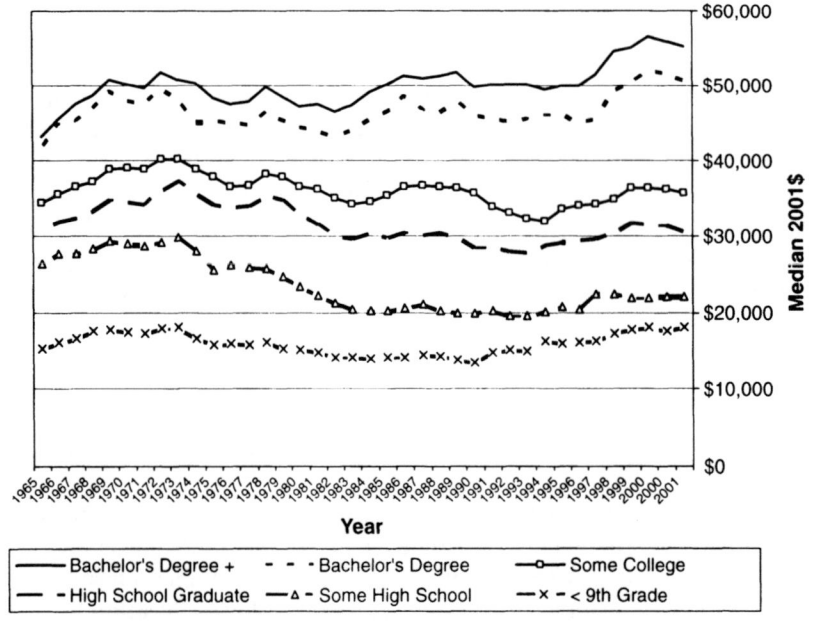

Fig. 2. Male Median Earnings by Education Level, 1965–2001, in 2001 Dollars.

earnings of non-college-educated men. This is a finding reported by others (cf. Galbraith, 2001; Freeman & Gottchalk, 2003). In fact, the size of the median earnings gap between high school educated men and college educated men doubles from 1965 to 2001 (Fig. 2). Our evidence is widely consistent with the reports of prior research (cf. Blau & Kahn, 1994; Buchmann & DiPrete, 2006; McCall, 2000).

The evidence for women is more clear-cut than the evidence for men (Fig. 3). If anything, education-based inequality among women is growing at a faster rate than educational inequality among men (see McCall, 2000). The earnings of all women, in real dollars, has risen from 1965 to 2001 due to increased labor-force participation and the opening up of labor-market opportunities (cf. Buchmann & DiPrete, 2006), but the increases in real-dollar returns to a college and post-graduate education for women have been spectacular. In short, there is clear evidence as to why women have incentives to attain a college education from a labor-market standpoint – their earnings, and the gap between the earnings of college graduates relative to high school graduates and dropouts, keep rising in real-dollar terms. The more puzzling question and the question our research proposes to address is why

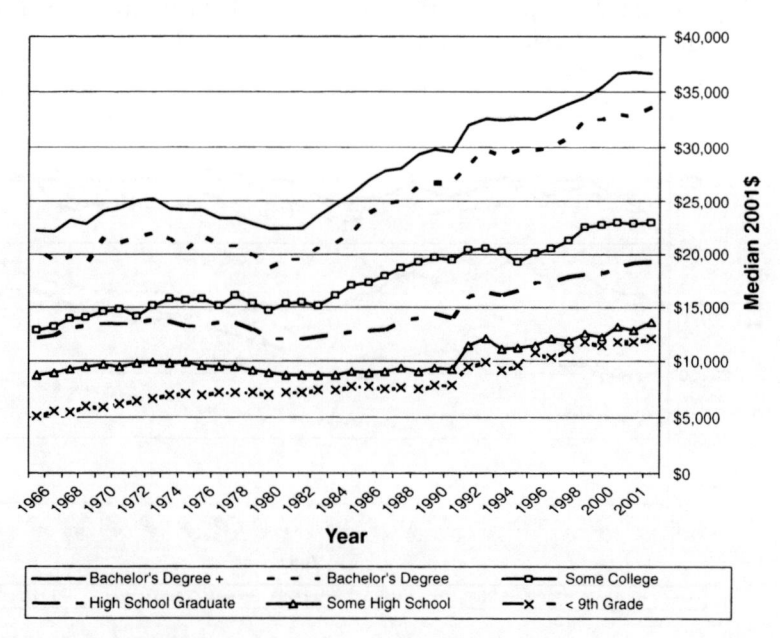

Fig. 3. Female Median Earnings by Education Level, 1965–2001, in 2001 Dollars.

men's participation in and completion of college is declining relative to women's. The answer does not seem to lie in declining returns to a college education for men.

There is, however, one dimension of the trends within genders that is interesting and that might have something to do with changing incentives to pursue a college education. Looking at Figs. 1 and 2, men's real returns to different levels of education for all groups except those with post-graduate education stagnates or falls; for women, real returns to different levels of education, and higher education in particular, rise. The relative shift is more apparent if we compare men and women's earnings by education levels directly (see Fig. 4).

In 1965, male high school graduates earned more in real terms than women who had gone to college and received degrees or even women with graduate educations. But notice what happens over time – almost all of the male trends are flat and many are declining, but all of the female trends are to differing degrees rising. This trend is so pronounced that by 2001, the relative ranking of median earnings by education and gender is substantially different than it is in 1965. The college educated female groups, nationwide, earn a median real wage that is higher than male high school graduates, and all college-educated groups out-earn all groups with less education, regardless of gender (see also Bernhardt, Morris, & Handcock, 1995).

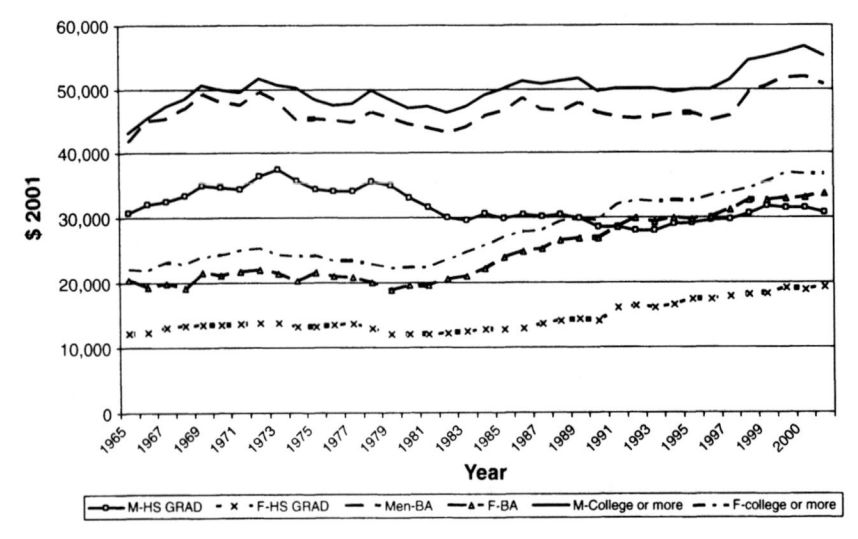

Fig. 4. Relationship between Gender and Education, 1965–2001, in 2001 Dollars.

Another way to read these trends is to look at the relative wage gaps between men and women with college and post-graduate educations. This gap has declined by almost half from 1965 to 2001, suggesting that educated women are slowly catching up with men in terms of the real earnings they can expect from a college education.

Clearly, there is something more complex going on with regard to men's and women's college attendance and completion rates than changes in returns to education. Men continue to receive high returns to a college education relative to non-college-educated men and non-college-educated women. Women receive high and rising returns to a college education relative to non-college-educated women and have surpassed the earnings of non-college-educated men. The one puzzle that we could point to, that might affect gender role inequalities in a non-material sense, is the lessened earnings disparities between men and women who are college educated. This effect might reinforce young men's perceptions that educational attainment and school performance are "something girls do" and that the advantages accruing to them are not what they once were, an explanation that points to the importance of gender identity to motivate college enrollment and performance.

Are Labor-Market Opportunities for Non-College Men Better than for Women?

A second plausible explanation regarding relative declines in men's college attendance is that young men now have options other than attending college that are better than they were at some previous time. As late as 1990, this argument would not have struck many analysts of labor markets as plausible – deindustrialization and economic restructuring had driven unemployment rates upward, and uneducated blue-collar workers (especially men) were the hardest hit by these trends (cf. Galbraith, 2001; Harrison & Bluestone, 1998). It is also obvious from our discussion above that, whatever else is happening, the earnings of non-college-educated men are not growing in real terms.

But these overall trends do not say very much about the labor market for young people, especially those in the range 17–24, the age group most likely to go to college. And the U.S. economy of the 1990s (from 1992 onward) experienced unprecedented growth and low unemployment rates, including very low unemployment rates for relatively unskilled workers (cf. Bureau of Labor Statistics, 2001).

Further, it is not clear what types of economic signals young people attend to when making decisions about the labor market. While existing studies do not support a labor-market explanation for diminishing male enrollments in colleges and universities, more fine-grained analyses of job opportunities for 17–24 year olds in recent years may shed more light. Although long-term returns from higher education may be substantial, relatively lucrative short-term employment opportunities may represent an enticing alternative to the student role. Do young men who forego college have more lucrative employment opportunities than do young women?

There is an additional issue that is related to this that we will address in the next section – do differences in labor-market activities by young men and women reflect relative signals they receive about the efficacy of higher education and their place in it? These signals might vary by race within gender groups as well as between genders. For example, African American men and European American men may receive quite different signals about the relative plausibility of higher education depending on how higher education institutions recruit students.

For now, let us return to the question of the relative labor-market opportunities for less-educated men. The preliminary evidence suggests that there is no compelling reason for men from different racial and ethnic backgrounds to view their labor-market prospects as improving relative to the college-educated. This indeed suggests that the gender identity explanation we propose below may be worth exploring.

Fig. 5 presents evidence regarding the hours worked by race and gender from 1976 to 1998 for 17–24 years old high school graduates and dropouts (data are from the March CPS).

This figure suggests that inequalities in hours worked by gender and racial groups are lessening. Importantly, if we view race-based advantages in potential access to higher education as an issue, *the median hours worked of young white men has declined, while the median hours worked of most other groups has risen.* If the hours one can work per week is a sign of employment opportunities, then these opportunities are not growing and (for white men in particular) might be declining.

But there is the possibility that the major differences in employment opportunities for this age group involve employment and unemployment, not what happens to the group that is employed and more importantly employed full time (cf. Clogg, Eliason, & Leicht, 2001). If unemployment rates are declining and especially if unemployment differences between genders and races among 17–24 year olds are declining to a uniformly low unemployment rate, this could be construed as evidence that employment opportunities have shifted in a better direction for at least some of the non-college-bound 17–24 years old age group.

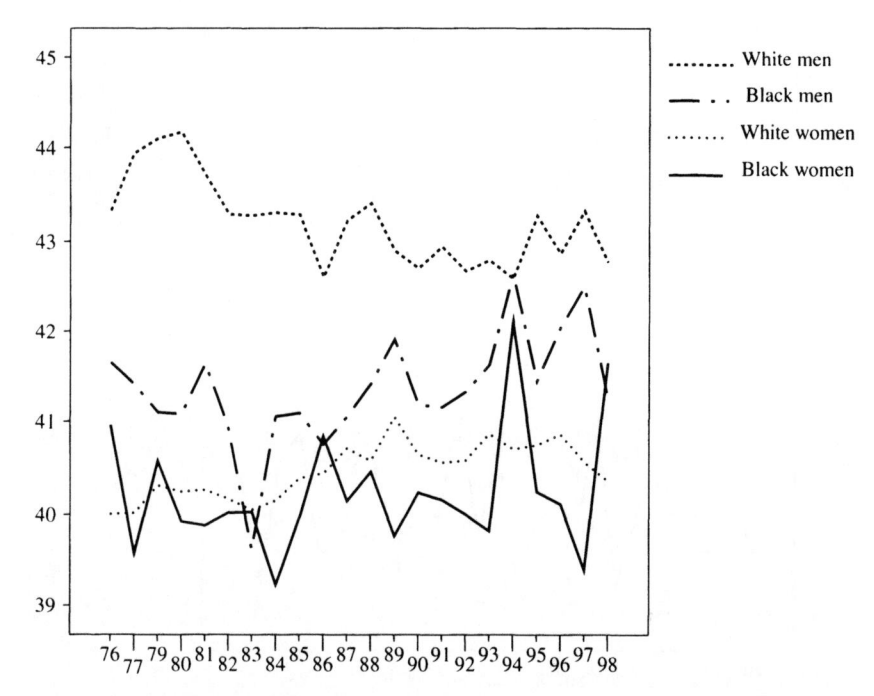

Fig. 5. Mean Hours Worked Per Week by Race and Sex, 1976–1998. Representation of Trends for People with the Following Characteristics: (1) 17–24 Years Old; (2) Employed Full-Time; and (3) Either Completed High School or Dropped Out.

Figs. 6 and 7 present evidence regarding these trends. Fig. 6 simply presents changes in unemployment rates over time by race and gender, and Fig. 7 expresses the same trend as Fig. 6 in terms of inequality between groups.

Using either one of these metrics, two trends are fairly clear for this group of young people: (1) inequalities in unemployment lessen and (2) unemployment moves in the direction toward a relative and uniformly low level for all race and gender groups. But notice, in particular, what happens to white male unemployment for this age group, from the high levels of unemployment during the early 1980s recession, when rampant deindustrialization was eliminating well-paying blue-collar jobs at an unprecedented rate, the prospects for finding a job have dramatically improved from the mid-1980s to 1998. Hence the relative perception that "I can get a job," especially among those with potentially marginal commitments to higher education, looks plausible.

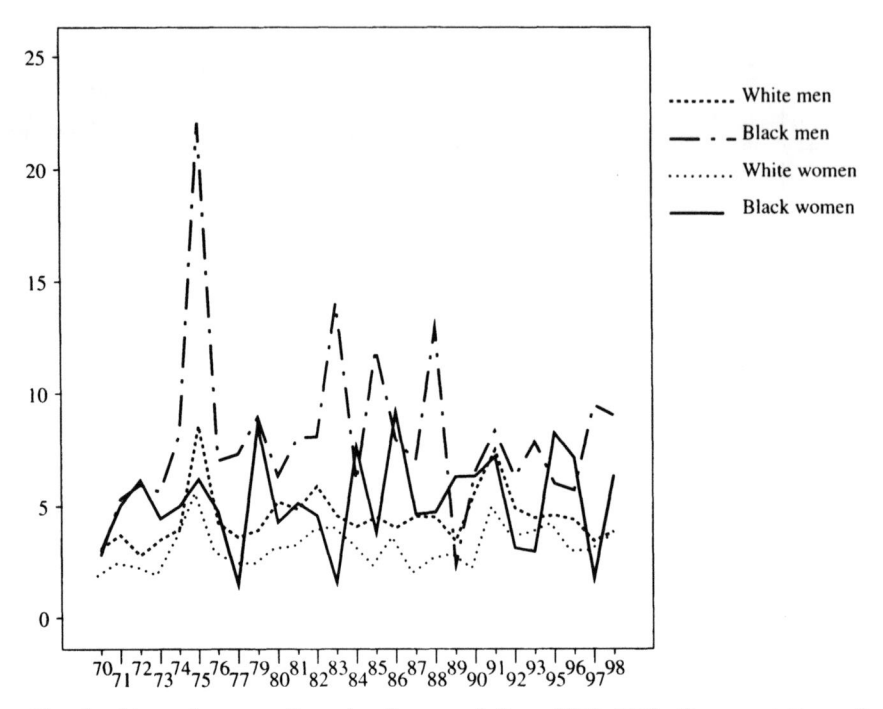

Fig. 6. Unemployment Rate by Race and Sex, 1970–1998. Representation of Trends for People with the Following Characteristics: (1) 17–24 Years Old; (2) Employed Full-Time; and (3) Either Completed High School or Dropped Out.

The final piece of the puzzle is to look at the relative median earnings of 17–24 years old non-college-educated workers. Figs. 8 and 9 provide relatively little evidence that labor-market prospects are improving for non-college-educated young people in the United States. Regardless of race or gender group, median income from wages for young people has declined. Further, inequalities between gender and racial groups have declined as well. Whatever else might be driving differences in college attendance and completion rates that advantage women, there is very little evidence regarding wages that would encourage men to refrain from going to college in numbers at least equal to those of women.

In the end, this brief descriptive analysis produced only one result that could be tied to men's declining relative college attendance rates – unemployment among non-college-educated men dropped over the course of the 1980s and 1990s, and unemployment inequalities between gender and

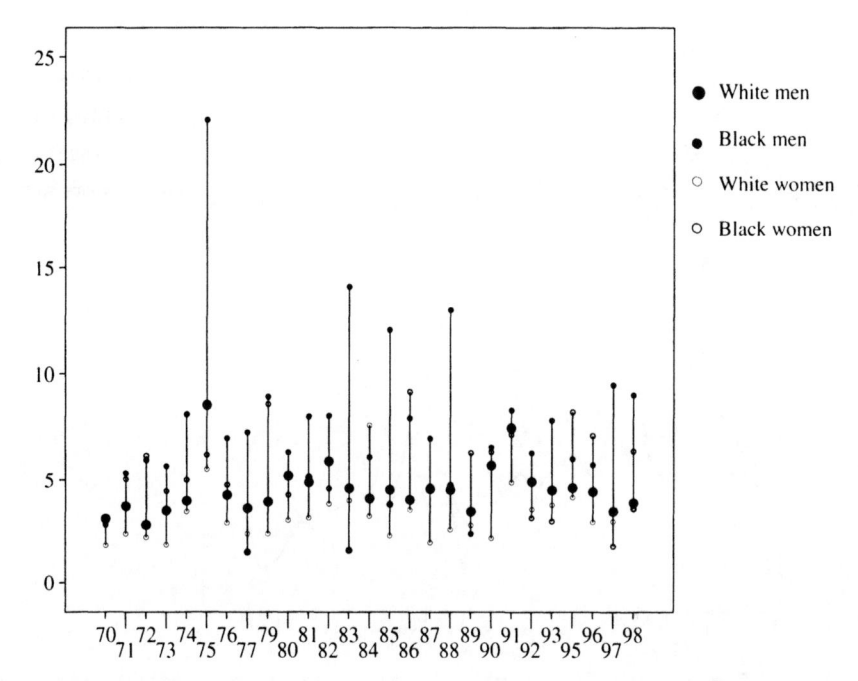

Fig. 7. Inequality in Unemployment Rates by Race and Sex, 1970–1998. Representation of Trends for People with the Following Characteristics: (1) 17–24 Years Old; (2) Employed Full-Time; and (3) Either Completed High School or Dropped Out.

racial groups declined. This suggests the possibility that there are short-term interests served by not entering college for men that do not exist for women, interests that are not tied to real earnings or potential hours of employment.

Trends in the Recruitment of Students into Higher Education

The final labor-market-related possibility for differences in college attendance and completion for young men and women is that there have been systematic trends in the recruitment of students into higher education, and these changes over time have come to favor young women over young men.

Tied to this possibility is the very real increase in the costs of a college education, and the portion of that education paid for by student loans compared to grants and other forms of financial aid that students do not have to pay back (Fig. 10).

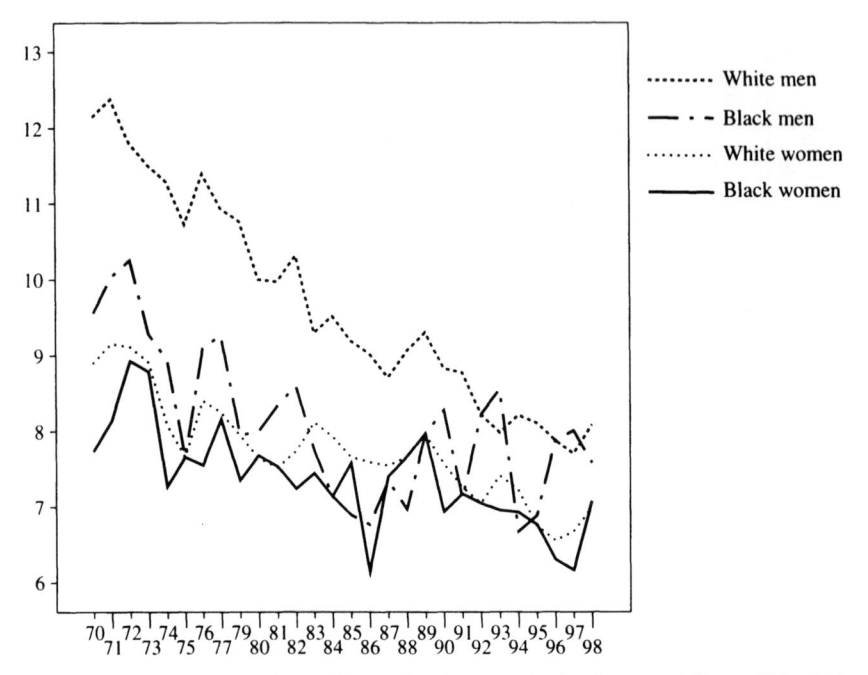

Fig. 8. Median Income from Wages (in Thousands) by Race and Sex, 1970–1998. Representation of Trends for People with the Following Characteristics: (1) 17–24 Years Old; (2) Employed Full-Time; and (3) Either Completed High School or Dropped Out.

Prior investigation has shown that college costs have risen at several times the inflation rate (Leicht & Fitzgerald, 2006; Phillips, 1992). But the other major shift has come in the mechanisms used to pay for college, with the overall shift overwhelmingly in favor of loans versus grants. This, in combination with the low unemployment rates of non-college-educated men, may be enough to tip the scales for marginally committed men away from pursuing a college degree. To explain women's current predominance in college enrollments, however, we must also assume that immediate employment and financial independence are more important for young men than for young women. The following sections develop a gender identity explanation for such a difference.

Prior research also points to other changes in the activities of colleges and universities, and trends in attendance rates associated with economic changes outside of university walls. David Karen's (1991) research suggests that

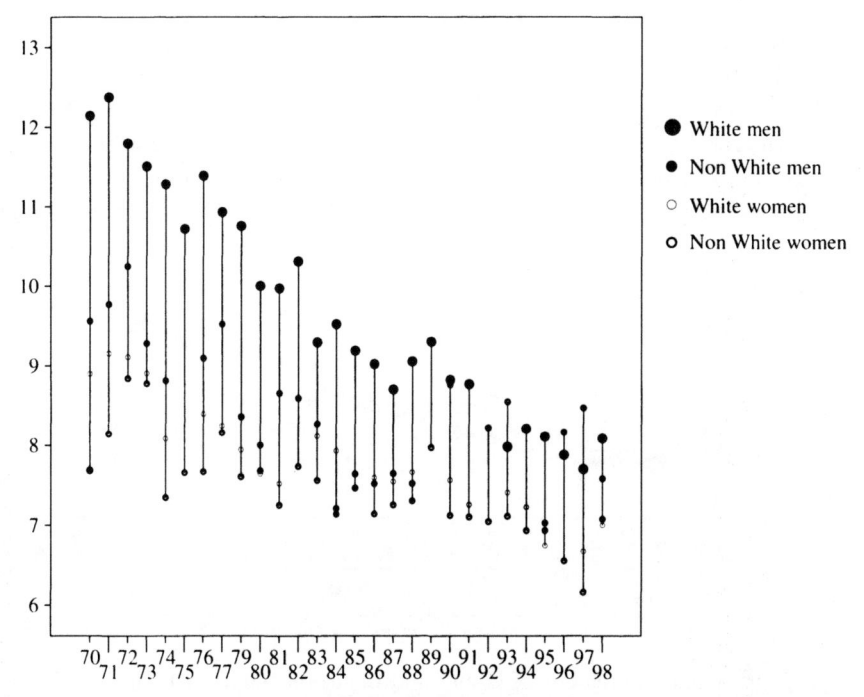

Fig. 9. Inequality in Median Wages (in Thousands) by Race and Sex, 1970–1998. Representation of Trends for People with the Following Characteristics: (1) 17–24 Years Old; (2) Employed Full-Time; and (3) Either Completed High School or Dropped Out.

recruitment into college and university education and its pursuit have been tilted in the direction of what he terms "officially socially recognized groups" (women and racial minorities) and away from or expressing indifference to low income, working class youth. This would especially disadvantage working class white men who then might be tempted to directly enter the labor market, and especially a labor market with low unemployment for 17–24 year olds.

Tian (1996) in his comparison of educational access and completion in the UK and US from 1970 to 1986, points to threats to traditional gender roles as a spur that changes higher education participation across these two English-speaking nations. In both cases, women's entry into higher education rises with the divorce rate, while men's does not. Men's college entrance rises with the unemployment rate, but women's does not. This leads

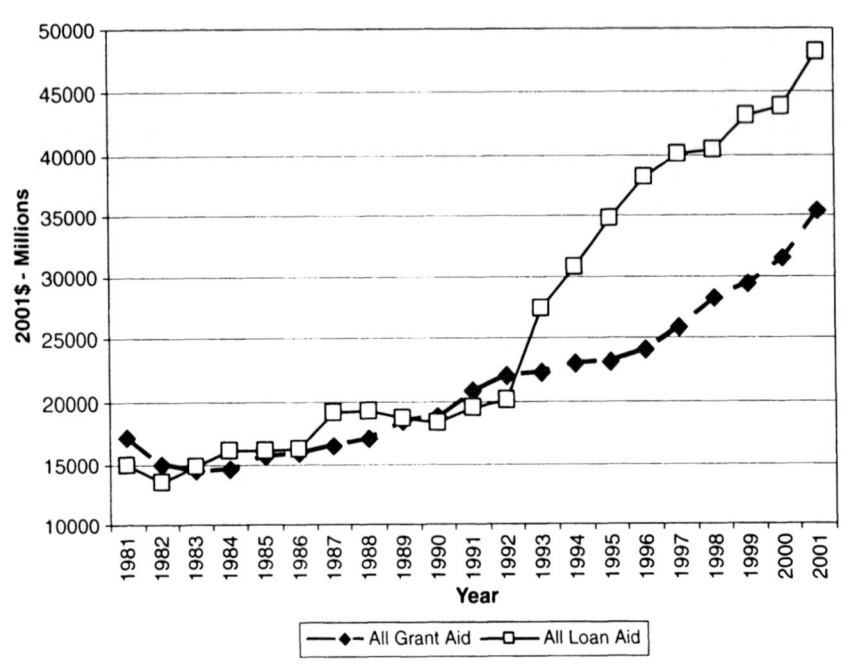

Fig. 10. Trends in the Use of Grants and Loans for Student Aid, in 2001 Dollars.

to his conclusion that men pursue higher education to continue in their traditional breadwinner roles when unemployment threatens their status, but that women enter colleges and universities when they are forced to abandon traditional gender roles, via divorce for example, and fend for themselves. This result is broadly consistent with our hypothesis that recent low unemployment rates for non-college-educated men may be contributing to relatively low male college attendance rates. It is also consistent with a more general gender identity explanation.

Powell and Parcel (1997) and Buchmann and DiPrete (2006) point to two other mechanisms that are labor-market and lifecourse related that may be affecting college attendance and completion rates. Powell and Parcell find that women's college attendance and educational attainment is much higher if girls come from families with two biological parents. Young men's college attendance is not affected by family structure at all. But then Buchmann and DiPrete (2006), in a much more comprehensive study of gender differences in college attendance and completion rates, find that declining male college attendance is especially pronounced among young men with absent or relatively uneducated fathers. The corresponding college attendance rates for girls from these same backgrounds rises. It seems highly likely that the same economic forces that would affect young male entrance into the labor market and college would be the same forces that would affect uneducated fathers' labor-market prospects. If uneducated fathers provide role models for their sons in an environment where unemployment is declining, this, combined with a lack of encouragement to attend college (and, as our figure suggests above, growing difficulties in paying for it), would tip the scales against men's college attendance. The corresponding increases in labor-market opportunities for young women would have the opposite effect.

In summary, there are three possible reasons for the changing salience of college education for young men and women. Most of this evidence still suggests that young men and women should be going to college because there are considerable earnings returns to doing so. However, the returns are no longer differentially distributed by gender as they once were, and unemployment rates for non-college-educated men, high during the deindustrialization of the 1980s, are now down to levels comparable to late 1960s and early 1970s.

GENDER IDENTITY AND THE COLLEGE STUDENT ROLE

The gender identities of college-age men and women may shape their decision to attend college, to persevere in it, and to perform well. We propose that the more consonant with an individual's gender identity is the college student role, the less resistance they will have to attending college and the more active they will be in pursuing academic success in college.

Following structural identity theory, we define identities as shared social meanings that individuals acquire about themselves and their behavior in social roles (Burke & Reitzes, 1991; Stryker & Burke, 2000). A fundamental proposition of identity control theory is that individuals behave in ways that sustain their identities (Burke 1991, 1997; Burke & Reitzes, 1991). Identity control theory (Burke, 1991; Burke & Reitzes, 1991; Burke & Stets, 1999) describes a process through which individuals sense discrepancies between their self conceptions, that is their identity standards, and information they receive about themselves. Identity standards are dispositional in the sense that they develop over time and become quite stable but respond to situational changes in information relevant to the identity (Burke, 2006). As gender identities develop during childhood, masculine becomes contrasted with feminine as boys and girls segregate (Boyle, Marshall, & Robeson, 2003;

Thorne, 1993). A status element emerges as well; for a girl, being a "tomboy" is not as relentlessly negative as being a "sissy" is for a boy (Thorne, 1993), which may explain the wider variety of girls' play activities noted by Boyle et al. (2003). In the informal social hierarchy of boys, status is tied closely with perceptions of masculinity especially physical prowess (Swain, 2002). It may be especially important for boys to avoid those activities seen as feminine. For example, Dutro (2002) observed that boys found it extremely important to avoid reading material seen as feminine, while girls were open to a wide variety of reading material without assessing its gender valence. We propose that to the extent the college student role and academic success are seen as feminine, young men resist engaging in academic activities.

Affect control theory (Heise, 1979; MacKinnon, 1994; Smith-Lovin & Heise, 1987) also supports our theoretical development. Both affect control theory and identity control theory develop from the premise that individuals behave in ways to maintain their identities (Burke, 1991; Burke & Reitzes, 1991; Burke & Stets, 1999). Affect control theory draws from work by Osgood, Tannenbaum, and Suci (1957) that proposes that people interpret meaning across three dimensions: evaluation (good to bad), potency (powerful to powerless), and activity (noisy/lively to quiet/still). Researchers using affect control theory obtain EPA (evaluation, potency, activity) profiles that measure fundamental sentiments about people in roles, objects, and behaviors (Smith-Lovin & Heise, 1987). Affect control theory assumes that the specific EPA profiles vary among cultures (Robinson & Smith-Lovin, 1999). In the United States, for example, the student identity is rated quite good, only slightly strong, and moderately active on EPA scales, producing an EPA profile of 1.49, .31, and .75 on semantic differential scales ranging from −4.33 to 4.33. In contrast, the identity of employee is rated as less good, stronger, and less active than the student identity (EPA rating, 1.16, .48, and .66). Young men have EPA profiles more powerful and less good than women in similar identities and roles.

Because the student identity EPA profile is quite good but only slightly strong in contrast to male identities generally which are less good but stronger than female identities, it follows that the student role is less consonant with a male identity than with a female identity. From the premise that individuals behave in ways to maintain their identities, it then follows that young men may not find academic activities and roles as attractive as do young women. The less good and more powerful role of employee may seem more attractive to men than does the college student role.

Social identity theory more directly relates the behavior motivated by gender identity to status differences between men and women (Abrams &

Hogg, 1990; Tajfel & Turner, 1986). Social identity theory proposes that individual self-concept is shaped by the status of the groups to which the individual belongs. The theory proposes that mere categorization is sufficient to produce derogation of out-group members. Gender differences, one of the most relevant categorizations motivating social interaction, might be expected to have effects on behavior predicted by the theory (Maass, Cadinu, Guarnieri, & Grasselli, 2003). An individual's social identity is threatened by the perception of association with a derogated out group (Ellemers, Spears, & Doosje, 2002). Thus men feel threatened when faced with the prospect of engaging in activities seen as feminine. The feminine activity not only undermines a masculine gender identity but threatens status loss as well.

Recent research by Youngreen, Childers, Conlon, Robinson, and Lovaglia (2003) shows that identities can have significant effects on academic performance. They found that when success on a standardized test was non-consonant with a student's identity, that student performed less well on the test than when the test was presented as consonant with the student's identity. Further, they found that it was not necessary for the non-consonant role to be seen as less valuable than an alternative more consonant role.

Youngreen et al. (2003) gave students a standard test of mental ability (the Raven Advanced Progressive Matrices). Before administering the test, they randomly assigned half of the participants to a condition that characterized the test as being an aptitude test capable of predicting success in a profession related to their college major. The other half of participants were given the same test characterized as an aptitude test capable of predicting success in a profession related to a contrasting major. For example, an education major might take the test thinking it could predict her success as a teacher; or in contrast, she might expect the test to predict her success in business. Business majors would also expect the same test to predict their success either in business or teaching depending on the condition to which they had been randomly assigned.

Youngreen et al. (2003) found that the anticipation of taking a test expected to show aptitude for their identity interfered with their identity as a college major, perhaps because of the possibility that a poor showing might disconfirm that identity. Doing well on the test, however, reaffirmed and strengthened that identity. These results supported the fundamental validity of Burke's (1991, 1997) identity control model. Moreover, participants taking a test they expected to be capable of predicting their success in their chosen field scored higher on a standard test of mental ability than did those who expected the test to predict success in a contrasting field.

If an identity such as college major can shape a student's mental ability test score, then it may well be that an identity as fundamental as gender might shape women's and men's decisions to enter and persevere in college as well as their motivation to perform well in it.

NEGATIVE EXPECTED CONSEQUENCES OF MEN IN COLLEGE

The attitudes of college students toward the consequences of their educational attainment can inform us about the potential difficulty that men face reconciling their masculine gender identity with the college student role. Mickelson (1990) identified an "attitude-achievement paradox" among black students. She found that although black students were as motivated to succeed in school and as aware of the rewards of academic success as white students, their academic achievement fell below that of their white peers. She found as well that black students did have some negative expectations about academic success. Such negative expectations about the consequences of academic success have been shown to impair performance on standardized tests (Lovaglia, Lucas, Houser, Thye, & Markovsky, 1998; Lovaglia et al., 2004) in addition to the well documented stereotype threat effect (Steele & Aronson, 1995). It seems likely that if college men have difficulty reconciling their college student role with their developing masculine identities, then they might express that conflict in the form of negative expectations for the consequences of academic success. That is, the objective financial and social returns from academic success might not be as important in determining the academic performance of men as their *expectations* for the consequences of academic performance.

Data collected to investigate the differential expected consequences for academic success of black and white students may inform us about the potential for role conflict in college men. Thompkins, Lucas, Thye, and Lovaglia (1999) surveyed college students at five universities in different regions of the United States to examine expectations they held for the consequences of their academic success. The survey included a series of items on three different dimensions: (1) Student motivation to succeed in school, (2) The rewards that students expect from academic success, and (3) The negative consequences that students expect will result from academic success. An example of an item that taps student motivation to succeed academically is "The surest way to achieve success in life is through higher education." Students rated how strongly they agreed with these statements on a scale from 1 to 6. An example item from the rewards of academic success scale is "I expect to earn more than $100,000 dollars a year as a direct result of higher education." The negative consequences of academic success are measured by items such as:

"If people see that you are successful in school, they will try to drag you down."

"My siblings and/or friends sometimes feel a need to discredit my academic accomplishments."

"My education makes some in my community think that I can be pushed around."

Thompkins et al. (1999) sought to resolve the attitude achievement paradox by proposing that realizing the value of education may make additional negative consequences of education more painful to contemplate. Worry about the negative consequences of academic success could sap black students' resolve and hamper concentration. They tested three hypotheses, all of which were supported:

Hypothesis A. Black students will express at least as much motivation to succeed academically as will white students.

Hypothesis B. Black students will expect rewards from academic success at least as high as will white students.

Hypothesis C. Black students will expect more negative consequences to result from academic success than will white students.

The results of Thompkins et al. (1999) can also test hypotheses regarding the differential expected consequences of academic success held by college men and women. If men have difficulty reconciling their student roles with their masculine identities, then we might predict their expectations to conform to the following three attitude (ATT) hypotheses:

ATT Hypothesis 1. Male students will express less motivation to succeed academically than will female students.

ATT Hypothesis 1 reflects the likelihood that gender role conflict could produce ambivalence and reduces the motivation to succeed in school.

ATT Hypothesis 2. Male students will expect rewards from academic success no higher than will female students.

ATT Hypothesis 2 reflects the likelihood that although men have traditionally received returns from each additional year of higher education that are higher than the returns of women, men will nonetheless expect returns equal to or lower than those expected by women.

ATT Hypothesis 3. Male students will expect more negative consequences to result from academic success than will female students.

ATT Hypothesis 3 reflects the likelihood that men will expect negative consequences from academic success in a variety of areas related to their identities.

We tested our three hypotheses using the data collected by Thompkins et al. (1999) with OLS regressions analysis of three dependent variables – scales representing: (a) motivation to succeed academically, (b) rewards expected from academic success, and (c) the negative expected consequences of academic success. Independent variables included race (Black = 1, other = 0), gender (male = 1, female = 0), and control variables year in school, parents' income/$10,000, and high school GPA.

The results in Table 1 support all three hypotheses (but note cautions in the following paragraph). With the Motivation to Succeed scale as the

Table 1. Regression Coefficients (and Standard Errors) Predicting Motivation to Succeed, Expected Rewards, and Expected Negative Consequences of Academic Success.

	Motivation to Succeed, $n = 1,339$	Expected Rewards, $n = 1,337$	Expected Negative Consequences, $n = 1,320$
Constant	4.49	3.89	2.45
	(.10)	(.05)	(.04)
Black	.05	.11	.51***
	(.07)	(.06)	(.05)
Male	−.11*	−.05**	.12***
	(.04)	(.04)	(.04)
Year in college	.00	−.07***	−.05***
	(.02)	(.02)	(.02)
Parents' income/$10,000	.00	.00	−.02*
	(.00)	(.00)	(.01)
High school GPA	.02	.00	.00
	(.03)	(.00)	(.00)
R^2	.01	.02	.08

*$p \leq 0.05$, two-tailed.
**$p \leq 0.01$, two-tailed.
***$p \leq 0.001$, two-tailed.

dependent variable, the coefficient for Male respondent is negative and significant ($-.11$, $p = .013$) suggesting that, controlling for high school GPA, college men in this sample have lower motivation to succeed academically than do college women. This supports ATT Hypothesis 1. With the Expected Rewards scale as the dependent variable, the coefficient for Male respondent was slightly negative and not significant ($-.05$, $p = .261$) suggesting that the college men in this sample expected rewards from academic success no larger than the rewards expected by the college women. This supports ATT Hypothesis 2 (but note the low R^2). The coefficient for Year in College was also negative but significant suggesting that progress in college tempers the rewards that students expect to receive as a consequence of academic success. With Expected Negative Consequences as the dependent variable, the coefficient for Male respondent is positive and significant ($.12$, $p = .001$). This supports ATT Hypothesis 3. In addition, the coefficient for Black respondent was positive and significant ($.51$, $p < .001$) suggesting that Black students expect more negative consequences of academic success than do others. The interaction of race and gender is not significant, perhaps due to a relatively small sample of black men. Expected negative consequences decreased with respect to year in school ($b = -.002$, $p = .001$).

Although all three hypotheses were supported, these results are at best mildly suggestive of an internal conflict between the college student role and young men's masculine identity. The data were collected for another purpose and some of the scale items are less relevant to male identities than to racial or ethnic identities. R^2 values are quite low suggesting that the most important variables in determining college student motivation, expected rewards, and expected negative consequences are left uncontrolled. Finally, this is not a representative sample, although universities in several regions were sampled and the results in each university were quite similar to the overall results. (Extensive analyses available on request from the first author.)

A PROPOSED EXPERIMENTAL STUDY OF GENDER IDENTITY AND ACADEMIC ROLE CONFLICT

An experimental setting is capable of providing more conclusive evidence about consonance or inconsonance between young men's gender identity and their success in college. We are developing a setting that allows more exploration than most laboratory experiments but that nonetheless provides the experimental control needed to assess the impact of gender identities on academic performance.

In the setting, the key elements of the academic role are reduced to two tasks, one in which students perform individually and in the other as members of a small group. Following previous studies, the individual task is a standardized test of mental ability (Raven Advanced Progressive Matrices) portrayed as an aptitude test that predicts performance in the subsequent group project.

More or Less Academic Group Tasks

Experimental conditions consist of a variety of group tasks to which participants have been randomly assigned. Type of task will range on two dimensions: perceived femininity or masculinity of the task and how academic it seems. The first experiment will comprise four group task conditions in a 2×2 design: (1) non-academic masculine, (2) academic masculine, (3) academic feminine, and (4) non-academic feminine. A non-academic masculine task would be building a tower out of irregularly shaped pieces of lumber without tools, the goal being to build the highest self-standing structure in a short time. An academic masculine task would be solving mathematical word problems involving ballistics, trains, and fast-moving rivers. An academic feminine task would be composing an essay on the feelings evoked by a famous poem. A non-academic feminine task would be arranging pictures of clothing items from fashion catalogs into clothing lines by designer and price point. Degree of success on all the tasks can be assessed objectively. Students will be informed that their performance will be graded against other individuals and groups that have completed the study.

In addition to a group performance score, team members will rate their own and each others contributions to the completion of the group task in terms of quality and quantity. Moreover, groups will be videoed while working and those videos coded to assess each members contributions to the team effort. The videos will allow us to explore ideas about gender interactions in task groups that have yet to rise to the level of formal hypothesis.

Gender composition of the group is one factor that may be important for a developing theory of gender identity impact on academic performance. As Dutro (2002) observed, it is important for boys to avoid activities seen as feminine. Avoiding activities that attract women is one way to reinforce a masculine identity. College men may gravitate toward majors with few women. More generally, as the percentage of women in the college student population increases, attending college may seem less attractive to men. At the group level, men may be reluctant to engage fully in group tasks where men are the minority of group members.

Size of the group is an important element of the experimental design. Because the design is more exploratory than most experiments, groups should be small enough to allow a reasonably large sample of groups in each experimental condition. Groups should also be large enough to provide a range of gender composition: all one gender, majority women, majority men, and perhaps equal numbers of women and men. Three-person groups allow for all types of gender composition except equal numbers of women and men. In our experience, increasing the size of a group increases geometrically the difficulty of assembling and running it in the laboratory (Kalkhoff, Youngreen, Nath, & Lovaglia, 2007). Thus our first experiment will be with three-person groups.

Our first Gender Identity Hypothesis (GID) is based on the proposal that men will gravitate toward activities that attract few women to protect their gender identities.

GID Hypothesis 1. On academic tasks men will participate more when the task group is majority male than they will when the task group is majority female.

Similarly, the premise that identities motivate behavior that confirms those identities leads to the second gender identity hypothesis.

GID Hypothesis 2. Men will participate more on masculine tasks than they will on feminine tasks while women will participate more on feminine than masculine tasks.

Gender Identity Impact on Individual Performance

Each participant's individual level of academic performance can also be assessed for every type of group task in the experiment. Recall that the standardized mental ability test (Raven Advanced Progressive Matrices) will be portrayed as an aptitude test for the type of group task that the participant will soon perform. The task will be described carefully in ways that emphasize how academic or practical it is and how masculine or feminine. The theoretical development of Youngreen et al. (2003) leads us to predict that students will score lower on the standardized test to the extent they see a high score disconfirming their gender identity. Specifically, male students will score lower on the standardized test when it is portrayed as an aptitude test for tasks they type as academic or feminine.

GID Hypothesis 3. Male students will score higher on a test presented as measuring aptitude for the non-academic masculine task than on the same test presented as measuring aptitude on the other three types of task.

GID Hypothesis 4. Male students will score higher on a test presented as measuring aptitude for the academic masculine task than they will on either the academic feminine task or the non-academic feminine task.

The richness and extent of the data collection possible with this design suggest that much more can be discovered about gender identity and its potential impact on college performance. For example, students can be administered individual masculinity and femininity personality scale instruments to assess whether these factors affect participation on various types of tasks and individual performance measures. Another area to explore is the extent to which men and women emerge as leaders in group work on various types of task and differences in the way men and women characterize the leadership of the group.

DISCUSSION AND CONCLUSION

The earnings of male college graduates remain strong and they continue to receive financial returns from each year of higher education that are as great or greater than the returns of female college graduates. More fine-grained analyses, however, show that the gap in earnings between men and women with college educations declined substantially since 1965. That is, women are slowly catching up.

A reduction in the historic advantage in wages enjoyed by college educated men over college educated women would not seem to explain the current predominance of women in college enrollments. College still advantages men more than it does women. Theoretical development other than rational choice seems necessary to explain the predominance of women in college.

Taking a gender identity approach, the lessened earnings disparities between men and women who are college educated might reinforce young men's perceptions that educational attainment and school performance conflict with a masculine self-image. Gender identity could be a strong motivator of college enrollment and performance, pushing women into college and drawing men out to endeavors more predominately masculine.

Another finding that supports the gender identity explanation is that unemployment rates seem to have a dramatic effect on men's but not women's college enrollment rates. Current low unemployment rates seem to entice men into the labor market and out of college, whereas women continue to enroll in college in ever higher numbers. If the gender identity of men place a higher value on immediate self-sufficiency and active occupation as opposed to the long-term investment of the more dependent student role, then that would account for the current predominance of women in college. Note also that men can work while going to school but for some reason more men than women choose to work only rather than trying to do both, suggesting that not only do men value paid labor more than do women, but also that men value higher education less – not because they expect lower financial returns from education than do women, but because going to college conflicts with a self-image that men cultivate.

Our preliminary evidence suggests that men do see more gender identity relevant negative consequences from success in higher education. Our proposed experimental setting could help to determine whether gender identity plays a major role in the current predominance of women in college enrollments.

REFERENCES

Abrams, D., & Hogg, M. (1990). *Social identity theory: Constructive and critical advances.* Hemel Hempstead, England: Harvester Wheatsheaf.
Bernhardt, A., Morris, M., & Handcock, M. S. (1995). Women's gains or men's losses? A closer look at the shrinking gender gap in earnings. *American Journal of Sociology, 101,* 302–328.
Blau, F., & Kahn, L. (1994). *At home and abroad: US labor market performance in international perspective.* New York: Russell Sage Foundation.
Boyle, D. E., Marshall, N. L., & Robeson, W. W. (2003). Gender at play. *American Behavioral Scientist, 46,* 1326–1345.
Buchmann, C., & DiPrete, T. A. (2006). The growing female advantage in college completion. *American Sociological Review, 71,* 515–541.
Burke, P. J. (1991). Identity processes and social stress. *American Sociological Review, 56,* 536–849.
Burke, P. J. (1997). An identity model of network exchange. *American Sociological Review, 62,* 134–150.
Burke, P. J. (2006). Identity change. *Social Psychology Quarterly, 69,* 81–96.
Burke, P. J., & Reitzes, D. C. (1991). An identity theory approach to commitment. *Social Psychology Quarterly, 54,* 239–251.
Burke, P. J., & Stets, J. E. (1999). Trust and commitment through self-verification. *Social Psychology Quarterly, 62,* 347–366.
Clogg, C., Eliason, S., & Leicht, K. T. (2001). *Analyzing the labor force: Concepts, measures and trends.* New York: Kluwer Academic Publishing.
DiPrete, T. A., & Buchmann, C. (2006). Gender-specific trends in the value of education and the emerging gender gap in college completion. *Demography, 43,* 1–24.

Dutro, E. (2002). But that is a girl's book! Exploring gender boundaries in children's reading practices. *The Reading Teacher, 55,* 376-384.
Ellemers, N., Spears, R., & Doosje, B. (2002). Self and social identity. *Annual Reviews of Psychology, 53,* 161-186.
Freeman, R., & Gottchalk, P. (2003). *Generating jobs: How to increase demand for less-skilled workers.* New York: Russell Sage Foundation Press.
Galbraith, J. (2001). *Created unequal: The crisis in American pay.* New York: Free Press.
Harrison, B., & Bluestone, B. (1998). *The great u-turn: Corporate restructuring and the polarizing of America.* New York: Basic Books.
Heise, D. R. (1979). *Understanding events: Affect and the construction of social action.* Cambridge: Cambridge University Press.
Jacob, B. A. (2002). Where the boys aren't: Noncognitive skills, returns to school, and the gender gap in higher education. *Economics of Education Review, 21,* 589-598.
Kalkhoff, W., Youngreen, R., Nath, L., & Lovaglia, M. J. (2007). Human participants in laboratory experiments in the social sciences. In: M. Webster, Jr. & J. Sell (Eds), *Laboratory Experiments in the Social Sciences.* New York: Elsevier. (forthcoming).
Karen, D. (1991). The politics of race, class, and gender: Access to higher education in the United States, 1960-1986. *American Journal of Education, 99,* 208-237.
Leicht, K. T., & Fitzgerald, S. T. (2006). *Post-industrial peasants: The illusion of middle class prosperity.* New York: Worth Publishers.
Lovaglia, M. J., Lucas, J. W., Houser, J. A., Thye, S. R., & Markovsky, B. (1998). Status processes and mental ability test scores. *American Journal of Sociology, 104,* 195-228.
Lovaglia, M. J., Youngreen, R., Lucas, J. W., Nath, L. E., Rutstrom, E., & Willer, D. (2004). Stereotype threat and differential expected consequences: Explaining group differences in mental ability test scores. *Sociological Focus, 37,* 107-135.
Maass, A., Cadinu, M., Guarnieri, G., & Grasselli, A. (2003). Sexual harassment under social identity threat: The computer harassment paradigm. *Journal of Personality and Social Psychology, 85,* 853-870.
MacKinnon, N. J. (1994). *Symbolic interactionism as affect control.* Albany, NY: State University of New York Press.
McCall, L. (2000). Gender and the new inequality: Explaining the college/non-college wage gap. *American Sociological Review, 65,* 234-255.
Mickelson, R. A. (1990). The attitude-achievement paradox among black adolescents. *Sociology of Education, 63,* 44-61.
Osgood, C. E., Tannenbaum, P. H., & Suci, G. J. (1957). *The measurement of meaning.* Urbana, IL: University of Illinois Press.
Phillips, K. (1992). *Boiling point: Republicans, democrats, and the decline of middle class prosperity.* New York: HarperPerennial.
Powell, M. A., & Parcel, T. L. (1997). Effects of family structure on the earnings attainment process: Differences by gender. *Journal of Marriage and the Family, 59,* 419-433.
Robinson, D. T., & Smith-Lovin, L. (1999). Emotion display as a strategy for identity negotiation. *Motivation and Emotion, 23,* 73-104.
Smith-Lovin, L., & Heise, D. R. (1987). *Analyzing social interaction: Advances in affect control theory.* New York: Gordon and Breach Science Publishers.
Steele, C. M., & Aronson, J. (1995). Stereotype threat and the intellectual test performance of African Americans. *Journal of Personality and Social Psychology, 69,* 797-811.

Stryker, S., & Burke, P. J. (2000). The past, present, and future of an identity theory. *Social Psychology Quarterly, 63*, 284–287.

Swain, J. (2002). The resources and strategies that 10–11-year-old boys use to construct masculinities in the school setting. *British Educational Research Journal, 30*, 167–185.

Tajfel, H., & Turner, J. C. (1986). The social identity theory of intergroup behavior. In: S. Worchel & W. G. Austin (Eds), *Psychology of Intergroup Relations* (pp. 7–24). Chicago, IL: Nelson-Hall.

Thompkins, D., Lucas, J. W., Thye, S. R., & Lovaglia, M. J. (1999). Race and the cost of academic success. Presented to the Annual Meeting of the American Sociological Association, August, Chicago, IL.

Thorne, B. (1993). *Gender play*. New Brunswick, NJ: Rutgers University Press.

Tian, Y. (1996). Divorce, gender role, and higher education expansion. *Higher Education, 32*, 1–22.

U.S. Bureau of Labor Statistics. (2001). *Current population survey*. Washington, DC.

Youngreen, R., Childers, K., Conlon, B., Robinson, D. T., & Lovaglia, M. J. (2003). Identity maintenance, deflection, and performance on a mental ability test. Presented to the Annual Meeting of the American Sociological Association. Atlanta, August.

GENDER AS A GROUP PROCESS: IMPLICATIONS FOR THE PERSISTENCE OF INEQUALITY

Cecilia L. Ridgeway

ABSTRACT

Gender is at core a group process because people use it as a primary frame for coordinating behavior in interpersonal relations. The everyday use of sex/gender as cultural tool for organizing social relations spreads gendered meanings beyond sex and reproduction to all spheres of social life that are carried out through social relationships and constitutes gender as a distinct and obdurate system of inequality. Through gender's role in organizing social relations, gender inequality is rewritten into new economic and social arrangements as they emerge, contributing to the persistence of that inequality in modified form in the face of potentially leveling economic and political changes in contemporary society.

Gender is often thought of as primarily an individual identity, albeit one that people acquire in response to broad social expectations. In the last decade, however, sociologists of gender have realized that to explain gender inequality and understand how it persists or is undermined we must recognize that gender itself is much more than a process that happens within individuals. Gender is better understood as system of social practices that implicate individuals but are rooted in the organization of social structures (Ferree, Lorber, & Hess, 1999; Lorber, 1994; Ridgeway, 1997; Risman, 1998, 2004). We can think of gender as an institutionalized *system* of social practices within society that constitute people as two significantly different categories, men and women, and organize relations of inequality on the basis of this difference (Ridgeway & Correll, 2004, p. 510). This system of social practices entails socioeconomic arrangements and cultural beliefs at the macro level, ways of behaving in relation to others at the interpersonal level, and selves and identities at the individual level.

Most social scientific approaches to gender inequality focus primarily on two levels of the multi-level gender system, the individual level of identity and the macro level of patterns like wage differences or widely held cultural beliefs about gender. Until recently, the intermediate level of interpersonal relations has received less attention. This is unfortunate because, as I will argue, gender is deeply implicated in the coordination of behavior in interpersonal settings and, consequently, in the organization of social relations among individuals. For this reason, I refer to gender as, at core, a *group process* – that is, a process that is integral to the organization of interpersonal groups – rather than primarily an individual process. In contrast to processes that are primarily intrapersonal, group processes are the *interpersonal* processes through which people develop systematic patterns or structures that they use to organize and regulate their mutual behavior toward one another, particularly in regard to shared goals or activities. People organize their behavior like this in the family, in social relations in the workplace, in schools and in almost all institutional and social contexts. To the extent that gender is at base a group process, it is inherently social psychological in nature.

Understanding gender's effects at the level of interpersonal group processes is central to explaining how the modern gender system works as a whole (Ridgeway & Correll, 2000). Gender's role in framing and organizing social relations, I will argue, provides the primary means by which gender spreads beyond individual interests to become a multi-level system of social practices that permeates social institutions of all sorts including the workplace and the political sphere. Furthermore, and central to the focus of this chapter, gender's effects in organizing social relations play an important role in maintaining and reproducing gender inequality in the modern world.

While gender inequality has declined in the U.S. over that last few decades, substantial inequality remains and progress toward equality has actually slowed since the 1990s (Cotter, Hermsen, & Vanneman, 2004; Padovic & Reskin, 2002). Yet, during this same period, forces at the economic and institutional level have increasingly worked against traditional distinctions between people based on gender (Jackson, 1998). As economic and political organizations grow ever larger, the rationalizing logics of their bureaucracies increasingly treat people as "workers" or "citizens" rather than as men and women. These tendencies are further reinforced by anti-discrimination legislation that gives organizations incentives to avoid treating people differently based on gender. Forces at the individual level also appear to be moving against gender inequality, as more people seek to raise girls to have similar opportunities as boys (Risman, 2004). If progress toward equality has actually slowed in the face of these leveling forces at the institutional and individual level, how has this happened? Some process must be working against the current to preserve inequality by continually recreating it in newly emerging jobs, organizational forms, and ways of living. What is this process?

I argue that the driving force behind gender as a distinct system of difference and inequality right now is at the interpersonal, group processes level. It derives from sex/gender's cultural construction as a primary frame for organizing a fundamental human activity: relating to another, be it in person, on paper, on the internet or, on a cell phone. The everyday use of sex/gender as a cultural tool for organizing social relations accounts, I will argue, for why cultural meanings associated with gender do not stay within the bounds of contexts associated with sex and reproduction. Instead the use of gender as a framing device spreads gendered meanings to all spheres of social life that are carried out through social relationships. Through gender's role in organizing social relations, I will argue, gender inequality is rewritten into new economic and social arrangements as they emerge, preserving that inequality in modified form over socioeconomic transformations.

To make this argument, I first describe how gender plays a role in coordinating behavior in social relations. Next, I consider how this coordinating role imports cultural meanings associated with gender into social relations and provide an account of how these cultural beliefs about gender shape actors' behaviors and judgments in those contexts. After drawing out the implications of these processes for gender inequality in the workplace and in the home, I return to the question of how gender inequality persists in the face of contemporary equalizing forces and consider the implications for the future.

GENDER AS A PRIMARY FRAME FOR SOCIAL RELATIONS

My first task is to explain what I mean by cultural tools or frames that people use for organizing social relations. People depend on relations with others to get most of what they want and need in life and often even for their very survival. These relations involve direct dealing with others either in person or via some medium like the internet. However, they also involve imaginative dealings with others in which people act alone but mentally calculate their behavior in relation to others because they expect to be socially evaluated for what they do.

To successfully relate to another in any of these ways, you must coordinate your behavior with that other. That is, you must find some way to anticipate how the other will behave in a given instance so that you can decide how to act yourself. For this to work, the other similarly needs a means to accurately anticipate your behavior. Essentially, the two of you need to make your behavior mutually predictable.

How is it that people solve the coordination problems that social relations present? Interestingly, the conclusions of symbolic interactionists who have studied how people organize interaction and the logical proofs of game theorists who have studied the formal problem of coordination point to the same answer. Goffman (1959, 1967) analyzed social interaction as a kind of drama or play that actors jointly perform. Just as actors draw upon a shared script to coordinate their performances, Goffman argued that people interact by developing an implicit shared definition of their situation that establishes "who" each of them is in the relationship and how each should therefore behave.

From a very different perspective, game theorists have sought to understand how people solve general coordination problems (Chwe, 2001). Coordination problems involve people who want to engage in joint activity, but exactly what they want to do depends on what the others will do. Coordination problems are often studied in regard to joint activities in which people want to engage in a behavior, say going to a party, but only if others will also engage in the same behavior (e.g., also go to the party). Logically, however, joint activities also involve situations in which someone wants to do something, but only if he or she knows another person will not do it. That, too, is a coordination problem. Activities can be even be imaginatively "joint" when a person acts alone if the person calculates his or her behavior based on what he or she expects others to do because the person expects to be socially evaluated for that behavior.

Simple communication, even when possible, among the actors involved will not solve coordination problems because each needs not only to communicate with the other but also to know that the other received the communication and that the other knows that the first person knows that the second person knows, and so on in an infinite regression. Consider the everyday coordination problem of scheduling a meeting between two people. In the easiest case, one person suggests a time and the second person agrees to that time. But to be sure the meeting is on, the second person still needs to know that the first person knows that second person has agreed to the time. And the first person similarly needs to know that the second person knows that first person got the second person's message of agreement. Until both actually show up at the appointed time, there is always a little remaining uncertainty and potential for confusion as many a mixed up appointment has demonstrated.

Game theorists have shown that the only practical solution to coordination problems such as this is that actors share "common" or public knowledge upon which they base their behavior (Chwe, 2001). Common knowledge is knowledge that all actors not only know but can assume that others know. It is, in effect, conventional cultural knowledge – that is, knowledge that is shared in a taken-for-granted way by members of a group or society.

To solve the problems of coordinating social relations, however, I argue that people need to share not just any common knowledge, but a *particular type* of such knowledge. What people need are shared cultural systems for categorizing and defining "who" you and the other in the situation "are," and, based on that categorization, how you are expected to behave. Category systems proceed by contrast. Something is this and belongs to the category and not that which does not belong. Category systems, therefore, are based on difference. Consequently, the coordination problem of social relations directs people's attention to differences among them, differences on which they can form shared category systems for making sense of one another.

I argue, then, that the inherent problem of organizing social relations in a population of people who must regularly deal with one another drives them to develop shared category systems based on culturally recognized standards of difference. To manage social relations in real time, some of these cultural category systems must be so simplified that they can be quickly applied as framing devices to virtually anyone in order to start the process of defining self and other in the situation. In fact, studies of social cognition suggest that a small number of cultural category systems, about three or four, serve as the primary categories of person perception in a society (Brewer & Lui, 1989; Fiske, 1998). These primary categories define the things a person in a given society must know about someone to render that someone sufficiently meaningful to initiate relating to them. In doing so they provide an initial frame of mutual understanding that allows actors to ask further questions of one another and understand the answers.

Sex/gender is a form of human variation that is highly susceptible to cultural generalization into a primary category for framing social relations.

It is associated with a bimodal distribution of physical traits that encourages a usefully simple, dichotomous category system that can be applied to anyone. The resulting sex category system has relevance to sexuality and reproduction and delineates a line of difference among people who must regularly coordinate their behavior, not only in the family but also in many contexts. Not surprisingly, then, evidence suggests that sex category is virtually always one of a society's primary category systems (Brewer & Lui, 1989; Glick & Fiske, 1999; Zemore, Fiske, & Kim, 2000). In the U.S., race and age are also primary categories (Schneider, 2004).

Social cognition research has in fact shown that people automatically and unconsciously sex categorize any concrete other that they cast themselves in relation to and do so almost instantly (Brewer & Lui, 1989; Stangor, Lynch, Duan, & Glass, 1992). They do this even when, as is often the case, more relevant and informative institutional roles, such as boss and employee are readily available to define self and other in the context. The evidence shows that actors' subsequent categorizations of one another according to institutional roles are nested within their prior understandings of each other as male or female and take on a slightly different meaning as a result (e.g., male clerk and female customer versus female clerk and male customer) (Brewer, 1988). We can think abstractly about an ungendered boss or employer, but we have difficulty relating, even imaginatively, to any specific boss or employee without gendering him or her first.

To gain a feel for the cultural importance of sex categorization for organizing social relations, consider how disturbed and confused people are when they must interact with some one they can not classify as male or female. Even a routine, trivial commercial exchange is difficult to complete with such a person. For one thing, our very language assumes that we know the sex of the other so that it becomes difficult to address the person. It is even more difficult to understand the meaning of the person's replies. The routine coordination of our behavior is at risk of failing because we lack the common working consensus about who we are that the initial framing device of sex categorization provides us.

At this point in the argument, some readers may be thinking that the sex categorization process I have emphasized must surely be effectively innate in people, given its relevance for sex and reproduction. I would agree that sex categorization must be something that we are biologically prepared to learn to do. My argument, however, is that the social problem of organizing interpersonal relations encourages people to make much broader cultural use of the physical male–female distinction than biology alone would logically require. *Indeed, the cultural tendency to use the sex distinction as a convenient tool to solve the coordination problem of social relations is an important means by which physical sex is culturally transformed into social gender.* As a result of this broad cultural amplification of the sex distinction, even the process of sex categorization itself becomes more social than physical in everyday encounters since it typically relies heavily on cultural cues of appearance such as dress and manner that are presumed to stand for physical sex differences (West & Zimmerman, 1987).

When sex category is culturally constructed as a fundamental tool for framing any social relation, the meanings associated with sex/gender are carried far beyond mating, reproduction, and the family. If we cannot comprehend someone sufficiently to relate to them without sex categorizing them first (and making salient our own sex category by implication), then sex/gender is pulled in some degree into every sphere of social life that is enacted through social relations. By this analysis, sex/gender's status as a primary framing device for social relations is what causes gender to be a force in all social institutions, not just the family but even those that make up the labor market and government too (Ridgeway, 1997). It is the use of sex/gender as a relational framing device that embeds (and, I will argue, continually re-embeds) gender in positional inequalities in political and economic as well as familial institutions. Yet, I argue, driven by its own logic as a framing device, gender brings its own dynamics to social relations so that it is never fully encapsulated by any given structure of political and economic inequalities (Ridgeway, 2006a). Gender becomes its own distinct system of difference and inequality in society.

CULTURAL BELIEFS ABOUT DIFFERENCE AND STATUS INEQUALITY

The utility of gender as a framing device lies in its focus on gender as a *difference*. The presumption is that actors classified in one category may be expected to behave differently from those classified in another category. The organizational requirement to construct the sexes as behaviorally different, however, does not necessitate that they be seen to differ in any *specific* way. As a consequence, the use of gender as a framing device does not itself dictate the content of our shared beliefs about gender difference.

Other aspects of how people cognitively process category systems based on difference do have an influence on the content of the cultural beliefs about gender difference that develop, however. As a large body of research has demonstrated, the mere classification of another as different evokes an evaluative response. Typically, this evaluative response is to favor one's own group (see Brewer & Brown, 1998, for a review). Notice, however, that in the case of sex categorization, this typical evaluative response to difference effectively creates competing views of the proper evaluative relation between males and females.

If gender is a system of difference for coordinating joint behavior among individuals, then competing views of who is "better" are an impediment to mutual relations that may be difficult to sustain over the long run. Mary Jackman has shown that under conditions of long term mutual dependence between groups, competing in-group preferences tend to be transformed by one means or another into shared status beliefs (Jackman, 1994). That is, members of both groups come to agree (or concede) that, as a matter of social reality, one group is more respected and status worthy than the other. In an achievement oriented society like the U.S., status evaluations like this are expressed and legitimated by corresponding assumptions about differences in general competence and instrumental expertise (Glick & Fiske, 1999). Thus contemporary status beliefs in the U.S. say that people in one group are more status worthy and competent, overall, than those in another group (Berger, Fisek, Norman, & Zelditch, 1977; Fiske, Cuddy, Glick, & Xu, 2002).

In comparison to groups created by most other social distinctions, there is an exceptional degree of mutual dependence between the sexes. Heterosexuality, reproduction, the way that sex cross-cuts kin relations, and the population division into two roughly equal sized gender groups all increase contact and dependence between the sexes. These conditions put unusually strong structural pressures on gender as a system of shared beliefs about difference to also be a system of shared beliefs about the status ranking of men and women. As a result of such structural pressures, shared cultural beliefs are particularly likely to describe gender differences in terms that establish one sex as more worthy of respect and as implicitly more competent in some ways than the other sex.

While this analysis suggests that cultural beliefs about gender difference tend to foster gender status beliefs about inequality, it does not presume male dominance. From an organizational perspective, the gender status beliefs that develop could be a set of specific status beliefs that advantage men in some social contexts and women in other contexts, but provide no overall advantage for either sex. The anthropological evidence suggests that small, technologically simple societies, especially foraging ones, tend to have gender status beliefs like this that result in a relatively egalitarian distribution of power between the sexes (see Wood & Eagly, 2002). In the

U.S. and other developed societies, however, we have diffuse, general status beliefs that attach higher status and competence overall to men than women (Glick et al., 2004; Williams & Best, 1990).

The historical origins of such male status dominance in western societies are unknown. However, research on how status beliefs develop has shown that when some factor gives members of one group a systematic advantage in attaining influence and power in their mutual dealings with members of another group, people from both groups develop shared status beliefs favoring the advantaged group (Ridgeway, Boyle, Kuipers, & Robinson, 1998; Ridgeway & Erickson, 2000). Many theories about the origins of male status dominance posit some factor, such as men's on average superior strength or the physical constraints faced by lactating mothers that could have resulted in a division of labor at some time in the past that provided men with an advantage in resources (cf. Wood & Eagly, 2002). Research on the development of status beliefs suggests that such a resource advantage would have given men a systematic influence advantage in their dealings with women which, in turn, would have fostered widely shared diffuse status beliefs favoring men (Ridgeway et al., 1998; Ridgeway, 2006b).

Whatever their origin, once diffuse, general status beliefs favoring men become culturally established, they root male advantage in group membership itself and, thus, advantage men even over their female peers who are just as strong as them and not lactating mothers. Because diffuse gender status beliefs root inequality in group membership, they constitute gender as a distinct organizing principle of inequality that is not fully reducible to other differences in power or material resources. With the development of diffuse gender status beliefs, then, gender becomes a dynamic of inequality on its own that, while it may be affected by material or political inequalities, is more than merely a reflection of them.

CULTURAL BELIEFS AS THE RULES OF THE GENDER GAME

Analyzing gender as a group process directs our attention to shared cultural beliefs about the distinguishing characteristics and behaviors of typical males and females as the fundamental factor that constitutes gender as a distinctive system of difference and inequality. Studies show that roughly consensual descriptive gender beliefs like this do indeed exist in the contemporary U.S. (Diekman & Eagly, 2000; Fiske et al., 2002; Glick et al., 2004; Lueptow,

Garovich-Szabo, & Lueptow, 2001; Spence & Buckner, 2000). They are, of course, stereotypes, but they are more than that as well. They are the social rules of the game of gender in contemporary America.

The social theorists, Anthony Giddens and William Sewell, have argued that social structures have a dual nature (Giddens, 1984; Swell, 1992). They consist, on one hand, of the implicit rules or cultural schemas by which people enact the structure and, on the other hand, of the arrangements of resources and power that result. Widely shared contemporary beliefs about gender are rules for structure in Giddens' and Sewell's sense. They are rules for enacting social relations in a manner that results in material arrangements between men and women that in turn uphold our current views of who men and women are and why they are unequal. As Alice Eagly and her colleagues have shown, the specific content of our gender beliefs is reciprocally related to the material arrangements, like the gendered division of labor and the structure of status relations embedded in that division of labor, that organize men's and women's lives (Eagly, Wood, & Diekman, 2000; Koenig & Eagly, 2006).

I have argued that it is the development of shared gender stereotypes, which in turn is driven by the use of gender as a framing device, that gives gender an independent dynamic as a system of inequality. That is, the development of gender stereotypes that incorporate gender status beliefs transform gender into a dynamic of inequality that is not simply tied to or a product of economic or political processes. Yet as Eagly's and others' work has shown, the actual content of these stereotypes themselves are nevertheless shaped and constrained by the material circumstances of men's and women's everyday experiences with one another (Eagly et al., 2000; Fiske et al., 2002). As I will discuss shortly, however, certain characteristics of the reciprocal link between cultural beliefs about gender and material arrangements between men and women give gender inequality substantial staying power in the face of material changes.

GENDER BELIEFS IN THE CONTEMPORARY U.S.

If shared cultural beliefs about gender are the rules of the gender game, it is useful to understand a bit more about their nature and effects in the current American scene. Studies show that men are presently seen as more agentic and competent overall and more competent at the things that "count most" in society (e.g., instrumental rationality) than the women. Women are viewed as less competent in general, but better at care-giving and communal tasks, even though these tasks themselves are less valued (Conway, Pizzamiglio, & Mount, 1996; Eagly & Mladinic, 1994; Glick et al., 2004; Koenig & Eagly, 2006). These stereotypes are consensual cultural knowledge in that most people know them and recognize them as the cultural rules by which they will be judged, whether or not they personally agree with them (Eagly & Karau, 2002). In fact, holding consensual stereotypes as descriptive beliefs is only modestly correlated with people's ideological beliefs about gender egalitarianism (Blair & Banaji, 1996; Rudman & Kilianski, 2000; Spence & Buckner, 2000).

The conceptions of men and women embedded in these contemporary stereotypes correspond rather closely to North American stereotypes of high-status and low-status actors in general. A variety of studies show that independent of gender, high-status actors in our society are seen as agentic and instrumentally competent, but less supportive than low-status actors, while low-status actors are thought to be more expressive and supportive, but less competent (Conway et al., 1996; Fiske et al., 2002; Wagner & Berger, 1997; Koenig & Eagly, 2006). Because of the way that gender is embedded in positional inequalities in the workplace, in educational and government institutions, and even in familes, network studies show that men and women in the U.S. typically interact with one another in status unequal role relationships such as boss and secretary, manager and subordinate, or older husband and younger wife (see Ridgeway & Smith-Lovin, 1999, for a review). For this reason and because of the status attached to gender itself, men and women experience one another most often as status unequals. Perhaps it is not surprising, then, that the content of gender stereotypes is closely linked to status. In comparison to other status distinctions, however, women are considered not only more expressive as all low-status actors are, but also distinctively warm and good. It seems likely that, as Eagly argues, this is related to women's almost exclusive association with childcare in our gender division of labor (Eagly et al., 2000).

As descriptions of the content of shared gender stereotypes show, these stereotypes represent themselves as universal depictions of "women" and "men" defined by a simple, stylized set of features. The cultural use of sex category as quick, first frame for social relations appears to encourage people to distill the concrete experience of interacting with real, multiattributed men and women into simplified, highly abstract categories. Given the cultural resources and power available to members of dominant groups in society, the descriptions of men and women that become inscribed in these simple, abstract cultural categories are ones that most closely describe white, middle-class, heterosexual men and women, if anyone. These gender beliefs are culturally hegemonic in that the descriptions of "women" and "men" that they contain are institutionalized in the media, legal definitions and policies, and normative images of the family (Ridgeway & Correll, 2004).

The institutionalized, hegemonic aspect of these shared understandings of "men" and "women" is what establishes them as the default rules of the gender game in public contexts. Since virtually everyone in our society knows these beliefs and expects that most others accept them, when they enter public settings that require them to define themselves in relation to others, their default expectation is that others will treat them according to hegemonic gender beliefs. Given the status distinction contained in hegemonic gender beliefs, then, men and women enter most social relational contexts expecting that others believe that men are generally more competent than women. This is important because people's sense of what others expect of them impacts behavior and biases judgments (Miller & Turnbull, 1986; Wagner & Berger, 1997).

Alternative gender belief systems exist in the culture along with hegemonic beliefs (Connell, 1995; Ridgeway & Correll, 2004). People from different racial, ethnic, political, or social class communities may have somewhat different or less polarized gender beliefs. They may, for instance, see women as more competent relative to men than the dominant stereotypes depict (Collins, 1991; Dugger, 1988). In a setting where people know they are around other likeminded people, such as in a gathering of co-ethnic associates, their shared alternative gender beliefs are likely to be evoked in the situation and shape their behaviors and evaluations rather than hegemonic gender beliefs. Even people with alternative gender beliefs, however, know and implicitly expect to be treated according to hegemonic beliefs when they move into more public settings or settings where they do not know the others well. Even for these people, then, hegemonic gender beliefs are a stubborn part of social reality that must be dealt with or accommodated in many contexts, even if not personally endorsed. This argument about when people rely on alternative rather than hegemonic gender beliefs has not been directly tested but is consistent with the current evidence (Filardo, 1996; Milkie, 1999).

GENDER AS A BACKGROUND IDENTITY

If hegemonic cultural beliefs provide a blueprint for enacting gender in most relational settings, how do they do so? What are their effects on people's behavior and judgments of others and themselves? I will first describe the general nature of gender's effects on behavior and judgments in social relations and then focus on the specific effects of gender status and competence beliefs since these are particularly relevant for gender inequality.

Social cognition research shows that sex categorizing another in a situation implicitly primes gender stereotypes and makes them cognitively available to affect judgments and behavior toward that person (Banaji & Hardin, 1996; Blair & Banaji, 1996; Kunda & Spencer, 2003). Thus the stereotypic rules of the gender game are virtually always implicit on hand to coordinate and shape behavior in social relations. Yet, the very factors that support sex/gender's utility as a quick, initial frame for making sense of another – its abstract, dichotomous nature – also limit its ability to provide an actor with much specific detail about who that other is and how best to relate to him or her. As a consequence, actors virtually always go on to categorize the other in more detailed and specific ways that carry more concrete and contextually relevant implications for behavior such as, for instance, institutional roles (Fiske, Lin, and Neuberg, 1999). These latter, more contextually specific categorizations of the other, however, are nested within the actor's initial understanding of the other as a man or woman and take on a slightly different meaning as a result (Brewer, 1988).

In most situations, it is these more concrete, contextually specific identities such as clerk and customer that are in the foreground of people's attention as they relate to one another. Even though actors start by sex categorizing one another, gender typically exerts its effects as a *background identity* in social relations that is not, by itself, the direct focus of the participants' concerns. This is actually important to the nature of gender's effects on behavior. Consider how gender is a background identity in student–teacher interactions in the classroom. The situationally focal identities of student and teacher define the actors' central behavior toward one another. But gender, as a framing identity in the background, draws in an added set of meanings that may implicitly modify or "color" how actors perform the activities defined by their focal identities. This is my understanding what it means to say that gender is a performance (West & Zimmerman, 1987). Gender is a way of performing otherwise ungendered activities, like teaching or playing the piano.

The extent to which gender stereotypes actually do modify or bias people's behavior and judgments in a given situation depends on the context (Deaux & Major, 1987; Wagner & Berger, 1997). It can vary from imperceptibly to substantially, as a wide variety of research shows (see Deaux & La France, 1998; Ridgeway & Bourg, 2004, for reviews). The more salient or relevant gender is for actors' in the setting, the greater its effects on their behavior. Salience in turn, depends on the extent to which gender in a given setting appears to provide useful clues about the other that help the actor figure out his or her own behavior. At a minimum, evidence suggests that gender is typically *effectively salient* for actors, that is, salient enough to measurably affect behavior, in mixed sex settings and in settings that are culturally linked to one sex or the other (Ridgeway & Bourg, 2004; Wagner & Berger, 1997). In these settings, widely shared gender stereotypes create implicit expectations for an actor's own as well as the others' behavior and these expectations often have self-fulfilling expectations on actual behavior (Miller & Turnbull, 1986). The impact of implicit gender expectations is especially consequential in the workplace and at home.

WORKFORCE AND HOME EFFECTS OF GENDER BELIEFS

When people work together on a shared goal, as is typical in the workplace or classroom but also in many family settings, a variety of evidences shows that influence hierarchies tend to develop among them that organize their goal oriented behavior (see Ridgeway, 2001). Research derived from expectation states theory has shown that these hierarchies are based on expectations actors form about their relative competence at goal related activities (Berger, Conner, & Fisek, 1974; Wagner & Berger, 2002). When gender is effectively salient, as it often is in these settings, cultural beliefs about men's greater instrumental competence, women's greater expressive competence, and men's greater status worthiness implicitly bias the expectations that the participants form for their own competence and status compared to others in the same situation. The strength of these biasing effects is proportional to the relevance of gender to the goals of the setting (Berger et al., 1977; Wagner & Berger, 1997). Thus cultural beliefs about gender bias competence and status expectations most powerfully in contexts that are culturally linked to one sex or the other, such as childcare, the military, nursing, or engineering.

Gender biased competence expectations, in turn, have been shown to bias, controlling for actual competence, the likelihood that people speak up in a situation, whether others attend to them if they do, how their suggestions are evaluated, whether they become influential, and the extent to which others and they, themselves, are willing to infer high ability in them based on their performance. The greater status worthiness associated with men also biases the extent which people accept men rather than women as legitimate authorities. This in turn affects the likelihood that men rather than women emerge as leaders, and shapes how they are received when they exercise power in a leadership position (see Correll & Ridgeway, 2003; Eagly & Carli, 2003; Ridgeway & Bourg, 2004, for reviews).

Taken together, these effects of gender status and competence beliefs on men's and women's behavior and judgments modestly advantage men over women in mixed-sex but gender-neutral settings and advantage men more strongly in male-typed settings, like engineering and math classes, but also home repair and home computing. In female-typed settings like nursing or childcare, gender status and competence beliefs slightly advantage women. Men, however, are advantaged for positions of actual authority (not just influence) even in female typed settings. An extensive body of evidence supports this pattern of gender effects (see Ridgeway & Bourg, 2004; Ridgeway & Smith-Lovin, 1999; Wagner & Berger, 1997, for reviews). In the workplace as well as the home, such effects create an array of often subtle processes that are everywhere and yet nowhere in that they are in the implicit, taken for granted background of what is happening.

These implicit stereotype biases affect not only how others treat a given man or woman, but also how that man or woman judges himself or herself (Correll, 2004). Consequently, in the labor force, they affect both "demand factors" like employer preferences, as well as "supply factors" like students' and workers' judgments of what they are good at and what they should pursue as a career. The demand and the supply processes created by implicit gender biases in social relations together promote the persistent tendency to gender type jobs, including newly developing jobs, sex segregation in jobs, the lower status of women's jobs compared men's, and gender inequality in workplace outcomes like pay and authority.

Implicit gender biases in social relations shape the sex segregation of jobs and inequality in pay and authority both through their primary effects on the everyday relations through which people carry out the work process and through secondary effects these relations have on the administrative procedures, job descriptions, pay evaluation schemes, job ladders, and so on that employers develop to organize the work process. Implicit gender biases shaping the behaviors and judgments of actors who are "at the table" when new administrative procedures and organizational structures are developed can cause these actors to produce procedures and structures that embody stereotypic assumptions about men and women and their relative status and competence (Nelson & Bridges, 1999; Steinberg, 1995).

When this happens, the resulting procedures and structures become independent agents of gender bias in the workplace that often persist through institutional inertia.

The same implicit biases that shape relations in the workplace also affect relations at home. As progress has been made in reducing gender inequality in the workplace, gender inequality in American society has increasingly rested upon social arrangements at home. There is evidence to suggest that cultural beliefs about men's greater status worthiness and women's greater communal skills are behind the stubborn inequality in the household division of labor. In particular, such beliefs appear to be behind men's persistent unwillingness to take on primary responsibility for care-giving tasks and some women's unwillingness to relinquish these responsibilities even in the face of women's greater involvement in the labor force (Berk, 1985; Brines, 1994). Taken for granted gendered expectations for self and other have been shown to undercut even committed gender egalitarians' efforts to equalize status and work at home (Risman, 1998).

THE PERSISTENCE OF INEQUALITY

Now let us return to my initial question about how gender inequality persists in the modern world in the face of potentially leveling changes at the economic and political level and increasingly egalitarian efforts at the level of individual socialization. I have argued that the use of sex/gender as a primary frame for organizing relations fosters the development and use of shared cultural beliefs about gender difference and inequality that, in turn, constitute gender as a distinct system of inequality in its own right. On the other hand, I have also cited evidence that the content of these gender beliefs generally reflects the social roles and material contexts in which men and women experience one another. The question then becomes, why do leveling economic and political changes simply not erode gender inequality by changing men's and women's experiences of one another and, therefore, their gender stereotypes?

The answer is that leveling economic and political change will indeed change stereotypes, or should do so eventually, but that the resulting change in shared gender stereotypes will substantially lag behind change in the material arrangements that organize men's and women's lives. Two factors contribute to the lag in stereotype change. First, as a lot of evidence shows, stereotypes create a wide variety confirmation biases that insulate them from disconfirming experiences (see Fiske, 1998; Schneider, 2004). Because people tend to see what they expect to see, they are less likely to notice aspects of another that do not fit the stereotype and if they do notice them, they are less likely to remember them later. And even if they do notice and remember men and women who disconfirm gender stereotypes, they tend to treat them as "exceptions" that have little to say about how "most" men and women are. Gender's typical role as a background rather than focal identity encourages the dismissal of exceptions by reducing the likelihood that people link someone's counterstereotypic behavior with gender rather than with some other aspect of that person's identity. They may say, for instance, that the person acts that way because he or she is a cop, not because of the person's gender. Of course, if more and more of the men and women that people meet are "exceptions" then the pressure on their stereotypes begins to build.

A second, less recognized factor also contributes to the lag in stereotype change. As I mentioned, widely shared gender stereotypes are institutionalized in the media, in the normative images of men and women embodied in laws and social policies, in the organization of public places and so on. The institutionalization of shared gender stereotypes encourages people to presume that "most others" hold these stereotypes even if they personally and those they know well no longer do so. And research shows that people's presumption that stereotypes are consensually shared is a major factor in their tendency to act on those stereotypes (Seachrist & Stangor, 2001). As a result, even as disconfirming experiences cause more and more individuals, as individuals, to decide that traditional gender stereotypes are not accurate, they may still presume that these stereotypes are the rules of the game in public places and act accordingly. This process then becomes self-fulfilling so that traditional gender stereotypes actually do continue to guide behavior in public settings despite their individual rejection. Eventually, this situation of growing pluralistic ignorance will become fragile and begin to crumble but the process will require time.

The lag in stereotype change, I argue, is what allows gender inequality to persist in the face of leveling economic and political changes. It does so because it creates a "window" of time in which old ideas about gender can be reinscribed into new ways of living. At the edge of social change, the contexts in which people first develop new ways of doing things and new types of economic activity are not typically formally structured, bureaucratic situations. Instead, these contexts of innovation are frequently more informally organized in terms of interpersonal relations among the participants. Think of the development of dot coms or start up companies of any kind. Such interpersonally organized situations, however, are precisely the ones in which gender stereotypes, made implicitly available for participants by routine sex categorization, are likely to measurably shape behavior and judgments. As a consequence, as the participants carry out the activities that innovate new types of jobs, of community organization, of technology, of businesses, and even of families, their behavior and judgments are shaped by taken–for-granted gender beliefs that are more traditional than their current, innovative circumstances. The effect is that they rewrite gender stereotypes into the new ways of doing things that they develop. As a result, the new economy or new forms of familial organization that emerge continue to embody gender inequality in their structures and practices. The degree of inequality may be altered in the process, but the ordinal hierarchy between men and women persists.

IMPLICATIONS FOR CHANGE

This argument suggests that gender inequality will be devilishly difficult but not impossible to stamp out. It is unlikely, in my view, that people will abandon the use of gender as a primary frame for coordinating social relations. However, the systematic inequality that results from the use of gender as framing device for social relations depends on cultural stereotypes about sex differences in overall competence and status. To the extent that stereotypes are modified to imply smaller competence differences, gender inequality will be reduced.

How can stereotypes be changed, given the confirmation biases and institutional forces that maintain them? Shelley Correll and I have argued that such stereotype modification is most likely to come about through constant, iterative changes in men's and women's material experiences with one another that in turn keep up the pressure on their cultural presumptions about sex differences in competence (Ridgeway & Correll, 2000). Such equalizing, iterative material changes are likely to result from the continuing efforts of individual women to push against the barriers they face in order to better their lives. They may also result from the efforts of organizational actors who intentionally or unintentionally act to undermine traditional gender assumptions in pursuit of economic or institutional goals. Continuing, iterative material changes can eat away at cultural presumptions of sex differences in competence just as a series of waves can eventually undermine a sand bar.

Women's increased labor market participation over the last few decades has been correlated with some slight changes of this sort in gender stereotypes. This period of time has witnessed the development of a distinct "business-professional woman" subtype who is stereotypically perceived as almost as agentic as men, although as not as nice as other women (Fiske et al., 2002; Glick & Fiske, 1999). Furthermore, over this same time period women have steadily increased in the agency and instrumental competence they attribute to themselves, if not in the competence they attribute to the typical woman (Spence & Buckner, 2000; Twenge, 2001).

There has been very little change in the expressive competence aspect of gender stereotypes, however (Spence & Buckner, 2000). Both men and women continue to see clear differences between the sexes in this regard and these cultural presumptions remain a major drag on the movement toward equality. At present, at least among younger women, differences between the wages of women who are responsible for motherhood duties at home and women without these duties are greater than the average wage differences between men and women (Budig & England, 2001). Indeed, the cultural battleground in the fight for gender equality now may be shifting to the arrangements we make for care giving and the implications these have for women's equality not only at home, but in the labor force as well.

We can see, then, that the role sex/gender plays in coordinating and organizing social relations – in other words, its nature as a group process – transforms gender into a distinct and obdurate system of inequality, although not an unchanging one. Because people use sex/gender as a primary frame for coordinating interpersonal relations, gender beliefs are carried into new arenas of activity at the edge of social change and gender inequality is reinscribed into new social practices and ways of doing things as they emerge. The continual regendering of new forms of social life, in turn, slows the leveling effects of economic and political forces that undermine gender inequality and gives the gender system of difference and inequality considerable but not unlimited staying power in the face of material change.

REFERENCES

Banaji, M. R., & Hardin, C. (1996). Automatic stereotyping. *Psychological Science, 7*, 136–141.

Berger, J., Conner, T. L., & Fisek, M. H. (Eds). (1974). *Expectations states theory: A theoretical research program.* Cambridge, MA: Winthrop.

Berger, J., Fisek, H., Norman, R., & Zelditch, M. (1977). *Status characteristics and social interaction.* New York: Elsevier.

Berk, S. F. (1985). *The gender factory: The apportionment of work in American households.* New York: Plenum.

Blair, I. V., & Banaji, M. R. (1996). Automatic and controlled processes in stereotype priming. *Journal of Personality and Social Psychology, 70*, 1142–1163.

Brewer, M., & Brown, R. J. (1998). Intergroup relations. In: D. T. Gilbert, S. T. Fiske & G. Lindzey (Eds), *Handbook of social psychology* (pp. 554–594). New York: McGraw-Hill.
Brewer, M. B. (1988). A dual process model of impression formation. In: T. Srull & R. Wyer (Eds), *Advances in social cognition* (Vol. 1, pp. 1–36). Hillsdale, NJ: Erlbaum.
Brewer, M. B., & Lui, L. (1989). The primacy of age and sex in the structure of person categories. *Social Cognition, 7,* 262–274.
Brines, J. (1994). Economic dependency, gender, and the division of labor at home. *American Journal of Sociology, 100,* 652–688.
Budig, M. J., & England, P. (2001). The wage penalty for motherhood. *American Sociological Review, 66,* 204–225.
Chwe, M. S.-Y. (2001). *Rational ritual: Culture, coordination, and common knowledge.* Princeton, NJ: Princeton University Press.
Collins, P. H. (1991). *Black feminist thought: Knowledge, consciousness, and the politics of empowerment.* New York: Routledge.
Connell, R. W. (1995). *Masculinities.* Berkeley, CA: University of California Press.
Conway, M., Pizzamiglio, M. T., & Mount, L. (1996). Status, communality, and agency: Implications for stereotypes of gender and other groups. *Journal of Personality and Social Psychology, 71,* 25–38.
Correll, S. J. (2004). Constraints into preferences: Gender, status, and emerging career aspirations. *American Sociological Review, 69,* 93–113.
Correll, S. J., & Ridgeway, C. L. (2003). Expectation states theory. In: J. Delamater (Ed.), *The handbook of social psychology* (pp. 29–51). New York: Kluwer Academic Press.
Cotter, D., Hermsen, J. M., & Vanneman, R. (2004). *Gender inequality at work.* New York: Russell Sage Foundation.
Deaux, K., & LaFrance, M. (1998). Gender. In: D. T. Gilbert, S. T. Fiske & G. Lindzey (Eds), *The handbook of social psychology* (4th ed., Vol. 1, pp. 788–828). New York: McGraw-Hill.
Deaux, K., & Major, B. (1987). Putting gender into context: An interactive model of gender-related behavior. *Psychological Review, 94,* 369–389.
Diekman, A. B., & Eagly, A. H. (2000). Stereotypes ad dynamic constructs: Women and men of the past, present, and future. *Personality and Social Psychology Bulletin, 26,* 1171–1188.
Dugger, K. (1988). Social role location and gender-role attitudes: A comparison of Black and white women. *Gender and Society, 2,* 425–448.
Eagly, A. H., & Carli, L. (2003). The female leadership advantage: An evaluation of the evidence. *The Leadership Quarterly, 14,* 807–834.
Eagly, A. H., & Karau, S. J. (2002). Role congruity theory of prejudice towards female leaders. *Psychological Review, 109,* 573–579.
Eagly, A. H., & Mladinic, A. (1994). Are people prejudiced against women? Some answers from research on attitudes, gender stereotypes, and judgments of competence. In: W. Stroebe & M. Hewstone (Eds), *European review of social psychology* (Vol. 5, pp. 1–35). New York: Wiley.
Eagly, A. H., Wood, W., & Diekman, A. B. (2000). Social role theory of sex differences and similarities: A current appraisal. In: T. Eckes & H. M. Trautner (Eds), *The developmental psychology of gender* (pp. 123–173). Mahwah, NJ: Earlbaum.
Ferree, M. M., Lorber, J., & Hess, B. B. (1999). Introduction. In: M. Ferree, J. Lorber & B. Hess (Eds), *Revisioning gender* (pp. xv–xxxvi). Thousand Oaks, CA: Sage.

Filardo, E. K. (1996). Gender patterns in African American and white adolescents' social interactions in same-race, mixed-sex groups. *Journal of Personality and Social Psychology, 71,* 71–82.

Fiske, S. T. (1998). Stereotyping, prejudice, and discrimination. In: D. T. Gilbert, S. T. Fiske & G. Lindzey (Eds), *The handbook of social psychology,* (4th ed., Vol. 2, pp. 357–411). Boston, MA: McGraw-Hill.

Fiske, S. T., Cuddy, A. J. C., Glick, P., & Xu, J. (2002). A model of (often mixed) stereotype content: Competence and warmth respectively follow from perceived status and competence. *Journal of Personality and Social Psychology, 82,* 878–902.

Fiske, S. T., Lin, M., & Neuberg, S. (1999). The continuum model: Ten years later. In: S. Chaiken & Y. Trope (Eds), *Dual process theories in social psychology* (pp. 231–254). New York: Guilford.

Giddens, A. (1984). *The Constitution of society: Outline of the theory of structuration.* Berkeley, CA: University of California Press.

Glick, P., & Fiske, S. T. (1999). Sexism and other "isms": Interdependence, status, and the ambivalent content of stereotypes. In: W. B. Swan, J. H. Langlois & L. A. Gilbert (Eds), *Sexism and stereotypes in modern society* (pp. 193–221). Washington, DC: American Psychological Association.

Glick, P., Lameiras, M., Fiske, S. T., Eckes, T., Masser, B., Volpato, C., Manganelli, A. M., Pek, J. C. X., Huang, L., Sakalli-Ugurlu, N., Castron, Y. R., Pereira, M. L., Willemsen, T. M., Brunner, A., Six-Materna, I., & Wells, R. (2004). Bad but bold: Ambivalent attitudes toward men predict gender inequality in 16 nations. *Journal of Personality and Social Psychology, 86,* 713–728.

Goffman, E. (1959). *The presentation of self in everyday life.* New York: Doubleday.

Goffman, E. (1967). *Interaction ritual.* Garden City, NY: Doubleday.

Jackman, M. R. (1994). *The velvet glove: Paternalism and conflict in gender, class, and race relations.* Berkeley, CA: University of California Press.

Jackson, R. M. (1998). *Destined for equality: The inevitable rise of women's status.* Cambridge, MA: Harvard University Press.

Koenig, A. M., & Eagly, A. H. (2006). *A unified theory of stereotype content: How observations of groups' social roles and intergroup relations produce stereotypes.* Unpublished manuscript. Northwestern University.

Kunda, Z., & Spencer, S. J. (2003). When do stereotypes come to mind and when do they color judgment? A goal-based theoretical framework for stereotype activation and application. *Psychological Bulletin, 129,* 522–544.

Lorber, J. (1994). *Paradoxes of gender.* New Haven, CT: Yale University Press.

Lueptow, L. B., Garovich-Szabo, L., & Lueptow, M. B. (2001). Social change and the persistence of sex typing: 1974–1997. *Social Forces, 80,* 1–36.

Milkie, M. A. (1999). Social comparison, reflected appraisals, and mass media: The impact of pervasive beauty images on Black and white girls' self-concepts. *Social Psychology Quarterly, 62,* 190–210.

Miller, D. T., & Turnbull, W. (1986). Expectancies and interpersonal processes. *Annual Review of Psychology, 37,* 233–256.

Nelson, R., & Bridges, W. (1999). *Legalizing gender inequality: Courts, markets, and unequal pay for women in America.* New York: Cambridge.

Padovic, I., & Reskin, B. (2002). *Women and men at work.* Thousand Oaks, CA: Pine Forge.

Ridgeway, C. L. (1997). Interaction and the conservation of gender inequality: Considering employment. *American Sociological Review, 62,* 218–235.
Ridgeway, C. L. (2001). Social status and group structure. In: M. A. Hogg & S. Tindale (Eds), *Blackwell handbook of social psychology: Group processes* (pp. 352–375). Maulden, MA: Blackwell.
Ridgeway, C. L. (2006a). Gender as an organizing force in social relations: implications for the future of inequality. In: F. D. Blau, M. C. Brinton & D. B. Grusky (Eds), *The declining significance of gender?* (pp. 265–288). New York: Russell Sage Foundation.
Ridgeway, C. L. (2006b). Status construction theory. In: P. J. Burke (Ed.), *Contemporary social psychological theories* (pp. 301–323). Stanford, CA: Stanford University Press.
Ridgeway, C. L., & Bourg, C. (2004). Gender as status: An expectation states theory approach. In: A. H. Eagly, A. E. Beall & R. J. Sternberg (Eds), *The psychology of gender* (pp. 217–241). New York: Guilford Press.
Ridgeway, C. L., Boyle, E. H., Kuipers, K., & Robinson, D. (1998). How do status beliefs develop? The role of resources and interaction. *American Sociological Review, 63,* 331–350.
Ridgeway, C. L., & Correll, S. J. (2000). Limiting gender inequality through interaction: The end(s) of gender. *Contemporary Sociology, 29,* 110–120.
Ridgeway, C. L., & Correll, S. J. (2004). Unpacking the gender system: A theoretical perspective on gender beliefs and social relations. *Gender and Society, 18*(4), 510–531.
Ridgeway, C. L., & Erickson, K. G. (2000). Creating and spreading status beliefs. *American Journal of Sociology, 106,* 579–615.
Ridgeway, C. L., & Smith-Lovin, L. (1999). The gender system and interaction. *Annual Review of Sociology, 25,* 191–216.
Risman, B. (1998). *Gender vertigo: American families in transition.* New Haven, CT: Yale University Press.
Risman, B. (2004). Gender as a social structure: Theory wrestling with activism. *Gender and Society, 18,* 429–450.
Rudman, L., & Kilianski, S. E. (2000). Implicit and explicit attitudes toward female authority. *Personality and Social Psychology Bulletin, 26,* 1315–1328.
Schneider, D. J. (2004). *The psychology of stereotyping.* New York: Guilford Press.
Seachrist, G. B., & Stangor, C. (2001). Perceived consensus influences intergroup behavior and stereotype accessibility. *Journal of Personality and Social Psychology, 80,* 645–654.
Sewell, W. H. (1992). A theory of structure: Duality, agency, and transformation. *American Journal of Sociology, 98,* 1–29.
Spence, J. T., & Buckner, C. E. (2000). Instrumental and expressive traits, trait stereotypes, and sexist attitudes: What do they signify? *Psychology of Women Quarterly, 24,* 44–62.
Stangor, C., Lynch, L., Duan, C., & Glass, B. (1992). Categorization of individuals on the basis of multiple social features. *Journal of Personality and Social Psychology, 62,* 207–218.
Steinberg, R. J. (1995). Gendered instructions: Cultural lag and gender bias in the hay system of job evaluation. In: J. A. Jacobs (Ed.), *Gender inequality at work* (pp. 57–92). Thousand Oaks, CA: Sage.
Twenge, J. M. (2001). Changes in women's assertiveness in response to status and roles: A cross-temporal meta-analysis, 1931–1993. *Journal of Personality and Social Psychology, 81,* 133–145.
Wagner, D. G., & Berger, J. (1997). Gender and interpersonal task behaviors: Status expectation accounts. *Sociological Perspectives, 40,* 1–32.

Wagner, D. G., & Berger, J. (2002). Expectation states theory: An evolving research program. In: J. Berger & M. Zelditch (Eds), *New directions in contemporary sociological theory* (pp. 41–76). New York: Rowman & Littlefield.
West, C., & Zimmerman, D. (1987). Doing gender. *Gender and Society, 1,* 125–151.
Williams, J. E., & Best, D. L. (1990). *Measuring sex stereotypes: A multination study.* Newbury Park, CA: Sage.
Wood, W., & Eagly, A. H. (2002). A cross-cultural analysis of the behavior of women and men: Implications for the origins of sex differences. *Psychological Bulletin, 128,* 699–727.
Zemore, S. E., Fiske, S. T., & Kim, H.-J. (2000). Gender stereotypes and the dynamics of social interaction. In: T. Eckes & H. M. Trautner (Eds), *The developmental psychology of gender* (pp. 207–242). Mahwah, NJ: Earlbaum.

Lightning Source UK Ltd.
Milton Keynes UK
09 April 2010

152517UK00001B/63/P